MATTHEW SARDON

# Prophecy Fulfilled

*How Jesus Completes the Messianic Promise*

THEOSIS HOUSE PRESS

Copyright © 2025 by Matthew Sardon

All rights reserved. No part of this publication may be reproduced, stored or transmitted in any form or by any means, electronic, mechanical, photocopying, recording, scanning, or otherwise without written permission from the publisher. It is illegal to copy this book, post it to a website, or distribute it by any other means without permission.

Matthew Sardon asserts the moral right to be identified as the author of this work.

First edition

This book was professionally typeset on Reedsy.
Find out more at reedsy.com

"For all the promises of God find their Yes in Him."

- 2 Corinthians 1:20

# Contents

Prologue     1

## I   THE SHAPE OF THE PROMISE

1. The First Gospel: The Seed Who Will Crush the Serpent     9
2. The Everlasting Throne: David and the Covenant of Kingship     27
3. The Prophet Like Moses: The Promise of a New Exodus     50
4. The Servant and the Son of Man: The Tension within Prophecy     72
5. The Priest of the New Covenant: Temple, Sacrifice, and...     93
6. When the Promise Enters History     114

## II   THE MESSIAH IN HISTORY

7. The Son of David Appears: Jesus and the Restoration of...     121
8. Greater Than Moses: Jesus the New Lawgiver and Redeemer     143
9. The High Priest Revealed: Sacrifice and the Torn Veil     166
10. The Servant Suffers: The Passion as Fulfilment of Prophecy     188
11. The Son of Man Enthroned: Resurrection, Ascension, and...     213
12. The Question of Authority     235

## III THE MESSIAH IN HIS OWN WORDS

13　Before Abraham Was, I AM: Jesus' Divine Self-Revelation　241
14　In All the Scriptures: Jesus as the Key to Prophecy　262
15　Vindicated on the Third Day: Resurrection as Fulfilment and...　281
16　A Sword That Divides　303

## IV THE MESSIAH REJECTED AND RECOGNISED

17　The Messianic Hope of Second Temple Judaism　311
18　Objections to Jesus: Genealogy, Suffering, Torah, and...　323
19　The Christian Response: Why the Messiah Had to Suffer　344
20　Israel and the Church: The Mystery of God's Faithfulness　361
21　The Promise Still Unfinished　377

## V THE PROMISE YET TO BE COMPLETED

22　The King Who Will Come Again: The Second Coming and Israel's...　383
23　Resurrection and Judgment: The Final Acts of the Messiah　399
24　A New Heaven and a New Earth: Creation Renewed in the...　412
25　The Question Fulfilment Cannot Avoid　425

## VI THE MESSIAH WHO IS GOD

26　The Architecture of Prophecy: Typology and Divine Design　431
27　Fulfilment, Not Replacement: Christ and the Story of Israel　448
28　Why Prophecy Matters: Faith, Evangelisation, and...　461

29　Conclusion　476

*About the Author*

# Prologue

From the moment Israel first heard the voice of God in the garden's aftermath, a certain expectancy entered the human story. It was not a philosophical curiosity or a cultural myth but a promise spoken by the Creator to a wounded creation. Scripture remembers that promise in the form of a struggle between the serpent and the seed, a struggle that would continue across generations until one particular descendant would deal a decisive blow to the powers that had ruptured humanity's communion with God. That first word of hope became the quiet thread running beneath every covenant, every deliverance, and every act of God in Israel's history. As Israel grew from a family into a nation, and from a nation into a kingdom, the promise did not diminish. It deepened. Abraham was told that through his descendants all nations would be blessed. Moses witnessed God's power to liberate His people and spoke of another prophet who would arise. David received the assurance of an everlasting throne, and the prophets spoke of a figure who would restore justice, heal Israel, and make God's presence known in a definitive way. Israel's Scriptures do not merely record history; they sustain hope. They cultivate the conviction that God is not finished with the world and that a particular person, chosen by God, will bring the story to its proper fulfilment.

This expectation shaped Israel's identity as much as land, law, or temple. It taught generations to live not only from memory but from anticipation, trusting that the God who acted in the past would act again in a manner even greater than before. The longing for the Messiah was not abstract. It was woven into festivals, psalms, prophetic oracles, and the very language of covenant. Through centuries of hardship—exile, foreign domination, internal division—Israel held onto this hope because it rested not on human optimism but on divine promise. Israel believed that God had bound Himself to His people and that He would one day send the anointed one who would vindicate that bond. Even when the shape of that figure seemed difficult to discern, the expectation persisted. It became the heartbeat of the Scriptures.

Christianity enters this story with a claim that stands at once in continuity with Israel's hope and in tension with it. Christians proclaim that the Messiah has come, that His name is Jesus of Nazareth, that His life reveals the fullness of God's covenant fidelity, and that His death and resurrection complete what the law and the prophets foretold. This claim did not appear in a vacuum. It emerged from the experience of those who lived with Him, followed Him, saw His works, heard His teaching, and encountered Him risen from the dead. They believed—not by gradual theological evolution but by the shock of divine action—that the promises given to Abraham, Moses, and David had reached their fulfilment. Their proclamation was simple and profound: the Messiah long awaited by Israel had walked among them.

Yet Judaism, reading the same Scriptures with reverence and fidelity, continues to await the Messiah. For many Jews, the world does not yet reflect the conditions anticipated by the prophets: peace has not prevailed, nations have not turned fully to the God of Israel, and the wounds of exile remain unhealed. For these reasons, the claim that the Messiah has already appeared seems premature, even contradictory to the prophetic vision. Here lies the great interpretive divergence. Two communities honour the same Scriptures, revere the same God, and cherish the same promises, yet arrive at opposite conclusions about whether those promises have been fulfilled. The identity of the Messiah becomes not a secondary theological point but the very question that both unites and divides Judaism and Christianity.

In our time, this question is often softened or ignored. Secular culture tends to treat religious claims as symbolic truths or private convictions rather than as statements that demand historical and theological clarity.

## PROLOGUE

Even many Christians have lost sight of the depth of Israel's longing and the intricate way in which prophecy shapes the identity of Jesus. Many imagine the Messiah as either a vague spiritual figure or a political ideal, forgetting that Israel expected a real person sent by God, anointed with divine authority, and capable of restoring the covenant in a definitive way. Likewise, some presume Christianity simply asserted Jesus' messiahship without attending to the careful and ancient pattern in Scripture. The result is a diminished understanding of both Judaism and Christianity, as if the question of the Messiah were an optional doctrinal detail rather than the centre of the biblical drama.

This book seeks to restore the gravity of that question. The Scriptures present messianic prophecy not as scattered predictions but as a unified narrative structure. Across centuries, through covenants, kings, prophets, poetry, and ritual, God forms a pattern that points toward a singular fulfilment. This pattern is not obvious at first glance, nor is it mechanical. It develops gradually, like a portrait whose contours become clearer with each stroke of divine revelation. Christians believe that Jesus stands precisely within this pattern and brings it to completion—not by coincidence, not by reinterpretation, but by the intrinsic coherence between His life and the promises of God.

Yet this claim must be approached with care, because it does not rest on sentiment or inherited assumption. It rests on Scripture. The only way to see whether Jesus fulfils the messianic hope is to enter the narrative that shaped that hope, to listen to the voices of the patriarchs and prophets, to understand the crises that forged Israel's expectations, and to consider how the New Testament presents Jesus not as a religious innovator but as the one who brings Israel's story to its intended end. The argument cannot begin with theological systems or later traditions. It must begin with the texts themselves, for it is within the Scriptures that the promise of the Messiah is formed, and it is within those same Scriptures that the question of fulfilment must be measured. Christians and Jews alike acknowledge that God speaks through these writings; therefore, any honest inquiry into the messianic identity must follow the shape of revelation rather than impose external assumptions upon it.

The claim that Jesus fulfils prophecy becomes meaningful only when we understand what prophecy is. Prophecy is not a divine guessing game in which isolated predictions await matching historical events. It is the unfolding of God's covenantal faithfulness across time. The prophets did not imagine disconnected moments in a distant future; they interpreted Israel's history in light of God's character, announcing that the same God who created, liberated, guided, and corrected His people would one day act with decisive finality. Prophecy is the theological architecture beneath the historical narrative. It prepares the mind and heart to recognise God's work when it appears. Jesus' life, death, and resurrection are presented by the New Testament not as an improvised conclusion but as the culmination of a pattern visible to anyone who reads the Scriptures with patience and trust in the God who does not abandon His promises.

Yet the Scriptures also display tension, ambiguity, and paradox. The Messiah is portrayed at times as a royal son of David, at other times as a suffering servant. He is depicted as a prophet like Moses, a priest like Melchizedek, a shepherd who gathers the lost, a judge of the nations, and a figure who shares in God's own authority. Israel expected deliverance, yet the form of that deliverance was not fully disclosed. The question that faced the first-century Jewish world was not whether God would send the Messiah, but what kind of Messiah God would send. Would He be a political liberator, a spiritual healer, a teacher of Torah, a restorer of the Temple, or an apocalyptic figure who ushers in the end of days? The prophetic texts hold these roles in an unresolved tension, leaving open the possibility that only God's own action could reveal how they belong together.

The proclamation of the early Christians was that this unity appears in Jesus. They believed that His teaching echoed the voice of the prophets, His authority surpassed that of Moses and David, His suffering corresponded to Isaiah's servant, His resurrection fulfilled the psalms of vindication, and His ascension revealed the heavenly Son of Man described by Daniel. They saw in Him the convergence of every strand of expectation. At the same time, they understood that this recognition was not automatic. It required reading Scripture through the lens of the resurrection and allowing God's final act to illuminate the earlier works He performed. This is why the apostles preached from the Scriptures and why Jesus Himself, according to the Gospels, interpreted the law, the prophets, and the psalms as witnesses to His identity. Their claim was not born out of theological creativity but out of continuity with the story they inherited.

This book follows that story. It begins where Scripture begins, with the earliest promises that shape Israel's hope, and traces their development across the covenants, the monarchy, the exile, and the prophetic age. It examines the life and ministry of Jesus in light of those promises and considers how His words, actions, and self-understanding fit within the framework of Israel's expectation. It addresses the reasons many Jews did not accept Him as the Messiah and explores how the early Church responded to those objections. It turns toward the promises that remain unfulfilled and asks how the Messiah's return completes the scriptural narrative. Finally, it reflects on the identity of the Messiah as more than an anointed king or prophet; He is the one in whom God's plan and presence become manifest.

The question of the Messiah is not a relic of ancient debate. It is the central question of biblical faith. It touches the character of God, the meaning of history, the hope of Israel, and the destiny of humanity. For Christians, Jesus is the answer to that question. For Jews, the answer is still awaited. The purpose of this book is not to force agreement but to consider carefully the story that gives rise to the question in the first place. If the Scriptures are to be trusted, then the Messiah stands at the centre of God's work in the world, and every reader, regardless of tradition, must reckon with the possibility that God has already revealed Him. The invitation is simple: follow the promises, listen to the prophets, and consider whether the figure who emerged in first-century Judea is indeed the one for whom Israel waited.

# I

# THE SHAPE OF THE PROMISE

# 1

# The First Gospel: The Seed Who Will Crush the Serpent

The story of the Messiah does not begin with a throne, a prophet, or a promise spoken in celebration. It begins with a wound. Scripture's first great drama unfolds in a garden where human beings, created for communion with God, find themselves estranged from the One who formed them. The serpent's whisper introduces a fracture into the harmony of creation, and when Adam and Eve turn from the voice of God to the voice of temptation, the consequences unfold with a sobering inevitability. Their eyes are opened, but not to glory; they see their own vulnerability and shame. The ground that once yielded fruit now resists them. The intimacy they shared with God becomes marked by fear. The peace woven into their relationship with each other becomes strained by blame. All of creation seems to tilt away from its Creator, as if echoing the disobedience that has entered the world through its stewards.

Yet within this scene of rupture, God does something unexpected. He speaks a word that both judges and heals, condemns and promises. He addresses the serpent first, identifying the true source of the rebellion. Then He declares that conflict will arise between the serpent and the woman, between the serpent's offspring and the woman's offspring, and that this conflict will culminate in a decisive victory. The serpent will strike, but the seed of the woman will crush its head. This is not a vague prediction. It is the first hint of redemption in Scripture, the first announcement that God will not allow evil to have the final word. Even before Adam and Eve hear their own sentence, they hear the promise that the story will not end in darkness. God steps into the chaos created by sin and plants a seed of hope that will grow through the entire biblical narrative.

This promise is astonishing in its simplicity. It does not name the deliverer, describe the timing, or outline the method of victory. It does something deeper. It introduces a trajectory. The victory will come through a human descendant, someone who stands within the lineage of the very people who have fallen. Redemption will not arrive as an external force unrelated to humanity; it will arise from within the human family itself. This is the mystery and the mercy of God's plan. He does not discard humanity because of disobedience. He binds Himself to humanity more deeply, promising that through the offspring of the woman, the power of evil will be confronted and defeated. The early chapters of Genesis do not yet reveal the face of this redeemer, but they establish the line along which He will come.

As Genesis unfolds, the motif of the seed becomes more than biological continuation; it becomes theological destiny. When Eve gives birth to Cain, her words reflect the hope that God's promise might be fulfilled through him. But Cain's heart darkens, and the first child born in hope becomes the first murderer in history. Abel, whose offering pleases God, becomes the victim of his brother's envy, and the seed of promise seems threatened almost immediately. Yet God responds with unexpected fidelity. Eve bears another son, Seth, and the narrative places significant emphasis on this new beginning. Through Seth, the line of hope continues, not because humanity shows sudden improvement but because God remains committed to His promise. The genealogies that follow, often skimmed by modern readers, function as theological scaffolding. They trace the line of the seed through generations, preserving the continuity of the divine promise even as humanity falters again and again.

The story of Noah reinforces this pattern. As wickedness spreads across the earth, it seems as though the corruption introduced by the serpent has overtaken humanity entirely. Yet Noah finds favour in the eyes of the Lord. He becomes a new Adam, stepping onto renewed ground after the floodwaters recede. His family represents a restart for the seed, a fresh beginning for the promise spoken in Eden. But even this new beginning carries the marks of human weakness. Noah plants a vineyard, becomes drunk, and falls into shame. The cycle of failure returns quickly, showing that no human effort, however promising, can fully restore what was lost. Still, God does not abandon His word. The covenant with Noah expands the horizon of divine fidelity, assuring creation that God will preserve life and continue the work He has begun. The seed survives not because humanity proves worthy, but because God remains faithful.

The call of Abraham marks a significant development in the story of the seed. God promises Abraham descendants as numerous as the stars, yet the heart of this promise lies not in quantity but in destiny. Through Abraham's offspring, God declares, all nations of the earth will be blessed. This echo of Genesis 3:15 now receives clearer contours. The seed will not only confront the serpent; it will bring blessing to the world. Abraham becomes the father of a people through whom God will shape history, reveal His character, and prepare the way for the Messiah. The promise narrows and widens simultaneously. It narrows to a particular lineage—Abraham, Isaac, Jacob—and it widens to embrace all nations through that lineage. This dual movement forms the core of biblical revelation: the God of Israel acts through a chosen people to redeem the world.

The unfolding of the patriarchal narratives reinforces this divine pattern. Isaac, born in circumstances that defy human expectation, becomes the bearer of the promise. Jacob, chosen despite his flaws, becomes Israel, giving his name to the people who will carry the seed. The twelve tribes emerge from his sons, each representing a facet of God's unfolding plan. Through their stories—marked by struggle, betrayal, reconciliation, and grace—the promise moves forward. Genesis ends not with fulfilment but with direction. The seed has been preserved through famine, exile, and familial strife, yet its ultimate purpose remains unfulfilled. The Messiah has not appeared. The serpent has not been crushed. But the line of promise is intact, waiting for the next stage of revelation.

As the story of Israel moves beyond Genesis, the early Jewish imagination does not forget the promise given in Eden. Far from fading into the background, the conflict between the serpent and the seed becomes a lens through which Israel understands the spiritual dimension of its history. The serpent, once a creature in the garden, becomes a symbol of the forces that oppose God's purposes in the world. The enmity God announces in Genesis 3:15 begins to appear in the patterns of Israel's story. Pharaoh, who enslaves God's people, embodies a serpent-like opposition to the divine plan. The chaos of the nations, the violence of human rebellion, and the recurring temptation toward idolatry all echo the primal conflict introduced in Eden. Israel's prophets and sages read their history not merely as political upheaval but as participation in a deeper struggle between God's promise and the destructive power of sin. In this way, Genesis 3:15 becomes more than an isolated verse; it becomes the theological backdrop for Israel's entire narrative.

Within this broad context, we find early Jewish interpretations that deepen the significance of the protoevangelium. The ancient Aramaic paraphrases of Scripture, known as the Targums, often expand the biblical text to offer explanatory or interpretive insights. In several of these, the conflict between the seed of the woman and the serpent is presented as a cosmic struggle that culminates in the days of the Messiah. The serpent is not simply an animal but a symbol of evil, hostile to God's purposes. The seed of the woman becomes a figure of deliverance who will ultimately triumph over the forces of darkness. This interpretive trajectory appears in various Second Temple writings as well. Though not uniform, these traditions bear witness to a growing expectation that God would send a deliverer who would confront and defeat the spiritual powers that held humanity in bondage. The promise of Eden thus becomes a foundation for later messianic hope, shaping Jewish eschatology long before the time of Jesus.

## THE FIRST GOSPEL: THE SEED WHO WILL CRUSH THE SERPENT

The Hebrew Scriptures themselves reinforce this expectation by repeatedly placing humanity's failure and God's fidelity side by side. Every major turning point in the early narrative highlights the depth of human brokenness. Cain's violence leads to further corruption among his descendants. The pre-flood world becomes filled with wickedness, prompting divine judgment. Noah's family falters almost immediately after stepping onto the renewed earth. The builders of Babel attempt to seize divine glory for themselves. Each scene reveals the persistent reality of sin and the inability of humanity to heal itself. Yet in every scene, God continues the work He began. He preserves the seed through Seth. He saves life through Noah. He scatters the nations in judgment but later calls Abraham to begin their healing. The pattern is unmistakable. Humanity's sin threatens the promise, but God's fidelity sustains it. The story of Scripture becomes a drama in which the promise survives not because of human virtue but because of divine mercy.

This theological pattern reaches a moment of profound clarity in the writings of the Church Fathers, who recognised in Genesis 3:15 the first announcement of the gospel. Irenaeus, writing in the second century, meditated deeply on the relationship between Adam and Christ. He described Jesus as the "New Adam" who retraces the steps of the first Adam but with obedience rather than disobedience. Through this recapitulation, Christ undoes the damage caused by the fall, restoring humanity to the path of communion with God. The Fathers also saw in Mary the "New Eve," whose faith stands in contrast to Eve's disobedience. While Eve listened to the serpent's deception, Mary listened to the word of God. While Eve's act introduced death, Mary's "yes" becomes the gateway through which life enters the world. The early Christians did not invent these parallels; they saw them emerging naturally from the biblical narrative and from the pattern of promise and fulfilment that begins in Genesis.

The connection between Christ and the serpent's defeat becomes especially vivid in the New Testament's reflection on the cross. Jesus speaks of His impending death as the moment when "the ruler of this world will be cast out," linking His sacrifice to a decisive victory over the forces of evil. Paul interprets the cross as the moment when God disarms the powers and principalities. The Book of Revelation portrays the risen Christ as the conqueror of the ancient serpent. These images do not arise in isolation; they reflect the conviction that the promise of Genesis 3:15 reaches its fulfilment in Jesus' victory over sin and death. The cross becomes the moment when the serpent strikes the heel, but the resurrection reveals the crushing of the serpent's head. In Christ, the cosmic conflict announced in Eden finds its resolution.

Even so, the narrative of Genesis does not leap immediately from the fall to the fullness of redemption. It traces a patient unfolding of God's plan. The earliest chapters of Scripture show God establishing a trajectory, not completing it. The seed is promised but not yet revealed. The enemy is identified but not yet defeated. The story leans forward, inviting the reader to anticipate what God will do next. By the time Genesis ends with Joseph's words about God bringing good out of evil, the reader has witnessed glimpses of divine faithfulness but has not yet seen the fulfilment of the promise. The groundwork has been laid. The expectation is alive. The stage is set for the next great movement in the drama of salvation.

When Israel's story continues in Exodus and beyond, the memory of Eden's promise remains embedded beneath the surface of every episode. Although Genesis 3:15 is rarely quoted directly in the rest of the Old Testament, its themes reappear like an echo through the great turning points of salvation history. The serpent's enmity resurfaces in every threat to God's people, every moment when darkness seems poised to extinguish the light of divine promise. Pharaoh's oppression embodies more than political tyranny; it reflects the ancient hostility between the forces of evil and the people through whom God intends to bless the world. His refusal to release Israel, his cruelty, and his defiance of God's command reveal a spirit aligned with the serpent's rebellion. The plagues, the Passover, and the deliverance through the sea all point to a God who contends with the powers that enslave humanity. What began as a promise in Eden continues as a lived reality in the life of God's people. Every redemption becomes a small foreshadowing of the greater victory that still lies ahead.

## THE FIRST GOSPEL: THE SEED WHO WILL CRUSH THE SERPENT

The wilderness years further highlight this dynamic. Israel faces the temptations of idolatry, fear, weariness, and rebellion. Each failure exposes the weakness of the human heart, yet each act of divine patience reveals God's commitment to the promise. The serpent's presence is not literal here, but the spirit of deception runs through the people's struggles. The desire to return to Egypt, the worship of the golden calf, and the dissatisfaction with God's provision all bear the marks of a deeper spiritual conflict. The promise of the seed is not merely about a future hero; it is about God confronting the underlying disorder that manifests in every generation. When Moses speaks of a prophet who will arise like himself, he is not introducing a new idea but building upon the expectation that God will provide a definitive answer to the problem of sin and deception. The Redeemer will not only liberate His people but lead them into true obedience, healing the rupture introduced by the serpent.

The monarchy brings another development in the shape of the promise. When God chooses David and establishes an everlasting covenant with him, Jews of the ancient world would have heard an echo of the ancient promise. The seed of the woman becomes the seed of Abraham, then the seed of Israel, and now the seed of David. The line narrows, but the hope broadens. The Davidic king is not simply a political leader; he becomes a symbol of God's faithful presence and protection. The psalms speak of a king who will rule with righteousness, who will crush the oppressor, who will shepherd the people, and who will inherit the nations. Some of these psalms even ascribe divine qualities to the coming king, blurring the lines between human and divine authority. In these poetic prayers, the serpent's power is not explicitly mentioned, but the expectation of a ruler who will establish justice hints at a deeper victory over the forces that distort the world.

The prophetic literature continues this pattern, often reflecting on Israel's failures and God's unwavering fidelity. Isaiah envisions a child born to bring light into the darkness, a king endowed with the Spirit, a servant who suffers on behalf of the people, and a figure who proclaims good news to the poor. The tension between exaltation and suffering becomes stronger here, suggesting that the Messiah's triumph will not follow the ordinary path of human conquest. Jeremiah speaks of a new covenant written on the heart. Ezekiel describes God renewing His people with a new spirit. Each promise adds depth to the hope announced in Genesis. The serpent's power, manifested through sin, idolatry, and injustice, will ultimately be broken. But the way this victory will unfold remains shrouded in divine mystery. The portrait of the Messiah grows ever more detailed, yet the full image is still incomplete.

Through all of this, the line of promise continues through fragile human vessels. The genealogical records preserved in Scripture may seem tedious to modern readers, yet they serve as vital testimony to God's fidelity. Each name is a link in a chain stretching back to the moment when God spoke hope into the ruins of Eden. The faithfulness of God, not the virtue of humanity, keeps the promise alive. Even the periods of exile, when Israel's identity and future seem most threatened, demonstrate that the promise cannot be undone. The prophets speak of a remnant, a faithful group preserved by God to carry the covenant forward. The seed remains intact. The serpent wounds but does not destroy. The promise endures.

By the time we arrive at the Second Temple period, the expectation of the Messiah has taken distinctive shape in Jewish thought. Although there is no single messianic doctrine in the Judaism of this era, several themes emerge consistently. Many Jews anticipate a Davidic king who will restore Israel's fortunes. Others expect a priestly figure who will purify the Temple and renew worship. Some imagine a prophetic leader who will reveal God's word in a final and definitive way. Still others ponder apocalyptic visions in which a heavenly figure descends to defeat evil. These hopes are diverse, yet they share a conviction rooted in the earliest pages of Scripture: God will act through a chosen one to defeat the forces that oppose His purposes. The serpent will be crushed. The seed will triumph. The world will be set right.

This expectation permeates the world into which Jesus is born. The promise of Genesis 3:15, carried through centuries of struggle and hope, forms the soil from which the New Testament sprouts. When the Gospel writers present Jesus' genealogy, they are not merely tracing biological heritage; they are identifying Him as the heir of the ancient promise. When they recount His victory over temptation in the wilderness, they are showing Him as the one who confronts the serpent's deception and emerges unscathed. When they describe His authority over demons, His healing of the sick, and His proclamation of the kingdom, they are portraying Him as the seed who has come to reverse the curse introduced in Eden. The life of Jesus cannot be understood apart from the scriptural story that precedes Him. He steps into a narrative already shaped by expectation, conflict, and hope.

What becomes even more striking is how Jesus embodies the very pattern that Genesis initiates. The New Testament does not treat the protoevangelium as a forgotten relic but as a foundational key for interpreting the mission of Christ. When Jesus enters the wilderness after His baptism, He confronts the tempter in a direct echo of the serpent's first deception. Yet where Adam fell in a garden of abundance, Jesus remains faithful in a place of hunger and desolation. His fidelity in the wilderness reverses the disobedience of Eden and reveals Him as the one capable of facing the serpent without yielding to its lies. This confrontation is not simply moral; it is messianic. It shows that the ancient conflict announced in Genesis continues and that Jesus stands as the champion of humanity in that battle.

Throughout His ministry, Jesus displays authority over the forces that the biblical tradition associates with the serpent's influence. He drives out unclean spirits with a word, revealing a sovereignty that surpasses the power of darkness. His healing of the sick, His opening of blind eyes, and His restoration of the broken all testify to the gradual undoing of the curse. Each miracle is a sign that the world is being set right, that the Messiah's victory is not only future but already taking shape in His presence. When Jesus speaks of binding the strong man before plundering his house, He is drawing on imagery that echoes the conflict between the seed and the serpent. The strong man is the one who holds humanity in bondage. The Messiah is the stronger one who enters the house of bondage, binds the oppressor, and frees the captives. This imagery would not have been lost on an audience steeped in the Scriptures; it reflects the unfolding of Genesis 3:15 in real time.

Jesus' teaching regularly invokes themes of new creation, restoration, and divine victory. When He proclaims the kingdom of God, He announces the beginning of a reign that will confront and overcome everything that has distorted creation since the fall. His parables often describe a world in which evil and good grow together until a final moment of separation, a world in which a hidden power spreads quietly yet irresistibly through the whole of creation. These teachings reflect a profound awareness of the ancient promise and its fulfilment. Jesus does not present Himself as one teacher among many or as a moral reformer attempting to improve society. He presents Himself as the one through whom God's reign breaks into history, fulfilling the trajectory of hope established in Eden.

The cross stands at the centre of this fulfilment. The early Christians understood Jesus' crucifixion not as a tragic end but as the moment when the serpent strikes the heel of the Messiah. The suffering of Christ is depicted in the Gospels as an assault by the powers of darkness. On the night of His arrest, Jesus declares that "the ruler of this world is coming," indicating that His passion involves more than human betrayal. Yet He also asserts His authority over that ruler, revealing that the apparent triumph of evil is only temporary. When Jesus dies on the cross, it appears to be the serpent's moment of victory. But the Scriptures teach that this strike becomes the moment of defeat. The resurrection, radiant and unexpected, reveals that the Messiah has crushed the head of the serpent by passing through death and destroying its power. Sin, death, and the forces of evil lose their dominion, not by being ignored or bypassed but by being confronted directly in the Messiah's self-offering.

The apostolic writings make this connection explicit. Paul speaks of God crushing Satan under the feet of His people, a reference that only makes sense in light of Genesis 3:15. In another letter, he describes Christ disarming the powers and exposing them through the cross. The author of Hebrews portrays Jesus as destroying the one who holds the power of death. The Book of Revelation culminates with the vision of the serpent, now identified as the ancient dragon, being cast down and ultimately destroyed. Across the entire New Testament, Jesus is presented as the fulfilment of the promise spoken in Eden. The seed of the woman has arrived, the serpent has been confronted, and the long conflict is drawing to its divinely appointed end.

Yet for all the clarity of this fulfilment, the mystery remains rich. The promise of Genesis 3:15 does not specify how the victory will occur. It simply declares that God will act through human descent to defeat evil. The Scriptures reveal that this act unfolds through humility rather than force, through suffering rather than conquest, through love rather than violence. Jesus' victory does not negate the natural order of creation but restores it from within. He enters the human story as one of us, bearing the full weight of human vulnerability, yet without sin. In doing so, He reveals the depth of God's commitment to His promise. The serpent is not defeated by arbitrary power but by the obedience of the Son, who unites divinity and humanity in an act of perfect fidelity.

This chapter has followed the path of that promise from its beginning in Eden, through the early narratives of Genesis, into the developing hopes of Israel, and finally into the life and ministry of Jesus. The protoevangelium, simple in form yet profound in meaning, establishes the foundation for everything that follows in Scripture. It shows that the Messiah is not an afterthought or a late addition to Israel's theology. He stands at the heart of God's plan from the very beginning. The rest of the biblical story expands this initial promise, adding layers of depth, symbolism, and revelation. The Messiah will not only defeat the serpent but will restore creation, redeem humanity, and reunite heaven and earth.

When we consider the protoevangelium within the larger sweep of salvation history, it becomes clear that God's first promise operates as the seed from which the entire narrative of redemption grows. Scripture does not treat the fall as an isolated tragedy followed by an unrelated plan of salvation. Instead, the promise in Genesis 3:15 becomes the axis around which the rest of the biblical story turns. The genealogies, covenants, prophetic visions, and rituals of Israel all develop as responses to that early announcement. Again and again, God reveals more of the identity of the promised figure, yet always within the dynamic of covenant. The Messiah will come from a particular people, through a particular line, embodying a particular mission that reflects the character of the God who promised Him. The seed is not an abstraction; it is a real lineage moving through history, and every stage of Israel's journey participates in the unfolding of that redemptive plan.

This is why the early chapters of Genesis carry such theological weight. They are not simply explanations for human origins; they are the theological foundation for messianic hope. The dynamic of human rebellion and divine faithfulness becomes the defining rhythm of Scripture. Each time humanity falls, God acts. Each time the promise seems threatened, God preserves it. Each time the world descends into violence or chaos, God maintains a remnant that carries the hope forward. This pattern reveals something essential about God's nature. He does not abandon His creation. He does not withdraw His promise. Even when the world opposes Him, He continues to work through the fragile, unpredictable lines of human history to bring forth the One who will heal it. The fall introduces a wound, but the promise points to a healer, and the rest of Scripture becomes a record of God preparing the world for that healing.

The theological richness of the protoevangelium becomes even more apparent when we recognise how the New Testament reads the Old. The Gospel writers do not treat Genesis as a distant prelude. They draw from it directly. Matthew begins his Gospel with a genealogy that traces Jesus' lineage back to Abraham and David, implicitly placing Him within the line of promise. Luke goes further, tracing the genealogy back to Adam, connecting Jesus not only to Israel but to humanity as a whole. These genealogies are not mere lists; they are theological statements. They proclaim that Jesus stands within the very line God has preserved since Eden. The evangelists are not introducing a new story; they are revealing the continuation of the only story Scripture has ever told: the story of the God who made a promise and has now fulfilled it in His Son.

The temptation narrative further strengthens the connection between Jesus and the promise of Genesis. When Jesus confronts the tempter, He relives the drama of Eden. The serpent approaches, now in the guise of Satan, offering shortcuts to power and glory. Adam failed in a garden of abundance. Israel faltered in the wilderness of testing. Yet Jesus remains faithful, refusing to turn from the word of God. His victory is not merely moral; it is representative. He stands in the place of Adam and Israel, succeeding where they failed, and in doing so, He discloses His identity as the one who can fulfil the promise of crushing the serpent. His fidelity becomes the first clear sign that the age of the Messiah has arrived.

The connection between Genesis and the New Testament continues through Jesus' works. When He heals the sick, restores the broken, and drives out demons, He demonstrates that the curse introduced in Eden is being undone. The serpent's influence is revealed in the suffering, disorder, and oppression that afflict humanity. Jesus' miracles serve not only as acts of compassion but as signs of messianic authority. They reveal that the seed of the woman has come and that the serpent's dominion is weakening. Every healing becomes a symbol of new creation. Every act of authority over evil becomes a proclamation that the long conflict is tipping toward victory. Jesus embodies the promise not only in His lineage and His teaching but in His very presence. The light He brings exposes the works of darkness and reveals that the world is being reclaimed for God.

The cross brings this revelation to its climax. The ancient promise speaks of two actions: the serpent striking the heel and the seed crushing the serpent's head. Jesus' passion reflects both movements. The serpent strikes through betrayal, suffering, humiliation, and death. Yet the cross, which appears to be a moment of triumph for evil, becomes the means of its defeat. The resurrection reveals that the serpent's strike cannot hold the Messiah. Death loses its power, and the humanity joined to Christ enters a new reality. The apostles interpret the cross and resurrection as the fulfilment of the protoevangelium because, through them, Jesus conquers the greatest enemy humanity faces: death itself. The head of the serpent is crushed in the moment when the Messiah rises, declaring that the powers of evil are defeated and that a new creation has begun.

This fulfilment does not erase the importance of the original promise; it illuminates it. Genesis 3:15 becomes the first note in a symphony that reaches its crescendo in Christ. The early Christians understood this instinctively. They did not see Jesus as one potential fulfilment among many. They saw Him as the fulfilment around which all other passages must be interpreted. The Scriptures, long read with anticipation, now spoke with clarity. What was whispered in Eden is proclaimed openly in the Gospels. What was foreshadowed in the lives of the patriarchs, kings, and prophets is now realised in the life of Jesus. The Messiah promised at the dawn of history has entered the world, and His victory has begun.

The Church Fathers saw in this fulfilment not only the restoration of humanity but the revelation of God's deeper intention for creation. When they described Jesus as the New Adam, they were not merely drawing parallels between two individuals; they were describing a cosmic renewal. Adam's disobedience introduced death into the world, but Christ's obedience introduces life. Adam's act fractured the bond between humanity and God, but Christ's fidelity restores that bond in a way that surpasses its original state. Through this lens, the protoevangelium is not simply the promise of a future victory; it is the announcement of a divine plan to recreate the human race from within. Christ's resurrection marks the beginning of a new humanity, one in which the serpent's power is broken and the possibility of union with God is reopened. In this sense, the promise of Genesis is fulfilled not only historically but ontologically. The very nature of humanity is renewed in Christ, who stands as the firstborn of the new creation.

This renewal also reveals why the story of Scripture unfolds as it does. The promise in Genesis does not lead immediately to the Messiah because humanity needs to be formed, instructed, and prepared to recognise the one who comes. The centuries between Eden and Bethlehem are not delays; they are the stage upon which God reveals the depth of His fidelity. Through the patriarchs, God demonstrates His commitment to a chosen people. Through Moses and the law, He teaches humanity the meaning of covenant faithfulness. Through the kings and prophets, He reveals both the consequences of sin and the hope of restoration. Every stage of Israel's history becomes part of the preparation for the Messiah. The promise grows in clarity, depth, and urgency. By the time Jesus appears, the expectations are mature, the longing is intense, and the pattern is unmistakable. The Messiah arrives not as a surprise but as the one who fits the only trajectory Scripture has ever offered.

This trajectory also explains the profound joy that marks the early Christian proclamation. When the apostles preached Jesus as the Messiah, they were not introducing a new religion. They were announcing that the promise God made in Eden had finally reached its fulfilment. Their message was not simply that a wise teacher had arisen or that a miracle worker had walked among them. Their message was that the long war between humanity and the serpent had reached its turning point. The enemy of the human race had been defeated, not by force or political power, but by the self-giving love of the Son of God. In their preaching, the apostles often returned to the theme of victory. They proclaimed Christ as the conqueror of death, the liberator of those enslaved by sin, and the one who now reigns at the right hand of God. Their joy was grounded in the conviction that the ancient promise had been kept and that the new creation had begun.

As we reflect on the protoevangelium, we begin to see why Scripture opens with such a promise and why the rest of the biblical story unfolds toward its fulfilment. Genesis introduces a world in need of healing, a humanity burdened by sin, and a creation longing for restoration. The promise of the seed becomes the answer to that longing. It reveals that God's response to sin is not abandonment but redemption. The entire narrative of the Bible flows from this revelation. The covenants, the sacrifices, the kingship, the prophecies, and the hopes of Israel all gather around the expectation that God will act decisively to overcome the serpent, restore humanity, and bring creation to its intended glory. Jesus stands at the centre of that divine action. His life, death, and resurrection reveal that the promise has been fulfilled in a way that transcends human expectation yet remains faithful to the deepest patterns of Scripture.

The seed promised in Eden has appeared. The serpent has been confronted. The victory has begun. And now the story moves forward, not only in the life of Christ but in the life of those who belong to Him. The crushing of the serpent's head is not a one-time event but a reality that continues as the kingdom of God spreads through the world. Every act of faith, every moment of repentance, every gesture of charity becomes an expression of the new creation that Christ inaugurated. The conflict continues, but its outcome has already been secured. The same promise that sustained Israel now sustains the Church, calling believers to live in the light of the Messiah's victory and to await the day when that victory will be made complete.

The first promise of Scripture, then, does more than introduce a theme. It establishes the framework through which the entire drama of salvation becomes intelligible. It reveals that God's response to human sin is not a retreat but a movement of deeper intimacy. By promising that the seed of the woman would triumph over the serpent, God commits Himself to a future in which humanity is not merely restored but elevated, drawn into a relationship that reflects His unchanging love and His desire to heal creation from its foundations. This promise becomes the lens through which we recognise the nature of God's activity in the world. It explains why the biblical narrative refuses to sever hope from history. The promise is rooted in the soil of human experience, carried through the generations, and fulfilled not in abstract speculation but in the flesh and blood of the Messiah.

The journey from Eden to Bethlehem is long, marked by sorrow, rebellion, and suffering, yet it is also marked by grace. Every moment in Israel's story, from the call of Abraham to the exile in Babylon, moves within the gravitational pull of that primordial word. The patriarchs carry the promise with imperfect hands. The kings bear it with fragile authority. The prophets speak of it with longing and clarity. Even Israel's failures become the stage upon which the depth of the promise is revealed. When hope seems lost, God renews it. When the seed seems threatened, God protects it. When humanity falters, God remains faithful. The protoevangelium is not a single thread but a tapestry woven into the entire fabric of Scripture, pulling the narrative toward its intended fulfilment.

In Jesus, the story reaches its turning point. He is not simply the next link in a chain of promise but the one to whom the chain has always pointed. His life reveals the meaning of the seed motif in its fullness. He enters the drama of human existence, confronts the serpent in temptation, undoes the effects of sin through healing and forgiveness, and takes upon Himself the very death introduced by the fall. In His resurrection, He reveals that death has been defeated and that the serpent's power has been broken. Through Him, the promise given in Eden is fulfilled not only in the victory of a single figure but in the restoration of all who belong to Him. The new creation begins in His risen life, and through the Spirit, it continues to unfold in the world until the final victory is made manifest.

The promise of Genesis 3:15 also invites us to understand our own lives within this same narrative. The battle between the serpent and the seed did not end at the resurrection; it now runs through the heart of every believer. The fidelity of Christ becomes the pattern for Christian discipleship, and the victory He won becomes the assurance that the struggles we face are neither meaningless nor hopeless. Every temptation resisted, every sin forgiven, every injustice confronted participates in the Messiah's triumph. The promise that God made at the dawn of history continues to shape the destiny of humanity. It anchors our hope in the God who keeps His word and draws us into a future where evil is overcome and creation is renewed.

As this book continues, we will explore how the promise narrowed through the covenants, how it shaped Israel's expectations, how it prepared the way for Jesus, and how He fulfils it in ways only God could accomplish. The first gospel spoken in Eden is not only the beginning of messianic prophecy; it is the beginning of the Gospel itself. Everything that follows in

Scripture will expand, clarify, and deepen this promise until its fulfilment becomes unmistakable. The seed has been revealed. The victory has begun. The Messiah stands at the centre of the story God has been telling since the beginning of time.

# 2

# The Everlasting Throne: David and the Covenant of Kingship

The rise of David marks one of the great turning points in the story of Israel, not because the people finally secure a king like the nations, but because God chooses this moment, this family, and this unlikely shepherd to reveal the form that His ancient promise will take. When the narrative first introduces David, he appears almost deliberately unimpressive—a youngest son, overlooked even by his own father, tending sheep in obscurity while the prophet Samuel searches for the one whom God has chosen. Yet Scripture insists that the Lord "sees not as man sees," for "man looks on the outward appearance, but the Lord looks on the heart" (1 Sam 16:7). The choice of David is already a repudiation of the worldly instinct to measure greatness by strength, stature, or influence. Israel's first king, Saul, embodied the external criteria the people desired, and his failure exposed the futility of that vision. The selection of David begins a new chapter in which kingship becomes not a concession to human longing but a canvas upon which God will paint the shape of His covenant.

David's early stories carry the marks of divine election. His triumph over Goliath is not merely a tale of courage but a theological proclamation. David comes to the battlefield "in the name of the Lord," declaring that the victory belongs to God rather than to military might (1 Sam 17:45–47).

The shepherd who protected his father's flock becomes the king who will shepherd Israel, a theme later remembered in Psalm 78, where God "chose David his servant" and brought him "to shepherd Jacob his people" with an integrity of heart and skilful hand. Already the portrait is clear: David's kingship derives not from human ambition but from the initiative of God. This divine initiative becomes the foundation upon which the most important promise of Israel's royal theology will be built.

That promise appears in a moment of apparent stillness, when David, now enthroned in Jerusalem, expresses a desire to build a house for the Lord. The prophet Nathan initially affirms this instinct, but God intervenes with a revelation that reverses the king's intention. David will not build a house for God; instead, God will build a house for David. The words that follow in 2 Samuel 7 form one of the central pillars of biblical theology. The Lord declares that He has taken David from the pasture, established him over Israel, given him rest from his enemies, and now promises something unprecedented. "Your house and your kingdom shall be made sure forever before me; your throne shall be established forever" (2 Sam 7:16). The triple emphasis on *house*, *kingdom*, and *throne*, each sealed with the term "forever," stretches royal expectation beyond any human horizon. No dynasty endures forever. No earthly throne escapes the erosion of time. Yet God binds Himself to David with a permanence that defies natural categories.

Jewish interpreters across the centuries have recognised the extraordinary weight of this promise. Rashi, commenting on this passage, notes that the word "forever" signals a covenant that cannot be annulled, even when later kings prove unworthy. The promise affects not only David's immediate son but projects forward to a figure whose reign will not end. Nachmanides reads 2 Samuel 7 as a direct messianic prophecy, insisting that the eternal throne can only be fulfilled in the Messiah who comes from David's line. These interpretations did not arise from Christian influence; they emerge from the intrinsic tension in the text itself. God promises something no mortal king could accomplish, and the centuries that follow force Israel to confront the depth of that tension.

## THE EVERLASTING THRONE: DAVID AND THE COVENANT OF KINGSHIP

The royal psalms deepen this mystery. Psalm 2 speaks of the Lord establishing His anointed on Zion and declares to this king, "You are my Son; today I have begotten you." The language of divine sonship here exceeds metaphor. Ancient Near Eastern kings were often called sons of gods as a political convention, but Israel's psalm places this sonship in the context of God's sovereign decree and ties it to the nations becoming the king's inheritance. The scope is universal, not regional. Psalm 72 expands this vision further, describing a king who will defend the poor, crush the oppressor, and extend peace "till the moon be no more." The language reaches toward an eschatological horizon, portraying a reign marked by justice and abundance that surpasses anything achieved in Israel's monarchy. Ibn Ezra, reflecting on Psalm 72, admits that no historical Davidic king fulfilled these descriptions fully, leaving the text open to future expectation. Psalm 89, meanwhile, holds together the promise of David's eternal throne with the anguish of Israel's suffering, asking how God's fidelity can be reconciled with the collapse of the kingdom. It is a psalm of crisis in which the covenant is not denied but thrown into question, forcing a deeper reflection on how God intends to keep His word.

Psalm 110 stands as perhaps the most startling of the royal texts. "The Lord says to my Lord: 'Sit at my right hand, until I make your enemies your footstool.'" A king of David speaks of another figure—his "Lord"—who is invited to share the authority of God Himself. Then comes the shocking declaration that this royal figure is "a priest forever according to the order of Melchizedek." The merging of kingship and priesthood is unprecedented in Israel, for the two offices were kept distinct by divine command. Yet the psalm envisions a ruler whose identity transcends the boundaries of Israel's institutions. Jewish tradition wrestled with this psalm. Some interpreters applied it to David himself, others to a future king, and still others to Abraham or the Messiah. The very diversity of readings reveals that the psalm presses the imagination beyond the familiar categories. It is no surprise that early Christians, following Jesus' own use of this text, saw in Psalm 110 a window into the mystery of the Messiah's divine authority.

As the royal theology of Israel grows, the narrative of the kingdom moves in the opposite direction. After the death of Solomon, the monarchy fractures. Injustice, idolatry, and political instability consume the land. Kings rise and fall with alarming speed, and the northern kingdom collapses under Assyrian conquest. Judah survives longer, yet its fate is sealed by the same spiritual unfaithfulness. The Babylonian invasion brings devastation: Jerusalem is destroyed, the Temple is burned, the Davidic line loses its throne, and the people are led into exile. For a nation whose identity is anchored in God's promise to David, this moment creates a theological crisis. Psalm 89's lament becomes the voice of Israel: "You have renounced the covenant with your servant... You have defiled his crown in the dust." If God's promise is unconditional, how can the throne lie empty? If the covenant is eternal, how can the kingdom fall? This tension does not weaken Israel's belief in the promise; it radicalises it. The expectation of a merely political king collapses, and the hope for a divinely appointed Messiah grows sharper.

The exile becomes the space in which Israel learns to read the Davidic covenant in a new key, not as a guarantee of earthly stability but as a pledge that God will intervene in a way that surpasses the failures of human kings. The covenant given to David contains a promise too large to fit within Israel's historical monarchy, and the collapse of the kingdom forces the people to confront this truth. The royal line has not been erased; it has been refined into expectancy. The throne stands empty because the one who will fill it must come from beyond ordinary succession, beyond political patterns, beyond the limits of fallen humanity. The eternal throne promised in 2 Samuel 7 beckons toward a future still unfolding, a promise awaiting the king who alone can bear its weight.

In the wake of the exile, the prophets step forward to reinterpret the shape of kingship, not by discarding the Davidic covenant but by unveiling its deeper meaning. Isaiah becomes one of the clearest voices in this transformation. Writing in a time of political instability and spiritual decline, he announces the birth of a child upon whose shoulders the government will rest, a child who will be called "Wonderful Counsellor, Mighty God, Everlasting Father, Prince of Peace" (Isa 9:6). These titles are not poetic exaggerations; they are theological assertions that strain the categories of ancient kingship. No king of Judah, however righteous, could bear the name "Mighty God." Yet Isaiah declares that "of the increase of his government and of peace there will be no end," and that he will sit "on the throne of David and over his kingdom" forever (Isa 9:7). This is not nostalgia for the golden age of David. It is an announcement that the Davidic covenant will be fulfilled by a figure whose identity transcends that of any earthly king.

Isaiah deepens this vision in chapter 11, where he describes a shoot emerging from the stump of Jesse. The monarchy, once a flourishing tree, has been cut down, reduced to a remnant. Yet from this remnant a new figure will arise, one upon whom "the Spirit of the Lord shall rest," a ruler who judges not by appearances but with perfect righteousness. His reign will bring harmony to creation itself—wolves dwelling with lambs, children playing where serpents once struck. Jewish commentary often interpreted these images symbolically, but the text's force lies in its assertion that the Davidic king will usher in a transformed world. Rashi recognised that this passage pointed to the Messiah, noting that the "shoot" and the "branch" are titles for the future redeemer. The Targum of Isaiah renders the passage with explicit messianic clarity, speaking not merely of a righteous ruler but of a king whose justice extends to the ends of the earth.

Jeremiah, writing on the threshold of exile, speaks with a similar intensity. He announces a coming king from David's line who will reign wisely and execute justice, and who will be called "The Lord is our righteousness" (Jer 23:6). This title is again astonishing. It implies not only that the king will do righteousness but that he will be righteousness itself for the people. The divine name is attached to the messianic king, suggesting that the covenant will be fulfilled by one who embodies God's saving presence. Ezekiel reinforces this hope by portraying the future restoration of Israel as centred on a shepherd-king called "David," who will rule over a reunited people, make a covenant of peace, and preside over a sanctuary filled with God's dwelling glory (Ezek 37:24–28). The use of David's name long after David's death reveals how thoroughly the prophetic imagination has elevated the figure of the Davidic king into the realm of eschatology.

As the prophetic vision grows, it becomes clear that Israel is no longer simply hoping for the return of a monarchy but for the arrival of a Messiah whose identity is inseparable from the promises of God Himself. The collapse of the kingdom has taught Israel to read the covenant not as a political guarantee but as a revelation of divine intention. The throne of David will endure forever because it will eventually be filled by a king who transcends mortality. The kingdom will not be established by military power but by the Spirit. The ruler will not merely enforce justice but embody it. Israel's hope becomes both more human and more divine, for the Messiah must be one of David's descendants, yet His attributes must reflect the very nature of God.

This expectation becomes visible in the literature of the Second Temple period, where the hope for a Davidic redeemer is expressed with remarkable vigour. The *Psalms of Solomon*, written in the first century before Christ, portray a coming king, "the Lord's Anointed," who will purge Jerusalem of sinners, gather the dispersed people, and rule the nations with justice. This king is described as perfectly righteous and empowered by God's Spirit. Notably, the text laments the corrupt Hasmonean kings, making clear that the author expects a Messiah who surpasses even the best historical rulers. The Dead Sea Scrolls likewise reflect this growing Messianism. The document known as 4QFlorilegium explicitly links 2 Samuel 7 with Psalm 2, interpreting the eternal throne and divine sonship as prophecies of the coming Messiah. In 4Q252, the expectation of a future Davidic king is stated without ambiguity, and in 4Q285—the so-called "Pierced Messiah" text—the Messiah appears as a suffering and victorious figure who executes judgment.

These writings show that by the time Jesus appears on the stage of history, the covenant with David has become the anchor of Israel's eschatological imagination. The people are not waiting for a theoretical figure; they are waiting for the fulfilment of God's oath. Even Josephus, writing as a historian rather than a prophet, acknowledges that there was a widespread belief in Judea that "one from their country would become ruler of the world," a reflection of the hope rooted in the Davidic line. Rabbinic writings after the destruction of the Temple continued this trajectory, with tractate *Sanhedrin* of the Talmud discussing the signs of Messiah's arrival and the "birth pangs" that would precede him. Though interpretations differ, the consensus remains: the Messiah must be Davidic, must restore justice, and must fulfill the covenant God made with David.

The New Testament does not introduce this hope—it assumes it. Matthew begins his Gospel by identifying Jesus as "the son of David, the son of Abraham," placing Him squarely within the line of promise. Gabriel tells Mary that her son "will be great and will be called the Son of the Most High," and that "the Lord God will give to him the throne of his father David," a kingdom with no end (Luke 1:32–33). The crowds who greet Jesus during His entry into Jerusalem shout, "Blessed is the coming kingdom of our father David," revealing that His ministry has been interpreted through the lens of messianic kingship. Even those who oppose Him understand the implications of His claims. When Jesus applies Psalm 110 to Himself, He exposes the inadequacy of merely human categories, forcing His listeners to recognise that the true son of David must also be David's Lord.

In this way, Israel's entire history of kingship becomes a preparation for the coming of Jesus. The patterns established in the life of David—the shepherd elevated, the anointed king, the covenant promise, the psalms that transcend earthly power—reach their fulfilment only in the Messiah. The royal line that once seemed broken becomes the channel through which God enters human history. The throne that stood empty becomes the sign of a kingdom not built by hands. God's promise to David, given in a moment of grace and sealed with the word "forever," finds its fulfilment in one who can finally bear the weight of eternity.

The more deeply we follow the arc of Israel's royal hope, the more clearly we see that the Davidic covenant forms the backbone of Israel's understanding of God's future action. The covenant in 2 Samuel 7 is not merely another promise woven into the story of Israel; it becomes the organizing centre of Israel's eschatological imagination. This is why the collapse of the monarchy does not extinguish hope but intensifies it. Israel does not interpret the exile as the failure of God's promise but as the failure of human kings to embody that promise. The throne may be vacant, but the covenant is not revoked. In fact, the absence of a king makes the divine promise stand out even more sharply. Psalm 89 becomes the anthem of this tension, lamenting the present disaster while insisting, "I will not violate my covenant, or alter the word that went forth from my lips" (Ps 89:34). The psalmist confronts God with His own faithfulness, daring to ask how an eternal throne can coexist with a shattered kingdom.

This tension becomes the furnace in which Israel's understanding of the Messiah is refined. Walter Brueggemann has observed that the prophetic imagination often arises precisely where the old structures have collapsed, allowing hope to expand into new theological territory. That is what happens with the Davidic covenant. Once the earthly monarchy has failed, the promises associated with it stretch beyond their historical embodiments. Isaiah's royal oracle, Jeremiah's "Lord our righteousness," and Ezekiel's future shepherd are not nostalgic fantasies—they are theological necessities born out of the conviction that God cannot lie. The exile does not weaken belief in the Messiah; it purifies it. Israel begins to long not merely for a king who can govern well but for a king who can heal the human condition, restore covenant fidelity, defeat injustice, and embody the presence of God among His people.

This longing grows in complexity as Jewish theological reflection continues. The Dead Sea Scrolls reveal that certain communities expected not one Messiah, but two—a priestly Messiah and a royal Messiah—each fulfilling distinct aspects of Israel's hope. This dual expectation does not contradict the Davidic covenant; it testifies to the depth of Israel's messianic yearning. The Davidic Messiah remains central, but his role is understood in increasingly transcendent terms. The community at

Qumran, for example, interpreted Psalm 2 messianically and linked it directly to the Davidic promise, seeing the royal figure as God's son in a special covenantal sense. In 4QFlorilegium, the declaration "You are my Son" is applied not to an ordinary king but to the coming Messiah, who will be installed on the throne promised to David. This interpretation shows that by the first century BCE, Jews were already reading the Scriptures with an expectation that the Davidic covenant would be fulfilled in a future, exalted ruler whose authority could rightly be called divine.

The *Psalms of Solomon* offer another window into this growing expectation. Composed in response to the corruption of the Hasmonean kings, these psalms do not reject kingship; they reject kings who violate the covenant. The psalmists cry out for a Messiah who will purge Jerusalem of wickedness, gather the dispersed tribes, rule the nations with justice, and rely entirely on God's righteousness rather than military power. Their Messiah is not a figure of political ambition but of covenant fidelity. He is righteous, wise, humble, and empowered by God's Spirit. He stands as the anti-type to failed kings, embodying everything the Davidic monarchs were meant to represent. Though not inspired Scripture, these psalms provide a vivid snapshot of messianic expectation in the generation before Jesus. They confirm that Israel's hope is not merely for restoration but for transformation—a king who restores the world's moral order and reconstitutes the people of God.

Rabbinic literature preserves this same expectation in a different key. The Talmud discusses the characteristics of the Messiah, the signs of His coming, and the conditions of the redeemed world. Although the rabbinic tradition is diverse, one theme remains constant: the Messiah must descend from David. The covenant cannot be forgotten or reinterpreted away. Even after the destruction of the Second Temple, Jewish teachers insisted that God would raise up a son of David who would rebuild the sanctuary, gather the exiles, and inaugurate an age of peace and obedience to the Torah. In *Sanhedrin 98*, the rabbis debate the Messiah's name, origins, and qualities, but they do not debate His lineage. The Messiah's Davidic identity is non-negotiable because it is grounded not in human expectation but in divine commitment. The rabbis may reject Christian claims about Jesus, but they affirm the same covenantal structure that Christians see fulfilled in Him.

This shared framework allows us to understand the New Testament not as an innovation but as a continuation. The evangelists present Jesus as the heir of David because that is the indispensable criterion for identifying the Messiah. Matthew's genealogy is a theological declaration that the long chain from Abraham to David to the exile to Joseph culminates in Jesus, who inherits the throne promised a thousand years earlier. Luke extends this genealogy all the way back to Adam, showing that the Davidic king is also the representative of all humanity. When Gabriel announces the birth of Jesus, his words echo the covenant of 2 Samuel 7 directly: the child will be called Son of the Most High, and God will give Him "the throne of his father David," and His kingdom will have no end. This is not symbolic language; it is covenant language. The early Christians believed that God had kept the promise He made to David not because they spiritualized the prophecy, but because they believed Jesus truly fulfilled it as the risen and exalted king.

Jesus' ministry confirms this identity in ways both unexpected and unmistakable. He accepts the title "Son of David" from those who call out to Him—blind men seeking mercy, crowds seeking healing—signalling that He does not reject the Davidic claim. But He also redefines kingship by embodying the justice, mercy, and self-giving love that the prophets associated with the coming Messiah. When He multiplies bread in the wilderness, He reveals Himself as the shepherd who feeds His flock. When He enters Jerusalem on a donkey, He enacts Zechariah's vision of the humble king who brings peace to the nations. When He teaches in the Temple, He exercises the authority of the one who has come to purify God's house. And when He speaks Psalm 110 in debate with the Pharisees, He reveals that the Messiah must be more than a son of David; He must be David's Lord, the one who shares in the authority of God Himself.

These claims cannot be dismissed as theological embellishment. They arise organically from the logic of the Davidic covenant, which promises an eternal throne to a son of David, yet requires that the one who occupies that throne possess a nature and authority surpassing anything that an ordinary descendant could bear. Jesus embodies this paradox because He alone unites human descent from David with divine sonship. His resurrection, which the apostles proclaim as the definitive act of God's vindication, reveals that He is the king whom death cannot hold—the true heir of the eternal kingdom. Peter's Pentecost sermon makes this explicit, arguing from Psalm 16 and Psalm 110 that David foresaw the resurrection of the Messiah and acknowledged Him as Lord. In this moment, the ancient promise becomes present reality. The throne of David, long empty and symbolically shattered, is restored in a way no one could have anticipated: not by political resurgence, but by the enthronement of Christ at the right hand of God.

Through this lens, the entire biblical narrative reveals its unity. God's covenant with David was never merely about preserving a dynasty; it was about preparing the world for a king whose reign would reconcile heaven and earth. The prophets, the psalms, the crises of Israel's history, and the longing of generations all converge on the figure of Jesus, who fulfills the promise not by seizing power but by offering Himself, not by claiming dominion but by manifesting divine sonship through obedience unto death. The throne of David becomes, in Him, the throne of the kingdom of God. The covenant becomes a revelation. The promise becomes flesh. The hope becomes a kingdom that cannot be shaken.

The early Church recognised this fulfilment not as a break from Israel's story but as its climax, the moment when the covenantal logic of Scripture finally reached its destination. The apostolic preaching in Acts repeatedly returns to the Davidic covenant as the interpretive key for understanding Jesus. Peter stands before the crowd at Pentecost and cites Psalm 16, insisting that David spoke of the Messiah's resurrection when he declared that God would not "let your Holy One see corruption." He then turns to Psalm 110, the psalm in which David calls his own descendant "Lord," and argues that this exaltation can only apply to the risen Christ, who has ascended to the right hand of God. For Peter, the resurrection is not merely a miracle—it is the enthronement of the son of David, the moment when the eternal throne promised in 2 Samuel 7 is occupied by its rightful king.

Paul echoes this same conviction when he enters the synagogue in Antioch and proclaims that God has fulfilled His promise to the fathers by raising Jesus from the dead, quoting Psalm 2's declaration, "You are my Son, today I have begotten you." In Paul's reading, the resurrection reveals Jesus as the Davidic heir, the one who receives the nations as His inheritance. When he writes to Timothy, he summarises the gospel itself as the announcement that Jesus Christ, "descended from David," has risen from the dead. For Paul, Jesus' Davidic identity is not a genealogical detail—it is the backbone of messianic fulfilment. The Messiah must come from David, and His resurrection reveals Him as the eternal king whose reign is indestructible. The apostles speak in continuity with Jewish expectation, but with a boldness that comes from witnessing the decisive act of God.

The Book of Revelation intensifies this vision by presenting Jesus as the lion of the tribe of Judah and the root of David, images drawn from Genesis and Isaiah that point toward the Messiah's royal authority. Yet the lion appears as a slain lamb, revealing that the victory of the Davidic king is achieved not through conquest but through sacrifice. The enthroned Lamb receives worship from all creation, fulfilling the promise of a king whose dominion extends over the whole earth. Revelation closes with Jesus identifying Himself as "the root and the descendant of David," a title that encapsulates the mystery of His identity. As the "descendant," He is the fulfilment of God's promise to David; as the "root," He is the one from whom David's kingship ultimately derives. The Messiah is both the heir of David and the source of David's hope, the human king who inherits the throne and the divine king who makes the throne eternal.

The Fathers of the Church seized upon this mystery with profound insight. Irenaeus, writing in the second century, argued that Christ recapitulates the entire history of Israel, fulfilling every promise made to the patriarchs and to David. For Irenaeus, the Davidic covenant finds its true meaning only in Christ, who becomes the obedient king that Israel could not produce on its own. Augustine, in *The City of God*, traces the unfolding of the two cities—earthly and heavenly—and shows how the promise to David anchors the hope of the heavenly city. He argues that the eternal throne promised in 2 Samuel 7 cannot apply to any earthly dynasty, for all earthly power is transient. It can refer only to Christ, whose kingdom is everlasting. Cyril of Jerusalem, in his catechetical lectures, insists that the title "Son of David" is not merely historical but theological, identifying Jesus as the long-awaited king of Israel who brings salvation to the world.

This patristic consensus emerges from a deep reading of Scripture itself. The Davidic covenant, understood in isolation, could be interpreted as a guarantee of national stability. But read within the full scope of Israel's story, it becomes a revelation that the Messiah must be a figure who unites heaven and earth. He must be human, to stand in David's line, yet He must possess a divine authority, because the throne promised to David is eternal. This is the paradox that the prophets glimpse, that the psalms sing, and that the New Testament proclaims openly. In Christ, this paradox is resolved. His humanity establishes Him as the true heir of David; His divinity establishes Him as the eternal king whose kingdom cannot pass away.

The logic of the covenant thus leads inexorably to the identity of Jesus. He is not simply one in a line of kings; He is the king toward whom the entire line pointed. The genealogy in Matthew is not a list of ancestors but a theological declaration that the Davidic story has reached its fulfilment. The angelic annunciation to Mary is not a poetic flourish but a covenant proclamation. The titles given to Jesus in the Gospels—Son of David, Lord, King of Israel—are not political slogans but revelations of His nature. When He teaches, He speaks with the authority of the king promised in the Scriptures. When He forgives sins, He exercises a prerogative belonging to God alone. When He lays down His life, He performs the act of the shepherd-king who saves His people. And when He rises, He shows that the throne of David has been filled by one who cannot be dethroned by death.

The Church has always understood the kingdom of Christ as the fulfilment of the Davidic covenant, not its cancellation. The throne is not abolished but transformed. The kingdom is not destroyed but universalised. What began as a promise to one family becomes the foundation for the redemption of the world. Christ reigns not from Jerusalem but from the right hand of the Father, yet His kingship is still profoundly Davidic. He is the shepherd-king, the anointed one, the ruler who brings justice, the prince of peace. The covenant's language of eternity, once a riddle, becomes a description of the risen Christ's indestructible life. The empty throne left by the exile becomes the sign of a kingdom that only God can inaugurate.

Seen in this light, the Davidic covenant is not merely one strand of messianic expectation—it is the heart that pumps life through the prophetic and psalmic visions of Israel. The expectation of a Messiah who is both human and more than human arises directly from the covenant's own terms. God promises an eternal king, and only the God-man can fulfil that promise. The entire biblical story presses toward this conclusion, and the Church recognises it not as an innovation but as the natural flowering of the seed planted in 2 Samuel 7. Jesus is the king who sits on David's throne forever, the ruler whose reign brings justice to the oppressed and peace to creation, the one who fulfils the hope of Israel and reveals the faithfulness of God.

The significance of this covenantal fulfilment becomes clearer when we examine how Jesus behaves as king. He does not seize authority; He receives it. His kingship is revealed not in self-exaltation but in self-emptying, echoing the paradox at the heart of Israel's royal theology. The prophets imagined a king who would be both exalted and humble, triumphant yet suffering, majestic yet meek. Jesus embodies each of these traits in ways that confound conventional expectations. When He enters Jerusalem on a donkey, He enacts Zechariah's prophecy of the humble king who brings peace to the nations. When He cleanses the Temple, He asserts the authority of the heir of David, fulfilling Malachi's vision of the Lord coming to purify His house. When He multiplies bread in the wilderness, He shows Himself to be the shepherd-king who provides for His flock, echoing the psalms that portray the Messiah as the one who satisfies the needs of the people.

Yet Jesus' kingship cannot be understood apart from His suffering. This is where the Davidic covenant reveals its deepest mystery. The Messiah must be both the victorious king and the suffering servant. The two roles are not opposed but intertwined. Isaiah's vision of the Servant, who bears the sins of the people and is pierced for their transgressions, stands alongside his vision of the royal child who bears divine titles. The early Church recognised that the Messiah could only be understood by holding these images together. The suffering of Christ is not a departure from His kingship but its expression. He conquers not by force but by love, not by domination but by obedience. His death becomes the moment when the serpent's apparent victory becomes its defeat, fulfilling the ancient promise of Genesis. The king from David's line crushes the head of the enemy not through political might but through sacrificial love.

This interpretation is not a later Christian invention but emerges naturally from the texts themselves. Even within the psalms, David's royal identity is frequently linked with suffering. Psalm 22, which Jesus quotes from the cross, is a Davidic psalm that moves from anguish to triumph, from seeming abandonment to victory. Psalm 69 portrays the righteous sufferer whose zeal for God's house consumes him, language that the New Testament applies directly to Jesus. Psalm 118, the psalm of rejected stone becoming the cornerstone, becomes a key text in early Christian preaching about the Messiah. These psalms reveal that suffering is not incompatible with kingship; it is often the means through which God's purposes are accomplished. The Davidic king is not spared trials; he passes through them to reveal the faithfulness of God.

The prophetic writings deepen this theme. Isaiah's servant songs, particularly Isaiah 52–53, describe a figure who bears the sins of many and makes intercession for transgressors. Jewish interpretation has varied on the identity of this servant—some see Israel collectively; others see a specific righteous remnant. But Christian interpretation, following the logic of the Davidic covenant, sees in the servant's suffering the means by which the Messiah accomplishes His mission. The prophets speak of a Davidic king who rules with justice and of a suffering servant who redeems through pain. These two images may seem dissonant, but in Christ they become harmonic. The Messiah is the king who suffers, the servant who reigns. The cross is His throne, and the resurrection is His enthronement.

Even within Judaism, before the time of Jesus, there were hints that some understood the Messiah to be a suffering figure. The Dead Sea Scrolls include texts in which the Messiah appears to be wounded or killed, only to rise or be vindicated by God. The "Pierced Messiah" fragment (4Q285) portrays a messianic leader who seems to suffer before executing judgment. Though scholars debate the interpretation of this text, its existence proves that messianic suffering was not outside the realm of Jewish expectation. The Targum to Isaiah 52–53 sometimes expands the servant passages in ways that highlight the suffering of the Messiah. Rabbinic sources record debates about whether the Messiah would come in humility or in glory, revealing that Jewish thinkers were grappling with the possibility of a Messiah whose path included suffering.

This background illuminates the logic of the Gospel passion narratives. When Jesus is hailed as "Son of David," He accepts the title. When He enters Jerusalem, He enacts the royal procession. When He debates the scribes about Psalm 110, He reveals that the Messiah must be greater than David. But when He suffers, He does so as the king who bears the fate of His people. The inscription on His cross—"Jesus of Nazareth, King of the Jews"—is meant as mockery, yet it speaks the truth. The crucifixion becomes the moment when the kingship of Christ is revealed in its paradoxical glory. The Messiah reigns by giving His life, and His triumph is unveiled in His resurrection.

The resurrection does more than reverse death; it vindicates the Davidic covenant. The eternal throne promised to David can only be occupied by one who has passed beyond death. No merely human king can reign forever. But Jesus, risen and glorified, becomes the living fulfilment of the covenant. When He appears to His disciples and declares that all authority in heaven and on earth has been given to Him, He speaks as the king whose dominion is universal and unending. The ascension is the enthronement of the Messiah. He takes His place at the right hand of God, fulfilling the imagery of Psalm 110 and establishing His rule over all creation. From this throne, He pours out the Holy Spirit, forming a people who live under His kingship and bear witness to His reign.

The kingdom of Christ thus becomes the continuation and perfection of the Davidic kingdom. It is not a political entity bound to geography or earthly power; it is a kingdom grounded in truth, righteousness, and divine authority. The Church Fathers recognised this transformation. Eusebius speaks of Christ as the one who fulfils the promise to David by ruling over a kingdom that extends to the ends of the earth. Tertullian argues that the prophetical expectations of a universal reign cannot apply to any earthly monarch but only to the Messiah. Athanasius sees in the resurrection the divine act that establishes Christ's eternal kingship. For all of them, the identity of Christ as David's son is inseparable from His identity as the Lord who reigns forever.

This reading also clarifies why the New Testament insists on calling Jesus "Lord," a title that, in the Greek-speaking world, could refer either to a human master or to the divine name. In the context of the Davidic covenant, the title takes on its full theological weight. To call Jesus "Lord" is to acknowledge that He shares the authority of God, that He sits on the eternal throne promised to David, and that His rule extends over all creation. His humanity roots Him in David's line; His divinity establishes Him as the king whose reign knows no end. The early Christians did not invent this theology; they inherited it from the logic of the covenant itself. The God who promised an eternal throne has fulfilled that promise in the risen Christ, who rules not from an earthly palace but from the right hand of the Father.

Through this fulfilment, the covenant with David becomes one of the clearest demonstrations of the faithfulness of God. The promise survives

Israel's disobedience, political collapse, exile, and centuries of longing. It survives the failures of kings, the destruction of the Temple, and the scattering of the nation. It endures because it rests not on human strength but on divine fidelity. In Christ, the promise stands revealed in its true form: an eternal king, a universal kingdom, a reign grounded in justice and love. The covenant that began with a shepherd-king in Bethlehem culminates in the risen Lord who reigns over heaven and earth, the one in whom all of God's promises find their "Yes."

The covenant's fulfilment in Christ also reshapes our understanding of what kingship means within the economy of salvation. Earthly kings rise and fall, secure borders, raise armies, and leave monuments, yet the biblical portrait of the Messiah reveals a king whose authority operates on a different plane. He does not govern by coercion but by truth. He does not guard His own life but lays it down for His people. He does not grasp at power but receives it from the Father. This inversion of worldly power is not a rejection of kingship but its perfection. The Davidic king was always meant to reflect the heart of God, to rule in justice, to defend the poor, to shepherd the people. The failure of David's descendants does not invalidate the ideal; it reveals the necessity of a king whose heart is perfectly aligned with the will of God. In Christ, the ideal becomes real. The king has come, not simply to rule over His people, but to recreate them in His own image, forming a kingdom grounded in righteousness and animated by the Spirit.

This transformation becomes evident in the way Jesus gathers disciples around Himself. He does not merely teach them; He forms them into a new Israel. The twelve apostles signify the restoration of the twelve tribes, revealing that the Messiah's kingdom is not an abstraction but a lived reality rooted in covenant renewal. When Jesus promises that they will "sit on twelve thrones, judging the twelve tribes of Israel," He speaks as the king who inaugurates the new age. His miracles, His teaching, His authority over demons, and His forgiveness of sins are not isolated acts but signs of the kingdom breaking into the world. Each moment reveals His identity as the heir of David, the one who brings order where chaos has reigned and healing where sin has wounded. He does not simply proclaim the kingdom; He embodies it.

The climactic display of this kingship comes in His death and resurrection. In the passion narratives, Jesus is repeatedly called "King of the Jews," a title meant to mock Him but which the evangelists present with deliberate irony. The Roman soldiers place a crown of thorns on His head, not knowing that in doing so they reveal a deeper truth: the king of Israel reigns through suffering love. His cross becomes His throne, the place where He conquers the enemies no earthly king could defeat—sin, death, and the ancient serpent who has opposed God's purposes since Eden. The victory He wins is not temporary but eternal, for death no longer holds dominion over Him. When He rises from the tomb, He inaugurates a new creation, fulfilling the promise that God would raise up a son of David whose kingdom would have no end.

The resurrection reveals the true dimensions of the Davidic covenant. Only one who has passed through death and emerged victorious can reign forever. Only one whose life is indestructible can occupy an everlasting throne. Only one who shares the authority of God can bring justice to the nations and restore creation. The covenant's language, which seemed impossible when first spoken, becomes clear in light of Christ. The Messiah must be human to fulfil the genealogy, the prophecies, and the promises to David. He must also be divine to fulfil the promise of an unending kingdom. The early Church understood this tension instinctively. When they confessed Jesus as "Lord," they were not merely offering Him respect; they were proclaiming that the son of David shares the divine identity. This conviction flows not from philosophical speculation but from the logic of Scripture itself. The God who promises an eternal king must Himself provide the king who can reign eternally.

The Church's worship bears witness to this reality. From the earliest hymns recorded in the New Testament, such as the one embedded in Philippians 2, Christians celebrated Christ as the exalted Lord whom every knee must bow to and every tongue confess. The Book of Revelation portrays Him as the Lamb who has conquered, the one worthy to open the scroll because He was slain and by His blood ransomed a people for God. The images of enthronement, victory, and universal dominion are not symbolic flourishes but the lived confession of a community that believes the king has taken His place on the eternal throne. The liturgy of the Church, East and West, continues this proclamation. Christ is hailed as the "King of Glory," the "King of Kings," and the "Son of David," titles that connect the worship of the Church directly to the covenant made with David in Jerusalem centuries before.

This continuity between Israel's hope and the Church's proclamation exposes the profound unity of Scripture. The Davidic covenant is not a relic of ancient history but a revelation of the way God chooses to rule His creation. He does not govern from a distance or through abstract decrees. He enters human history, binds Himself to a particular family, and fulfils His promise through the incarnation of His Son. The throne of David becomes the throne of Christ. The kingdom of Israel becomes the kingdom of God. The covenant that seemed to shatter in exile becomes unbreakable through the resurrection. Every strand of the biblical narrative, from the promise to Abraham to the psalms of David to the visions of the prophets, converges on this moment when the king is enthroned in glory, ruling from the right hand of the Father and interceding for His people.

As the implications of this fulfilment unfold, a new reality emerges for those who belong to the Messiah. They are not subjects of an earthly empire but citizens of a heavenly kingdom. Their allegiance is not to a transient ruler but to a king whose reign is eternal. Their hope is not in political restoration but in the renewal of creation itself. In Christ, the covenant with David extends to all nations, fulfilling the promise that Abraham's descendants would bless the world. The kingdom becomes a people gathered from every tribe and tongue, united not by ethnicity or territory but by faith in the one who reigns forever. The Davidic covenant thus becomes the foundation for Christian identity. To confess Jesus as Lord is to confess that the promise to David is fulfilled, that the eternal king has come, and that His kingdom will never pass away.

What becomes unmistakable, once the covenant's logic is traced from

David to Christ, is that the hope for a Messiah is not a poetic flourish layered late onto Israel's imagination. It is the structural consequence of God's own fidelity. The Davidic covenant carries within itself a kind of divine momentum, pressing history toward a king who can bear the weight of eternity. The failures of the monarchy do not diminish the promise—they expose its true scope. When David's sons prove unfaithful, the promise remains because it does not depend on their righteousness. When Jerusalem falls, the promise remains because it was never bound to the survival of an earthly regime. When the throne sits empty, the promise remains because God Himself has sworn an oath. The Messiah is not the outcome of Israel's longing; He is the outcome of God's commitment. History moves not by human aspiration but by divine promise, and the promise given to David becomes the compass by which Israel interprets both its suffering and its hope.

This is why, in the fullness of time, the New Testament does not hesitate to proclaim Jesus as the fulfilment of the covenant. The evangelists announce Him not as a new idea but as the answer to an ancient oath. The apostles preach Him not as a symbolic heir but as the risen king seated at God's right hand. The early Church worships Him not as a gifted teacher but as the Lord of Psalm 110, the son of David who is also David's Lord. Every title ascribed to Jesus—Christ, Lord, Son of God, Son of David—makes sense only within the framework of the covenant. The incarnation itself becomes intelligible in this light. God becomes man not simply to dwell among His people but to fulfil a promise He made in the days of David. The eternal Son takes on the lineage of Jesse so that the throne promised to David might be occupied forever by the one who shares the life of God.

This fulfilment also reveals something essential about the character of God. He is not a distant sovereign who issues decrees from beyond the world. He is a God who binds Himself to humanity, who makes promises with real consequences, who enters history to keep those promises. The Davidic covenant shows that God does not hesitate to align His purposes with the fragility of human lineage in order to bring forth the salvation of the world. The covenant is not merely a legal contract; it is an expression of divine love. God does not abandon His people even when they abandon Him. He does not revoke His promise even when His chosen kings fall. The everlasting throne reveals the everlasting fidelity of God, a fidelity that culminates in the person of Christ, whose very identity is the union of divine faithfulness and human descent.

In Christ, the throne of David becomes the throne from which all creation is governed. His reign is not limited by geography or bound by time. It extends over the living and the dead, over heaven and earth, over angels and powers. His kingdom is not secured by swords but by the victory of the cross, not sustained by tribute but by the gift of the Spirit. The Church, formed by His word and nourished by His body, becomes the visible expression of that kingdom in the world. Believers live under a king who reigns not by coercion but by charity, not by fear but by truth. Their allegiance is not demanded but invited, not enforced but embraced. This is the paradox of the Messiah's kingship: the more He gives of Himself, the more His kingdom grows; the more He serves, the more His authority is revealed; the more He suffers, the more His glory shines.

From Bethlehem to Golgotha, from the empty tomb to the right hand of the Father, the story of Jesus is the story of the Davidic covenant brought to its divine fulfilment. The shepherd-king has become the universal Lord. The promised son has become the eternal ruler. The oath sworn by God has become flesh and blood, risen and glorified, reigning now and forever. In Him, the hope of Israel and the longing of the nations converge. In Him, the promises given to Abraham, Moses, and David find their unity. In Him, the kingdom of God takes its visible and everlasting form. The covenant that began in the courts of Jerusalem now spans the world, inviting every nation to share in the reign of the Son of David, the Christ, the Lord, the King whose throne shall never be shaken.

Thus the Davidic covenant, once entrusted to a single man and a single dynasty, becomes the cornerstone of salvation history. It reveals the kind of God who makes promises He alone can fulfil, the kind of king who rules by love rather than force, and the kind of kingdom that expands through mercy rather than conquest. The Messiah promised to David, awaited by Israel, and revealed in Jesus is the one through whom all creation will be renewed. His throne is everlasting because His life is everlasting, and His reign brings to completion the purpose for which the world was made. In the light of this king, every hope finds its fulfilment, every promise its "Yes," and every longing its rest.

# 3

# The Prophet Like Moses: The Promise of a New Exodus

Israel never tells its origin story as a tale of human ingenuity or political brilliance. It tells it as the story of a God who bends down to rescue His people from bondage, revealing Himself not through abstractions but through a liberator, a covenant, and a journey that becomes the template for all future redemption. From the moment Moses steps onto the stage of Scripture, the shape of salvation is disclosed: God raises a deliverer, confronts the oppressive power, breaks the chains, forms a people, gives them His law, and leads them toward a promised inheritance. This is why Moses is not only Israel's first great prophet but the mould into which every future hope is cast. The book of Numbers describes him with a uniqueness unparalleled in Scripture: "If there is a prophet among you, I the LORD make myself known to him in a vision… Not so with my servant Moses… With him I speak mouth to mouth" (Num 12:6–8). And Deuteronomy seals this testimony at the close of Moses' life: "There has not arisen a prophet since in Israel like Moses, whom the LORD knew face to face, none like him for all the signs and wonders that the LORD sent him to do" (Deut 34:10–12).

This portrait is not literary embellishment; it reflects the way Israel understood the very nature of divine revelation. Moses is the mediator of the covenant at Sinai, standing between God and the people as the one who receives the commandments, transmits the words of the Lord, establishes the sacrificial rituals, and intercedes when the people fall into sin. The book of Exodus presents him as the man who ascends the mountain into the consuming fire to receive the law (Exod 24:15–18), whose face shines with reflected glory after speaking with God (Exod 34:29–35), and who pleads for the people when they have made gods of their own hands. The golden calf incident, far from showing Moses as a mere administrator, reveals him as the intercessor whose fidelity sustains the covenant. He stands before God and says, astonishingly, "If you will not forgive their sin, blot me out of your book" (Exod 32:32), a depth of self-offering that early Christians would later hear as a foreshadowing of Christ's own intercession.

Jewish tradition amplifies this unique status. The Targum Onkelos—the most authoritative Aramaic rendering of the Torah—consistently heightens the dignity of Moses, calling him repeatedly "the prophet of the LORD" and emphasizing the intimacy of his communion with God. Philo of Alexandria, writing in the first century, describes Moses as "king, legislator, high priest, and prophet" (*Life of Moses* 2.2), presenting him as the ideal fusion of roles necessary to guide the people of God. Midrash Rabbah goes further, stating, "God spoke to Moses clearly and not in riddles; no other prophet has arisen to match him," echoing the biblical declaration that Moses' prophetic authority is singular. These traditions do not exalt Moses for his own sake but because through him Israel experienced God's redeeming power. Moses becomes the prism through which Israel learns what it means for God to save.

The exodus event itself shapes Israel's understanding of salvation with an enduring clarity. It begins with God hearing the cry of the oppressed (Exod 2:23–25) and sending Moses with the divine commission, "I will send you to Pharaoh that you may bring my people... out of Egypt" (Exod 3:10). Liberation unfolds through signs and wonders—plagues that dismantle the oppressive order and reveal the impotence of Egypt's gods. The crossing of the Red Sea becomes the great moment of deliverance, celebrated in

Psalm and prophecy as the defining act of God's kingship. The wilderness becomes the place where the people learn dependence, where God feeds them with manna and gives them water from the rock, revealing Himself not only as liberator but as provider. And Sinai becomes the centre of covenant formation, where God declares, "I am the LORD your God who brought you out of Egypt" (Exod 20:2), grounding the law not in abstract morality but in the memory of redemption.

Moses embodies every dimension of this drama. As liberator, he confronts Pharaoh not with political leverage but with the authority of God's word. As mediator, he receives the Torah, establishing Israel's identity as a covenant people. As miracle-worker, he performs signs that validate his commission. As intercessor, he pleads for mercy when Israel sins, revealing that the covenant is sustained not by human fidelity but by divine compassion offered through a chosen servant. This is why later biblical authors continually return to the exodus as the pattern of future salvation. As Frank Moore Cross remarks, the exodus becomes "the central metaphor of Yahweh's kingship," a theological blueprint that the prophets will later expand into the hope for a new and greater redemption.

Because Moses stands at the intersection of liberation, revelation, and covenant, Scripture itself begins to anticipate someone who will one day fulfil these roles in a definitive way. The clearest promise appears in Deuteronomy, where Moses, knowing his death is near, tells Israel: "The LORD your God will raise up for you a prophet like me from among your brethren; to him you shall listen" (Deut 18:15). He continues, speaking in God's voice, "I will put my words in his mouth, and he shall speak to them all that I command him" (v. 18). This is no casual prediction. It is the announcement of a future figure who will stand in continuity with Moses yet surpass him in authority. The passage itself recalls the theophany at Sinai, where the people begged not to hear the terrifying voice of God directly. The new prophet will speak with that same divine authority, mediating God's word as Moses did. And the warning attached to the promise intensifies its significance: "Whoever will not listen to my words which he shall speak in my name, I myself will require it of him" (v. 19).

## THE PROPHET LIKE MOSES: THE PROMISE OF A NEW EXODUS

Jewish commentators have long wrestled with the meaning of this passage. Rashi interprets "a prophet like me" as referring to the line of prophets who follow Moses but acknowledges an ultimate fulfilment in the Messiah. Maimonides, in *Hilchot Melachim*, describes the Messiah as a prophet of unparalleled clarity whose authority echoes Moses' unique intimacy with God. The Targum Jonathan strengthens the messianic reading by paraphrasing the passage with references to a future "prophet of righteousness," signalling that Deut 18 was read in antiquity with an eye toward a coming redeemer. In the Dead Sea Scrolls, the community at Qumran expected the Prophet, distinct from the priestly and royal Messiahs, who would interpret the law with divine authority and reveal God's will for the final days (1QS 9:11). This expectation emerges directly from the Mosaic promise. Israel knew that Moses was unmatched, yet Deuteronomy explicitly said another would come. The space between these truths becomes one of Israel's deepest hopes—a prophetic figure who would inaugurate a new era of revelation and redemption, a redeemer like Moses, yet greater.

This expectation did not remain confined to Deuteronomy. The rest of the Torah itself begins to echo forward, hinting that Moses' mission is both foundational and anticipatory. The exodus, far from being a self-contained event, becomes the grammar of redemption through which Israel learns to recognise God's saving patterns. When the prophets speak of God's future acts, they do so by drawing Moses forward—not by reproducing the past, but by expanding it. The book of Isaiah becomes the clearest voice of this expectation. As Israel enters the trauma of exile, Isaiah does not simply recall the memory of the Red Sea; he uses it as the canvas for a greater deliverance. "Thus says the LORD, who makes a way in the sea... 'Remember not the former things... behold, I am doing a new thing; now it springs forth, do you not perceive it?'" (Isa 43:16–19). The "new thing" is not the erasure of the first exodus but its transformation—an act of God that will make the earlier deliverance appear as a prelude.

Isaiah speaks repeatedly of a highway in the wilderness, rivers flowing in the desert, and creation itself opening to the approach of the redeemed.

These images are not poetic inventions; they are prophetic reapplications of the exodus pattern. Israel's liberation from Egypt becomes the model for her liberation from exile, and by extension, for the ultimate liberation still to come. Jewish tradition recognised this immediately. The rabbis noted that just as God redeemed Israel from Egypt with wonders, so the final redemption would come with signs surpassing those of old. The Mekhilta de-Rabbi Ishmael, commenting on the Song at the Sea, declares: "As the first Redeemer was, so shall the final Redeemer be." This refrain—"as the first, so the last"—runs like a thread through rabbinic eschatology. Moses becomes the pattern for the Messiah, not because Moses is the ideal end of salvation history, but because the Messiah will bring to perfection what Moses began.

Jeremiah makes the same claim with startling clarity. He declares that the day will come when Israel's redemption will no longer be described as "the LORD who brought up the people of Israel out of Egypt," but as "the LORD who brought up and led the descendants of Israel out of the north country" (Jer 23:7–8). In other words, the new deliverance will overshadow the first. The prophet even describes a new covenant, "not like the covenant I made with their fathers… when I took them by the hand to bring them out of the land of Egypt" (Jer 31:32). The new covenant will be characterised not by tablets of stone but by hearts transformed by God Himself—"I will put my law within them, and I will write it upon their hearts" (Jer 31:33). This shift from external inscription to internal transformation corresponds to the shift from Moses to the prophet like Moses. The first mediator gave the law written by God's finger; the final mediator will give the law written by God's Spirit.

Ezekiel likewise frames Israel's future salvation as a new exodus. He speaks of God gathering His scattered people from the nations, purifying them with clean water, giving them a new heart, and placing His Spirit within them so that they can walk in His statutes (Ezek 36:24–27). He even describes God leading His people "into the wilderness of the nations" and entering into judgment with them "as I entered into judgment with your fathers in the wilderness of the land of Egypt" (Ezek 20:35–36). This is unmistakable exodus imagery, deliberately invoked to show that the coming redemption will follow the ancient pattern. The prophet also envisions a restored sanctuary filled with divine glory, recalling Moses' Tabernacle where "the glory of the LORD filled the tent" (Exod 40:34). Once again, Moses becomes both the foundation and the prophecy of what is to come.

Second Temple Judaism inherited this prophetic imagination and developed it with even greater intensity. The *Wisdom of Solomon* recounts the exodus as a template for God's future actions, describing how He "made His people to pass through a marvellous sea" and will again judge the wicked and vindicate the righteous (Wis 19). The Book of Jubilees amplifies the exodus into cosmic significance, treating it as the axis around which the history of the world turns. The Dead Sea Scrolls repeatedly speak of a coming "visitation" in which God will perform wonders like those of the past. The sect at Qumran explicitly awaited a new Moses, a prophet who would interpret the law with perfect clarity and restore its true meaning. In the *Rule of the Community* (1QS 9:11), they speak of awaiting "the Prophet," "the Messiah of Aaron," and "the Messiah of Israel," showing that the expectation of a Mosaic-like figure was not marginal but essential to their eschatological worldview.

Some texts sharpen this expectation even further. The *Testament of Moses* speaks of a future time when God will raise up a leader who will again stand against oppressive nations and bring judgment upon idolatry, echoing Moses' confrontation with Pharaoh. The *Testament of Levi* and *Testament of Judah* anticipate figures who, like Moses, combine teaching, judgment, and divine authority. Jewish theologian Michael Fishbane has shown that this "inner-biblical exegesis"—the way later texts reinterpret earlier ones—reveals that Moses was already becoming, within Israel's own canon, a pattern awaiting fulfilment.

All of this prepares for the central claim of the chapter: that Moses is not merely the beginning of Israel's story but its prophetic shape. His life—his call, his miracles, his mediation, his intercession, his covenant, his ascent of the mountain, his intimacy with God—creates a pattern that

Israel understands as the blueprint for future salvation. The people expect a deliverer who will echo Moses in form but surpass him in power. They expect a teacher who will reveal God's will as Moses did, but with greater clarity. They expect a redeemer who will confront oppressive powers, but with deeper authority. They expect a covenant, but one written not on stone but on the heart. They expect a Passover, but one whose deliverance will never fade. They expect, in short, a new Moses.

Among all the institutions of Israel's life, none preserved the memory of Moses more vividly than Passover. This feast did more than recall a distant event; it formed Israel's identity around liberation, sacrifice, judgment, and covenant. Exodus 12 establishes the Passover as a perpetual memorial, commanding each generation not merely to remember the redemption from Egypt but to enter it. The liturgy of the Haggadah, shaped across centuries, expresses this with striking clarity: *"In every generation, a person must see himself as if he came out of Egypt."* By binding each generation to the original act of deliverance, Passover became a living prophecy. The redemption of the past was a rehearsal for the redemption yet to come. The blood of the lamb, the unleavened bread, the bitter herbs, the four cups, the questions of the child—each element belonged not only to the memory of Moses but to the expectation of the Messiah.

Jewish tradition recognized this explicitly. The Mekhilta on Exodus teaches that "as the first redeemer was, so shall the last redeemer be," meaning that the final deliverance of Israel will mirror and surpass the exodus of old. The Targum to Exodus 12 amplifies the sacrificial lamb as a symbol of God's future act of salvation. Rabbinic homilies often speak of redemption unfolding "in the month of Nisan," the month of the exodus, because the first salvation sets the calendar for the last. Even the Passover cup known as *kos shel Eliyahu*—the cup of Elijah—expresses the conviction that redemption is not complete until the Messiah comes. Elijah, the forerunner, must appear to herald the new Moses, the final deliverer whose mission will transform the world.

The Second Temple texts deepen this expectation by expanding the symbolism of Passover into eschatological imagery. The writings found at Qumran speak of a future "Messianic banquet," an eschatological feast in which the Messiahs of Aaron and Israel preside over a renewed covenant meal (1QSa 2). This meal draws directly from the pattern of Passover, where covenant and sacrifice are united. The community believed that the final redemption would include a renewed celebration of God's deliverance, but one that surpassed the historical exodus as sunlight surpasses dawn. Jubilees recounts the Passover as a heavenly archetype, a festival observed not only by Israel but by the angels, suggesting that the exodus belongs to the cosmic structure of God's plan. In the *Wisdom of Solomon*, the crossing of the Red Sea becomes a symbol of God's judgment upon the wicked and salvation for the righteous—a pattern that the final redeemer will replicate.

Within this web of expectation, the promise of a prophet like Moses takes on greater significance. The anticipation is no longer merely for a teacher, or a national liberator, or a miracle-worker, but for a figure who embodies all the roles that Moses held in unity. The prophet like Moses must confront oppressive power—just as Moses confronted Pharaoh. He must perform signs and wonders—not to entertain, but to authenticate divine purpose. He must mediate a covenant—not written on stone like Sinai, but inscribed upon hearts by the Spirit, as Jeremiah foretold. He must lead a unity of God's people—not only a physical exodus from land, but a spiritual exodus from sin. He must intercede—standing between God and His people with a devotion that mirrors and surpasses Moses' plea, "blot me out of your book" (Exod 32:32). The new redeemer must therefore be both like Moses and greater than Moses, fulfilling Moses' words and surpassing his works.

This expectation saturates the Gospel narratives. When John the Baptist appears in the wilderness, the priests and Levites ask him plainly, *"Are you the Prophet?"* (John 1:21), referring directly to Deuteronomy 18. Their question reveals that the category of "the Prophet like Moses" remained alive and distinct within Jewish messianic expectation. John denies the title, pointing instead to the one who will come after him. When Jesus feeds the five thousand, the crowd declares, "This is indeed the Prophet who is to come into the world" (John 6:14). The multiplication of bread is not merely a miracle; it is a Mosaic sign, echoing the manna of the wilderness and revealing that a new Moses has begun to feed the people of God. When Jesus teaches with unparalleled authority in the Sermon on the Mount, proclaiming, "You have heard that it was said... but I say to you" (Matt 5), He does not abolish Moses—He reveals Himself as the one who can speak with the same divine authority Moses mediated. Matthew's entire narrative is structured as a Mosaic typology: Jesus escapes a murderous king as Moses did, passes through water at His baptism as Israel did, is tested in the wilderness for forty days as Israel was tested for forty years, ascends a mountain to give law, and forms a covenant people through His teaching.

The Transfiguration becomes the moment when the typology is unveiled in full clarity. Jesus ascends the mountain with three companions, as Moses ascended with Aaron, Nadab, and Abihu. His face shines like the sun, recalling Moses' radiant face after speaking with God. Moses himself appears alongside Elijah, representing the law and the prophets, and the divine voice declares, "This is my beloved Son... listen to Him!" (Matt 17:5). The command "listen to Him" is the exact fulfilment of Deuteronomy 18:15—Moses once said, "To him you shall listen," and now the Father speaks the same command from the cloud. The prophet like Moses has arrived, and He stands not beside Moses as an equal but above Moses as the Son.

As the Gospels unfold, the imagery of a new exodus intensifies. Luke uses the word "exodus" to describe Jesus' impending passion in Jerusalem (Luke 9:31), indicating that His death and resurrection will not merely evoke the exodus—they will be the exodus in its perfect form. Jesus confronts demonic powers as Moses confronted Pharaoh. He frees the oppressed, heals the wounded, restores the outcast, and proclaims liberty to captives. He gathers a new people around a new covenant meal—the Last Supper—which He intentionally institutes during Passover. "This is my blood of the covenant" (Matt 26:28) echoes both Sinai and Jeremiah 31, revealing that what Moses mediated through sacrifice, Jesus now mediates through

His own self-giving. The new covenant is not ratified by the blood of bulls but by the blood of the Lamb of God.

The shape of redemption is unmistakable. Jesus does not merely resemble Moses; He fulfils Moses. The signs He performs, the covenant He inaugurates, the liberation He brings, the teaching He gives, and the death He offers all reveal that the exodus Moses began reaches its divine completion in Him. He leads humanity out of bondage to sin as Moses led Israel out of bondage to Pharaoh. He feeds the people with heavenly bread as Moses fed them with manna. He intercedes for sinners as Moses pleaded for Israel after the golden calf. And as Gregory of Nyssa observed, He leads the soul "from shadow to truth, from bondage to freedom, from earth to heaven," accomplishing what Moses prefigured but could not complete.

This is why the early Church proclaimed Christ not merely as Messiah but as the new Moses. He is the prophet like Moses promised in Deuteronomy 18, the teacher whose authority surpasses every prophet, the mediator of the new covenant, the redeemer of a new exodus, the giver of the true Passover, and the one who leads God's people into the promised inheritance of eternal life. The story Moses began in Egypt finds its fulfilment in the One who stands on the mountain of transfiguration, whose word is the very voice of God, and whose sacrifice opens the way not to a land but to a kingdom that will never end.

Yet none of these parallels reaches the heart of the matter until we examine the nature of Moses as covenant mediator and how that role becomes the deepest measure for identifying the Messiah. Moses stands between God and the people not merely as a messenger but as the human instrument through which God establishes Israel's entire covenantal life. At Sinai, the people tremble before the divine voice and beg Moses to speak on their behalf. "You speak to us, and we will hear; but let not God speak to us, lest we die" (Exod 20:19). Moses ascends the mountain alone, enters the cloud of divine presence, receives the commandments, and returns with the law that forms Israel as a holy nation. The book of Deuteronomy recalls this moment with solemn gravity: the people heard the voice of

God but saw no form, and Moses alone was permitted to approach the fire (Deut 4:12, 5:5). The covenant depends upon a mediator, one who ascends to God and descends to the people with a word that is not his own.

This mediation becomes one of the essential features of the expected redeemer. If the Messiah is to inaugurate a new covenant, He must stand in the place of Moses—ascending to the divine presence, bringing revelation, and establishing a bond between God and His people. Jeremiah's promise of a "new covenant" is impossible without a new mediator. The early rabbis recognised this logic. In their reflections on Jeremiah 31, they taught that the new covenant would restore Sinai's glory but elevate it: "The Torah will be renewed by the future redeemer," declares Exodus Rabbah (6:4), implying that the Messiah must bring a revelation equal to or surpassing Sinai. This expectation harmonises perfectly with Deuteronomy 18, where Moses speaks of a prophet who will mediate God's words with the same authority he possessed. The new Moses must therefore embody the same intimacy with God that marked Moses' face when it shone with borrowed glory.

The patristic writers saw this connection with luminous clarity. Origen commented that the people could not endure the full radiance of divine truth, so God sent Moses as "a tempered light" through whom the Word reached Israel. In Christ, however, the light shines not by reflection but by its own source. Augustine, preaching on the Gospel of John, wrote: "Moses was the servant, Christ the Lord; Moses the bearer of the tablets, Christ the giver of grace." The distinction does not deny their continuity; rather, it reveals the very structure of salvation history. Moses foreshadows Christ precisely by being what Christ will bring to perfection. Gregory of Nazianzus captures it even more succinctly: "Moses lifted the serpent; Christ was lifted up. Moses saved from temporal death; Christ from eternal."

But the clearest fulfilment of Mosaic mediation appears in the upper room on the night of the Passover. At Sinai, Moses took the blood of sacrificed animals, sprinkled it upon the people, and said, "Behold the blood of the covenant which the LORD has made with you" (Exod 24:8).

It was the moment when Israel became God's covenant nation. In the Last Supper, Jesus lifts the cup and echoes Moses directly: "This is my blood of the covenant" (Matt 26:28). The parallel is precise, deliberate, and unmistakable. Moses sealed the covenant with the blood of bulls; Jesus seals it with His own. Moses mediated a law engraved on stone; Jesus mediates a law engraved on hearts by the gift of the Spirit. Moses ascended Sinai and returned with commandments; Jesus ascends Calvary and rises with a new creation.

This is where the typology sharpens into identity. Jesus not only parallels Moses; He supersedes him as the mediator of a covenant of eternal life. The Letter to the Hebrews makes this explicit when it states, "Jesus has been counted worthy of more glory than Moses" (Heb 3:3), not by diminishing Moses' greatness but by revealing the greater reality to which Moses pointed. The author of Hebrews describes Moses as a faithful servant "in God's house," but Christ as the Son "over God's house" (Heb 3:5–6). The point is not merely hierarchical. It reveals the ontological difference between the shadow and the substance. Moses mediated the covenant as a servant; Christ mediates the covenant as its divine source. Moses carried the tablets; Christ writes the law into the human soul. Moses lifted his hands to intercede for Israel against Amalek; Christ lifts His pierced hands to intercede forever for His people at the right hand of the Father.

Within this theological framework, the exodus itself becomes a prophecy of Christ's paschal mystery. At the Red Sea, Moses stood with raised arms while the waters parted, offering Israel a passage from death to life. The early Christians saw this as the anticipation of baptism, where believers pass from the kingdom of darkness into the kingdom of God's beloved Son. Paul draws the parallel explicitly: "All were baptized into Moses in the cloud and in the sea" (1 Cor 10:2). If the first exodus was a baptism into Moses, the new exodus is a baptism into Christ. The manna in the wilderness becomes the foreshadowing of the Eucharist. The water from the rock becomes the foreshadowing of the Spirit, for Paul writes, "The Rock was Christ" (1 Cor 10:4). The bronze serpent lifted up for healing becomes a prophecy of Christ crucified, as Jesus Himself teaches: "As

Moses lifted up the serpent in the wilderness, so must the Son of Man be lifted up" (John 3:14).

Every dimension of Moses' mission thus expands into the contours of Christ's. Moses confronted Pharaoh, the embodiment of oppressive power; Christ confronts the powers of sin, death, and the devil. Moses led Israel out of Egypt; Christ leads humanity out of the dominion of darkness. Moses instituted Passover; Christ becomes the Passover Lamb whose blood shields His people from judgment. Moses built the tabernacle; Christ builds the living temple of His body, the Church. Moses interceded for Israel; Christ intercedes eternally for the world He redeems. Moses could look upon the promised land but not enter it; Christ rises into the heavenly inheritance and opens it to all who follow Him. Moses delivered Israel from a foreign tyrant; Christ delivers humanity from the ancient serpent.

The magnitude of this fulfilment explains why the early Church was unwavering in confessing Jesus as the prophet like Moses. Justin Martyr, debating Trypho the Jew in the second century, repeatedly cites Deuteronomy 18 and insists that the signs, teachings, and death of Jesus fulfil the Mosaic pattern in a way no other figure in history ever approached. He argues that the command "to him you shall listen" finds its definitive meaning in Christ, the one whose words carry the authority of God Himself. This theological conviction did not arise from allegorical imagination but from a profound engagement with Scripture. The earliest Christians were Jews who knew the Torah intimately. They recognised that Jesus accomplished the works of Moses in a form so elevated that only the Messiah could do them. They saw that He not only delivered Israel but delivered creation, not only taught the law but fulfilled it, not only mediated a covenant but embodied it in His own life and death.

If Moses is the archetype of redemption, the ultimate measure of the new redeemer is not simply whether he performs wonders or teaches with authority, but whether he accomplishes the final exodus—the liberation that all previous deliverances only prefigured. This expectation is deeply Jewish and profoundly rooted in Scripture. Isaiah's prophecies of a highway through the desert, of captives released, of a servant who leads nations, all take the exodus form and elevate it into eschatology. Ezekiel's vision of a people cleansed and given a new heart places the new deliverance not merely on the plane of national restoration but of spiritual transformation. Jeremiah's new covenant prophecy situates the new exodus at the level of the human heart, where God Himself will inscribe His law with divine intimacy. These visions collectively point to a redeemer who stands at the intersection of liberation, revelation, covenant, and divine presence.

The Gospels present Jesus in precisely this light. When He begins His ministry, He chooses the wilderness as the place of confrontation, echoing Moses' preparation on Horeb and Israel's formation in the desert. His forty days mirror Israel's forty years, but unlike Israel, He remains faithful in every temptation. When He proclaims the kingdom, He announces good news to the poor, liberty to captives, recovery of sight to the blind, and the year of the Lord's favour (Luke 4:18–19), a mosaic of Isaianic images that Jews of the time recognised as the vocabulary of the new exodus. His miracles are not random acts of compassion but theological acts—signs that the age of deliverance has begun. The blind see, the lame walk, lepers are cleansed, the deaf hear, and the dead are raised. These miracles echo the promise of Deut 18:18, that the prophet like Moses would speak God's word and authenticate His mission through divine works.

One of the clearest new exodus demonstrations is the feeding of the five thousand. Jesus does not simply multiply bread; He reenacts the giving of manna, revealing Himself as the one who feeds the people of God in the wilderness. The crowd's response is instantaneous: "This is indeed the Prophet who is to come into the world!" (John 6:14). Their recognition is explicitly Mosaic. They see in Jesus the signs that Moses performed and the promises Moses made. But Jesus takes the typology deeper still. In His Bread of Life discourse, He declares, "It was not Moses who gave you the bread from heaven; my Father gives you the true bread" (John 6:32). The manna was a sign; He is the substance. Moses fed Israel for a time; Jesus offers Himself as the bread that leads to eternal life.

The Sermon on the Mount amplifies this Mosaic identity even further. The scene is unmistakably Sinai: a mountain, a gathered people, and a lawgiver who speaks with divine authority. But Jesus does not merely repeat the commandments; He deepens them. "You have heard that it was said... but I say to you" (Matt 5) is the language of divine prerogative. It reveals that the one speaking is not another prophet in Moses' line but the one who stands behind Moses, the giver of the law itself. As Augustine observed, "Moses spoke in the name of the Lord; Christ speaks as the Lord." The law Jesus gives is not written on stone but inscribed upon hearts through the Spirit—a fulfilment of Jeremiah's promise and a transformation that Moses himself longed for when he cried, "Would that all the LORD's people were prophets, and that the LORD would put His Spirit upon them!" (Num 11:29).

Yet the new exodus could not be accomplished merely through teaching or miracles. The first exodus required the blood of the Passover lamb; the final exodus requires a sacrifice of infinitely greater depth. This is why Jesus chooses Passover for His climactic act. At the Last Supper, He takes the elements of the Passover meal and redefines them around His own person. "This is my body, which is given for you... This cup is the new covenant in my blood" (Luke 22:19–20). The Passover of Moses was a memorial of deliverance; the Passover of Christ becomes deliverance itself. The lamb that was slain in Egypt foreshadows the Lamb of God who takes away the sins of the world. The blood painted on doorposts to avert judgment becomes the blood poured out from the side of Christ to redeem humanity. The meal eaten in haste before a journey becomes the Eucharistic feast that sustains believers on their pilgrimage to the heavenly kingdom.

When Jesus rises from supper and leads His disciples into Gethsemane, He is not departing from Passover but entering its deepest mystery. The evangelists present His passion with unmistakable exodus overtones. John notes that when Jesus is condemned, it is "about the sixth hour" on the day of Preparation for Passover (John 19:14), the moment when the lambs were slaughtered in the Temple. The seamless tunic He wears evokes the high priest's vestment, suggesting that He offers not only the sacrifice but Himself as priest and victim. The darkness that covers the land recalls the plague that preceded Israel's liberation. The cry, "It is finished" (John 19:30), signals not defeat but completion— the fulfilment of the exodus pattern and the inauguration of the new covenant promised by Jeremiah.

The new exodus reaches its climax not in the crucifixion alone but in the resurrection. Just as the first exodus reached its defining moment when Israel passed through the waters into freedom, so the new exodus reaches its fulfilment when Christ passes through death into life. His resurrection is the victory over the final oppressive power: not Pharaoh, not Babylon, not Rome, but death itself. Paul describes Christ as "the first fruits of those who have fallen asleep" (1 Cor 15:20), implying that His resurrection is the beginning of a harvest that includes all who belong to Him. The new Moses has led the way through the waters of death, opening a path that no human power could cross. Gregory of Nyssa described this moment as the true exodus: "He renewed human nature by His resurrection, leading it up from the tyranny of death to the blessed life."

Yet even resurrection is not the conclusion of this Mosaic typology. Moses ascended the mountain to behold the promised land from afar, unable to enter because of Israel's sin. Christ, the new Moses, ascends not to a mountain but to the right hand of the Father, entering the heavenly inheritance that He then opens to His people. His ascension accomplishes what Moses could only foreshadow. He enters the true promised land and prepares a place for all who follow Him. In the ascended Christ, humanity finally enters what the first exodus could never achieve: communion with God. The Letter to the Hebrews describes Him as the one who has "passed through the heavens" (Heb 4:14) and entered the heavenly sanctuary as the perfect mediator. This ascent completes the exodus pattern: liberation, covenant, sacrifice, passage, and entrance into the inheritance.

The continuity is astonishing. Every major moment of Jesus' life corresponds to Moses' mission, but with a magnitude that reveals the divine source. Moses was sent; Jesus is begotten. Moses revealed God's will; Jesus reveals God Himself. Moses interceded for Israel; Jesus intercedes for all humanity. Moses offered the blood of sacrifices; Jesus offers His own blood. Moses led Israel out of Egypt; Jesus leads creation out of death. The first exodus birthed a nation; the final exodus births the new creation. In this fulfilment, the early Church did not merely see parallels; they saw prophecy accomplished.

This is why the early Christian proclamation, from its earliest strata, identifies Jesus in explicitly Mosaic terms. Peter, preaching in the Temple in Acts 3, does not introduce a new interpretive category; he reaches directly for Deuteronomy 18. After healing the lame man, he declares to the gathered crowd: "Moses said, 'The Lord God will raise up for you a prophet like me from your brethren. You shall listen to Him in whatever He tells you.' ... God, having raised up His servant, sent Him to you first, to bless you by turning every one of you from your wickedness" (Acts 3:22, 26). The sequence is deliberate. Peter does not treat Deuteronomy 18 as fulfilled in a general prophetic tradition; he applies it with precision to the resurrection of Jesus. This is the prophet like Moses because this is the one whom God has raised. The exodus Moses initiated now continues through the risen Christ, who turns His people from sin and leads them into the blessing promised to Abraham.

Stephen, in Acts 7, expands the Mosaic typology further. In his long recital of Israel's history, he presents Moses as rejected by his own people, yet chosen by God to deliver them. "This Moses, whom they rejected... this man God sent as both ruler and redeemer" (Acts 7:35). Stephen's language is not accidental. The Greek words *archonta* (ruler) and *lytrōtēn* (redeemer) match the roles that Christ embodies. But Stephen goes further still. He quotes Moses' own words: "God will raise up for you a prophet from your brethren as He raised me up" (Acts 7:37). Here, Moses' rejection becomes a typology of Christ's rejection; Moses' acceptance becomes a prophecy of Christ's vindication. Stephen reads the story of Moses as a prefiguration of the story of Jesus, and in doing so he reveals how the earliest Christians understood the unity of Scripture: Moses himself pointed toward the one who would fulfil his mission in perfection.

The Gospel of John makes this identification unmistakable through its narrative structure and theological claims. It opens with a contrast: "For the law was given through Moses; grace and truth came through Jesus Christ" (John 1:17). This is not a condemnation of Moses but a revelation of fulfilment. Moses mediated the law; Jesus embodies grace and truth, a phrase echoing God's self-revelation to Moses in Exodus 34:6. John presents Jesus as the one who reveals the Father fully, in the way Moses could only mediate in part. When Jesus says, "If you believed Moses, you would believe Me, for he wrote of Me" (John 5:46), He does more than assert continuity; He asserts prophetic fulfilment. Moses' writings contained the seeds of a redemption only Christ could bring to fruition.

The climactic moment in John's Gospel where the Mosaic pattern becomes explicit is the Transfiguration's Johannine counterpart: the revelation of divine glory in Christ's passion. When Jesus is lifted up on the cross, John uses the same verb (*hypsōthēnai*) that the Septuagint uses for Moses lifting up the bronze serpent (Num 21:9). Jesus Himself draws the connection: "As Moses lifted up the serpent in the wilderness, so must the Son of Man be lifted up" (John 3:14). The serpent lifted for healing becomes the crucified Christ lifted for the healing of the world. The sign of Moses becomes the salvation of humanity. And just as those who looked upon the bronze serpent were healed from death, so those who look to Christ crucified receive life eternal. The typology is not symbolic ornamentation; it is the logic of salvation history unfolding in its fullness.

The Epistle to the Hebrews crystallises the Mosaic-Christological connection by presenting Christ as the definitive mediator. Hebrews 3 begins by asking believers to "consider Jesus, the apostle and high priest of our confession," and immediately compares Him to Moses. "Moses was faithful in all God's house as a servant… but Christ is faithful over God's house as a Son" (Heb 3:5–6). The distinction is not one of opposition but of degree and identity. Moses belongs to the household of God; Christ is the heir. Moses is a servant; Christ is the Son. Moses mediated the old covenant; Christ mediates the new, "enacted on better promises" (Heb 8:6). The author of Hebrews cites Jeremiah 31 at length, showing that the new covenant Moses anticipated and Jeremiah predicted is fulfilled in Christ, whose sacrifice inaugurates the definitive relationship between God and humanity.

In that same epistle, the structure of the new exodus becomes unmistakable. Christ is portrayed as the true Passover Lamb (Heb 9:12–14), whose blood cleanses the conscience in a way animal sacrifices never could. He is the greater high priest who enters not an earthly tabernacle, patterned after the heavenly, but the heavenly sanctuary itself (Heb 9:24). Moses built the tabernacle according to the pattern shown on the mountain; Christ enters the reality that Moses could only imitate. The exodus, with its liberation, covenant, sacrifice, and sanctuary, becomes the shadow; Christ brings the substance. Hebrews 11 recalls how Moses chose "to be mistreated with the people of God rather than to enjoy the fleeting pleasures of sin" because he saw Him who is invisible (Heb 11:25–27). This sight of the invisible becomes literal in Christ, for He reveals the Father directly. In Him, the longing of Moses to behold God's glory is granted to all who believe.

The apostolic preaching thus presents Jesus not merely as a figure reminiscent of Moses, nor as a teacher in Moses' tradition, but as the very fulfilment of Moses' prophetic hope. He is the new mediator, the new deliverer, the new lawgiver, the new source of heavenly bread, the new healer lifted upon the wood, the new one who speaks face to face with God because He is the eternal Son. He surpasses Moses not by diminishing him but by bringing to completion what Moses began. As Chrysostom wrote, "Moses saved a slave people; Christ saves the world. Moses lifted up the serpent; Christ crushed the serpent's head." The new exodus is not a metaphor but a divine event, and Jesus stands at its centre.

The pattern is so complete, the fulfilment so extensive, that the early Church Fathers did not hesitate to speak of Moses as the *type* and Christ as the *truth*. Irenaeus, arguing against the Gnostics, grounded his theology of recapitulation in this very structure: "As through Moses God led the people out of Egypt, so through Christ He leads humanity out of death" (*Against Heresies* 4.9.1). Moses becomes the miniature in which the full portrait of Christ can already be seen. Likewise, Melito of Sardis, in his great second-century *Homily on Pascha*, declares: "He who led you out of Egypt and delivered you from the bitter tyranny of Pharaoh, this is He who has made heaven and earth... this is the Passover of our salvation." Melito reads the exodus not as a merely historical event but as a Christological revelation—already whispering the name of the one who would one day accomplish redemption in its final form.

Gregory of Nyssa, whose *Life of Moses* shaped Christian spirituality for centuries, took this insight further by presenting the entire ascent of Moses—from his flight to Midian, to his vision of God in the burning bush, to his ascent of Sinai—as a pattern of the soul's journey into God. For Gregory, Moses is the archetype of the pilgrim of faith, but Christ is the archetype fulfilled: the one who ascends not into cloud and darkness but into the uncreated light of the Father's glory. Moses enters the cloud and hears God's voice; Christ is the voice made flesh. Moses reflects God's glory; Christ radiates it inherently as "the brightness of the Father's glory" (*Adv. Eunomium* 2.10). In Gregory's hands, the typology becomes an ascent: Moses leads up the slope; Christ carries the soul into the homeland of divinity.

Origen, preaching on Exodus, insists that Moses' intercession after the golden calf was a foreshadowing of Christ's priestly mediation: "Moses stood in the breach and averted wrath, but Christ stands forever, for He is the eternal high priest" (*Hom. Exod.* 12). The gap Moses filled temporarily, Christ fills eternally. The forgiveness Moses begged for trembling Israel becomes the forgiveness Christ secures once for all through His own self-offering. Augustine, in turn, sees in the giving of the law through Moses and the giving of grace through Christ the structure of salvation history. "The law was given through Moses," he writes, "not that it might justify, but that it might make the proud guilty; grace and truth came through Jesus Christ, that the guilty might be justified" (*Tractates on John* 3.10). Augustine does not set Moses against Christ; he shows how Moses prepares for Christ by revealing humanity's need for the Redeemer who brings what the law could not confer.

This sweeping testimony—biblical, Jewish, apostolic, patristic—

converges on one conclusion: the Messiah cannot be understood apart from Moses, and Moses cannot be understood apart from the Messiah. The exodus was never merely an event; it was a prophecy. The Passover was never merely a festival; it was a foreshadowing. The wilderness was never merely a journey; it was an icon of the human pilgrimage from slavery to freedom. The mediator who ascended Sinai, received the law, and interceded for Israel was not the final mediator but the one who showed what the final mediator would be. The prophet like Moses was not simply a future teacher but the One in whom revelation, liberation, covenant, sacrifice, and divine presence would reunite in a single person.

In Jesus of Nazareth, this hope takes flesh. He is the deliverer who confronts not Pharaoh but the spiritual powers of sin and death. He is the liberator who opens not the Red Sea but the tomb. He is the mediator who ascends not a mountain of stone but the heavenly sanctuary, entering the presence of the Father on our behalf. He is the lawgiver who writes not on tablets but on human hearts by the Holy Spirit. He is the Passover Lamb whose blood does not protect a single night but redeems the world. He is the new Moses whose face does not reflect borrowed glory but radiates the very glory of God. Every thread of Mosaic prophecy converges in Him because every thread of salvation history was woven to prepare for Him.

The exodus Moses accomplished was great; the exodus Christ accomplishes is absolute. Moses brought Israel out of Egypt; Christ brings the world out of death. Moses gave Israel the law; Christ gives humanity divine life. Moses built the tabernacle; Christ builds the Church. Moses interceded for Israel; Christ intercedes eternally at the right hand of the Father. Moses glimpsed the promised land from a mountain peak; Christ enters the true promised land and brings His people with Him. The old exodus created a nation; the new exodus creates a new creation.

This is why the question of Jesus' identity is inseparable from the question of Moses' prophecy. Either Jesus is the prophet like Moses, inaugurating the definitive redemption, or the expectation of Scripture collapses into fragments. But the witness of Scripture, tradition, and history stands united: Jesus does not merely resemble Moses; He fulfils

## THE PROPHET LIKE MOSES: THE PROMISE OF A NEW EXODUS

Moses. He is the One Moses spoke of, anticipated, foreshadowed, and longed for. In Him the exodus reaches its divine purpose, and in Him the covenant reaches its eternal fulfilment. Jesus is the prophet like Moses—but more than Moses, more than prophet, more than mediator. He is the Lord of the exodus, the Word made flesh, the Lamb who was slain, the Redeemer of the world. In Him, the ancient promise becomes the everlasting salvation.

# 4

# The Servant and the Son of Man: The Tension within Prophecy

Israel's Scriptures hold together a vision of God's saving work that is at once majestic and disquieting. On one hand, the prophets speak of a figure who will rise in splendour, receive dominion from the Ancient of Days, and reign over all nations with everlasting authority. On the other, the same Scriptures speak of a figure who is despised, rejected, wounded, silent before His oppressors, and crushed for the sins of the people. These two portraits—one glorious, one humiliated—stand within the prophetic canon without explanation, inviting contemplation yet defying easy synthesis. They form a paradox at the heart of Israel's hope, a tension that demanded resolution yet remained unresolved until the coming of Jesus of Nazareth.

The first portrait arises with piercing clarity in the writings of Isaiah, particularly in the passages traditionally called the Servant Songs. "Behold my servant, whom I uphold, my chosen, in whom my soul delights" (Isa 42:1). The tone begins with gentleness—He does not cry aloud, nor break a bruised reed—but the mission quickly intensifies. In Isaiah 49, the Servant speaks of being called from the womb, fashioned by God to restore Israel and to become "a light to the nations" so that "salvation may reach to the ends of the earth" (Isa 49:6). Yet woven into this grandeur is a thread of agony: the Servant laments, "I have laboured in vain; I have spent my strength for nothing and vanity" (Isa 49:4). The mission is glorious; the experience is crushing.

By the time Isaiah reaches chapters 52–53, the Servant's suffering becomes the defining feature of his mission. "His appearance was so marred, beyond human semblance" (Isa 52:14). "He was despised and rejected by men, a man of sorrows and acquainted with grief" (Isa 53:3). The text speaks not merely of suffering but of substitution: "He was wounded for our transgressions, crushed for our iniquities... and the LORD has laid on him the iniquity of us all" (Isa 53:5–6). Nowhere else in the Hebrew Scriptures is the theology of atonement rendered with such existential intensity. The Servant suffers not as a tragic hero nor as a martyr for truth but as a sacrificial figure whose pain becomes redemptive. And yet, the song does not end in defeat. "He shall see his offspring... the will of the LORD shall prosper in his hand" (Isa 53:10). The Servant dies, yet somehow lives; is crushed, yet somehow triumphs. Humiliation sinks downward into death only for exaltation to rise upward into vindication.

Parallel to this path of sorrow stands a second prophetic portrait—one not of suffering but of transcendent glory. In the book of Daniel, amid visions of beasts and kingdoms, a figure appears who is neither angel nor mere man: "one like a son of man" who comes "with the clouds of heaven" (Dan 7:13). He is presented before the Ancient of Days, and to Him "was given dominion and glory and kingdom, that all peoples, nations, and languages should serve him" (Dan 7:14). The word "serve" (*pelach*) in Aramaic is used elsewhere in Daniel for worship offered to God alone. The figure, though human in appearance, receives a divine prerogative. His dominion is everlasting; His kingdom shall not be destroyed. There is no hint of suffering here—only triumphant exaltation, heavenly authority, and cosmic rule. The scene is a coronation above the clouds, a revelation of messianic glory set in the court of heaven itself.

Within the canon of Israel, these two portraits are allowed to stand side by side without explanation. The Servant suffers; the Son of Man reigns. The Servant is crushed; the Son of Man is enthroned. The Servant is silent before His executioners; the Son of Man comes with the clouds of heaven. The Scriptures provide no narrative to merge them, no prophet to harmonise them, no sage to show how the afflicted Servant and the exalted Son of Man belong to a single identity or mission. The tension remains open, pressing its weight upon every mind that seeks to discern the shape of the Messiah. Jewish interpreters across the centuries wrestled with the dissonance. Some treated the Servant as Israel collectively, others as a righteous remnant, others as a prophet or priest. But the Son of Man in Daniel was almost universally read in messianic and even divine terms, especially in the apocalyptic literature of the Second Temple period.

Indeed, writings such as *1 Enoch* and *4 Ezra* (2 Esdras) offer some of the clearest windows into Jewish messianic expectation before the time of Jesus. In *1 Enoch* 48, the Son of Man is described as a pre-existent figure hidden with God before creation, who will judge the kings of the earth and dwell among the righteous. In *1 Enoch* 62, He sits on a throne of glory and receives worship from all nations—a direct expansion of Daniel's vision. Likewise, in *4 Ezra 13*, the man from the sea—a figure closely tied to Daniel's Son of Man—destroys the enemies of God, gathers the dispersed tribes, and inaugurates the age to come. These texts confirm that by the first century, Jewish theology had elevated Daniel's Son of Man into a central messianic figure, one whose heavenly origin and universal authority set Him apart from all earthly deliverers.

Yet during this same period, Isaiah's Servant continued to provoke debate. Some traditions, including Targum Jonathan on Isaiah 52:13, identified the Servant explicitly with the Messiah—"Behold, my servant the Messiah shall prosper." This reveals that at least some strands of Jewish interpretation saw the Servant as a messianic figure. Others, especially after the rise of Christianity, emphasised a corporate reading, interpreting the Servant as Israel suffering among the nations. Still others recognised the Servant as an individual righteous sufferer whose pain brings atonement, as reflected in Midrash Rabbah, which teaches: "The sufferings of the righteous bring healing to the world." But no tradition in Judaism before Jesus successfully integrated the Servant's humiliation

## THE SERVANT AND THE SON OF MAN: THE TENSION WITHIN PROPHECY

with the Son of Man's exaltation into one coherent messianic identity. The prophetic canon holds a paradox without providing the key.

The tension is profound. A Messiah who suffers and dies seems incompatible with the expectation of a Messiah who rules with everlasting dominion. A Messiah crushed by iniquity seems irreconcilable with a Messiah who judges the nations. A Messiah rejected and despised seems at odds with a figure worshipped by every people and language. If these prophetic strands describe two different figures, then the Scriptures divide their hope. If they describe one figure, then the Messiah must embody both humiliation and glory in a sequence that no interpreter before Jesus ever imagined.

The paradox grows sharper the closer one reads the details of Isaiah's Servant. This figure is not portrayed merely as a righteous sufferer in the general sense familiar to Israel's history; he suffers with a specificity and intentionality that sets him apart from every prophetic profile. Isaiah 53, the most controversial passage in the Jewish–Christian dialogue, presents a suffering that is not only unjust but substitutionary. "Surely he has borne our griefs and carried our sorrows" (Isa 53:4). The Hebrew verbs *nasa* (to lift, to carry) and *saval* (to bear a burden) both imply a carrying of something not one's own. The Servant is pierced not for his own crimes but "for our transgressions" (v. 5). The chastisement that brings peace to others falls upon him; the healing of the many comes through his wounds. This is not the suffering of a nation in exile nor the martyrdom of a prophetic witness; it is the suffering of one who takes upon himself the consequences of another's sins.

Early Jewish sources bear witness to this interpretation. The Targum of Jonathan to Isaiah 52:13 reads, "Behold, my servant the Messiah shall prosper." The Aramaic paraphrase does not hesitate to see the Servant as the anointed Redeemer. The Midrash on Ruth, commenting on "the man of sorrows," identifies the Servant with the Messiah who endures grief for Israel's sake. Even the Babylonian Talmud contains passages (Sanhedrin 98b) describing the Messiah seated among the poor, afflicted with wounds, binding his sorrows one at a time—an image drawn directly from Isaiah's vocabulary. These interpretations varied in nuance, but all recognised that the Servant's suffering transcended ordinary historical categories. His pain had redemptive quality; his wounds had salvific force.

Yet Jewish tradition simultaneously preserved the exalted expectations of Daniel 7. The figure who ascends with the clouds is granted dominion that outlasts empires. In the Book of Enoch, which predates the ministry of Jesus by at least a century, the Son of Man is described as pre-existent, enthroned beside God, and receiving worship from the nations. "All who dwell on earth will fall down and worship before Him" (*1 Enoch* 62:6). This is no ordinary human being; this is a heavenly figure who acts with divine authority. In *4 Ezra 13*, the Son of Man appears riding on the clouds, a direct allusion to Daniel, and destroys the enemies of God by the mere sound of his voice. Rabbinic tradition preserved the memory of this expectation as well. In *Sanhedrin* 98a, the Messiah is described as one who may come "on the clouds of heaven"—a direct link to Daniel's prophecy. This shows that the exalted Messiah was not a Christian invention; it belonged to the Jewish imagination long before Jesus.

Between these two trajectories—one descending into humiliation, the other ascending into glory—no synthesis existed. The prophets provided no timeline, no narrative arc, no unifying explanation that could reconcile the Servant's pain with the Son of Man's dominion. The Jewish imagination preserved both but held them apart. The Messiah, if he came, was expected either to restore the kingdom of David with power or to suffer in solidarity with the nation, but not to do both in a single mission. A Messiah who would die seemed incompatible with a Messiah who would reign forever. A Messiah rejected seemed irreconcilable with a Messiah exalted. And so the tension persisted, unresolved, awaiting an interpreter who could reveal that the Servant's humiliation and the Son of Man's exaltation were not two destinies but two movements of one redemptive path.

Jesus steps into this tension not as an external analyst but as the very figure in whom both visions converge. When He refers to Himself more than eighty times as "the Son of Man," He is invoking Daniel's exalted figure, not simply a generic phrase for "human being." The context makes this clear. When He heals the paralysed man, He declares, "The Son of Man has authority on earth to forgive sins" (Mark 2:10), a claim of divine prerogative that scandalises the scribes. When He speaks of His return, He says, "They will see the Son of Man coming on the clouds of heaven with power and great glory" (Matt 24:30), echoing Daniel 7 with deliberate precision. When He stands before the high priest at His trial, He is asked, "Are you the Messiah, the Son of the Blessed?" Jesus responds with the most explicit self-identification in the Gospels: "I am, and you will see the Son of Man seated at the right hand of Power and coming with the clouds of heaven" (Mark 14:62). The Sanhedrin tears its robes not because Jesus has made a vague claim but because He has placed Himself in the centre of Daniel's heavenly throne-room, claiming divine authority, divine worship, and divine dominion.

Yet this same Jesus identifies Himself with the Servant in ways equally intentional. When He speaks of His mission, He says, "The Son of Man came not to be served but to serve, and to give His life as a ransom for many" (Mark 10:45). The term "ransom for many" (*lytron anti pollōn*) is a clear echo of Isaiah 53:12—"He bore the sin of many." When He institutes the Eucharist, He uses the language of Isaiah's Servant: "This is my blood of the covenant, poured out for many" (Mark 14:24). The phrase "poured out for many" again derives from Isaiah's description of the Servant who pours out his life unto death. Luke cites Isaiah 53:12 directly and applies it to Jesus, declaring, "This scripture must be fulfilled in Me: 'He was numbered with the transgressors'" (Luke 22:37). Every layer of the Gospel testimony reinforces the claim: Jesus embraces the Servant's humiliation as the path to the Son of Man's exaltation.

This integration reaches its climax in the passion predictions. Jesus tells His disciples that "the Son of Man must suffer many things" (Mark 8:31). The juxtaposition is revolutionary. Daniel's Son of Man is the figure who receives everlasting dominion; Isaiah's Servant is the figure who is crushed. No Jewish interpreter before Jesus had ever fused the two. Jesus does so as the core of His mission. The Son of Man must suffer. The Son of Man must be rejected. The Son of Man must be killed. And the Son of Man will rise. The Servant's descent becomes the Son of Man's ascent. Humiliation becomes the doorway to glory. The two great streams of prophetic expectation, long divergent, flow together into a single narrative: suffering unto glory, death unto resurrection, cross unto throne.

The apostles absorbed this synthesis with astonishment, for it revealed a coherence in Israel's Scriptures that no prior interpreter had seen. Peter's earliest preaching presents Jesus' death not as a tragic contradiction to messianic expectation but as its fulfilment. On the day of Pentecost he proclaims that Jesus, "delivered up according to the definite plan and foreknowledge of God," has been raised and exalted to the right hand of the Father (Acts 2:23, 33). The language is Danielic — exaltation, enthronement, divine right hand — yet the path to that exaltation is Isaianic, marked by suffering, rejection, and voluntary self-offering. Peter's later epistles make the same claim with even greater clarity. Reflecting on Christ's passion, he writes, "He committed no sin; no guile was found on His lips... He Himself bore our sins in His body on the tree" (1 Pet 2:22, 24), an explicit quotation of Isaiah 53. Here the suffering Servant is not in tension with the enthroned Lord; He is the enthroned Lord. The Servant's wounds become the pathway to the Son of Man's glory, the means by which dominion is gained not through conquest but through sacrificial love.

Paul, too, sees in this union the very structure of the gospel. In the great Christ-hymn of Philippians 2, he sings of one who "emptied Himself, taking the form of a servant... becoming obedient unto death, even death on a cross." This descent into humiliation echoes Isaiah's Servant, who yields himself without resistance. Yet immediately Paul continues: "Therefore God has highly exalted Him and bestowed on Him the name above every name... that every knee should bow... and every tongue confess that Jesus Christ is Lord" (Phil 2:6–11). This exaltation mirrors Daniel's vision of the Son of Man receiving universal allegiance. Paul weaves together Isaiah's humiliation and Daniel's enthronement into a single narrative arc: the one who suffers is the one who reigns; the Servant is the Son of Man; the cross leads to the throne. Scholars across the centuries have recognised this intentional fusion. Richard Bauckham describes Philippians 2 as "the most explicit early Christian integration of the divine identity of Christ with the suffering Servant and the exalted Son of Man," showing that humiliation and exaltation are not two episodes but one revelation.

The author of the Epistle to the Hebrews deepens the relationship further. He portrays Christ as the one who shares the suffering of humanity so that He might lead humanity into glory. "It was fitting that He, for whom and by whom all things exist, in bringing many sons to glory, should make the pioneer of their salvation perfect through suffering" (Heb 2:10). The Servant's suffering becomes the means by which the Son of Man leads His people into the heavenly inheritance. Hebrews connects the Isaianic Servant's voluntary death with Danielic dominion in one bold affirmation: "We see Jesus, who for a little while was made lower than the angels, crowned with glory and honour because of the suffering of death" (Heb 2:9). Glory because of suffering — here the paradox finds its resolution. The humiliation does not undermine the exaltation; it enables it. The suffering Servant and the exalted Son of Man are not two figures but one mission seen from different vantage points.

The Book of Revelation, the final testament of the New Covenant, renders this union in its most dramatic imagery. John sees in heaven "a Lamb standing as though it had been slain" (Rev 5:6), and all creation falls in worship before Him, declaring that He is worthy "to receive power and wealth and wisdom and might and honour and glory and blessing" (Rev 5:12). The one who was slain is now enthroned; the victim is the ruler. The Lamb receives the same worship given to God Himself, echoing Daniel's vision where "all peoples, nations, and languages" serve the Son of Man. The sacrificial imagery of Isaiah converges with the heavenly enthronement of Daniel in a single vision: the Lamb who suffered is the Lord who reigns. Gregory of Nazianzus captured this mystery with exquisite economy: "He is lifted up as the serpent, yet He rules as God. He suffers as servant, yet He is glorified as Son."

This Christian synthesis did not arise from external philosophical pressure or from arbitrary harmonisation. It arose from the historical reality of Jesus' life, death, and resurrection — and from the apostles' conviction, taught by Christ Himself, that "everything written about Me in the Law of Moses and the Prophets and the Psalms must be fulfilled" (Luke 24:44). On the road to Emmaus, the risen Lord rebukes the disciples for failing to see that "it was necessary that the Christ should suffer these things and enter into His glory" (Luke 24:26). This is the hermeneutical key: not humiliation or exaltation, but humiliation *unto* exaltation. The Servant's suffering is not the negation of the Son of Man's authority; it is the means by which the Son of Man receives His dominion. The two trajectories are not parallel but sequential, not contradictory but complementary.

Before Jesus, no interpretive framework existed to unify these prophetic threads. After Jesus, the integration becomes the very heart of Christian proclamation. The early Church Fathers understood this with acute clarity because they recognised that the unity of Scripture hinges upon the unity of the Messiah. Justin Martyr, in his *Dialogue with Trypho*, argues repeatedly that "the same one who came in humility will come again in glory," identifying Isaiah's Servant with Daniel's Son of Man. Origen saw in the apparent contradiction of the prophetic visions a divine pedagogy: God reveals the Messiah through paradox so that His identity cannot be reduced to earthly categories. Athanasius, preaching on the incarnation, declared that Christ "makes low the heights and raises the lowliness," binding Isaiah's abasement with Daniel's enthronement in a single, seamless movement of redemption.

Modern scholarship, far from diminishing the force of this synthesis, has strengthened it. Joseph Ratzinger writes that the New Testament's use of Daniel 7 and Isaiah 53 is not creative reinterpretation but deep perception: Jesus' life reveals the hidden unity of these texts. J.J. Collins, the foremost scholar of apocalyptic literature, acknowledges that Daniel's Son of Man stands as a unique heavenly figure within Second Temple Judaism, awaiting a concrete historical fulfilment. Brevard Childs observes that Isaiah's

## THE SERVANT AND THE SON OF MAN: THE TENSION WITHIN PROPHECY

Servant Songs anticipate a redemptive agent whose suffering transforms the destiny of the people in ways that surpass corporate interpretations. When these strands are read together in light of the historical Jesus, the coherence becomes unmistakable.

What emerges is not a Messiah who happens to suffer and then happens to reign, but a Messiah whose suffering is the very path to His reign. The Servant and the Son of Man are not two messianic candidates but two prophetic windows through which the same figure is seen — first in His humiliation, then in His exaltation. The cross and the clouds belong to one story. The pierced one and the enthroned one are the same. The Lamb who was slain is the Son of Man who comes with the clouds.

The force of this integration becomes even clearer when one considers how Jesus *embodies* the Isaianic and Danielic roles rather than merely *claiming* them. His ministry unfolds as a living exegesis of prophecy. When He heals the sick, opens the eyes of the blind, proclaims good news to the poor, and sets captives free, He is enacting the mission of Isaiah's Servant, who is anointed "to bring forth justice to the nations" and "to open the eyes of the blind" (Isa 42:1, 7). Matthew explicitly cites Isaiah 42 as fulfilled in Jesus' gentle, restorative works: "He will not break a bruised reed... and in His name the nations will hope" (Matt 12:20–21). This is no political revolutionary nor mere moral teacher; this is the Servant whose quiet authority heals the wounded world.

At the same time, Jesus' miracles carry Danielic overtones of eschatological authority. When He casts out demons, the crowds marvel that He commands unclean spirits with a word. In the apocalyptic worldview of the Second Temple period, exorcism was not simply therapeutic; it was a sign of the inbreaking kingdom. Daniel's visions depict the Son of Man as the divine agent who defeats the monstrous powers symbolised by the beasts. Jesus' authority over demonic forces becomes a present manifestation of the Son of Man's dominion. He Himself makes the connection explicit: "If I cast out demons by the Spirit of God, then the kingdom of God has come upon you" (Matt 12:28). The kingdom of the Son of Man is manifest not in political upheaval but in the overthrow of the spiritual tyrannies that enslave humanity.

His teaching also reveals the dual trajectory of the Servant and the Son of Man. When He forgives sins, He acts in the mode of Daniel's exalted figure who exercises divine prerogatives. The scribes rightly ask, "Who can forgive sins but God alone?" (Mark 2:7). Jesus answers not with argument but with demonstration: "But that you may know that the Son of Man has authority on earth to forgive sins..." (v. 10). The healing that follows is not merely compassionate; it is doctrinal, affirming the Son of Man's divine authority. Yet the same Son of Man teaches of His forthcoming rejection: "The Son of Man must suffer many things and be rejected by the elders and chief priests and scribes, and be killed" (Mark 8:31). The disciples are bewildered because no Jewish expectation united suffering with heavenly authority. Jesus is not merely interpreting prophecy; He is reconfiguring the messianic horizon itself by revealing the path through which the Son of Man will attain His dominion.

His entry into Jerusalem sharpens this tension to a razor's edge. Riding on a donkey in fulfilment of Zechariah 9:9, He comes as a Servant-King whose humility hides His majesty. Yet the crowds cry out, "Hosanna to the Son of David!" affirming His royal identity. Jesus then goes to the Temple and exercises a cleansing judgment that mirrors both Isaiah's prophetic rebuke and Daniel's apocalyptic authority. Malachi foretold that the Lord would "suddenly come to His temple" (Mal 3:1), bringing purification; Jesus enacts precisely this prophecy when He overturns tables and drives out those who profane the sacred courts. This is the Servant bringing justice; this is the Son of Man asserting divine authority. The Temple scene unites humiliation and glory, suffering and sovereignty, as Jesus is acclaimed by children yet opposed by priests, honoured by the poor yet plotted against by the powerful.

Still, the deepest convergence of Isaiah and Daniel appears at the Last Supper. When Jesus identifies His broken body and poured-out blood as the covenant sacrifice "for many" (Mark 14:24), He directly invokes Isaiah 53: "He bore the sin of many." The Servant's mission becomes sacramentally present in the bread and the cup. But in the same discourse

## THE SERVANT AND THE SON OF MAN: THE TENSION WITHIN PROPHECY

He also speaks of drinking anew in "My Father's kingdom" (Matt 26:29), invoking Daniel's everlasting dominion. The supper is both sacrifice and promise, humiliation and expectation: the Servant gives His life even as the Son of Man anticipates His enthronement. The Eucharist becomes the hinge of the prophetic paradox — the place where the suffering Servant offers Himself and the exalted Son of Man pledges the coming kingdom.

The passion narratives intensify this interplay with remarkable intentionality. Jesus is silent before His accusers, fulfilling Isaiah's image of the oppressed Servant who "opened not His mouth" (Isa 53:7). He is numbered among the transgressors as foretold (Isa 53:12). He bears the sins of many in the very moment He is stripped, beaten, mocked, and crucified. Yet even in His humiliation, the Son of Man theme erupts through the cracks of suffering. When adjured under oath by the high priest to declare His identity, Jesus responds with the most charged and explosive words He ever uttered: "You will see the Son of Man seated at the right hand of Power and coming with the clouds of heaven" (Mark 14:62). Here, in the midst of Isaianic humiliation, He declares Danielic exaltation. The one who stands bruised and bound before earthly authorities proclaims His future enthronement before the Ancient of Days. The Servant stands revealed as the Son of Man.

The crucifixion itself becomes the decisive moment in which the prophetic paradox is resolved not in theory but in blood. Isaiah's description of the Servant "pouring out His soul unto death" plays out in real flesh and real agony. At the same time, Jesus' cry, "It is finished" (John 19:30), is a declaration of fulfilment — not defeat but completion of the mission that leads inevitably to exaltation. The cosmic signs that accompany the crucifixion — darkness over the land, the tearing of the Temple veil — echo Daniel's apocalyptic imagery. Heaven and earth bear witness that what takes place on Golgotha is not merely tragic but transformative. The humiliation of the Servant becomes the cosmic turning point through which the Son of Man will receive His eternal kingdom.

The resurrection is where the paradox flowers into its full theological meaning. If the crucifixion embodies the Servant's humiliation, the resurrection unveils the Son of Man's exaltation. Isaiah hinted that after the Servant's suffering, "He shall see light" and "He shall prolong His days" (Isa 53:10–11), a cryptic promise of life beyond death. Daniel foresaw the Son of Man receiving glory and dominion from the Ancient of Days (Dan 7:14). In the resurrection, these two trajectories converge. Jesus rises, not as a resuscitated mortal, but as the vindicated Servant and enthroned Son of Man, the one upon whom God has bestowed everlasting authority. His body bears the wounds of the Servant and the glory of the Son. The empty tomb is the hinge between humiliation and exaltation, the moment when the Servant's obedience is crowned with the Son of Man's dominion.

The New Testament insists that the resurrection is not merely the reversal of death but the divine proclamation that Jesus is indeed the figure foreseen by Isaiah and Daniel. Peter declares on Pentecost that God has "made Him both Lord and Messiah" (Acts 2:36) through the resurrection. Paul writes that Jesus "was declared to be the Son of God in power... by His resurrection from the dead" (Rom 1:4). The resurrection is the moment in which the Son of Man's heavenly enthronement begins. In Ephesians, Paul describes Jesus as seated "far above all rule and authority and power and dominion" (Eph 1:21), reflecting Daniel's vision of a kingdom that surpasses all earthly kingdoms. The risen Christ embodies the Servant's suffering and the Son of Man's sovereign glory in one divine-human person.

The ascension intensifies this reality. When Jesus is taken up and a cloud receives Him out of the apostles' sight (Acts 1:9), the imagery is unmistakably Danielic. The Son of Man comes with the clouds of heaven — not to earth, but "to the Ancient of Days" (Dan 7:13). The direction of Daniel's vision is into heaven, and Luke's account mirrors that movement. Jesus' ascension is the enthronement ceremony foreseen in Daniel, the moment when the one who suffered now receives "dominion and glory and kingdom." The Fathers of the Church perceived this instantly. Athanasius notes that Christ "ascends with the humanity He assumed," lifting human nature into the sphere of divine glory. Cyril of Alexandria remarks that the ascension "fulfils Daniel's prophecy, for He who comes with the clouds approaches the Ancient of Days to receive the throne." The Servant rises; the Son of Man reigns.

What follows from this enthronement reveals even more clearly the unity of the Isaianic and Danielic missions. The risen and ascended Jesus pours out the Holy Spirit at Pentecost, inaugurating the new covenant promised by Jeremiah and Ezekiel. Isaiah foresaw that the Servant would bring justice to the nations and be a "light for the Gentiles"; now the nations begin to hear the gospel proclaimed in their own languages. Daniel foresaw that the Son of Man's kingdom would gather peoples of "every nation and language"; now the Church begins to form as a transnational kingdom bound not by ethnicity but by the Spirit. The descent of the Spirit is the sign that the Servant's sacrifice has been accepted and the Son of Man's reign has commenced. Humiliation has borne fruit; exaltation has become participation.

The apostles never treat these developments as separate theological currents. They see them as one unified revelation. In 1 Peter 3:22, Christ is described as the one "who has gone into heaven and is at the right hand of God, with angels, authorities, and powers made subject to Him." This is Danielic enthronement expressed in post-resurrection language. Yet the same apostle had only verses earlier spoken of Christ suffering once for sins, "the righteous for the unrighteous" (1 Pet 3:18), lifting directly from the vocabulary of Isaiah 53. Peter sees no contradiction because the cross and the throne are not two missions but two stages of one mission. The Servant is the pathway by which the Son of Man becomes King.

The Book of Revelation renders the same conviction with apocalyptic vividness. John sees "one like a son of man" walking among the lampstands (Rev 1:13), echoing Daniel's vision almost verbatim. This exalted figure holds the keys of death and Hades (Rev 1:18), symbolising His victory over the last enemy. Yet the same enthroned Christ is "the Lamb who was slain" (Rev 5:6), bearing the marks of the Servant's suffering forever. The nations worship Him with a doxology that fuses the theology of Isaiah and Daniel: "Worthy is the Lamb who was slain… to Him who sits upon the throne"

(Rev 5:12–13). This is Isaiah's wounded healer and Daniel's eternal King, united in one person whose kingship is grounded not in violence but in sacrifice.

The early Church Fathers continued this line of interpretation with remarkable unanimity. Ignatius of Antioch speaks of Christ as "both of Mary and of God, first passible and then impassible" — the Servant's suffering followed by the Son of Man's immortality. Irenaeus writes that Christ "sums up in Himself both the humbling of Adam and the dominion of God," joining Isaiah's redemptive sorrow with Daniel's rule. Tertullian argues that the Messiah must necessarily suffer and then reign, because prophecy demands both movements. Origen explicitly links the Servant's atonement with the Son of Man's ascent: "He descended as the Servant, He ascended as the Son of Man." The theological synthesis that had eluded centuries of Jewish interpretation becomes the bedrock of Christian proclamation.

What emerges across Scripture, tradition, and the witness of the early Church is this: the humiliation and exaltation of the Messiah are not competing narratives but complementary dimensions of one divine plan. The Servant and the Son of Man are not rival identities but two prophetic angles on the same redeeming figure. The Servant reveals the depth of God's love; the Son of Man reveals the height of His glory. The Servant shows God entering human suffering; the Son of Man shows humanity entering God's life. The Servant descends into the misery of sin; the Son of Man rises into the majesty of heaven. Only in Jesus do these motions meet, in a single person whose obedience unto death becomes the very means by which all authority in heaven and earth is given to Him.

This unified vision becomes even more striking when we examine the way Jesus applied these titles to Himself. His preferred self-designation, *the Son of Man*, was not a humble circumlocution meaning merely "a human being" but a deliberate invocation of Daniel's heavenly figure. Scholars such as J. J. Collins and Larry Hurtado have shown that in first-century Judaism, "Son of Man" carried apocalyptic weight, signalling a transcendent, eschatological redeemer. Jesus uses the title not only when speaking of His future glory but when speaking of His impending suffering. In saying, "The Son of Man must suffer many things... be killed, and after three days rise again" (Mark 8:31), He inserts the Servant's humiliation directly into the Son of Man's narrative. No rabbi, no interpreter of the Second Temple period fused these trajectories. Jesus alone revealed that the one who is enthroned with the Ancient of Days is the one who must first be pierced and crushed for the sins of the people.

This reconfiguration forces a profound rereading of Isaiah's Servant. Isaiah speaks of one who "will justify many" (Isa 53:11), a phrase that Paul adopts explicitly when he describes Christ as the one whose obedience makes many righteous (Rom 5:19). The Servant "bears iniquity" (Isa 53:6), and Christ becomes "the one who knew no sin yet was made sin for our sake" (2 Cor 5:21). The Servant "pours out His soul unto death" (Isa 53:12), and Jesus speaks of His blood poured out "for many for the forgiveness of sins" (Matt 26:28). The Servant's mission is substitutionary; Jesus' mission is sacrificial. The prophetic and historical lines overlap perfectly. What Isaiah foretold, Jesus enacts: the suffering of one becomes the salvation of many.

At the same time, Daniel's vision unfolds in the resurrection and ascension of Christ. The one who appears "like a son of man" and receives from the Ancient of Days eternal dominion finds precise fulfilment in Jesus' exaltation. Paul describes Christ as seated "at the right hand of God... above every name that is named" (Eph 1:20–21), a Danielic enthronement if ever there was one. Hebrews speaks of Him as the one who "sat down at the right hand of the Majesty on high" (Heb 1:3). Peter proclaims on Pentecost that He has been exalted to the right hand of God and has poured out the Spirit (Acts 2:33), thereby exercising the authority of Daniel's enthroned figure. In Revelation 1, John sees "one like a son of man" whose face shines like the sun and who holds the keys of death and Hades (Rev 1:13–18). These are not symbolic flourishes; they are the direct continuation of Daniel's expectation, realised in the risen Christ.

But the final proof of the prophetic integration appears not only in Christ's identity but in His *judgment*. Daniel's Son of Man is the figure who presides over divine judgment, receiving authority to judge the nations. Jesus claims this prerogative explicitly: "The Father judges no one, but has given all judgment to the Son... because He is the Son of Man" (John 5:22, 27). The reason for His universal authority is not His divine nature alone but His incarnate mission as the suffering Redeemer. He judges the world not as a detached celestial being but as the One who bore the world's sin. His right to judge flows from His willingness to be judged. He possesses dominion because He accepted humiliation; He wields authority because He embraced obedience unto death. This is the profound theological centre of the prophetic paradox: the servant redeems, and the Son reigns; the Son reigns because the servant redeems.

The early Church continued this interpretive line with extraordinary coherence. Justin Martyr, using Isaiah and Daniel against his Jewish interlocutors, insisted that the Scriptures foretold both the suffering and the glory of the Messiah. "The same one," he wrote, "who is said to suffer is also declared to come on the clouds of heaven." Origen argued that the Servant's humiliation "purifies those who believe," while the Son of Man's exaltation "confers immortality," two aspects of one salvific act. Cyril of Alexandria taught that Christ "humbled Himself as man yet remained exalted as God," uniting Servant and Son in a single hypostatic identity. Athanasius declared that He "took on the bonds of servitude" so that humanity might "share His royal freedom." Each of these Fathers saw in Jesus not a harmonised contradiction but a revealed unity: humiliation and exaltation are two movements of the divine descent and ascent, the kenosis and glorification of the same Lord.

This also clarifies why the earliest Christian creeds emphasise both suffering and glory. "Crucified under Pontius Pilate" is immediately followed by "He ascended into heaven and sits at the right hand of the Father." The creed itself reflects the journey from Servant to Son of Man, from the cross to the clouds. The Church confesses that Christ suffered according to the Scriptures — Isaiah's Scriptures — and rose in fulfilment of the Scriptures — Daniel's Scriptures. The integrated reading of prophecy becomes the basis of Christian worship, theology, and identity.

## THE SERVANT AND THE SON OF MAN: THE TENSION WITHIN PROPHECY

Yet this synthesis is not merely doctrinal; it is spiritual. The pattern of humiliation leading to exaltation becomes the path of discipleship. Jesus teaches that whoever would follow Him must take up the cross, entering the Servant's descent in order to share the Son's glory. Paul expresses this trajectory when he writes, "If we suffer with Him, we shall also be glorified with Him" (Rom 8:17). The Servant's obedience becomes the believer's imitation; the Son of Man's exaltation becomes the believer's hope. The prophetic unity revealed in Christ thus shapes the very structure of Christian life: descent into love, ascent into glory; cross before crown; death before resurrection.

Through all of this, the Scriptures maintain their integrity. Isaiah does not need re-interpretation; Daniel does not need dilution. Their words stand as written, their claims as given. What was obscure becomes luminous not because their meaning changed but because the one they foretold has come. Christ reveals that the Servant's suffering and the Son of Man's exaltation are two sides of the same coin of redemption. In Him, the paradox resolves without collapsing. In Him, the prophetic voices harmonise without losing their distinctive tones. In Him, the humiliation becomes the seed of exaltation, the suffering the prelude to glory, the cross the throne from which the Son of Man reigns forever.

The coherence of this revelation becomes even more striking when one considers that Jesus Himself consistently framed His mission around both strands of prophecy, drawing them together with an intentionality that no prior interpreter had imagined. When He spoke of His suffering, He did not present it as an unfortunate deviation from His mission but as the necessary fulfilment of Scripture. "The Son of Man goes as it is written of Him" (Mark 14:21). The phrase "as it is written" refers not to a single verse but to the entire Isaianic witness: the Servant's rejection, His silent endurance, His bearing of sins, His death with the wicked, and His vindication by God. Jesus does not see His suffering as contradictory to His messianic identity; He sees it as essential to it. The Son of Man — the Danielic figure of heavenly dominion — goes to His destiny *because* the Servant's path demands it.

This explains why, after the resurrection, Jesus opens the Scriptures to the disciples on the road to Emmaus and asks the question that becomes the theological key to the entire prophetic tradition: "Was it not necessary that the Christ should suffer these things and enter into His glory?" (Luke 24:26). This question is the axis upon which the entire messianic expectation turns. The suffering is not optional; it is necessary. The glory is not incidental; it is inevitable. The necessity of suffering arises from Isaiah; the inevitability of glory arises from Daniel. Jesus reveals that the true Messiah must pass through the valley of the Servant to ascend the mountain of the Son of Man. Suffering is the doorway to dominion; humiliation the path to exaltation; the cross the ladder to the throne. The paradox becomes a prophecy fulfilled and a theology unveiled.

The apostles never recovered from this revelation. It shaped their proclamation, their worship, their understanding of Christ, and their interpretation of Scripture. When Paul writes that Christ "humbled Himself... even to death on a cross" and therefore God "highly exalted Him" (Phil 2:8–9), he is not constructing a new theological idea; he is summarising the entire prophetic arc. When Peter proclaims that Christ's sufferings and subsequent glories were foretold by the Spirit (1 Pet 1:11), he is identifying the Servant and the Son of Man as two movements of one divine narrative. When John sees the Lamb enthroned, he is witnessing Isaiah's sacrificial victim crowned with Daniel's everlasting dominion. The New Testament is not inventing a Messiah who suffers and reigns; it is unveiling the Messiah to whom the prophets bore witness all along.

This unity also clarifies the Jewish–Christian disagreement that followed. Judaism preserved the vision of a triumphant Messiah, drawn from Daniel and the royal psalms. Christianity proclaimed that the triumph had come, but through the route Isaiah described. The disagreement was not over whether Daniel's Son of Man would reign, but over whether Isaiah's Servant could be the same person — and whether His suffering could be redemptive. Christianity's claim rested on the historical event of Christ's passion and resurrection: the Servant had suffered, and God had exalted Him. If God raised Jesus from the dead, He validated both His identity and His mission. If God exalted Him to His right hand, He fulfilled Daniel 7 in Him. The resurrection becomes the hermeneutical miracle that binds the Servant and the Son of Man forever in one Lord.

The Fathers of the Church understood this with crystalline conviction. They did not treat Isaiah and Daniel as competing visions but as complementary revelations whose unity becomes intelligible only in Christ. Justin Martyr argued that Isaiah foretold Christ's first coming in humility and Daniel His second coming in glory, both belonging to the same Messiah. Irenaeus taught that the Servant's obedience restores what Adam lost, while the Son's exaltation brings creation into its final destiny. Athanasius declared that Christ descends to bear the curse and ascends to bestow glory, uniting divine condescension with divine exaltation. Cyril of Alexandria saw in Christ the one who "does not abandon His humility even in His glory," whose wounds remain visible in His risen body as the eternal testimony of His redeeming love.

What emerges from this rich theological tapestry is not a Messiah constructed from selective readings or harmonised fragments, but the very figure whom the prophets foresaw in mystery and whom Jesus revealed in history. The Servant and the Son of Man stand not as two candidates for messiahship but as two prophetic lenses focused on the same person. Through Isaiah we see His descent — the compassion that leads Him into human suffering, the obedience that carries Him into death, the sacrifice that heals the nations. Through Daniel we see His ascent — the authority granted by the Ancient of Days, the dominion over all peoples and languages, the everlasting kingdom that shall not pass away. Through Jesus we see the whole — the Servant's wounded hands raised in the Son's eternal glory.

This chapter began with a tension, a paradox, a seeming contradiction at the heart of Israel's messianic hope. It ends with a resolution so profound that it reveals not merely the identity of the Messiah but the character of God Himself. The God of Israel does not save by bypassing suffering but by entering it. He does not establish His kingdom through domination but through self-giving love. He does not crush His enemies with earthly force but conquers the greater enemies — sin, death, the devil — through the humility of the cross. The Servant shows us the depth of God's compassion; the Son of Man shows us the height of God's majesty. Together they form the full revelation of the Messiah, the one in whom humiliation and glory embrace, the one whose suffering redeems and whose dominion renews creation, the one who is both Lamb and Lord, Servant and Son.

# 5

# The Priest of the New Covenant: Temple, Sacrifice, and Atonement

The story of Israel is a story of worship before it is a story of kings, prophets, or nations. From the moment the Lord calls Abraham out of Ur, sacrifice becomes the language of covenant, the means by which God and man draw near. Abraham builds altars wherever God appears to him. Isaac blesses and sacrifices. Jacob erects pillars and pours oil upon them. Long before Israel has a king, before it has a land, before it even has a law, it has a priestly identity that binds it to the God who has chosen it. The question of sacrifice is therefore not peripheral but central, not ceremonial but theological. It expresses the deepest truth of the human condition: that communion with God must be restored through atonement, and that atonement requires mediation, offering, and blood. This truth runs like a scarlet thread through the Scriptures, shaping Israel's imagination and forming the foundations of its messianic hope.

The earliest and most enigmatic figure in this priestly world is Melchizedek, king of Salem, who appears without genealogy, blesses Abraham, and offers "bread and wine" as priest of God Most High (Gen 14:18–20). His presence is brief, yet the implications are immense. He is both king and priest — a union forbidden in later Israelite law, where kings come from Judah and priests from Levi. Melchizedek stands outside that structure, older than it, deeper than it, pointing to a priesthood that exists before the Mosaic covenant and surpasses it in dignity. The author of Hebrews calls him "without father or mother or genealogy… resembling the Son of God" (Heb 7:3), not because he is literally eternal, but because Scripture presents him as a type, an archetype of a priesthood not bound by lineage or law. Psalm 110, the great messianic coronation psalm, seizes upon this figure with prophetic precision: "The LORD has sworn and will not change His mind: 'You are a priest forever after the order of Melchizedek'" (Ps 110:4). The same psalm declares, "The LORD said to my Lord: Sit at my right hand" (Ps 110:1). Kingship and priesthood converge in a single messianic figure, an eternal priest-king whose authority transcends the old covenant and whose priesthood is not inherited but bestowed by divine oath.

This is the first great signal that the Messiah would not only rule but reconcile, not only govern but sanctify. Jewish tradition itself recognised the extraordinary nature of Melchizedek. Philo calls him "king of peace" (*Legum Allegoriae* 3.79), and the Dead Sea Scrolls magnify him even further. In the fragment known as 11QMelchizedek, Melchizedek becomes an eschatological deliverer who proclaims the Jubilee, judges evil powers, and brings atonement to the people — functions that belong not merely to priests but to God Himself. The text interprets Isaiah 61:1, "to proclaim liberty to the captives," as a prophecy fulfilled by Melchizedek, who is described in language approaching divinity. While this does not imply that ancient Judaism believed the Messiah would be divine, it does reveal that Jewish thinkers were willing to imagine a priestly redeemer whose role far surpassed the limitations of the Aaronic priesthood. Melchizedek therefore becomes a seedbed of messianic expectation: a priest who blesses, who brings peace, who mediates, who reigns.

If Melchizedek hints at the possibility of a priestly Messiah, the Temple reveals the necessity of one. Israel's sanctuary is the architectural embodiment of creation's purpose: a place where God dwells with His people. The Tabernacle is built according to a heavenly pattern revealed to Moses on Sinai (Exod 25:9), a microcosm of the universe, adorned with garden imagery that recalls Eden. The Holy of Holies becomes the meeting place of heaven and earth, where the presence of God rests upon the mercy-seat between the cherubim. When Solomon dedicates the Temple, the glory of the Lord fills it so powerfully that the priests cannot stand to minister (1 Kings 8:10–11). Israel's identity becomes inseparable from this sacred space. To be God's people means to draw near in sacrifice, to ascend in worship, to be reconciled through priestly mediation. The Temple is not merely a national symbol; it is the theological heart of Israel's existence.

Yet the Temple also reveals a problem at the core of humanity: sin creates distance, and distance demands sacrifice. Every day priests offer burnt offerings, grain offerings, peace offerings, sin offerings, and guilt offerings, each with its own purpose and symbolism. The people draw near, but never fully. The veil remains, the distance persists, the blood flows without end. On Yom Kippur, the Day of Atonement, the high priest enters the Holy of Holies once a year and only with blood, offered "for himself and for the errors of the people" (Heb 9:7). He sprinkles the blood before the mercy-seat, confesses the sins of Israel over the scapegoat, and sends it into the wilderness. This ritual is the high point of Israel's sacrificial system, the moment when the nation is cleansed and restored. Yet its repetition year after year reveals its incompleteness. As Hebrews laments, "It is impossible for the blood of bulls and goats to take away sins" (Heb 10:4). The sacrifices cleanse externally but cannot transform the heart; they restore ritual purity but cannot bestow eternal life.

The rabbis knew this tension well. Mishnah *Yoma* describes the trembling of the high priest as he enters the Holy of Holies, his garments adorned with bells so that the people might hear him and know he still lived. A rope, tradition says, was tied around his ankle lest he die in God's presence and need to be pulled out. The entire nation waits outside, listening, hoping, praying. The high priest emerges alive, and Israel rejoices — yet they know it must happen again next year. The system builds longing into its very structure. If the sacrifices must be repeated, then sin has not been definitively abolished. If the priest must continually offer blood, then reconciliation is still partial. The covenant is real, the forgiveness is real, but the restoration is not yet complete. Israel begins to look beyond the cycle toward a definitive atonement, a final priest, a perfect sacrifice.

This longing is intensified by the prophetic critiques. Jeremiah rebukes the people for relying on the Temple while ignoring righteousness: "Do not trust in these deceptive words: 'This is the temple of the LORD'" (Jer 7:4). Isaiah thunders that God hates sacrifices offered with unjust hearts (Isa 1:11–17). Hosea declares, "I desire mercy, not sacrifice" (Hos 6:6), not because sacrifice is abolished, but because sacrifice without mercy contradicts its own purpose. Malachi laments the corruption of the priesthood, their polluted offerings, their contempt for the altar (Mal 1–2). Yet even as the prophets expose the inadequacies of the sacrificial system, they also kindle hope for a renewed priesthood and a purified offering. Malachi promises that the Lord Himself will "suddenly come to His temple" and "purify the sons of Levi" so that the offering of Judah "will be pleasing as in former days" (Mal 3:1–4). Jeremiah announces a new covenant in which God will write His law upon the heart and remember sin no more (Jer 31:31–34). Daniel foresees that "atonement will be made for iniquity" and "everlasting righteousness" will be established (Dan 9:24). The sacrificial world of Israel does not end in critique but in promise, not in despair but in expectation.

The expectation of a renewed priesthood did not fade after the exile; it intensified. Israel returned to its land, rebuilt the Temple, restored the sacrifices, and reestablished the priestly line, but something was missing. The glory that once filled the sanctuary in the days of Moses and Solomon did not return in visible splendour. Ezekiel had seen the glory depart (Ezek 10), but the Scriptures never describe it returning in the same way. The Second Temple stood, but it lacked the radiance that once made priests fall to the ground. This absence was not merely architectural; it was theological. It signalled that Israel's restoration was real but incomplete, that the covenant remained open, awaiting a deeper fulfilment. The sacrifices continued, yet the heart of Israel remained unhealed. The priesthood functioned, yet the promise of a new heart and a new spirit had not yet come. The Temple stood as both hope and ache — a sign of God's nearness and a reminder of humanity's distance.

This tension produced one of the most remarkable developments in Jewish thought: the growing expectation of a priestly Messiah. While modern readers often assume that Jews of the Second Temple period expected only a political king, the evidence tells a richer story. The Dead Sea Scrolls, reflecting the theology of the Qumran community, speak repeatedly of a coming priestly figure. In the *Rule of the Community* (1QS), members are instructed to obey both "the messiah of Aaron" and "the messiah of Israel," a dual-messiah expectation in which the priestly messiah holds primacy. In 1QSa, the "Prince of the Congregation" defers to the coming high priest, who presides over the eschatological banquet. Most striking is 11QMelchizedek, which identifies the eschatological deliverer with Melchizedek himself, proclaiming liberty to the captives and executing divine judgment on wicked powers. Here the priestly messiah is not merely a reformer; he is the agent of final atonement and cosmic liberation.

This expectation is not limited to sectarian writings. The *Testament of Levi*, a Jewish work from around the second century BC, describes a future priest who will open the gates of paradise, give access to the tree of life, and atone for the sins of the righteous. The *Testament of Aaron* portrays a glorious priest whose star rises in heaven and who brings purification to Israel. Even Josephus, though careful to avoid messianic speculation, acknowledges the centrality of priesthood to Jewish identity, describing the high priest as the one who "represents the nation before God" and mediates divine favour. Taken together, these sources reveal a Jewish imagination increasingly focused not only on kingship but on priesthood, not only on political liberation but on spiritual reconciliation. The hope for a definitive priest does not arise in Christian hindsight; it is already embedded within the Jewish worldview that Jesus Himself enters.

With this context in place, the meaning of the Temple becomes clearer. The Temple is not simply the place where sacrifices occur; it is the place where God and humanity meet. It is the visible sign of the invisible covenant. Its architecture mirrors Eden: the menorah as the tree of life, the cherubim guarding the sanctuary, the high priest entering the Holy of Holies as Adam once walked with God. Yet unlike Eden, access is restricted. Sin has introduced distance, and the sacrificial system expresses both the reality of that distance and the hope of its healing. Every offering is a confession that reconciliation requires death. Every priestly act is an admission that mediation is necessary. Every feast, fast, and ritual purification acknowledges the truth that sin is not merely a legal problem but a relational rupture. The Temple thus reveals the human condition with theological clarity: humanity longs for communion but cannot restore it by its own power.

Because the Temple dramatizes this longing, the prophets begin to speak of a time when God Himself will provide the perfect priest and the perfect sacrifice. Jeremiah declares that God will make a new covenant in which "I will forgive their iniquity, and I will remember their sin no more" (Jer 31:34). Ezekiel promises that God will cleanse His people with water, give them a new heart, and place His Spirit within them (Ezek 36:25–27). Zechariah foresees a day when God will remove the guilt of the land "in a single day" (Zech 3:9), a striking prophecy that points to a definitive act of atonement rather than an annual ritual. The very structure of Israel's worship anticipates its own fulfilment. The sacrifices are shadows awaiting reality; the priests are mediators awaiting the true High Priest; the Temple is a symbol awaiting the actual place where God dwells among His people.

All of this converges upon Jesus of Nazareth, whose life unfolds as the embodiment and fulfilment of Israel's priestly story. Yet before the New Testament proclaims Him as High Priest, it portrays Him as the new Temple — the dwelling place of God among men. When He declares, "Destroy this temple, and in three days I will raise it up" (John 2:19), He is not merely predicting His resurrection; He is revealing that His body is the true locus of divine presence. John underscores this earlier when he says that the Word "dwelt among us" (John 1:14), using the verb *eskēnōsen*, meaning "tabernacled." Jesus is the Tabernacle in flesh, the place where

God meets humanity, the reality toward which the entire sacrificial system pointed. If the Temple is where God dwells with His people, then Jesus is the Temple in person. If the Temple is where atonement is made, then Jesus will make atonement in Himself. If the Temple is where the priest enters on behalf of the people, then Jesus will enter not with the blood of animals but with His own.

This identity explains why Jesus cleanses the Temple with prophetic authority, why He calls it "My Father's house," and why the veil is torn from top to bottom at His death. The tearing of the veil is not merely a sign of judgment; it is a declaration that access to God has been opened through the offering of Christ. The barrier between God and humanity, symbolised in architecture, is removed in blood. The place of separation becomes the place of communion. Christ's death is therefore not only prophetic fulfilment or moral example; it is priestly action — the moment when the true High Priest enters the true Holy of Holies and accomplishes what generations of priests could not: definitive atonement.

Before we reach that climax, however, the chapter must establish the full weight of the sacrificial system and the longing it generated. The need for reconciliation lies at the core of the human heart and at the centre of Israel's worship. Every sacrifice, every burnt offering, every drop of blood, every trembling priest on Yom Kippur testifies to the truth that sin separates and only God can restore. Israel lives inside this truth daily, yearly, continually. The longing becomes the lens through which the Messiah must be recognised. To understand who Jesus is, we must see Him not only as king and prophet but as priest and sacrifice — the one who reconciles heaven and earth in His own flesh.

The priestly identity of Jesus begins to emerge even in the early years of His ministry, though not through the expected channels. He does not belong to the tribe of Levi, and He is not trained in the Temple courts. Yet His actions, His words, and His very presence exhibit a priestly authority that transcends the hereditary boundaries of the old covenant. He touches lepers and makes them clean — a reversal of the Levitical order, where contact with impurity renders one unclean. He forgives sins directly, a prerogative reserved for God and mediated only through sacrifice. When the paralytic is lowered through the roof, Jesus pronounces, "Your sins are forgiven" (Mark 2:5), prompting the scribes to protest: "Who can forgive sins but God alone?" Their outrage is theologically correct. Forgiveness requires atonement; atonement requires sacrifice; sacrifice requires a priest. For Jesus to claim the authority to forgive is to claim implicitly the authority to reconcile, which is the heart of priesthood. His subsequent healing of the paralytic serves as a visible sign of an invisible priestly act: "that you may know that the Son of Man has authority on earth to forgive sins" (Mark 2:10). In one moment, the messianic roles begin to interlace. The Son of Man exercises priestly authority; the healer enacts the work of atonement.

The Sermon on the Mount furthers this priestly dimension by redefining purity not as ritual compliance but as inner transformation. "Blessed are the pure in heart, for they shall see God" (Matt 5:8). Purity is no longer achieved through washings and offerings but through an interior cleansing that only God can accomplish. Jesus teaches with the authority of a lawgiver and the insight of a priest who knows the true condition of the human heart. His declaration that "something greater than the temple is here" (Matt 12:6) is not merely comparative; it is ontological. He is the reality toward which the Temple points. His presence consecrates; His mercy restores; His teaching illumines. He embodies what every priestly act symbolised: communion with God made possible through divine initiative.

The clearest expression of His priestly mission emerges in His self-identification as the Good Shepherd in John 10. The shepherd imagery recalls David and the royal office, yet Jesus frames it in sacrificial terms: "The Good Shepherd lays down His life for the sheep" (John 10:11). In the Hebrew Scriptures, shepherds lead, guide, and protect; they do not die in place of the flock. The language of substitution belongs to sacrifice. Jesus describes His death as voluntary, authoritative, and obedient: "No one takes it from Me, but I lay it down of My own accord" (John 10:18). This is not martyrdom but priesthood. He offers Himself, not by compulsion but by divine will. He is both priest and victim, agent and offering. This union of roles is without precedent in Israel's history and reveals a category that only Melchizedek had foreshadowed: a priest who offers not something else but himself.

This self-offering becomes explicit at the Last Supper. The night before He dies, Jesus gathers His disciples and performs an act that surpasses the entire sacrificial system of Israel. Taking bread and wine — the very elements offered by Melchizedek — He identifies them with His body and blood, declaring, "This is My blood of the covenant, which is poured out for many for the forgiveness of sins" (Matt 26:28). The phrase "poured out for many" echoes Isaiah 53:12, where the Servant "poured out His soul unto death" and "bore the sin of many." Here Jesus fuses the priestly and prophetic strands of Israel's hope. He is the Servant whose suffering atones for sin, and He is the priest whose offering inaugurates the new covenant. The Last Supper is therefore not merely a farewell meal; it is the institution of a new liturgy, the moment when the true High Priest reveals the form His sacrifice will take. The Eucharist becomes the anticipatory participation in His self-offering, a sacrament that unites priest, victim, and altar in one divine act.

The passion narratives intensify the sacrificial imagery. Jesus' agony in Gethsemane echoes the priestly burden of bearing the sins of the people. His prayer, "Not My will, but Yours be done" (Luke 22:42), is the obedience the old covenant priests symbolised but could never perfect. At His arrest, He stands as the innocent one yielding Himself to fulfill the Scriptures. At His trial, He is condemned not for moral failure but for messianic identity. Pilate finds no guilt in Him, yet hands Him over to satisfy the demands of the crowd. The injustice of His death, emphasised by all four Gospels, aligns Him with the unblemished offerings required for sacrifice. When He is scourged, mocked, stripped, and nailed to the cross, He becomes the paschal victim, the lamb led to the slaughter, the scapegoat bearing the sins of the people. The high priest tears his garments in outrage at Jesus' confession, yet it is Jesus who becomes the true high priest by offering His own body outside the city, just as sin offerings were burned outside the camp (Lev 16:27; Heb 13:11-12).

At the moment of His death, the veil of the Temple is torn from top to bottom. The symbolism is immediate and immense. The barrier that separated God and humanity is removed not by human hands but by divine action. Access to the Holy of Holies — the place where the high priest entered once a year — is now opened permanently through the sacrifice of Christ. The tearing of the veil is the visible sign of the invisible truth: the old covenant priesthood has reached its fulfilment and termination. The priestly ministry of Jesus has accomplished what the Levitical priesthood could never achieve — direct and eternal access to God. The Temple continues to stand for a few more decades, but its inner meaning has passed into the flesh and blood of Christ, who becomes the locus of worship, the site of reconciliation, the true Holy of Holies.

When Jesus breathes His last and declares, "It is finished" (John 19:30), He is not describing the end of His life but the completion of the sacrificial work He came to perform. The phrase echoes the conclusion of priestly offerings and the fulfilment of covenant obligations. What is finished is not the story but the sacrifice, not the mission but the offering that makes the mission effective. The blood of Christ, poured out upon the cross, becomes the foundation of the new covenant, fulfilling Jeremiah's prophecy and surpassing the blood of bulls and goats with the blood "that speaks a better word than Abel's" (Heb 12:24). The cross is therefore not a tragic interruption of Jesus' ministry; it is the climactic act of His priesthood, the moment when the true High Priest passes through the heavens by passing through death.

The resurrection does not negate the priesthood of Christ; it perfects and reveals it. When God raises Jesus from the dead, He vindicates not only His identity but His sacrifice. Resurrection is the divine affirmation that Christ's offering has been accepted, that sin has been atoned for, that death has been conquered. The empty tomb is not merely a sign of victory but of completed atonement. It is the high priest emerging from the Holy of Holies alive, signalling that the sacrifice has been effective. Just as Israel waited with bated breath for the high priest to return on

Yom Kippur, so the disciples encounter the risen Lord as the One who has passed through death and returned with peace. His first words, "Peace be with you" (John 20:19), carry priestly resonance. Peace is the fruit of atonement, the restored harmony between God and humanity. He breathes the Holy Spirit upon them, echoing both the creation of Adam and the ordination of priests, who were consecrated for service through sacred anointing. The resurrection therefore inaugurates not merely a new phase of Jesus' life but a new economy of worship, in which Christ becomes the living Temple and His disciples become participants in His priestly mission.

This new economy reaches its theological summit in the Ascension and the heavenly priesthood of Christ. The letter to the Hebrews presents the ascended Christ not as a distant ruler but as the eternal High Priest who ministers in the true sanctuary. "We have a great high priest who has passed through the heavens, Jesus the Son of God" (Heb 4:14). He does not enter a man-made sanctuary but the heavenly reality of which the earthly Temple was a shadow (Heb 8:5). He enters "by means of His own blood" (Heb 9:12), obtaining "eternal redemption." The contrast is absolute: the earthly high priest enters repeatedly; Christ enters once for all. The earthly high priest offers blood that is not his own; Christ offers His own blood. The earthly high priest stands because his work is never done; Christ sits at the right hand of God because His work is finished. The heavenly throne is both His seat of authority and His priestly dwelling, for in Christ kingship and priesthood are no longer divided. He reigns by virtue of His sacrifice; He intercedes by virtue of His enthronement.

The imagery Hebrews uses is drawn directly from the architecture and rituals of the Temple. The Holy of Holies, accessible only once a year, becomes the symbol of heaven itself. The veil that once separated humanity from God becomes the body of Christ, torn on the cross so that believers may "enter the sanctuary by the blood of Jesus" (Heb 10:19–20). The mercy-seat, the place of sprinkled blood, becomes the throne of grace to which Christians now draw near with confidence (Heb 4:16). The high priestly intercession, once a trembling ritual performed by a mortal man, becomes the perpetual ministry of the risen Christ, who "always lives to make intercession" (Heb 7:25). For Hebrews, the entire sacrificial system of Israel is a divinely instituted prophecy of Christ. The law is a shadow; Christ is the substance. The sacrifices are copies; Christ is the reality. The priesthood is temporary; Christ's priesthood is eternal.

This priesthood also explains the indestructibility of the new covenant. Covenants were sealed with blood, and the new covenant is sealed with Christ's. Because His blood is incorruptible, the covenant is unbreakable. Because His life is indestructible, His priesthood is forever (Heb 7:16). Because His offering is perfect, no further sacrifice remains. The Eucharist, far from being a repetition of the cross, is the sacramental participation in the once-for-all offering of Christ, the means by which His priestly mediation becomes present in every age and every place. When the Church gathers to break the bread and share the cup, it does so not as a new sacrifice but as entry into the eternal sacrifice of Christ, who remains both priest and victim in heavenly glory.

The early Church absorbed this priestly vision with profound clarity. Ignatius of Antioch speaks repeatedly of Jesus as the one "who is truly our high priest," whose sacrifice gathers the Church into unity. Justin Martyr describes the Eucharist as the pure offering foretold by Malachi, made possible by Christ's priesthood. Irenaeus presents Christ as the one who restores Adamic communion with God through His obedient self-offering. Athanasius, in *On the Incarnation*, emphasises that Christ's death is not an accident but a priestly act offered freely for the life of the world. Cyril of Jerusalem instructs catechumens that in the Eucharist, they partake of the "spiritual incense" of Christ's sacrifice and enter the Holy of Holies. Chrysostom, preaching on Hebrews, declares that Christ "offered Himself once and sanctified the whole world," a priesthood unparalleled in history or imagination. Augustine, synthesising these traditions, writes that Christ is both "priest and sacrifice, sacrificer and victim," the one through whom all true worship is offered.

In this light, the identity of Jesus as Messiah cannot be restricted to kingship or prophecy. Without the priestly dimension, the messianic identity is incomplete, and the logic of Israel's Scriptures remains unresolved. The Messiah must restore communion with God, and communion cannot be restored without sacrifice and priesthood. If Jesus is the Messiah, He must not only rule and teach; He must reconcile. And if He reconciles definitively, He must be the High Priest who offers the perfect sacrifice. It is not enough for Him to be a prophet like Moses or a king like David. He must be the priest like Melchizedek, the Temple in flesh, the sacrifice that truly atones, the mediator who brings humanity into the very presence of God.

Yet the full force of this truth becomes most apparent when we consider the relationship between Jesus' priestly work and the longing embedded within Israel's worship. Every aspect of the sacrificial system expressed a hope beyond itself. The morning and evening offerings expressed a hope for perpetual communion. The Day of Atonement expressed a hope for total forgiveness. The Temple expressed a hope for unbroken presence. The priesthood expressed a hope for perfect mediation. All of these hopes converge in the person of Christ. In Him, communion becomes perpetual, forgiveness becomes total, presence becomes incarnate, mediation becomes perfect. The shadows dissolve before the substance; the copies fade before the original; the longing finds its fulfilment.

The priestly mission of Christ also reframes the meaning of sacrifice itself. In the ancient world, sacrifice could be misunderstood as an act by which humans attempted to change the divine disposition, to appease an offended deity, or to secure favour through ritual exchange. But Israel's Scriptures always placed sacrifice within the context of covenant, not transaction. Sacrifice was not about manipulating God but about restoring communion. The blood of the animal was a symbol of life offered back to the Giver of life, a gesture of trust, repentance, and reconciliation. Yet the sacrificial system—precisely because it dealt in symbols—could not accomplish what it signified. The life of a bull or goat could point toward atonement, but it could not achieve it. The sacrifices were "a shadow of the good things to come" (Heb 10:1), powerful in meaning but limited in effect. They revealed the need for forgiveness and expressed the desire for restoration, but they awaited the moment when God Himself would provide the true offering.

Jesus fulfills sacrifice not by abolishing it but by revealing its true depth. Sacrifice is not ultimately about the death of the victim but the love expressed in the offering. What God desires is not blood for its own sake but the surrender of the heart. "Behold, I have come to do Your will, O God" (Heb 10:9). The obedience of the Son—freely given, lovingly embraced—is the essence of true worship. In Gethsemane, when Jesus prays, "Not My will, but Yours be done," He offers the perfect interior sacrifice, the alignment of human will with divine will, the restoration of the obedience lost in Adam. On the cross, this interior offering becomes exterior in the shedding of blood. The physical sacrifice expresses the spiritual reality. Christ's death is therefore not a detached ritual but the consummation of His entire life of obedience, a priestly act that unites love and offering in one seamless gift.

This deepened understanding of sacrifice also illuminates the mystery of Christ as both priest and victim. In the old covenant, these roles were necessarily separate. The priest offered; the victim was offered. The priest acted; the animal was acted upon. But in Christ, the priestly agency and sacrificial self-gift converge. He is the one who offers and the one who is offered. He acts freely even as He submits to death. The cross is not something that happens to Him; it is something He embraces. The Gospel of John highlights this agency with extraordinary clarity: "No one takes My life from Me; I lay it down of My own accord" (John 10:18). The divine Son becomes the human priest who offers Himself as the sacrifice that heals the world. This unity of priest and victim is the heart of Christian worship and the foundation of the Eucharistic mystery.

The resurrection and ascension reveal yet another dimension of Christ's priesthood: His intercession. In the old covenant, the priest's work did not end when the sacrifice was offered; he continued to bear the people's needs before God. He blessed them, prayed for them, represented them. The high priest, bearing the names of the tribes upon his breastplate, carried

Israel into the presence of God symbolically. In Christ, this intercession becomes perpetual and personal. Hebrews proclaims that He "always lives to make intercession" (Heb 7:25). His priesthood does not end because His life does not end. His sacrifice remains eternally present because His risen body bears the marks of His offering. The wounds are not erased in glory; they become the eternal signs of mercy, the visible evidence of His priestly mediation. He does not simply offer His blood once; He brings the power of that offering into eternal life, where it continues to reconcile, heal, and sanctify.

This heavenly priesthood also explains the Church's sacramental life. The Eucharist is not a repetition of Calvary but a participation in it. The one sacrifice of Christ becomes present sacramentally, not by being re-crucified but by drawing the faithful into the eternal offering He now presents before the Father. This was the conviction of the earliest Christians. Ignatius of Antioch calls the Eucharist "the medicine of immortality," not because the elements change by human power but because Christ the High Priest is present in them, giving His life to His people. Justin Martyr describes the Eucharist as the pure offering foretold by Malachi, the sacrifice offered among the nations in every place (Mal 1:11). Irenaeus sees in the Eucharist the restoration of creation itself, for the bread and wine—"the fruit of the earth and the work of human hands"—become instruments of divine communion. The Church becomes, in this sacramental vision, a priestly people united to the priesthood of Christ, offering not bloody sacrifices but the sacrifice of praise and the faithful participation in the one offering that saves.

The implications of Christ's priesthood for the forgiveness of sins are equally profound. In the old covenant, forgiveness was mediated through the priesthood and tied to the sacrificial system. But the forgiveness was partial, symbolic, anticipatory. In Christ, forgiveness becomes absolute and personal. When He forgives sins during His earthly ministry, He does so with the authority of the true High Priest. After His resurrection, He breathes upon the apostles and gives them the authority to forgive sins in His name (John 20:21–23). The Church's ministry of reconciliation is therefore not a human invention but a participation in Christ's own priestly work. Confession becomes the place where the merits of the cross touch the sinner's life, where Christ's sacrifice becomes effective in individual hearts, restoring communion one person at a time.

All of this reveals that the priesthood of Christ is not an abstract title or a metaphor. It is the key to understanding the entire economy of salvation. The Messiah is not merely the fulfiller of Davidic kingship or Mosaic prophecy; He is the fulfiller of the priesthood that undergirded Israel's covenantal identity. Without this priestly dimension, the messianic narrative would have power but no reconciliation, authority but no atonement, glory but no healing. Israel's deepest need was not political restoration but communion with God, and this communion required priesthood and sacrifice. The Messiah had to be the one who restores the presence of God among His people and who removes the barrier of sin that separates humanity from the divine life.

Jesus fulfills this mission not by entering an earthly sanctuary but by becoming the sanctuary; not by offering an external sacrifice but by offering Himself; not by securing temporary forgiveness but by accomplishing eternal redemption. His priesthood is the hinge of the new covenant, the bridge between God and humanity, the reality toward which every altar, every offering, every priest, every feast, and every drop of sacrificial blood pointed. In Him, Israel's worship reaches its goal, and the longing of the human heart finds its answer.

The priestly identity of Christ also exposes the inner logic of God's plan in a way that reveals both the tenderness and the severity of divine love. The old covenant sacrificial system was never meant to endure forever; it was pedagogical. It taught Israel the gravity of sin, the cost of reconciliation, and the holiness of God. It taught that communion with God could not be restored through moral effort alone, nor maintained through mere ritual compliance. It taught that reconciliation requires mediation, that forgiveness requires blood, and that sin is not a superficial blemish but a rupture at the heart of creation. Yet even as it taught these truths, the system carried within itself the seeds of its own transcendence.

Its rituals revealed their own inadequacy; its priests revealed their own mortality; its sacrifices revealed their own limitation. The entire structure pointed beyond itself toward a priest and a sacrifice capable of achieving what the symbols could only signify.

Christ steps into this structure not as a reformer of ritual but as its fulfillment. He does not abolish sacrifice; He reveals its true meaning. He does not reject priesthood; He embodies its perfection. He does not dismantle the Temple; He becomes the Temple in which humanity and God are united. In Him, the pedagogical becomes actual, the symbolic becomes real, the anticipated becomes fulfilled. The old covenant, with its cycles of atonement and its rhythms of offering, becomes the foundation for a new covenant in which forgiveness is not temporary but eternal, and access to God is not seasonal but perpetual. The cross is the moment where the bare structure of sacrificial theology becomes flesh, where the eternal Son takes on the role of the priest and assumes the form of the victim. In that single act, the entire economy of worship is transformed.

This transformation extends far beyond the bounds of Israel, for Christ's priesthood is not tribal, national, or genealogical. It is cosmic. Melchizedek's priesthood predated Israel and embraced the nations; Christ's priesthood fulfills that universality. The Temple embodied the meeting of heaven and earth; Christ actualises that meeting in Himself. The Day of Atonement secured Israel's forgiveness for a year; Christ's offering secures forgiveness for the world for eternity. The priesthood of Christ therefore stands at the centre of a new creation. In the resurrection, He emerges as the "firstborn from the dead," not only restored to life but exalted into a mode of existence in which His priestly mediation becomes eternal. In the ascension, He carries human nature into the presence of God, sanctifying humanity's destiny and revealing that the purpose of priesthood is not simply reconciliation but glorification.

This is why the New Testament insists that the Church shares in Christ's priesthood. Peter declares that believers are a "royal priesthood" (1 Pet 2:9), echoing Exodus 19:6 but elevating it through union with Christ. The Church does not replace the Levitical priesthood; it participates in Christ's heavenly priesthood. The sacramental life of the Church, especially Baptism and the Eucharist, draws believers into the priestly pattern of Christ's death and resurrection. Baptism unites the faithful to His paschal sacrifice, crucifying the old self and raising a new creation. The Eucharist unites them to His ongoing self-offering, allowing them to share in the sacrifice by which the world is redeemed. Even the moral life becomes priestly. When Paul urges believers to offer their bodies as "a living sacrifice, holy and acceptable to God" (Rom 12:1), he is not speaking metaphorically. He is describing the shape of Christian existence in union with the High Priest.

This shared priesthood, however, never diminishes the uniqueness of Christ's own. He alone offers the sacrifice that atones for sin. He alone mediates between God and humanity (1 Tim 2:5). He alone holds the eternal priesthood promised in Psalm 110. The ministerial priesthood of the Church participates in His priesthood, but never replaces it. This is why the Eucharist is efficacious—not because of human power, but because Christ acts through His ministers to make present the sacrifice He eternally offers. The priest at the altar does not stand in the place of Christ as if the Lord were absent; he stands in the presence of Christ, through whom the sacrifice is offered "once for all." The faithful do not repeat Calvary; they are gathered into the eternal priesthood that flows from Calvary.

This priestly participation extends into the Church's mission of reconciliation. When Jesus breathes the Spirit on the apostles and grants them the authority to forgive sins (John 20:21–23), He establishes a sacramental extension of His own priestly work. Confession becomes the continuation of the High Priest's ministry of mercy. The absolution spoken over the penitent echoes the declaration of peace spoken in the upper room. The reconciliation granted in the sacrament is not a human judgment but a participation in the eternal atonement accomplished by Christ. The priest speaks, but it is Christ who forgives; the penitent kneels, but it is Christ who restores; the words are earthly, but the grace is heavenly.

Even the eschatological imagery of the New Testament reflects Christ's priesthood. When Revelation describes the heavenly liturgy, it presents the risen Christ as both Lamb and Priest. He stands "as though slain," revealing His sacrificial identity, yet He reigns from the throne, revealing His divine authority. The twenty-four elders fall before Him with golden bowls of incense, "which are the prayers of the saints" (Rev 5:8), symbolising His mediating role. The worship of heaven is priestly, sacrificial, and Christocentric. The entire cosmos becomes the Temple, and Christ becomes its High Priest. Humanity is redeemed not merely from sin but into worship, into communion, into priestly participation in the life of God.

Through all these dimensions, the priesthood of Christ illuminates a single, stunning truth: salvation is not merely deliverance from guilt but restoration to communion. It is not merely legal pardon but relational intimacy. It is not merely the removal of sin but the sharing of divine life. Priesthood exists for this purpose. Sacrifice exists for this purpose. Atonement exists for this purpose. Christ fulfills all three, not by offering something external but by offering Himself. His priesthood reveals the heart of God: a love that descends into the depths of human brokenness to lift humanity into the heights of divine glory.

In this light, the entire sweep of Scripture takes on a new coherence. What begins with the enigmatic priest-king Melchizedek blossoms into the universal priesthood of Christ. What begins with Abraham building altars culminates in the offering of the Lamb who was slain before the foundation of the world. What begins with the Tabernacle overshadowed by the cloud finds its fulfillment in the Word made flesh who "tabernacles" among us. What begins with the high priest trembling before the mercy-seat ends with the risen Lord entering the true Holy of Holies with confidence and authority. The story that once seemed fragmented—altars here, sacrifices there, rituals scattered across centuries—reveals itself as a single narrative of divine descent and human ascent, made one in the priestly mission of the Messiah.

Christ does not stand outside this story as a critic of an ancient system. He stands within it as its fulfiller and interpreter. His life is the living exegesis of Israel's worship. In His body, the Temple finds its meaning; in His blood, the sacrifices find their truth; in His priesthood, the covenant finds its consummation. The humility of His incarnation, the obedience of His ministry, the agony of His passion, the triumph of His resurrection, and the glory of His ascension are not separate episodes loosely connected by theology. They are the stages of a single priestly act, the movements of a liturgy written from eternity and enacted in time, the unveiling of a divine intention older than creation itself.

What this means for the messianic question is decisive. A Messiah who does not reconcile humanity to God is no Messiah at all. The royal promises to David, the prophetic expectations of Moses, the apocalyptic visions of Daniel, and the Servant's suffering in Isaiah all point toward a world made right—but none of these hopes can be fulfilled without atonement. Liberation without reconciliation is incomplete; restoration without forgiveness is superficial; kingship without sacrifice is hollow. Israel's deepest longing was not merely for a ruler who would defeat its enemies but for a priest who would defeat its sin. The Messiah had to be the one who could restore Eden's lost communion, who could reopen the way into the presence of God, who could bridge with His own life the infinite distance between divine holiness and human frailty.

Jesus alone accomplishes this. He offers the sacrifice no other priest could offer: Himself. He enters the sanctuary no other high priest could enter: the heavenly Holy of Holies. He establishes the covenant no other mediator could establish: a covenant sealed not with the blood of animals but with the blood of God-made-man. He fulfills the deepest ritual, theological, and spiritual structures of Israel's worship, not by abolishing them but by embodying them. In Him, the priestly office becomes eternal; the sacrifice becomes perfect; the Temple becomes indestructible.

Through this priestly mission, the messianic identity of Jesus becomes unmistakable. His kingship rests not on conquest but on mercy; His prophecy is confirmed not only by His words but by His wounds; His authority flows not from political strength but from sacrificial love. The cross becomes His throne, the resurrection His vindication, the ascension

His enthronement. In Him, the priesthood of Melchizedek finds its heir, the Temple finds its Lord, and the world finds its reconciliation. Nothing in Israel's story remains loose or orphaned; every thread, every symbol, every sacrifice finds its completion.

What emerges, therefore, is a Messiah whose glory is inseparable from His priesthood and whose priesthood is inseparable from His love. A Messiah who does not merely teach truth but embodies it, who does not merely command holiness but imparts it, who does not merely represent humanity before God but joins humanity to God. A Messiah who, in offering Himself, reveals the very heart of God—a heart that pours itself out for the life of the world.

# 6

# When the Promise Enters History

From the moment the first promise was spoken in Eden, the Scriptures have been reaching forward. A trajectory forms, not as a straight line but as a widening arc, gathering stories, covenants, symbols, and longings into a single, swelling expectation. The seed who would crush the serpent, the son who would sit on David's everlasting throne, the prophet who would speak with God's own authority, the Servant who would suffer, the Son of Man who would reign, the priest who would reconcile—each of these figures rose from Israel's history like silhouettes against the horizon, distinct yet strangely convergent. No single chapter of Israel's story exhausted them. No king, prophet, or priest fulfilled the shape of the promise. Instead, the hope grew larger with every generation, pressing beyond its historical containers, demanding a figure greater than the past yet wholly faithful to it.

The earliest pages of Scripture set the pattern. Humanity falls, yet God speaks a word that refuses to let the story end in defeat. The promise of a seed introduces not merely optimism but destiny. The battles of Cain and Abel, the renewal with Noah, the calling of Abraham, and the long genealogies that mark the movement of grace are not digressions but developments of that first word. Through the patriarchs, the theme of continuity emerges: God preserves a line not because of human fidelity but despite human failure. The story of Israel begins with a miracle of preservation. If the line survives, it is only because God holds it.

With David, the promise takes on royal form. God binds His fidelity to a throne, swearing an oath that outlasts every political collapse. The royal psalms lift the expectation even higher, speaking of a king who reigns over the nations, who is called God's Son, whose dominion extends to the ends of the earth. Yet the monarchy itself crumbles. Exile shatters every earthly assurance. And still the promise remains. The prophets reinterpret the covenant in ways unimaginable before: the future king will not simply restore Israel's political fortunes but will bring justice to the nations, gather the scattered, heal the broken, and renew creation. The throne grows larger even as the kingdom disappears.

Then comes Moses, not merely as the founder of Israel's worship but as the archetype of mediation. In him, the pattern expands again. A prophet like Moses will arise—one who knows God face to face, who reveals God's will, who leads the people into a deeper exodus than the first. The later prophets seize upon the memory of Moses to frame the hope of a future deliverance. Liberation from Egypt becomes the blueprint for liberation from sin; the giving of the Torah becomes the template for a law written on the heart. Israel begins to look not only for a king but for a teacher, not only for a ruler but for a redeemer who will draw the people into a renewed covenant.

Yet even these images cannot contain the fullness of the promise. Isaiah's Servant enters the scene with disarming humility, bearing the sins of the people and healing them through His wounds. Daniel's Son of Man rises in the clouds, receiving everlasting dominion from the Ancient of Days. These visions do not compete; they coexist, held in tension by the prophetic imagination. Israel is confronted with two figures—one humiliated, one exalted—yet both essential to the world's salvation. No interpreter can merge them; no history can reconcile them. The paradox stands like a riddle placed at the centre of the Scriptures, waiting for the moment when its solution will appear in flesh and blood.

Temple and sacrifice add their own voice to the promise. The entire sacrificial world reveals that the deepest wound of humanity is not political oppression but separation from God. The Temple stands as both gift and ache: the place where God dwells with His people and the sign that they cannot yet dwell with Him fully. The priests minister daily, yet the veil remains. The sacrifices cleanse, yet they cannot transform. Yom Kippur reconciles the nation, yet it must happen again and again. Israel learns through worship what it cannot learn through history: atonement is necessary, but no earthly priest can accomplish it. The longing for a definitive priest, a final sacrifice, a perfect reconciliation becomes the silent heartbeat of Israel's worship.

When the prophets speak of a new covenant, of a day when God will write His law upon human hearts and remember sin no more, they are not abandoning the old patterns but disclosing their destiny. The covenant with Abraham, the throne of David, the prophecy of Moses, the suffering of the Servant, the glory of the Son of Man, the priesthood of Melchizedek, the sacrificial system of the Temple—none of these is complete on its own. Each is a fragment of a larger truth. Each stands as a sign of something more. Part I of this story, the story of Israel's expectation, ends not with a figure but with a silhouette, a converging outline drawn from a thousand years of revelation. The Scriptures have constructed a portrait through promises: a redeemer who will crush evil, a king who will reign forever, a prophet who will reveal God's heart, a servant who will suffer for many, a son of man who will be enthroned in glory, a priest who will reconcile humanity to God. The Messiah cannot be less than this. He must somehow be all of this.

The stage is set, but the figure has not yet stepped onto it. Part I shows the longing; Part II shows the arrival. The first half of this book has traced the architecture of expectation: the deep roots of the protoevangelium, the royal covenant that shaped Israel's hope, the prophetic patterns that illuminated its future, the paradoxes that refused reduction, the priestly yearnings that no ritual could satisfy. Yet expectation cannot save. A silhouette cannot heal. A prophecy cannot forgive. Israel's Scriptures lead the reader to the edge of revelation, to the threshold where promise must become presence.

## WHEN THE PROMISE ENTERS HISTORY

Part II crosses that threshold. The Messiah appears not as an abstract fulfilment but as a living man in a particular place and time—born in the line of David, raised in Galilee, stepping into the baptismal waters of the Jordan, proclaiming the kingdom with authority that echoes Sinai, healing the sick with compassion that fulfils Isaiah, standing in the Temple as its true Lord, offering Himself in a sacrifice that fulfils every altar, suffering as the Servant foretold, rising as the Son of Man anticipated, and ascending to receive the dominion Daniel envisioned. History becomes the arena where every strand of Scripture converges, where the silhouette takes on form, where the Messiah reveals Himself through deed and word, sign and wonder, suffering and glory.

The God who promised in Eden, who swore an oath to David, who spoke through Moses and the prophets, who accepted the sacrifices of generations, now enters His own story. The Messiah long awaited is not simply the fulfilment of prophecy; He is the fulfilment of Israel itself, the one in whom the entire purpose of creation reaches its meaning. Part II unfolds this revelation. It is the story of a king who reigns by serving, a prophet who teaches with divine authority, a priest who offers Himself, a servant whose suffering redeems, a son of man whose glory transforms the world. It is the story of Jesus of Nazareth, in whom every promise becomes flesh, every expectation finds its answer, and every hope discovers that it was waiting for Him all along.

# II

# THE MESSIAH IN HISTORY

# 7

# The Son of David Appears: Jesus and the Restoration of Kingship

The story of Jesus enters history beneath the weight and wonder of a promise that long predates His birth. The Scriptures had shaped Israel to expect a king—one born of David, rooted in covenant, anointed with divine authority, and destined to restore the people to God. When the Gospels open, they do not begin with miracle or parable but with lineage, because messianic identity cannot be detached from the covenant God swore to David: "I will establish the throne of his kingdom forever" (2 Sam 7:13). Matthew therefore begins his Gospel with a bold declaration, "The book of the genealogy of Jesus Christ, the son of David, the son of Abraham" (Matt 1:1), front-loading David because the entire narrative will hinge on whether this man truly fulfills the royal promise. The genealogy is crafted with astonishing precision, arranged in three movements—Abraham to David, David to the exile, the exile to Christ (Matt 1:17)—as if Matthew were saying that Israel's whole history flows toward this moment, the arrival of the rightful king.

Luke's genealogy complements this by tracing the line through Nathan, another son of David (Luke 3:31), preserving Davidic descent even as it emphasizes Jesus' solidarity with all humanity by reaching back to Adam (Luke 3:38). Early Jewish historians confirm the cultural significance of such lineage. Josephus remarks that Jewish families, especially those of priestly or royal significance, kept public genealogical records to establish legitimacy (*Contra Apion* 1.30–36). In this world, lineage was not a trivial detail; it was the ground upon which any claim to kingship stood. The evangelists are therefore not offering sentimental family trees. They are issuing a theological argument: the child who appears in the Gospels does so as the heir of David's everlasting dynasty.

Yet the Davidic claim does not rest on genealogy alone. It must take form within the geography of promise. The Messiah was expected to arise from Bethlehem, the city of David, because the prophet Micah had declared, "From you shall come forth for me one who is to be ruler in Israel" (Mic 5:2). Matthew reinforces this connection when he narrates the birth: "Jesus was born in Bethlehem of Judea in the days of Herod the king" (Matt 2:1), and he explicitly cites the prophecy to demonstrate that this is no accidental birthplace but the fulfillment of an ancient word (Matt 2:5–6). Bethlehem, though small, was loaded with symbolic meaning. It was where David was anointed; it was the cradle of Israel's royal hope. By entering the world in this humble town, Jesus steps quietly yet decisively into the royal story.

From Bethlehem the path leads north to Galilee, a region dismissed by the elite yet central to prophetic expectation. Isaiah had spoken of a day when "in the latter time he has made glorious the way of the sea, the land beyond the Jordan, Galilee of the nations" (Isa 9:1). The place associated with humiliation would become the site of dawning light: "The people who walked in darkness have seen a great light" (Isa 9:2). Matthew sees this fulfilled in Jesus' decision to begin His ministry not in Jerusalem, the seat of power, but in Galilee, the borderland where Jews and Gentiles mingled (Matt 4:12–16). This geographical pattern is already a royal sign: the king enters His kingdom not from its political centre but from its margins, gathering the lost and forgotten before confronting the religious and political powers in Jerusalem.

Jesus' message appears with the force and clarity of royal proclamation. His first words in Mark's Gospel carry an unmistakable tone: "The time is fulfilled, and the kingdom of God is at hand" (Mark 1:15). He does not announce merely a moral program or spiritual insight. He declares the arrival of God's reign, an event long anticipated by Israel's prophets. Daniel had foreseen a moment when God would establish a kingdom that "shall never be destroyed" (Dan 2:44) and grant everlasting dominion to "one like a son of man" (Dan 7:13–14). Isaiah envisioned the beauty of the herald who brings "good news" and proclaims, "Your God reigns" (Isa 52:7). Jesus steps into this prophetic stream and speaks with the voice of the king whom Israel has awaited.

His words are not the mere rhetoric of a teacher. They carry an authority that astonishes His hearers. Matthew records that "He taught them as one who had authority, and not as their scribes" (Matt 7:29). In the Sermon on the Mount, Jesus does not simply interpret Torah; He speaks from above it: "You have heard that it was said... but I say to you" (Matt 5:21–22). Such claims place Jesus in continuity with, yet far beyond, any Davidic figure before Him. Solomon spoke with wisdom; the prophets spoke with divine commission; but Jesus speaks as the lawgiver Himself. When He declares that "something greater than Solomon is here" (Matt 12:42), He is not being provocative; He is stating the truth of His identity. The one who stands before Israel is not only David's son but David's Lord (Matt 22:45).

The royal authority of Jesus is not confined to His teaching. His works reveal the presence of the kingdom in action. Isaiah had foretold that in the age of salvation, "the eyes of the blind shall be opened, and the ears of the deaf unstopped" (Isa 35:5), and Jesus fulfills these signs in abundance. The Gospels describe Him giving sight to the blind (Mark 10:46–52), cleansing lepers (Matt 8:2–3), making the lame walk (Luke 5:17–26), and even raising the dead (Mark 5:35–43). These miracles are not displays of power for their own sake. They are royal deeds—acts of dominion over creation, acts of compassion toward the suffering, acts that reveal the heart of the king who restores His people.

Exorcisms reveal another dimension of His kingship. When Jesus casts out demons, His opponents accuse Him of acting by Satan's power, but He responds with a declaration that strikes at the core of the messianic question: "If it is by the Spirit of God that I cast out demons, then the kingdom of God has come upon you" (Matt 12:28). In other words, the king has entered His territory and the powers of darkness are being driven out. His reign is not political but cosmic. His authority extends not merely over Israel but over the spiritual forces that enslave humanity. Josephus records that exorcism in Jewish culture was seen as a sign of divine empowerment (*Antiquities* 8.45–49). Jesus' exorcisms, then, are not fringe events— they are messianic indicators, revelations of a king who conquers evil not with armies but with a word.

In all these actions—His lineage, His birthplace, His message, His authority, His compassion, His dominion—Jesus reveals Himself as the Son of David. Yet everything He does also presses beyond the expectations of a political liberator. Israel longed for a king who would defeat Rome; Jesus reveals a king who defeats sin, sickness, Satan, and death. Israel expected a throne in Jerusalem; Jesus proclaims a kingdom that begins in the human heart and extends to the ends of the earth. Israel looked for a warrior; Jesus appears as a healer, a shepherd, a servant.

The king has arrived, but He does not rule as the world rules. He rules with mercy, authority, humility, and divine power. He rules through His very presence.

The moment arrives when Jesus makes His kingship visible, not through a coronation but through a procession that reinterprets every royal expectation. As He approaches Jerusalem for the final Passover, He enacts a prophecy that had been waiting for centuries. Zechariah had spoken of a future king who would come to Zion "righteous and having salvation, humble and mounted on a donkey" (Zech 9:9). This was no ordinary prophecy. It belonged to the era of restoration when God would defeat Israel's enemies and establish His rule in peace. When Jesus deliberately instructs His disciples to fetch the colt (Matt 21:1–3), He is not seeking transportation. He is declaring identity. Matthew writes that this act "took place to fulfill what was spoken by the prophet" (Matt 21:4–5), and all four Gospels record the event, signalling its centrality (Mark 11:1–10; Luke 19:28–40; John 12:12–15).

The crowds respond instinctively in messianic language. "Hosanna to the Son of David! Blessed is he who comes in the name of the Lord!" (Matt 21:9; cf. Ps 118:26). Palm branches, used in the Maccabean period as symbols of national liberation (1 Macc 13:51; 2 Macc 10:6–7), fill the streets. The people cry out not for a teacher, not for a prophet, but for the Davidic king who would restore Israel. This scene is a royal entry, but it is unlike any the ancient world had ever seen. There is no chariot, no warhorse, no procession of soldiers. The king enters His city in humility, proclaiming peace rather than conquest.

Jesus accepts the acclamation but refuses to turn it into political revolution. His first royal act is not to confront Rome but to confront the Temple, the heart of Israel's worship. He enters the courts and drives out the merchants, declaring, "My house shall be called a house of prayer, but you make it a den of robbers" (Matt 21:13; Jer 7:11). This is the authority of a king, but it is not the authority of Herod or Caesar. It is the authority of the Lord of the Temple Himself. Malachi had foretold a day when "the Lord whom you seek will suddenly come to His temple" (Mal 3:1). Jesus now fulfills that vision, revealing a kingship inseparable from divine presence.

Even the children recognize Him. "Hosanna to the Son of David!" they cry in the Temple courts (Matt 21:15). The chief priests and scribes rebuke them, but Jesus answers by citing Psalm 8:2: "Out of the mouth of babes and infants you have brought forth praise" (Matt 21:16). The king has entered His sanctuary, and only innocence has enough clarity to acknowledge Him.

Yet Jesus' kingship continues to confound expectations. His parables reveal a royal authority grounded not in domination but in invitation—a kingdom likened to a wedding feast (Matt 22:1–14), a vineyard entrusted to tenants (Matt 21:33–46), a mustard seed that grows beyond imagining (Mark 4:30–32). These parables situate His kingship within the horizon of divine generosity. The kingdom He inaugurates is expansive, unexpected, open to those who would never have been admitted to earthly courts. The tax collectors and prostitutes enter ahead of the religious elite (Matt 21:31).

In His kingdom, authority and mercy are inseparable.

This unity of mercy and authority exposes the deeper nature of His royal identity. Jesus is not merely a successor to David; He is the fulfillment of David's role as the shepherd of Israel. When He looks upon the crowds, the Gospels say He is "moved with compassion for them, because they were like sheep without a shepherd" (Mark 6:34). This is royal language. In Ezekiel 34, God promises to shepherd His people Himself and to set over them "one shepherd, My servant David" (Ezek 34:23–24). Jesus heals, teaches, and feeds out of this shepherding identity, not as a distant king but as one who carries the burdens of His people.

Even His identity is interrogated through royal categories. When blind Bartimaeus cries out, he does not call Jesus "prophet" or "teacher" but "Jesus, Son of David, have mercy on me!" (Mark 10:47). He recognizes that the true king is not the one who seizes power but the one who restores sight. And Jesus responds with the generosity of the king Israel had awaited: "Your faith has made you well" (Mark 10:52). In this moment, the Davidic throne is not an abstraction; it is mercy embodied.

But the royal identity of Jesus reaches its most striking expression in the trial before Pilate. The Roman governor interrogates Him directly: "Are You the king of the Jews?" (John 18:33). Jesus refuses to answer in political terms: "My kingdom is not of this world" (John 18:36). He does not reject kingship; He redefines it. His kingdom does not arise from worldly systems or coercive force. It arises from truth: "For this purpose I have come into the world—to bear witness to the truth" (John 18:37). Pilate is puzzled; Jesus is not. The reign He inaugurates is the reign of God restored in the hearts of humanity.

It is here, in this courtroom, that the paradox of the Davidic Messiah reaches its climax. The man who should be enthroned is condemned. The man who fulfills every covenantal expectation is judged unworthy by His own people. The one who restored the blind, healed the sick, raised the dead, taught with authority, and entered Jerusalem as king is handed over to be crucified. Yet the Gospels insist that Jesus remains king even in His humiliation. The soldiers mock Him with a purple robe and a crown of thorns (John 19:2). Their cruelty becomes unintended coronation. Pilate orders the inscription for the cross: "Jesus of Nazareth, King of the Jews" (John 19:19). What was meant as sarcasm becomes a proclamation of truth.

The cross is not the negation of His kingship; it is the revelation of it. Augustine writes, "He mounted the cross as a king mounts his throne" (*Tractates on John* 36.1). The crucifixion is the moment when the Davidic promise meets the depth of divine love. Israel looked for a king who would defeat Rome; God gave a king who would defeat death. The throne promised to David becomes the wood of the cross; the dominion promised in the psalms is exercised through self-giving love.

Here, in the crucified king, the promise reaches its turning point. But it is the resurrection that unveils its fullness. Peter, on the day of Pentecost, interprets the risen Christ through the Davidic psalms: "Being therefore exalted at the right hand of God… God has made Him both Lord and Messiah, this Jesus whom you crucified" (Acts 2:33, 36). The resurrection is not merely vindication; it is enthronement. The king rejected by His people is crowned by His Father.

In this way, Jesus emerges not simply as a Davidic heir, but as the Davidic fulfillment—greater than David, greater than Solomon, greater than the entire line of kings that preceded Him. His kingdom is eternal because His life is eternal. His reign is universal because His resurrection is universal in scope. His authority is divine because His kingship is divine.

The resurrection does not terminate the royal narrative; it inaugurates a new chapter in it. Israel's Scriptures had spoken of a king who would reign forever, but no earthly dynasty could sustain such a promise. Jesus, risen from the dead, enters a mode of existence in which death no longer has claim over Him, and therefore His kingship can no longer be threatened by the rise and fall of nations. Paul expresses this with lapidary precision: the Gospel is "about His Son, who was descended from David according to the flesh and declared to be the Son of God in power… by His resurrection from the dead" (Rom 1:3–4). In other words, the resurrection is not merely proof of divine favour; it is the moment of royal declaration. What had been hidden in humility is now revealed in glory. The Davidic title "Son of God" becomes manifest with cosmic force.

This is exactly how the earliest Christians preached. Peter, addressing the crowds in Jerusalem during Pentecost, roots his proclamation firmly in Davidic expectation. He cites Psalm 16, in which David says, "You will not abandon my soul to Hades, nor let your holy one see corruption" (Ps 16:10), and argues that David could not have been speaking about himself, since "he both died and was buried" (Acts 2:29). Instead, David "foresaw and spoke about the resurrection of the Messiah" (Acts 2:31). On this basis, Peter declares that God has exalted Jesus and fulfilled the covenant oath to David that "one of his descendants would sit on his throne" (Acts 2:30). The resurrection is the enthronement; Pentecost is the public announcement.

This royal exaltation is echoed by Paul in his sermon at Antioch: "We bring you the good news that what God promised to the fathers, this He has fulfilled to us their children by raising Jesus" (Acts 13:32–33). Paul immediately cites Psalm 2—"You are my Son, today I have begotten you"—a coronation psalm historically applied to the kings of Judah. In the resurrection, Jesus becomes the definitive heir of this royal declaration. The psalm that once celebrated mortal kings now finds its true subject in the immortal Son. The ancient covenant has finally reached its target.

But the restoration of kingship cannot be reduced to resurrection alone. The ascension is the moment when the royal symbolism becomes unmistakable. Daniel had seen "one like a son of man" coming with the clouds of heaven, entering the presence of the Ancient of Days, and receiving "dominion, glory, and a kingdom" that would never pass away (Dan 7:13–14). The New Testament implicitly identifies the ascension with this enthronement. Jesus is lifted up, not as a departure but as an arrival. He enters the heavenly court as the triumphant king who has defeated sin, death, and the powers of darkness. Acts describes Him being taken up and seated at the right hand of God (Acts 2:33; 7:56), the position of royal authority. Hebrews echoes the same truth: "After making purification for sins, He sat down at the right hand of the Majesty on high" (Heb 1:3). The king has been enthroned, not in earthly Jerusalem but in the heavenly

## THE SON OF DAVID APPEARS: JESUS AND THE RESTORATION OF...

temple from which His reign extends over all creation.

This understanding is not a later theological development; it is embedded in the earliest confessions of the Church. When Paul summarises the Gospel he preaches, he includes among its essentials that Jesus "was raised on the third day" and "appeared" to many witnesses (1 Cor 15:4–8). But in his pastoral letters and homilies, he interprets this resurrection as the royal enthronement foretold in Scripture. To Timothy, he says, "Remember Jesus Christ, risen from the dead, descended from David" (2 Tim 2:8). The Davidic identity remains essential even in the age of the resurrection. Christ's kingship is not a metaphor; it is the concrete fulfillment of the covenant God swore to David a thousand years earlier.

The Book of Revelation presents the most dramatic depiction of Jesus' kingship. John calls Him "the ruler of the kings of the earth" (Rev 1:5) and "the Lion of the tribe of Judah, the Root of David" (Rev 5:5). Yet when John turns to see this Lion, he beholds instead "a Lamb standing, as though slain" (Rev 5:6). This paradox captures the essence of Jesus' kingship. He conquers not by violence but by sacrifice; He reigns not by domination but by self-giving love. The heavenly court worships Him with words that echo the Davidic psalms: "Worthy is the Lamb who was slain, to receive power and wealth and wisdom and might and honour and glory and blessing!" (Rev 5:12). Here the crucified king is adored with royal acclamations, enthroned at the centre of heaven's liturgy. The kingship that began in Bethlehem, that was misunderstood in Galilee, that was mocked in Jerusalem, is revealed in its true form before the hosts of heaven.

This royal vision reshapes the way the early Church speaks of salvation. To be saved is not merely to be forgiven; it is to enter the kingdom of the Son. Paul writes that God "has delivered us from the dominion of darkness and transferred us into the kingdom of His beloved Son" (Col 1:13). This is regal language. Salvation is relocation—movement from one domain to another, from tyranny to royal freedom, from exile to home. The Messiah is not simply the teacher of a moral way; He is the king who inaugurates a new realm of existence.

This is why the earliest Christian creed was not a complex doctrinal formula but a royal confession: "Jesus is Lord." In the Greek-speaking world, *Kyrios* was the title of emperors; in the Greek Old Testament, it was the divine name applied to God. When Christians proclaimed Jesus as Lord, they were not uttering a polite religious phrase; they were declaring that He is the true king of Israel and the ruler of the nations. This confession united Jews and Gentiles, not because it downplayed Jesus' Davidic identity but because His Davidic kingship was the means by which God fulfilled the universal promise of salvation: "In your seed all the nations of the earth shall be blessed" (Gen 22:18).

The Davidic promise thus becomes the hinge upon which the universal mission turns. Jesus' kingship is rooted in Israel but extends beyond Israel. His throne is promised to one nation but destined for all nations. His authority fulfills the psalm that declares, "Ask of me, and I will make the nations your heritage, and the ends of the earth your possession" (Ps 2:8). This is not allegory; it is the structure of the Gospel itself. The Messiah begins in the cradle of David, but His kingdom knows no borders.

Through all these layers—lineage, geography, proclamation, miracles, passion, resurrection, and ascension—the same truth emerges: Jesus is the king Israel expected and the king the world did not know it needed. His kingship is more than restoration; it is revelation. More than political hope; it is divine action. More than national identity; it is cosmic renewal. In Him, the promise to David attains its full stature, and the kingdom of God takes on a human face.

The kingship of Jesus displays itself not only in His public ministry and heavenly enthronement but in the way He gathers a people to Himself. Every king forms a kingdom, but Jesus forms one unlike anything in Israel's previous experience. He calls twelve apostles—not an arbitrary number, but a deliberate sign of restored Israel. The twelve tribes fractured in exile; the twelve apostles signal their reunification under the Messianic king. Jesus Himself makes the connection explicit when He tells the apostles, "You who have followed me will sit on twelve thrones, judging the twelve tribes of Israel" (Matt 19:28). This is Davidic language—

restoration, governance, renewal. The kingdom Jesus inaugurates is not merely internal or symbolic; it is a structured community, gathered around the king and sharing in His authority.

This reconstitution of Israel is further revealed in Jesus' choice of a prime ministerial figure. In the ancient Davidic kingdom, the king appointed a royal steward—*al ha-bayit*, "the one over the house"—who wielded the keys of authority (Isa 22:20–22). Jesus replays this Davidic pattern when He says to Simon, "I will give you the keys of the kingdom of heaven" (Matt 16:19). This is not a metaphor floating free of context. The language of keys, binding, and loosing belongs to royal administration. By granting Peter this authority, Jesus reveals that His kingdom has real governance, real structure, real continuity. The Messiah does not merely teach; He builds.

Even His moral and ethical demands carry a distinctly royal quality. When Jesus proclaims the Beatitudes (Matt 5:3–12), He does not offer generic spiritual advice but announces the constitution of His kingdom. The poor in spirit, the meek, the merciful—these are the citizens who will inherit the earth, see God, and be called His children. This is royal legislation expressed in grace rather than force. The Sermon on the Mount as a whole reads like the charter of a king laying out the ethos of His realm. Its authority surpasses that of Moses because its giver surpasses Moses. "You have heard...but I say to you" (Matt 5:21–22) is not the voice of a reformer but of the king who stands within the law and brings it to fulfillment.

The royal identity of Jesus becomes even clearer in the confrontations with religious authorities. They challenge His actions, interrogate His authority, and attempt to trap Him with questions. Yet each time, He responds with the dignity and wisdom befitting the son of David. After His parable of the wicked tenants, He cites Psalm 118:22—"The stone the builders rejected has become the cornerstone"—and declares that the kingdom will be taken from those who reject Him and given to those who bear its fruit (Matt 21:42–43). This is judicial authority, the authority of the king to judge His people. It mirrors the prerogatives of David and

Solomon but surpasses them, because the judgment Jesus pronounces is not historical but eschatological.

His teaching on the kingdom carries this same royal gravity. When He speaks of the final judgment, He does so in explicitly kingly terms: "When the Son of Man comes in His glory, and all the angels with Him, then He will sit on His glorious throne" (Matt 25:31). The imagery echoes Daniel 7—the heavenly court, the enthroned figure, the nations assembled before Him. Jesus identifies Himself as that Son of Man, the king who separates sheep from goats, who renders a verdict not on political allegiance but on love expressed in concrete acts of mercy. This is kingship as divine justice. This is authority exercised not through military conquest but through moral discernment. The Davidic promise expands here into a cosmic horizon: the king of Israel is revealed as judge of the nations.

Even Jesus' parables of the kingdom assume royal themes. The parable of the talents (Matt 25:14–30) depicts a master entrusting authority to his servants and rewarding fidelity. The parable of the wedding feast (Matt 22:1–14) portrays a king whose invitation widens beyond expected guests to include the poor and forgotten. The parable of the vineyard tenants (Mark 12:1–12) reveals a royal son sent to claim what belongs to him—rejected, killed, yet vindicated by the lord of the vineyard. These are not abstract stories; they are windows into Jesus' self-understanding as the rightful king.

And yet the king remains hidden in humility until the right moment. This is the paradox that permeates the Gospels. Jesus performs deeds that reveal divine authority—stilling the sea, multiplying bread, casting out demons, forgiving sins. People respond with royal titles: "Son of David" (Matt 21:9), "Lord" (Kyrios), even "My Lord and my God" (John 20:28). But Jesus continually redirects the enthusiasm of those who would crown Him prematurely. After feeding the five thousand, the crowd attempts to make Him king by force, but He withdraws to the mountain alone (John 6:15). The Messiah cannot be seized; He must be revealed. His kingship is not validated by popular acclaim but by divine appointment.

This slow unveiling culminates in a moment that the Gospels treat with extraordinary reverence: the Transfiguration. On a mountain—David's sons were often enthroned on Mount Zion—Jesus reveals a glory that surpasses anything associated with the ancient monarchy. His face shines like the sun; His garments become dazzling white (Matt 17:2). Moses and Elijah appear, representing the prophetic and lawgiving traditions that prepared Israel for the Messiah. And a voice from the cloud declares, "This is My beloved Son; listen to Him" (Matt 17:5). This is coronation language echoing Psalm 2:7. The king is revealed as the Son in whom the Father delights, standing between the old covenant figures as their fulfillment. The disciples fall prostrate because they are witnessing royalty of divine origin.

The royal identity unveiled on the mountaintop remains hidden in the valley below, but it determines the shape of everything that follows. Jesus now speaks openly of His death and resurrection because the king must take His throne by way of suffering. The Gospels emphasize the necessity of this path. "The Son of Man must suffer many things…and be killed, and on the third day be raised" (Luke 9:22). The word *must* (*dei* in Greek) signifies divine purpose. The king's suffering is not an interruption of His mission; it is the mission. Isaiah had foretold that the Servant would be "pierced for our transgressions" (Isa 53:5), and Daniel had spoken of a Messiah who would be "cut off" (Dan 9:26). Jesus now gathers these threads and weaves them into the royal tapestry. The king is the servant; the throne is the cross; the coronation is crucifixion.

This is why the New Testament never separates Jesus' kingship from His passion. When James and John request positions of honour, Jesus replies, "You do not know what you are asking… Can you drink the cup that I drink?" (Mark 10:38). Kingship requires participation in suffering. The cup is royal, but it is filled with sacrifice. Even His entry into Jerusalem, royal as it is, is overshadowed by His prophecy of destruction and judgment. He weeps over the city because its refusal to recognize the king will lead to devastation (Luke 19:41–44). Royal authority does not shield Him from sorrow; it deepens it.

Everything now moves toward the cross, where the paradox of the

Davidic Messiah reaches its most luminous expression. The crown is of thorns; the throne is of wood; the acclamation is mockery; the inscription is meant as insult. But the truth shines through human scorn. The one crucified is indeed the King of the Jews. And because He is king not by human appointment but by divine identity, His reign extends beyond death.

From the cross, the king exercises His royal authority in a manner that overturns all earthly categories. The soldiers divide His garments as though stripping a defeated ruler of his dignity (John 19:23–24), yet in doing so they fulfill Psalm 22:18, a psalm that begins in dereliction and ends in triumph. The chief priests mock Him, saying, "He is the King of Israel; let Him come down now from the cross" (Matt 27:42). They speak more truth than they understand. For if He were the kind of king they expected—one who preserves Himself through force—He would indeed come down. But the Messiah God promised is the king who saves others rather than Himself. His refusal to descend is not impotence but sovereignty. Augustine captures this inversion with startling clarity: *"For our sakes He endured mockery, for our sakes He hung upon the cross; His throne was a gibbet, yet from there He ruled the nations"* (Sermon 47).

The royal dignity of Jesus is most evident in His final acts of mercy. To the repentant thief, He grants not merely forgiveness but royal fellowship: "Today you will be with Me in Paradise" (Luke 23:43). The king opens His kingdom to a dying criminal, fulfilling Isaiah's prophecy that He would "make many righteous" and "divide the spoil with the strong" (Isa 53:11–12). To His mother and the beloved disciple, He bestows a new covenantal family (John 19:26–27), acting with the authority of a patriarch even as He hangs upon the cross. To His executioners, He offers intercession: "Father, forgive them, for they know not what they do" (Luke 23:34). No king of Israel ever ruled in such a manner. The cross is not the collapse of His kingship; it is its purest revelation.

When Jesus breathes His last, the earth responds as though the true ruler has released a cosmic command. Darkness descends (Mark 15:33). The Temple veil is torn from top to bottom (Matt 27:51). Rocks split, tombs open, and the centurion—Rome's representative—confesses, "Truly this was the Son of God!" (Matt 27:54). The centurion's words echo Psalm 2, where the nations rage but the Lord enthrones His Son despite their rebellion. In the crucifixion of Jesus, the kingship promised in that ancient psalm is revealed in paradoxical glory. The nations do not enthrone Him; the Father does.

But the Father's enthronement becomes visible only on the third day. The resurrection is the divine vindication of Jesus' royal identity. When the women arrive at the tomb, they are greeted with the words, "He is not here, for He has risen" (Matt 28:6). The risen Christ declares to His disciples, "All authority in heaven and on earth has been given to Me" (Matt 28:18). This is the language of kingship in its fullest sense. No Davidic monarch ever spoke such words. The dominion described in Daniel 7—"all peoples, nations, and languages should serve Him"—now finds its realization in the risen Son of Man. The kingdom Jesus proclaimed in Galilee is now manifest in glory; His authority extends over creation itself.

This royal authority shapes the mission He entrusts to His disciples. The Great Commission is not merely an instruction to evangelize; it is the royal edict of a universal king: "Go therefore and make disciples of all nations" (Matt 28:19). This fulfills Psalm 72, which envisioned a messianic king whose reign would extend "from sea to sea" and whose name would be blessed among all the nations (Ps 72:8, 17). Jesus, risen and enthroned, becomes the living fulfillment of this Davidic hope. He reigns not from Jerusalem's palace but from the right hand of the Father, yet His rule is no less real. It is more real, because it is eternal.

The ascension completes this upward movement. Luke describes Jesus being lifted up and received into the cloud (Acts 1:9), an image resonant with Daniel 7:13, where the Son of Man is granted dominion in the heavenly court. The cloud is not atmospheric; it is theophanic. It signifies divine presence and enthronement. Hebrews echoes this vision by declaring that Jesus has entered "behind the veil" as a priest (Heb 6:19–20) and taken His seat as king (Heb 1:3). Priesthood and kingship converge in the ascended Christ; the royal Son now reigns through His intercessory love, ruling the world by mediating it to the Father.

Yet even this heavenly enthronement is not distant. The king who reigns at the right hand of God remains present with His people. Revelations 1 depicts Him as walking among the lampstands—the churches—holding their angels in His hand (Rev 1:12–16). His voice is like rushing waters; His eyes burn with fire; His face shines like the sun. This is the royal Christ who governs history, judges the nations, sustains the faithful, and ultimately brings creation to its consummation. His kingship is not postponed until the end of time; it is active now, shaping every age with the quiet force of divine sovereignty.

This is why the early Christians spoke of the Gospel primarily in terms of kingship. Mark begins his account with the words, "The beginning of the gospel of Jesus Christ, the Son of God" (Mark 1:1). In the Roman world, "gospel" (*euangelion*) was the public announcement of a new king's accession. The evangelists adopt this word deliberately. They proclaim that the true king has come—not Caesar, not Herod, but Jesus of Nazareth. His kingship relativizes all earthly power, judges all earthly injustice, and offers a kingdom built not on violence but on grace. As Paul declares, every throne, dominion, and power is subject to Him (Col 1:16). Human kingdoms rise and fall, but the kingdom of the Son endures forever.

In this light, the crucifixion and resurrection of Jesus do not merely fulfill prophecy; they reveal the nature of God's own kingship. Israel expected a son of David who would defeat its enemies. God sent a Son who defeated death. Israel sought a throne restored in Jerusalem. God established a throne in the heavens. Israel clamored for liberation from Rome. God liberated humanity from sin and death. The Messiah they received was infinitely greater than the messiah they imagined. In Him, the promise given to David reaches beyond Israel's borders and embraces the world.

What emerges is a stunning theological truth: Jesus is the king Israel longed for, the king Israel failed to recognize, and the king the world cannot live without. His kingship is the heart of the Gospel. Every healing, every teaching, every confrontation, every parable, every miracle, every sorrow, and every triumph reveals the reign of the God who has become man for the salvation of His people. The son of David has appeared, and with Him, the kingdom of God has entered history.

The royal identity of Jesus unfolds even more fully when we consider the kind of kingdom He establishes. Earthly kings secure their rule through military strength, diplomatic alliances, taxation, and the consolidation of land. Jesus secures His kingdom through forgiveness, conversion, and the transformation of the human heart. This is why He speaks repeatedly of the kingdom not merely as a realm but as a reality that takes root within the person—"The kingdom of God is within you" (Luke 17:21)—or, as some translations render it, "in your midst." His reign is internal before it is external, spiritual before it is geopolitical. The Davidic promise remains intact, but its fulfillment expands into the realm of divine communion.

Jesus' parables emphasize this interior quality of His kingship. The kingdom is like leaven hidden in three measures of flour until all is leavened (Matt 13:33), like a mustard seed that begins insignificantly but grows into a tree where the birds of the air make their nests (Matt 13:31–32). These images convey not only growth but gentleness. The Messiah exercises dominion quietly, almost imperceptibly, until the full reality bursts into view. In this, He embodies the promise of Isaiah: "A bruised reed He will not break, and a faintly burning wick He will not quench" (Isa 42:3). The king fulfills prophecy not through force but through gentleness, not through coercion but through mercy. His authority shapes rather than crushes, heals rather than wounds.

Yet His gentleness is never weakness. Jesus confronts the powers of darkness with absolute authority. When the Gerasene demoniac meets Him, the demons cry out, "What have You to do with me, Jesus, Son of the Most High God?" (Mark 5:7). They recognize Him instantly and submit to His command. In this confrontation, we see a glimpse of the cosmic kingship described in Psalm 89: "O LORD God of hosts, who is mighty as You are?" (Ps 89:8). The Son of David rules not only Israel but the unseen realms. His sovereignty extends beyond the visible world, because His kingship is rooted in divine identity.

This divine identity becomes clearer as Jesus accepts titles and actions that belong only to God. He forgives sins (Mark 2:5–12), a prerogative the scribes rightly acknowledge as divine: "Who can forgive sins but God alone?" He accepts worship (Matt 14:33; John 9:38), something unthinkable for a mere king of Israel. He stills storms with a word (Mark 4:39), echoing Yahweh's dominion over the chaotic waters in Psalm 107:29. He multiplies bread in the wilderness (John 6:1–14), surpassing Moses and prefiguring the Eucharistic banquet of the new covenant. In all these acts, the Davidic Messiah is revealed not as a gifted human leader but as God's own Son, exercising divine authority in human flesh.

This is why Jesus repeatedly challenges His hearers with the question of His identity. In Matthew 22, He asks the Pharisees, "What do you think of the Messiah? Whose son is He?" They reply, "The son of David." Jesus then cites Psalm 110: "How is it then that David, in the Spirit, calls Him Lord?" (Matt 22:42–45). The implication is clear: the Messiah is not only David's descendant but David's Lord. Royal lineage alone cannot explain Him. The king expected by Israel must be greater than Israel itself—greater than Abraham (John 8:58), greater than Jacob (John 4:12), greater than the Temple (Matt 12:6). Jesus inhabits the Davidic promise while transcending it, fulfilling it in an unexpected and divine way.

One of the most striking manifestations of this divine kingship occurs during Jesus' trial before the Sanhedrin. When asked directly, "Tell us if You are the Messiah, the Son of God," Jesus responds with a fusion of Daniel 7 and Psalm 110: "From now on you will see the Son of Man seated at the right hand of Power and coming on the clouds of heaven" (Matt 26:63–64). This answer is a declaration of enthronement. He identifies Himself not only as David's heir but as the heavenly Son of Man who receives universal dominion from the Ancient of Days. The high priest tears his garments because the claim is either blasphemy or revelation. No middle category exists. The king of Israel stands before His people and reveals that He is the king of heaven.

Yet the earthly response is rejection. The true king is condemned as a traitor. The Messiah promised to Israel is handed over to Gentiles. But even this rejection fulfills prophecy. Isaiah had foretold that the Servant would be "despised and rejected by men" (Isa 53:3). Zechariah had spoken of the shepherd struck and the sheep scattered (Zech 13:7). Jesus enters His kingly glory not by avoiding these prophecies but by embracing them. The king must suffer before He reigns. His crown must be woven of thorns before it gleams with divine light.

What makes this kingship unlike any other is that Jesus invites His followers to share in it—not in its power, but in its pattern. When James and John petition Him for seats of honour, Jesus asks, "Are you able to drink the cup that I drink?" (Mark 10:38). The kingdom He offers is not a hierarchy of privilege but a communion of self-giving love. "The Son of Man came not to be served but to serve, and to give His life as a ransom for many" (Mark 10:45). Here the nature of divine kingship is revealed with absolute clarity: authority exists for the sake of service, dominion for the sake of redemption, kingship for the sake of love.

This inversion of worldly power becomes the foundation of Christian discipleship. Those who enter the kingdom must do so through humility (Matt 18:3-4), forgiveness (Matt 18:21-22), and sacrificial charity (Matt 25:31-46). The laws of the new kingdom are not imposed externally but written in the heart through grace, fulfilling the promise of Jeremiah 31:33. Jesus, the royal lawgiver, does not legislate as Moses did; He transforms as only God can.

The transformation He effects becomes visible in the Church He establishes. The kingdom is not an abstract idea but a concrete community gathered around the king and animated by His Spirit. The Church becomes the sphere in which His kingship is exercised on earth, not in political terms but sacramentally and morally. When Jesus says, "All authority in heaven and on earth has been given to Me" (Matt 28:18), He immediately commissions the apostles to baptize and teach (Matt 28:19-20). This is royal delegation. The king extends His reign not through armies but through apostles; not by conquering territories but by converting hearts.

This dynamic kingship continues in the life of the early Church. The book of Acts portrays a community living under the authority of the risen king. The apostles heal in His name (Acts 3:6), preach His resurrection (Acts 4:33), suffer joyfully for His sake (Acts 5:41), and proclaim Him as "Lord of all" (Acts 10:36). Paul describes Christ as the head of the body (Col 1:18), the one in whom all things hold together (Col 1:17), the one under whose feet all powers are placed (1 Cor 15:25–27). This is Davidic kingship expanded to cosmic scale. What David did for Israel, Christ now does for creation.

In this cosmic expansion of kingship, the deepest meaning of the Davidic promise comes into view. When God swore to David, "Your throne shall be established forever" (2 Sam 7:16), the words could not be contained within the lifespan of any mortal king. They were already straining toward a future figure whose reign would endure beyond time, whose dominion would not collapse under sin or death, and whose kingdom would embrace not only Israel but the nations. The prophets sensed this. Psalm 72 prays that the royal son will "have dominion from sea to sea" (Ps 72:8) and that "all nations shall call Him blessed" (Ps 72:17). Isaiah foresees a king whose rule will bring endless peace and justice, upheld "with righteousness from this time forth and forevermore" (Isa 9:7). These promises were not poetic exaggerations; they were glimpses of the Messiah whose kingship would exceed the boundaries of any earthly dynasty.

Jesus fulfills these hopes by embodying a kingship that is human in lineage, divine in authority, sacrificial in method, and eternal in scope. In Him, the throne of David is not merely restored; it is transfigured. He reigns through a heart that knows human weakness and through a power that conquers death. His rule does not end when His earthly life ends, because His resurrection inaugurates a kingdom that death cannot touch. His ascension establishes that kingdom in the heavens, where no enemy can dethrone Him and no earthly catastrophe can threaten His reign. The Davidic covenant was a promise of permanence; Jesus turns permanence into glory.

But the grandeur of this kingship does not obscure its intimacy. The risen king continues to shepherd His people with the tenderness He showed in Galilee. He calls disciples by name (John 20:16), breaks bread with them in hidden places (Luke 24:35), restores the fallen with mercy (John 21:15-17), and sends His Spirit to dwell within their hearts (Acts 2:1-4). His reign is not distant or abstract; it is personal, immediate, and transformative. The kingdom He establishes is not a geopolitical state but the restoration of communion between God and humanity. As Paul writes, "The kingdom of God is righteousness and peace and joy in the Holy Spirit" (Rom 14:17). These are not qualities imposed from without; they are the interior fruits of living under the rule of a king who gives Himself entirely for the life of His people.

This inward transformation extends outward into the mission of the Church. The king who reigns from heaven continues His work on earth through the members of His body. The apostles preach His Gospel, not as philosophers offering insights but as heralds announcing the accession of a king. Their message is not simply that Jesus taught wisely or acted compassionately; it is that God "has made Him both Lord and Messiah" (Acts 2:36). The kingship of Christ becomes the interpretive centre of Christian proclamation. Every baptism is an act of royal incorporation; every Eucharist is a participation in the feast of the kingdom; every act of mercy is a sign that the reign of God is breaking into the world. The crucified and risen king continues to extend His dominion, not by force but by grace, not through conquest but through conversion.

This is why the New Testament describes Christian existence in emphatically royal terms. Believers are called "a chosen race, a royal priesthood, a holy nation" (1 Pet 2:9). They are seated with Christ in the heavenly places (Eph 2:6), share in His sufferings so that they may share in His glory (Rom 8:17), and overcome the world through faith in Him (1 John 5:4-5). The kingdom Jesus inaugurates is not merely His; it becomes theirs. He reigns not to dominate but to elevate, not to hoard authority but to distribute it, transforming His followers into participants in the divine life. The promise God made to David—that his son would build a house for the Lord—finds its fullness in the Church, the living temple constructed from the hearts of those redeemed by the king.

Yet the kingdom remains both already and not yet. Jesus reigns now, but His reign is not yet acknowledged by all. The nations still rage (Ps 2:1), empires still rise and fall, and human hearts still resist the gentle authority of Christ. But the Scriptures assure us that the kingdom inaugurated in His resurrection will one day be manifest in its totality. Paul speaks of the moment when Christ "must reign until He has put all His enemies under His feet" (1 Cor 15:25). John sees a vision of the Lamb who is also the Lion of Judah—the Davidic king—standing in the centre of heaven's throne, receiving worship from every tribe and tongue (Rev 5:9–14). The end of history is not the dissolution of Christ's kingship but its universal recognition.

All this reveals that Jesus is not simply the fulfillment of the Davidic promise; He is its meaning. Every earlier king was a shadow; every royal hope was a fragment. David conquered enemies; Jesus conquers death. Solomon ruled with wisdom; Jesus is wisdom incarnate. Josiah restored the covenant; Jesus establishes the new covenant in His blood. The kings of Israel rose and fell; Jesus rises never to fall again. The promise of an everlasting throne was never meant for a merely earthly monarch. It was the promise of a divine-human king whose reign would heal creation.

In Him, the royal line reaches its perfection. In Him, the kingdom becomes indestructible. In Him, the promises to David and the hopes of Israel find their fulfillment. He is the Son of David who restores the kingdom, the Son of Man who receives dominion, the Lord who reigns from the cross, and the risen king whose glory fills heaven and earth. The long-awaited Messiah has appeared, and with Him the dawn of the eternal reign promised from the beginning. Through His kingship, the ancient story enters its climax, and the world is invited to step into a kingdom where justice and mercy are no longer opposed, where authority is exercised as love, and where God reigns not from a distant throne but from a pierced and resurrected heart.

# 8

# Greater Than Moses: Jesus the New Lawgiver and Redeemer

From the beginning of Israel's story, Moses stands as the towering mediator between God and His people—the liberator who confronts Pharaoh, the prophet who ascends the mountain of fire, the lawgiver who receives the covenant sealed in God's own words, the intercessor who pleads for Israel's life when judgment looms. No figure before Jesus carries such concentrated authority, and no figure shapes Israel's imagination more profoundly. This is why Deuteronomy closes with the haunting line, "There has not arisen a prophet since in Israel like Moses, whom the LORD knew face to face" (Deut 34:10). The Scriptures themselves create an expectation suspended in midair: Moses was unsurpassed, yet God promised another who would be "like him" (Deut 18:15–19). The people waited for one who would speak with God's voice, who would reveal His will with clarity deeper than Sinai, who would lead a liberation greater than the first exodus. Moses becomes both the summit of Israel's past and the silhouette of its future.

It is into this expectation that Jesus steps, not merely recalling the deeds of Moses but embodying and surpassing them. His ministry unfolds as a deliberate re-enactment of Israel's foundational story, revealing that He is not simply a teacher within the Mosaic tradition but the One to whom

Moses' entire mission pointed. The Gospel of Matthew makes this plain from the outset. Jesus survives a massacre of infants at the hands of a tyrant (Matt 2:16–18), echoing the childhood of Moses under Pharaoh's decree (Exod 1:22). He returns from Egypt so that the prophecy "Out of Egypt I have called my son" (Hos 11:1) might be fulfilled (Matt 2:15). Like Moses, He passes through water before beginning His mission—Moses through the Red Sea (Exod 14), Jesus through the Jordan (Matt 3:13–17). Moses fasted forty days before receiving the law (Exod 34:28); Jesus fasts forty days before proclaiming the kingdom (Matt 4:1–2). Each narrative choice announces the same truth: the story of Israel is being recapitulated in the life of its Messiah, but in a way that presses beyond the limits of the first covenant.

This becomes clearest when Jesus ascends a mountain to teach. Just as Moses climbed Sinai to receive the law amid thunder and cloud (Exod 19–20), Jesus "went up on the mountain" (Matt 5:1) and opened His mouth to deliver the charter of the new covenant. The Sermon on the Mount is not a commentary on the Mosaic law; it is the renewal and interiorization of it. Where Moses spoke commandments carved in stone, Jesus speaks words meant to be carved upon hearts (cf. Jer 31:33). "You have heard that it was said... but I say to you" (Matt 5:21–22). No prophet had ever spoken this way. None had ever dared reinterpret the divine law with divine authority. The crowd senses the difference immediately: "He taught them as one who had authority, and not as their scribes" (Matt 7:29). Jesus does what Moses never did—He speaks as the giver of the law, not merely its mediator.

Yet Jesus insists He has not come to abolish the law or the prophets but to fulfill them (Matt 5:17). Fulfillment does not negate; it perfects. In Moses, the law was external, a boundary that disciplined behavior. In Jesus, the law becomes internal, transforming the heart that desires, the will that chooses, and the love that gives itself. Anger is addressed not only in murder, but in its earliest stirrings (Matt 5:22). Adultery is confronted not only in the act but in the gaze that distorts another's dignity (Matt 5:28). Oaths, retaliation, and hatred—all the areas where the law restrained sin—

are now caught up into a greater righteousness that reflects the character of the Father Himself: "Be perfect, as your heavenly Father is perfect" (Matt 5:48). This is Sinai transfigured. The covenant given in fire becomes a covenant written in love.

But Jesus does more than teach a new law; He performs signs that mirror and surpass the wonders wrought through Moses. When Moses fed Israel with manna in the wilderness, it was bread given from heaven, a sign of God's sustaining mercy (Exod 16). When Jesus feeds the multitude with five loaves and two fish, the people recognize the Mosaic echo and declare, "This is indeed the prophet who is to come into the world" (John 6:14), referencing Deuteronomy 18. Yet Jesus presses beyond the sign, declaring that He Himself is "the bread of life" (John 6:35) and that the manna was but a foreshadowing of the true food that gives eternal life (John 6:48–51). Moses mediated provision; Jesus becomes provision. The miracle is not only external multiplication but revelation of His identity.

Moses stretched out his hand over the sea, and the waters parted (Exod 14:21). Jesus rebukes the winds and waves, and they obey (Mark 4:39). The disciples ask the only question that makes sense: "Who then is this, that even wind and sea obey Him?" (Mark 4:41). In the Old Testament, mastery over the chaotic waters belongs to God alone: "You rule the raging of the sea; when its waves rise, You still them" (Ps 89:9). Jesus demonstrates not merely prophetic power but divine authority. His dominion over nature does not repeat the exodus—it surpasses it. Moses divided the sea by God's command; Jesus commands the sea by His own word.

The liberation Jesus brings, like Moses', includes deliverance from oppressive powers, but the enemy He confronts is deeper than Pharaoh. Again and again, He drives out demons with effortless authority (Mark 1:27; Matt 12:28). Moses delivered Israel from political bondage; Jesus delivers humanity from spiritual enslavement. He enters the "strong man's house" and binds him (Mark 3:27), an image that evokes both Egypt and the primordial serpent. The new exodus is not a metaphor. It is the defining drama of salvation history—bondage, confrontation, liberation, covenant, and journey into communion with God. In Jesus, each movement is recast and fulfilled.

These signs, these teachings, these acts of authority build toward a revelation that could not occur at Sinai: the Transfiguration. Moses' face had shone after speaking with God, but the light was reflected, borrowed (Exod 34:29–35). When Jesus is transfigured before His disciples, "His face shone like the sun, and His garments became white as light" (Matt 17:2). This is not reflected glory. It is the radiation of divine identity bursting through His humanity. Moses and Elijah appear, representing law and prophecy, not as equals but as witnesses. The voice that once thundered on Sinai now speaks from the cloud again, but with a new and greater declaration: "This is My beloved Son… listen to Him!" (Matt 17:5). The command to listen echoes Deuteronomy 18: "To Him you shall listen." The prophecy is fulfilled in a moment of unveiled light. Jesus is not simply like Moses—He is greater than Moses because He is the Son in whom the fullness of God's glory dwells.

The disciples fall on their faces because they witness what Israel longed for yet could never behold. Moses had asked to see God's glory, but he was shown only the divine "back," the afterglow of presence (Exod 33:18–23). Peter, James, and John see what Moses could not—the glory of God in the face of Jesus Christ (2 Cor 4:6). The new covenant is already beginning to dawn.

What Moses glimpsed only in shadows, Jesus now fulfills openly as He leads a new exodus that surpasses the liberation from Egypt in both scope and depth. The first exodus freed Israel from political slavery, but the new exodus frees humanity from sin, death, and the demonic powers that enslave the heart. This movement becomes explicit at an astonishing moment in Luke's Gospel. During the Transfiguration, as Jesus stands in radiant glory conversing with Moses and Elijah, Luke alone records the content of their divine conversation: "They spoke of His *exodus* which He was to accomplish at Jerusalem" (Luke 9:31). The Greek term—*exodos*—is deliberate. Jesus' Passion is not merely a tragic execution or a martyr's fate; it is the true exodus, the moment when redemption reaches its definitive form. Moses once led Israel out of slavery into covenant; Jesus will lead humanity out of the slavery of sin into the eternal covenant sealed in His blood.

This new exodus unfolds step by step throughout His ministry. When Jesus feeds the multitudes in the wilderness, the scene mirrors Israel receiving manna after crossing the Red Sea. The crowds follow Him into a deserted place (Mark 6:31–34), and He feeds them with an abundance that leaves twelve baskets of fragments—a symbolic gesture toward the restored tribes of Israel. But unlike manna, which perished with the dawn, the bread Jesus gives points toward an imperishable gift: "Whoever eats this bread will live forever" (John 6:51). The manna sustained a people walking toward a promised land; the Eucharistic bread sustains a people walking toward eternal life. Moses prayed; Jesus gives. Moses mediated; Jesus embodies.

The exodus motif deepens through Jesus' mastery over the sea. When He walks upon the waters and calms the storm with a simple rebuke (Matt 14:25; Mark 4:39), He reveals mastery over the forces that had once threatened Israel in its flight from Egypt. The sea in Scripture is not merely geographical; it is symbolic of chaos, disorder, and death—the hostile powers that resist God's creative and redemptive work. In the exodus, God made a "way in the sea" (Isa 43:16), but even then, Israel passed through only because the Lord fought for them. Jesus walks on the water without fear because the chaos is subject to Him. Where Moses stretched out his hand and waited upon divine intervention, Jesus exercises divine prerogative directly. The disciples' question—"Who is this?" (Mark 4:41)—is the right question, for Psalm 77:19 speaks of Yahweh alone whose "way was through the sea" and whose "path through the great waters" revealed His power. Jesus now enacts this divine authority in human flesh.

The new exodus becomes unmistakable when Jesus liberates those oppressed by demonic bondage. Moses confronted Pharaoh, a tyrant who held power over Israel's bodies; Jesus confronts Satan, the ancient serpent who holds power over humanity's souls. His exorcisms are not mere displays of spiritual authority but demonstrations that the kingdom of God has broken into enemy territory. "If it is by the Spirit of God that

I cast out demons, then the kingdom of God has come upon you" (Matt 12:28). This is liberation at its deepest. The new Moses confronts a greater oppressor than Egypt, and the new Passover Lamb will break chains that iron shackles could never touch.

All of this prepares for the moment when Jesus redefines covenant itself. Moses mediated the covenant through words etched in stone; Jesus mediates the covenant through His own body and blood. At the Last Supper—which takes place during Passover—He takes bread, blesses it, breaks it, and says, "This is My body, which is given for you" (Luke 22:19). Then He takes the cup and declares, "This cup is the new covenant in My blood" (Luke 22:20). With these words, He fulfills and surpasses every covenant gesture of the Old Testament. The blood of lambs marked Israel's homes during the first Passover (Exod 12); the blood of Jesus marks the hearts of His disciples in the new Passover. The first Passover saved Israel from temporal death; the new Passover saves humanity from eternal death. The first covenant was sealed by sacrifice; the new covenant is sealed by the sacrifice of the Son of God.

Here the superiority of Jesus to Moses becomes undeniable. Moses carried tablets down from Sinai; Jesus carries the cross up Calvary. Moses sprinkled the people with the blood of animals and declared, "This is the blood of the covenant" (Exod 24:8); Jesus declares, "This is My blood of the covenant" (Mark 14:24). Moses interceded for Israel and turned away God's wrath (Exod 32:11–14); Jesus intercedes by offering Himself as the atoning sacrifice (Heb 9:14). Moses lifted up the bronze serpent to heal the dying (Num 21:9); Jesus says, "The Son of Man must be lifted up, that whoever believes in Him may have eternal life" (John 3:14–15). The typology is not subtle. Every movement of Moses anticipates a greater fulfillment in Christ.

Even the geography and rhythm of Jesus' actions echo the exodus narrative. Israel wandered in the wilderness for forty years; Jesus spends forty days in the desert, confronting the devil who had once ensnared Adam and Israel alike (Matt 4:1–11). Israel failed in its testing, but Jesus triumphs. Israel grumbled for water; Jesus offers living water that wells up to eternal life (John 4:14). Israel was guided by a pillar of cloud and fire; Jesus promises the Holy Spirit who will lead His people into all truth (John 14:26). Israel entered the promised land through the leadership of Joshua—literally "Yehoshua," a name meaning "The LORD saves." Jesus bears the same name in its Greek form, *Iēsous*, because He brings the true and final salvation Joshua's conquest only foreshadowed.

But if the Sermon on the Mount is the new Sinai, then the Passion is the new Red Sea. At Sinai, God revealed Himself in thunder and cloud, yet remained veiled; at Calvary, God reveals Himself in the broken body of the crucified Son. At the Red Sea, the waters parted so Israel could pass through death into life; on the cross, Jesus passes through death itself to open the way to eternal life for all humanity. Paul makes this parallel explicit when he writes that believers are "baptized into Moses" through the sea (1 Cor 10:1–2) but are now baptized into Christ through His death and resurrection (Rom 6:3–4). The imagery is unmistakable: baptism is the new crossing of the sea, the sacramental entrance into the new exodus Jesus has accomplished.

When Jesus dies, the veil of the Temple is torn from top to bottom (Matt 27:51), just as the sea once split at God's command. The tearing of the veil reveals what Moses could only prefigure: the barrier between God and humanity has been removed. Access to the divine presence is no longer restricted to the high priest once a year; it is opened through the pierced heart of the true mediator. The exodus was the beginning of covenant life; the tearing of the veil marks the dawn of a new creation.

This new exodus reaches its climax in the resurrection. Moses led Israel out of slavery, but it was the risen Christ who led humanity out of death, the final and most ancient captivity. In Him, the promise spoken through Hosea—"I shall redeem them from death" (Hos 13:14)—is fulfilled in a manner far surpassing Israel's expectations. Death is defeated not by plague or parted waters but by divine life bursting from a sealed tomb. Jesus becomes the firstborn of the new creation, the leader of a humanity liberated not once but forever.

The resurrection completes the new exodus, yet it also launches a new pilgrimage, because liberation without direction is only half a deliverance. Just as Israel journeyed from the Red Sea toward the promised land under Moses, so the disciples now journey under the risen Christ toward the fullness of the kingdom. But unlike the Israel of old, which walked behind a mediator who himself remained outside the final inheritance, the new Israel follows a mediator who has already entered glory. Moses died on Mount Nebo, seeing the land from afar (Deut 34:1–5); Jesus rises from the dead and ascends to the Father, seated at the right hand of God (Acts 1:9; Eph 1:20–22). The promised land for which Moses longed becomes, in Christ, the inheritance of the redeemed—a participation in the divine life itself.

This is why the Letter to the Hebrews draws a direct comparison between Jesus and Moses: "Moses was faithful in all God's house as a servant…but Christ is faithful over God's house as a Son" (Heb 3:5–6). The distinction is decisive. Moses was a servant within the household; Jesus is the heir who owns the house. Moses mediated the old covenant; Jesus mediates the new and better covenant "enacted on better promises" (Heb 8:6). Moses sprinkled the people with the blood of calves and goats (Exod 24:8); Jesus enters the heavenly sanctuary "by His own blood, thus securing an eternal redemption" (Heb 9:12). The superiority of Christ's mediation is not a matter of comparison in degree; it is a comparison in kind. Jesus does not simply improve upon Moses; He fulfills and surpasses him.

Yet for Jesus to be the new lawgiver and redeemer, He must also reveal the true depth of God's law, exposing the inner meaning that lay veiled under the Mosaic covenant. Moses delivered commandments from God; Jesus reveals God Himself. Moses spoke of God's will; Jesus embodies it in His person. It is in this sense that He declares, "Do not think that I have come to abolish the law… I have not come to abolish them but to fulfill them" (Matt 5:17). Fulfillment here means bringing the law to its intended completion by revealing its divine heart. The Torah given through Moses was a gift, but it was provisional, preparing a people for the fullness that would come in the Messiah. Paul captures this with clarity when he writes that the law served as a "pedagogue," a guardian until Christ came (Gal 3:24). The law restrained sin and revealed God's holiness, but it could not heal the heart. Jesus heals the heart by giving the Spirit, who writes the law within (Rom 5:5; 2 Cor 3:3–8).

This interiorization becomes visible in Jesus' teachings. When He intensifies the commandments—addressing not only murder but anger, not only adultery but lust—He is not adding burdens but revealing what Moses already longed for: a people transformed from within. Moses could exhort Israel to love the Lord with all their heart (Deut 6:5), but he could not give the new heart necessary to do so. Jesus gives that heart by pouring His Spirit into those who belong to Him. The new covenant promised by Jeremiah—"I will put My law within them, and I will write it upon their hearts" (Jer 31:33)—finds fulfillment not in a new scroll or set of commands but in the indwelling of God's own life. In this, Jesus is the lawgiver who not only commands but empowers, not only teaches but transforms.

To grasp the magnitude of Jesus' mission, we must also consider His role as intercessor. Moses interceded on behalf of Israel after the golden calf, standing between divine judgment and the people's destruction (Exod 32:11–14). His prayer saved the nation. But Moses himself acknowledged his inadequacy when he said, "If now I have found favour in Your sight, O Lord, please let the Lord go in the midst of us, for this is a stiff-necked people" (Exod 34:9). Moses could mediate forgiveness temporarily; he could not change the human heart. Jesus, by contrast, intercedes not merely with words but with His own self-offering. On the cross, He prays, "Father, forgive them" (Luke 23:34), fulfilling Isaiah's prophecy that the Servant "made intercession for the transgressors" (Isa 53:12). But His intercession does not end with His death. Risen and glorified, He "always lives to make intercession" for His people (Heb 7:25). The mediator of the new covenant does not plead from the outside; He advocates from within the Godhead, His humanity now fully united with divine life.

This union also explains why Jesus' authority transcends that of Moses. Moses revealed God's law; Jesus reveals God's identity. When He says,

"Before Abraham was, I AM" (John 8:58), He invokes the divine name spoken to Moses from the burning bush (Exod 3:14). The implications are staggering. Moses encountered the flame that burned without consuming; Jesus is the eternal fire of divine being assuming human flesh. Moses removed his sandals before the holy ground; Jesus brings the holy ground into the world by His presence. The authority He wields is not conferred but inherent. This is why He can deepen the law with a single phrase: "But I say to you." No prophet, no scribe, no rabbi ever spoke this way. Jesus speaks not as one interpreting the divine will but as its source.

This divine authority becomes the foundation for the new covenant community. Moses gathered Israel around the commandments; Jesus gathers disciples around Himself. Moses appointed elders to assist in governing the people (Num 11:16–17); Jesus appoints apostles and gives them authority to bind and loose (Matt 16:19; 18:18). Moses erected a tabernacle where God's presence would dwell; Jesus becomes the living temple and promises that His followers will become temples of the Spirit (John 2:19–21; 1 Cor 6:19). Moses led Israel to the edge of the promised land; Jesus promises His disciples that He goes to prepare a place for them in His Father's house (John 14:2–3). The structure remains, but the substance is transformed.

The new covenant also reconfigures the understanding of sacrifice. Moses oversaw the institution of Passover and the sacrificial system that defined Israel's worship. Jesus becomes the Passover Lamb Himself. John the Baptist identifies Him from the beginning: "Behold, the Lamb of God who takes away the sin of the world!" (John 1:29). At the Last Supper, Jesus reclines as the true Paschal Lamb whose blood seals the eternal covenant. On the cross, as the Passover lambs are being slaughtered in the Temple, Jesus is lifted up, fulfilling the pattern declared in Exodus—"not one of His bones will be broken" (Exod 12:46; cf. John 19:36). This is not coincidence; it is fulfillment. Moses instituted sacrifice; Jesus perfects it. Moses commanded Israel to remember its deliverance; Jesus gives His Church a sacrament in which the Redeemer Himself becomes present. The Eucharist is the food of the new exodus, sustaining God's people on their journey not to earthly Canaan but to the eternal kingdom.

This movement from type to fulfillment, from shadow to substance, reaches a crescendo when Jesus reveals that He is the way, the truth, and the life (John 14:6). Moses taught the way; Jesus is the way. Moses mediated truth; Jesus embodies truth. Moses delivered life-giving law; Jesus gives life itself. The categories begin to collapse because the fulfillment has exceeded the frame. The new Moses stands before Israel not as a renewed prophet but as the incarnate Word through whom the Father speaks once and for all.

The surpassing of Moses becomes even clearer when Jesus ascends another mountain, not to teach and not yet to suffer, but to reveal His identity in a moment of unveiled majesty. The Transfiguration is not an isolated miracle; it is the turning point where the comparison between Moses and Jesus becomes an open contrast between servant and Son, shadow and substance, anticipation and fulfillment. When the Gospel records that "His face shone like the sun" and "His garments became white as light" (Matt 17:2), the reader is meant to recall Exodus 34, where Moses' face shone after speaking with God. Yet the difference is as striking as it is theologically decisive. Moses reflected a glory that was not his own; Jesus radiates the glory that belongs to Him by nature. Moses veiled his face because the people could not bear the brilliance (Exod 34:33); Jesus stands unveiled as the eternal Word made flesh, illuminating the darkness rather than shrinking from it (John 1:5,14).

The presence of Moses and Elijah at this moment reveals the entire story of Israel converging upon Christ. Moses represents the law, Elijah the prophets. Both stand beside Jesus not as equals but as witnesses. They fade when the Father speaks from the cloud, "This is My beloved Son… listen to Him!" (Matt 17:5). The command is not "listen to them," nor "listen to My law," but "listen to Him." The voice from the cloud repeats the promise of Deuteronomy 18—that God would raise up a prophet like Moses, to whom the people must listen—but now with the clarification Moses could never speak: the prophet to come is the beloved Son, the One who reveals the Father in perfect truth (John 1:18). The revelation is unmistakable.

The new lawgiver is not merely the successor of Moses; He is the Son who fulfills every expectation Israel carried.

Yet this outpouring of glory does not distract Jesus from the path that lies ahead. The road to the new exodus runs not only through miracles and mountains but through suffering, rejection, and death. Moses lifted up the bronze serpent to heal the afflicted (Num 21:9), providing a remedy for their mortal wounds. Jesus declares that He must be lifted up in the same manner, "that whoever believes in Him may have eternal life" (John 3:14–15). The typology is seamless—and scandalous. The instrument of death becomes the instrument of healing. Where Moses raised a symbol of salvation, Jesus raises His own body to redeem the world. The cross becomes the new staff, wielded not against a tyrant of flesh and bone but against the power of sin and death itself.

The depth of this comparison becomes clearer when considering how Moses described Israel's rebellion and need for atonement. The people were "a stiff-necked nation" (Exod 32:9), prone to forget God's mercy and turn to idols. Moses interceded on their behalf, offering himself as a substitute—"blot me out of Your book" (Exod 32:32)—yet God did not accept the offer. The logic is simple and devastating: a sinful man cannot atone for a sinful nation. The mediator needed to be without sin, capable of offering a sacrifice of infinite worth. Jesus becomes this mediator not only by living a life of perfect obedience but by offering that life in perfect love to the Father. The Letter to the Hebrews captures this mystery: "He offered Himself without blemish to God" (Heb 9:14). The contrast with Moses is not a matter of merit or devotion but of nature. The Son offers what the servant never could.

Even the language Jesus uses at the Last Supper reflects a deliberate surpassing of the Mosaic covenant. When Moses ratified the first covenant, he sprinkled the blood of sacrificial animals on the altar and the people and declared, "Behold the blood of the covenant" (Exod 24:8). At the table with His disciples, Jesus deliberately echoes this formula: "This is My blood of the covenant, which is poured out for many for the forgiveness of sins" (Matt 26:28). The old covenant purified the flesh externally and temporarily; the new covenant purifies the heart internally and eternally (Heb 9:13–14). Moses used the blood of animals; Jesus offers His own. Moses ascended a mountain to receive the covenant; Jesus ascends Calvary to establish it.

The sacrifice of Christ is the turning point where the entire Mosaic economy finds its fulfillment. The old sacrifices had to be repeated daily and yearly because they could not perfect the worshiper (Heb 10:1–4). Jesus' sacrifice, offered once for all, accomplishes what those countless offerings could only signify. Moses entered the earthly tabernacle made with hands; Jesus enters "the greater and more perfect tent" of heaven itself (Heb 9:11). Moses sprinkled the people with blood that symbolized cleansing; Jesus' blood actually cleanses the conscience from dead works (Heb 9:14). The mediator of the new covenant not only reveals God's will but restores the relationship Adam forfeited, leading humanity out of the Egypt of sin into the promised freedom of divine life.

This movement from shadow to fulfillment also explains why Jesus repositions the entire understanding of authority within the covenant community. Moses stood outside the people as their leader and judge. Jesus gathers His disciples around Himself and appoints apostles not merely to assist Him but to share in His own authority. When He says to Peter, "I will give you the keys of the kingdom of heaven" (Matt 16:19), He uses imagery rooted in Isaiah 22:22, the office of the royal steward in the house of David. Moses had no authority to confer the kingdom; Jesus possesses the kingdom and bestows authority within it. The people followed Moses through signs and wonders; the disciples follow Jesus through the gift of His own Spirit, who brings them into the intimacy of the Father and the Son (John 14:16–20). Authority under Moses was structured around the law; authority under Christ is structured around communion.

This communion is what Moses longed for when he said, almost with sorrow, "Would that all the Lord's people were prophets, that the Lord would put His Spirit upon them!" (Num 11:29). Moses desired a people filled with the Spirit but could not bring it about. Jesus promises exactly this: "I will ask the Father, and He will give you another Paraclete, to be with you forever" (John 14:16). The new covenant is defined not simply by obedience to divine commandments but by participation in divine life. Moses mediated a covenant mediated by tablets; Jesus mediates a covenant mediated by the Spirit, written upon the human heart.

Even the geography of Jesus' final days mirrors and surpasses the narrative arcs of Moses' story. Moses died outside the promised land, his work unfinished, his hope deferred (Deut 34:4). Jesus dies within the land but rises to lead His people into a kingdom not bound by territory. Moses' tomb was hidden from Israel (Deut 34:6); Jesus' empty tomb becomes the proclamation of the Gospel itself. Moses left behind a people still prone to rebellion; Jesus leaves behind a people who receive the Holy Spirit and become His witnesses to the ends of the earth (Acts 1:8). The contrast is not between good and better, but between promise and fulfillment, between preparation and consummation.

Still, the pattern Moses set matters because without it the fullness of Christ's mission could not be grasped. Moses entered the cloud of divine presence; Jesus descends from it. Moses bore the radiance of God's glory on his face; Jesus is the radiance of the Father's glory in His very being (Heb 1:3). Moses wrote the words of the covenant; Jesus is the Word made flesh. Moses lifted his hands to win victory over Amalek (Exod 17:11–13); Jesus stretches out His hands on the cross to win victory over sin, death, and the devil. Moses struck the rock so that water flowed for the thirsty (Num 20:11); Jesus is struck on the cross, and from His pierced side flow blood and water, the sacraments that give life to the Church (John 19:34). The parallels are exhaustive yet always asymmetrical, always tilting toward the glory of the One who fulfills what Moses could only foreshadow.

The entire pattern crystallises in the moment Jesus interprets the Scriptures after His resurrection on the road to Emmaus. Two disciples walk away from Jerusalem in sorrow, convinced that the one they believed to be the redeemer had failed (Luke 24:21). Jesus draws near unrecognised and rebukes them not for doubt in itself, but for failing to grasp what Moses had already made known. "O foolish men, and slow of heart to believe all that the prophets have spoken!" (Luke 24:25). Then comes the decisive revelation: "Beginning with Moses and all the prophets, He interpreted to them in all the Scriptures the things concerning Himself" (Luke 24:27). The risen Christ identifies Moses' writings as the foundation of His own messianic identity, for Moses bore witness to Him long before Bethlehem or Calvary. The exodus, the Passover, the covenant, the law, the wilderness, the priesthood, the sacrifices—every thread of Moses' ministry finds its fulfillment in the person walking beside the disciples. The one Moses prefigured is now alive, explaining to hearts slowly awakening how the entire story points to Him.

The Emmaus moment is not an appendix to the Gospel but the interpretive key to it. Moses becomes intelligible only through Christ, and Christ becomes luminous through the testimony of Moses. Jesus had said earlier, "If you believed Moses, you would believe Me, for he wrote of Me" (John 5:46). This is not metaphor or allegory. It is a historical and theological claim that the Mosaic covenant, in all its complexity, anticipated a redeemer whose mission would both mirror and surpass Moses' own. The first liberator led slaves to freedom through the blood of lambs; the final liberator leads humanity to eternal life through His own blood. The old covenant wrote commandments on stone; the new covenant writes the law within by the Spirit poured into hearts. The first mediator entered the earthly tabernacle; the final mediator enters the heavenly sanctuary with the fullness of divine authority.

In this light, the Sermon on the Mount appears not as a moral manifesto but as the revelation of the divine will in its original purity. Jesus does not abolish Moses; He reveals Moses' deepest intention. When He intensifies the law, He does not contradict the Torah but uncovers its heart: the formation of a people who mirror the holiness of God. Moses taught Israel to love God; Jesus reveals the God who loves Israel to the point of incarnation. Moses taught the people to avoid idols; Jesus exposes every hidden idol of the heart and offers Himself as the one worthy object of total devotion. Moses commanded righteousness; Jesus imparts the grace necessary to attain it. What the law demanded, Christ empowers.

This is why Jesus declares, "Something greater than Moses is here," though He phrases it indirectly through other figures—greater than the Temple (Matt 12:6), greater than Jonah (Matt 12:41), greater than Solomon (Matt 12:42). Each comparison is a revelation of the same truth. The one who stands among the people of Israel is not merely a teacher, prophet, or wonder-worker but the one in whom the fullness of God dwells bodily (Col 2:9). Moses reflected divine glory; Jesus is divine glory. Moses revealed God's will; Jesus reveals God's face. Moses brought the covenant written on stone; Jesus becomes the covenant incarnate.

The binding of the new covenant is therefore not limited to commands or rituals but established in the very person of Christ. This is why He can call disciples not simply to obey, but to follow Him—something Moses never commanded regarding himself. To follow Moses was to follow God's law; to follow Jesus is to follow God Himself. Such an invitation would be blasphemous in the mouth of any prophet. In Jesus, it becomes the hinge upon which human destiny turns.

This makes sense only in the context of the new exodus. When Moses led Israel out of Egypt, he led them from slavery into covenant. When Jesus leads humanity out of sin, He leads them not merely into a renewed covenant but into divine sonship. The people of Israel were called God's firstborn (Exod 4:22), but the disciples of Jesus are made children of God by adoption, receiving the Spirit who cries "Abba, Father!" (Rom 8:15). Moses could lead people to the border of the promised land; he could not make them sons. Jesus grants a share in His own relationship with the Father, fulfilling the words of Deuteronomy 14:1—"You are children of the LORD your God"—in a depth previously unimaginable. The new lawgiver does not just form a people; He forms a family.

Moses taught Israel to remember its redemption annually through the Passover feast. Jesus transforms the Passover into the Eucharist, not as a memorial of liberation already accomplished but as a sacrament of liberation continually enacted. Each time the Church celebrates the Eucharist, it participates in the new exodus, for the same Christ who died and rose now gives Himself as the food for the journey. The manna in the wilderness sustained Israel until they reached Canaan; the Eucharist sustains believers until they enter the heavenly kingdom. The old exodus concluded with the giving of the land; the new exodus concludes with the gift of God Himself.

This movement toward union with God is what sets the mission of Jesus apart from the mission of Moses. Moses could reveal the path to life; Jesus is life itself. Moses could speak God's truth; Jesus is the truth incarnate. Moses could show the way; Jesus is the way. These distinctions are not poetic flourishes but theological realities that define the difference between servant and Son. The ministry of Moses was a gift, but it was preparatory. It pointed beyond itself. It created a hunger that only the Messiah could satisfy. Jesus fulfills every longing Israel carried through the centuries, not by matching Moses step for step, but by doing in fullness what Moses could do only in shadow.

This is why the Gospel writers frame so many of Jesus' actions in Mosaic terms. When He sits to teach, He does so as the new Moses. When He ascends a mountain, He does so as the new Moses. When He performs signs of power, He does so as the new Moses. When He establishes a covenant in blood, He does so as the new Moses. But in every case, Jesus takes the pattern and extends it beyond the horizon Moses could see. The authority He wields is the authority of God Himself. The redemption He accomplishes is universal rather than national. The covenant He inaugurates is eternal rather than provisional. The exodus He leads is climactic rather than preparatory.

From this vantage point, the Passion and Resurrection become the interpretive centre of all Moses foreshadowed. The new Moses accomplishes the new exodus not by defeating a foreign king but by conquering the final enemies—sin and death. He does not lead a march through parted waters but passes through death and opens a path no human had ever walked. He does not enter a tent made of earthly materials but ascends into heaven as the true high priest. He does not sprinkle the people with the blood of bulls but offers His own blood, which speaks "more graciously than the blood

The contrast between Moses and Jesus reaches its sharpest clarity when the Gospel of John frames the entire history of Israel within a single decisive comparison: "For the law was given through Moses; grace and truth came through Jesus Christ" (John 1:17). This is not a dismissal of the law but a revelation of its purpose. Moses delivered the divine will; Jesus delivers the divine life. Moses conveyed commandments that revealed sin; Jesus gives grace that overcomes sin. Moses articulated truth in words inspired by God; Jesus is the truth in person, the Word made flesh who dwells among His people as the living tabernacle of divine presence (John 1:14). The distinction is as vast as the difference between shadow and substance, preparation and fulfillment, promise and its final realization.

The new exodus can be seen not only in Jesus' actions but also in the transformation He brings to the human condition. Israel's liberation from Egypt changed their circumstances; Jesus' liberation from sin changes human nature. The old covenant formed a people externally through law and ritual; the new covenant forms them internally through the Spirit. What Moses longed to see—the law written on the heart, the Spirit resting upon all God's people, the transformation of the stiff-necked into the obedient—Jesus accomplishes through His death, resurrection, and gift of the Spirit at Pentecost. The wilderness of the human heart becomes the dwelling place of God. The inner landscape once marked by rebellion becomes a place of communion.

Moses' mission reveals the limits of even the greatest human mediator, for he stood before God as a servant, pleading for mercy on behalf of a disobedient people. Jesus stands before the Father as the Son, offering His own life for the salvation of the world. The difference in their intercession reveals the difference in their being. Moses begged God to turn away His wrath (Exod 32:11–14); Jesus absorbs that wrath into His own self-offering, fulfilling the prophecy that the Servant would bear the iniquities of many (Isa 53:11–12). Moses asked God to forgive; Jesus grants forgiveness from the cross. Moses spoke words that mediated life; Jesus speaks words that are spirit and life (John 6:63). The mediator greater than Moses does not guide from a distance—He enters the fullness of human suffering, sanctifying it from within and transforming it into the path of divine glory.

The identity of Jesus as the new Moses also emerges in the vast scope of His mission. Moses liberated one nation; Jesus liberates all. Moses confronted the might of Egypt; Jesus confronts the prince of this world and triumphs. Moses established a covenant with Israel; Jesus establishes a covenant for all nations. The promise to Abraham—that all families of the earth would be blessed (Gen 12:3)—comes to fruition not through Sinai but through Calvary. The new exodus is not bound by geography, ethnicity, or historical moment. It is the cosmic liberation of humanity through the blood of the Lamb who takes away the sin of the world.

This universal dimension is already hinted at in Moses' own story. When Israel left Egypt, "a mixed multitude went up with them" (Exod 12:38), suggesting that liberation was never meant to be the exclusive possession of Israel alone. The prophet Isaiah later declares that the Servant will be "a light to the nations" (Isa 49:6). What Moses began in seed form, Jesus fulfills in universal scope. His teaching is not confined to Israel; it extends to all who hunger and thirst for righteousness. His miracles are not signs of national deliverance but manifestations of the kingdom breaking into the entire world. His death is not the tragedy of one nation's rejected prophet but the sacrifice through which God reconciles the cosmos to Himself (Col 1:20).

The universality of Jesus' mission does not undermine or bypass the Mosaic covenant but completes it. Moses brought the people to the edge of the land promised to Abraham; Jesus brings the redeemed into the eternal inheritance promised in Him before the foundation of the world. Moses built a tabernacle filled with God's glory; Jesus forms a Church that becomes the living temple of His presence. Moses wrote the words of the covenant on scrolls; Jesus writes the covenant on human hearts by the Spirit. Moses gave Israel a priesthood; Jesus becomes the great High Priest whose kingdom consists of priests drawn from every tribe and tongue (Rev 1:5–6).

In this way, Jesus not only fulfills Moses but reveals Moses' true purpose.

The law was not an end but a pedagogue, a guardian leading the people to Christ (Gal 3:24). The exodus was not an end but a prefigurement of the greater deliverance to come. The Passover lamb was not an end but a symbol of the Lamb who would shed His blood for the salvation of the world. The bronze serpent was not an end but a sign of the healing that would flow from the crucified Messiah. Every movement of Moses' ministry becomes intelligible only in the light of Christ, for Christ is the telos—the fulfillment—of the law (Rom 10:4).

This fulfillment radiates with particular brilliance in the Johannine imagery of the feast of Tabernacles. Moses had led Israel through the wilderness, where God provided water from the rock and light through the pillar of fire. During the feast, Israel remembered these gifts through water ceremonies and the lighting of great lamps in the Temple courts. On the last and greatest day of the feast, Jesus stands and cries out, "If anyone thirsts, let him come to Me and drink" (John 7:37). He identifies Himself as the true source of living water, a role Moses never claimed. The next day, in the very place where the lamps blazed at night, Jesus declares, "I am the light of the world" (John 8:12). The signs of the wilderness journey point once again to Him. The water Moses drew forth from the rock becomes living water that flows from Christ; the light that guided Israel becomes the eternal light that shines in darkness.

Yet the greatest sign of all emerges not in the wilderness or on the mountain but on the cross. Moses lifted up a serpent to heal the dying; Jesus is lifted up to give eternal life. Moses stretched out his hands in intercession; Jesus stretches out His hands in surrender to death, conquering the very force that enslaved humanity. Moses struck the rock and water flowed; Jesus' side is pierced and blood and water pour forth, the sacramental signs of the new creation. Moses faced a tyrant who sought to destroy Israel's firstborn; Jesus becomes the firstborn raised from the dead, the beginning of the new humanity. The entire drama of salvation finds its centre in this moment of self-offering, where the new Moses does what the old Moses never could: He reconciles God and humanity in His very being.

It is in this same moment that Jesus reveals the full depth of the new covenant. When He cries out, "It is finished" (John 19:30), He does not mean simply that His suffering is over. The phrase signifies that His mission has reached its telos. The exodus is complete. The liberation is accomplished. The covenant is sealed. The new people of God are formed not by circumcision or descent but by union with the crucified and risen Christ. Moses commanded the people to obey the law; Jesus commands them to remain in His love (John 15:9). Moses revealed God's commandments; Jesus reveals God's heart.

The resurrection then becomes the vindication of everything Jesus claimed and accomplished. Moses led a people who constantly murmured, rebelled, and faltered; Jesus forms a community that begins in fear but becomes bold in the Spirit, carrying the good news of the kingdom to the ends of the earth. The disciples who once trembled behind locked doors become living stones of the new temple. The Spirit who rested upon Moses and then departed rests permanently upon those united to Christ. The new covenant community becomes the embodiment of the new exodus, journeying not toward an earthly land but toward the new Jerusalem, where the Lamb Himself is the light and the glory of God is its sun (Rev 21:23).

The glory of the risen Christ not only surpasses Moses but reveals the ultimate aim toward which Moses had always been pointing: communion with God that transforms the human person into a living participant in divine life. Moses entered the cloud of God's presence alone, while the people trembled from afar. Jesus draws His disciples into the very communion He shares with the Father, promising them the Spirit who will dwell within them and make them sons in the Son. The ascent Moses made toward God in fear becomes, in Christ, an ascent made by grace, as those united to Him share in His own filial boldness. The face Moses veiled for the sake of the people becomes, in Paul's words, a vision unveiled for all who turn to the Lord, for "we all, with unveiled face, beholding the glory of the Lord, are being changed into His likeness from glory to glory" (2 Cor 3:18). The transformation Moses glimpsed but could never grant becomes the inheritance of the new covenant people.

This transformation is made possible because Jesus does not merely mediate divine commandments but communicates divine life. Moses taught Israel how to walk with God; Jesus enables humanity to dwell in God. Moses warned Israel against idolatry; Jesus reveals the Father so that the human heart may finally adore the One for whom it was made. Moses appointed a priesthood that could offer sacrifices for sin; Jesus becomes both priest and sacrifice in a single act of love. Moses established a tabernacle where God's presence dwelt in shadow; Jesus establishes a Church where His presence dwells in sacrament. Moses led Israel through a desert toward a land flowing with milk and honey; Jesus leads the redeemed through the wilderness of this age toward the kingdom where death is no more, and God will be all in all.

The final declaration of Jesus in Matthew's Gospel illuminates the fullness of this fulfillment: "All authority in heaven and on earth has been given to Me" (Matt 28:18). Moses spoke with authority derived from God; Jesus possesses authority inherent to God. Moses governed a people within a defined covenant; Jesus commissions the apostles to make disciples of all nations, extending His dominion to the ends of the earth. Moses' authority ceased with his death; Jesus' authority endures forever, sustained by His resurrection and the eternal life He shares with the Father. The One who stands upon the mountain in Galilee at the end of Matthew's Gospel is the lawgiver, the redeemer, the prophet, the priest, the king—the complete fulfillment of every office Moses embodied in fragmentary form.

This universal authority reveals that the new exodus is not only a liberation from sin but an invitation into mission. Those who follow Christ do not simply walk out of bondage; they become heralds of the kingdom He inaugurates. The disciples are sent not with stone tablets but with the living word of the Gospel, not with the blood of goats but with the sacramental power of Christ's own life, not with a pillar of fire above them but with the fire of the Spirit within them. The new lawgiver does not simply lead a people; He multiplies Himself through them, extending

His saving work through their proclamation, their witness, their sacrificial love. The exodus from Egypt ended at Sinai; the exodus through Christ extends until the end of the age, gathering the nations into the household of God.

In this way, the story of Moses reaches its final and definitive meaning. What began with the cry of slaves in Egypt culminates in the cry of victory from the empty tomb. What began with a burning bush culminates in the tongues of fire that descend upon the apostles at Pentecost. What began with a covenant carved upon tablets culminates in a covenant written by the Spirit upon human hearts. What began with the blood of lambs painted on doorposts culminates in the blood of the Lamb of God poured out for the life of the world. The entire drama Moses inaugurated finds its fulfillment in Jesus, for He is the true liberator, the true mediator, the true teacher, the true prophet, the true priest, the true king—the one to whom Moses himself bore witness.

The comparison, in the end, yields a single conclusion. Moses brought the people to the threshold of the promised land but could not enter with them. Jesus opens the way into the eternal inheritance by entering it first. Moses saw the glory of God reflected; Jesus is the glory of God revealed. Moses interceded for a rebellious nation; Jesus intercedes for the world by offering His own life. Moses delivered a law that disciplined the heart; Jesus gives a Spirit that transforms it. Moses led one people out of one bondage; Jesus leads all humanity out of the bondage of sin into the freedom of divine sonship.

The new exodus is thus the fulfillment of every hope Israel carried across centuries of longing. The new Moses has come, not to repeat the work of the old but to perfect it. The covenant has reached its fullness. The mediator has appeared in glory. The one whom Moses foretold now stands revealed. The age of shadows has given way to the age of grace. The people of God are invited to walk not behind a servant, but with the Son, who leads them not toward a land but toward the very life of God.

# 9

# The High Priest Revealed: Sacrifice and the Torn Veil

From the moment Israel received the commandments at Sinai, the heart of its worship pulsed within the walls of a sanctuary designed not by human imagination but by divine instruction. The Lord said to Moses, "Let them make Me a sanctuary, that I may dwell in their midst" (Exod 25:8). The Tabernacle—and later the Temple—stood as the visible sign of God's desire to dwell with His people, yet that presence was veiled, shielded, mediated at every turn. A curtain woven from blue, purple, and scarlet yarn (Exod 26:31–33) separated the Holy Place from the Holy of Holies. Only one man—the high priest—could pass through it, and only once each year on the Day of Atonement (Lev 16:2, 34). This architecture proclaimed both intimacy and distance: God was near, yet unapproachable; present, yet hidden; dwelling among His people, yet separated from them by a veil thick with the memory of sin.

    The priesthood of Israel developed precisely because this veil existed. Humanity could not enter the presence of God without mediation. The high priest bore the names of the tribes upon his breastplate (Exod 28:29), carried blood from the sacrifice into the sanctuary (Lev 16:14–15), and performed rites "to make atonement for the holy sanctuary" and "for all the people of the assembly" (Lev 16:33). Yet even these sacred acts could not purify fully. The Letter to the Hebrews later observes that these rituals "cannot perfect the conscience of the worshiper" (Heb 9:9) and that the blood of goats and calves offered year after year "can never take away sins" (Heb 10:4). The entire sacrificial system was a divine mercy, but it was also a divine prophecy—a sign pointing forward, a shadow awaiting its substance.

This longing saturates the Old Testament. The prophets lament a priesthood grown corrupt (Mal 2:8), sacrifices offered without justice (Isa 1:11–17), and a Temple that, though filled with glory in Solomon's day (1 Kings 8:10–11), eventually witnessed the departure of the divine presence in Ezekiel's vision (Ezek 10:18–19). Israel yearned for restoration, not only of land and kingdom, but of worship—a purified priesthood, a renewed covenant, a return of God's glory. Malachi foretold that "the Lord whom you seek will suddenly come to His Temple" (Mal 3:1). Ezekiel envisioned a future sanctuary from which living water would flow (Ezek 47:1–12). Isaiah prophesied a Servant who would "make many to be accounted righteous" by bearing their iniquities (Isa 53:11). All of these strands—Temple, priesthood, sacrifice, atonement—wove themselves into a tapestry of expectation that could not be fulfilled within the boundaries of Israel's earthly worship.

It is into this sacred context that Jesus steps. His first recorded action in the Gospel of John after the wedding feast at Cana is to ascend to Jerusalem and enter the Temple (John 2:13). There, in an act both prophetic and priestly, He drives out the money changers and overturns their tables, declaring, "Take these things away; do not make My Father's house a house of trade!" (John 2:16). The Synoptic Gospels add the words of Isaiah and Jeremiah to His declaration: "My house shall be called a house of prayer for all nations, but you have made it a den of robbers" (Mark 11:17; cf. Isa 56:7; Jer 7:11). This cleansing is not a moment of anger but a moment of revelation. The one who speaks does so with an authority greater than priest or prophet. He speaks as the Lord of the Temple itself.

When challenged by the authorities, Jesus utters the cryptic yet earth-shattering words: "Destroy this Temple, and in three days I will raise it up" (John 2:19). John clarifies, "He spoke of the Temple of His body" (John 2:21). In this single statement, Jesus relocates the entire geography of Israel's worship. The meeting place between God and man is no longer a building of stone, however holy, but the incarnate body of the Son. The Temple had always been a sign of Emmanuel—God with us—but the reality now stands before them in flesh and blood. The Temple is fulfilled because the presence it signified has arrived.

The priestly overtones of Jesus' ministry become clearer as His public work continues. He speaks of giving His life "as a ransom for many" (Mark 10:45), echoing the language of sacrificial substitution. He identifies Himself as the Good Shepherd who "lays down His life for the sheep" (John 10:11), fulfilling Ezekiel's prophecy of God Himself shepherding His people (Ezek 34:11–16). He forgives sins not by offering sacrifice but by His own divine authority (Mark 2:5–7), something no priest ever dared to do. When questioned about this power, He appeals not to Levitical ordination but to His unique relationship with the Father: "The Son of Man has authority on earth to forgive sins" (Mark 2:10). The one who stands before Israel is not merely a priestly reformer; He is the priest long anticipated—the one whose ministry will not be confined by genealogy or lineage but grounded in divine sonship.

All these signs—purified Temple, authority over sin, identity as ransom and shepherd—lead toward a single, decisive moment: the institution of the Eucharist. On the night He was betrayed, Jesus takes bread, blesses it, breaks it, and says, "This is My body which is given for you" (Luke 22:19). He takes a cup and declares, "This cup is the new covenant in My blood, which is poured out for many" (Luke 22:20; cf. Matt 26:28). These words echo Moses' gesture at Sinai, where he sprinkled blood on the people and declared, "Behold the blood of the covenant which the LORD has made with you" (Exod 24:8). Yet Jesus does what Moses never could: He offers His own blood. He interprets His death before it occurs, revealing it as sacrifice, covenant, priestly act, and gift. The Eucharist is not merely a meal but the sacramental unveiling of His priestly identity.

In this gesture, Jesus unites priest and victim. Augustine captured this

## THE HIGH PRIEST REVEALED: SACRIFICE AND THE TORN VEIL

mystery succinctly: "He is both priest and sacrifice; priest, by offering Himself; sacrifice, by being offered" (*City of God*, 10.20). The high priest of Israel carried blood not his own into the Holy of Holies; Jesus carries the offering of His own life. The Eucharist becomes the liturgical form of this self-giving, the moment where He reveals that His body will be the place of atonement and His blood the seal of the new covenant.

This is the beginning. Batch 2 will take us into Gethsemane and toward the cross as the true Day of Atonement.

The priestly character of Jesus' mission intensifies in Gethsemane, where the contours of His sacrifice rise into view with unflinching clarity. In the garden, He withdraws from His disciples "about a stone's throw," kneels, and prays, "Father, if You are willing, remove this cup from Me; nevertheless not My will, but Yours, be done" (Luke 22:41–42). The language He uses is steeped in the vocabulary of sacrifice, for the "cup" in the prophets signifies the cup of judgment that the nations must drink (Isa 51:17; Jer 25:15–16). Jesus takes into His hands what no high priest had ever touched—the full burden of humanity's sin, the bitterness of estrangement from God—yet He receives it with a human will offered freely in love. The Letter to the Hebrews reflects on this moment: "In the days of His flesh, Jesus offered up prayers and supplications, with loud cries and tears... and He was heard for His godly fear" (Heb 5:7). The agony of Gethsemane is not a crisis of identity but the consecration of His priesthood, for it is here that He subjects His human will entirely to the Father, fulfilling what Adam failed to do and healing the root of human disobedience.

Gregory Nazianzen understood the depth of this obedience when he wrote, "What has not been assumed has not been healed" (*Epistle 101*). Jesus assumes the full anguish of a humanity that recoils before suffering, and in assuming it, He heals it. His "not My will" is not defeat but victory—the triumph of a human will at last aligned perfectly with divine love. Moses offered intercession for a sinful people; Jesus offers His own obedience as the first movement of the sacrifice that will save the world.

The garden scene also echoes the consecration of the high priest described in Leviticus, where the anointed mediator stands between God and the people on the threshold of the sacrificial rite (Lev 8–9). Jesus stands not before an altar made of bronze but before the altar of His own self-offering. The high priest of old bore the names of Israel upon his breastplate; Jesus bears the whole of humanity within His heart. The high priest washed himself before approaching the sanctuary; Jesus is "the one without stain or blemish" (Heb 7:26), whose entire life has been a preparation for this hour. The high priest entered the Holy of Holies with fear and trembling; Jesus goes forth from the garden with resolute calm, having surrendered Himself to the Father with a love stronger than death.

From Gethsemane Jesus is led to trial, and from trial to Golgotha, where He completes the work prefigured in every sacrifice, every priest, every drop of blood shed upon Israel's altars. At the moment the Lamb of God is lifted up, the Gospel of Mark records, "Jesus uttered a loud cry and breathed His last. And the veil of the temple was torn in two, from top to bottom" (Mark 15:37–38). With this one sentence, the evangelist reveals more than an architectural incident. The veil, which had for centuries symbolized humanity's separation from the presence of God, is ripped apart at the very moment Jesus dies. No human hand performs the action; it is torn "from top to bottom," a divine act inaugurating a new order of worship. The rending of the veil is the visible sign that the barrier of sin has been removed, that atonement has been accomplished, that access to God is now open not once a year to one priest but through Christ to all who enter Him by faith.

This tearing must be understood against the backdrop of the Day of Atonement described in Leviticus 16. Once each year the high priest entered beyond the veil with the blood of a bull for himself and a goat for the people. He sprinkled the blood upon the mercy seat, symbolically atoning for Israel's sins (Lev 16:14–15). He then confessed the sins of the nation over the head of the scapegoat, which was led into the wilderness "to bear all their iniquities away" (Lev 16:21–22). These rituals were powerful yet incomplete. The priest who offered sacrifice was himself sinful; the victims were mere animals; the effects of the ritual were temporary. But the pattern foreshadowed a greater day when a priest without sin would offer a sacrifice of infinite worth, entering not an earthly tent but "the greater and more perfect tent... not made with hands" (Heb 9:11).

It is precisely this pattern that the New Testament identifies in the Passion of Christ. The Letter to the Hebrews declares that Christ entered "once for all into the Holy Place, taking not the blood of goats and calves but His own blood, thus securing an eternal redemption" (Heb 9:12). The sacrifice of Calvary is not one offering among many but the singular, definitive act that ends the entire sacrificial economy. "Where there is forgiveness of these, there is no longer any offering for sin" (Heb 10:18). The high priest of old could not remain in the Holy of Holies; his work was momentary. Christ, however, enters the heavenly sanctuary and remains there forever as the eternal mediator, "a priest forever, according to the order of Melchizedek" (Heb 7:17; Ps 110:4). The entry that once belonged to the high priest alone is now granted to all who are united to Christ, for through Him "we have confidence to enter the sanctuary by the blood of Jesus" (Heb 10:19).

This sheds new light on the manner of Jesus' death. The evangelists note that He was crucified outside the city (John 19:17; Heb 13:12–13), recalling the scapegoat driven into the wilderness, bearing the sins of the people away. His blood, poured out on the cross, parallels the blood sprinkled within the sanctuary. His cry of abandonment—"My God, My God, why have You forsaken Me?" (Mark 15:34)—echoes the agony of the suffering Servant who bore the sins of many (Isa 53:12). Every detail of the Passion conforms to the sacrificial architecture of Israel's worship, yet surpasses it. The victim is willing. The priest is perfect. The sanctuary is heavenly. The atonement is eternal.

Even the small, vivid moments recorded by John are charged with sacrificial meaning. When Jesus, knowing that all was accomplished, said, "I thirst," He was offered sour wine on a hyssop branch (John 19:28–29). Hyssop had been used to smear the blood of the Passover lamb upon Israel's doorposts (Exod 12:22). When the soldier pierced His side with a spear, "at once there came out blood and water" (John 19:34), recalling both the blood of sacrifice and the water used in purification rites (Num 19:17–19). The evangelist emphasizes that "not one of His bones will be broken" (John 19:36), fulfilling Exodus 12:46, the instruction concerning the Passover lamb. Jesus is not simply a victim; He is the Lamb of God in whom every symbol of Israel's worship converges.

At the heart of all this stands the truth that Jesus does not merely offer sacrifice—He *is* the sacrifice. He does not merely approach the sanctuary—He *is* the sanctuary. He does not merely mediate—He *is* the mediator. Through His crucified body the presence of God becomes accessible, for He is the Temple not made with hands, the priest not tainted by sin, the Lamb without blemish, the scapegoat who bears iniquity, and the high priest who brings humanity into the very life of God.

The crucifixion must be seen, therefore, not merely as the tragic end of a righteous man, but as the climactic liturgical act toward which all of Israel's worship had been moving from the moment Moses erected the first altar in the wilderness. The entire sacrificial economy—lambs and goats, unleavened bread, sprinkling of blood, incense rising before the veil—was a divine pedagogy preparing humanity to recognise the perfect offering when it appeared. The prophets had already sown hints of this final act. Isaiah spoke of a Servant who would be "wounded for our transgressions" and "bruised for our iniquities," adding that "the LORD has laid on Him the iniquity of us all" (Isa 53:5–6). The psalmist, anticipating the horror of Golgotha, wrote of hands and feet pierced and garments divided by lot (Ps 22:16–18), words that would echo beneath the Roman nails and the soldiers' games. Zechariah foretold a pierced one over whom the people would mourn (Zech 12:10). These were not isolated predictions but the articulation of a pattern woven into Israel's Scriptures: salvation would come through suffering, atonement through sacrifice, reconciliation through the offering of a life.

Yet the novelty of Jesus' sacrifice lies not only in the fulfillment of prophecy but in the identity of the one who suffers. No animal could take away sin; no human being, stained with sin, could offer a perfect sacrifice. Only one who is both fully human and entirely without sin could stand in the place of humanity, bearing its burdens, and only one who is divine could offer a sacrifice of infinite value. This is why the Letter to the Hebrews insists that "it was fitting that we should have such a high priest, holy, blameless, unstained, separated from sinners, exalted above the heavens" (Heb 7:26). Jesus is priest not by lineage but by nature; victim not by coercion but by love. He is the priest who offers, and the offering that is given. His humanity allows Him to act on our behalf; His divinity makes His act universally efficacious. The altar upon which He offers Himself is the cross. The sanctuary into which He carries His offering is heaven itself.

The torn veil reveals this mystery with dramatic clarity. In the Temple, the veil separated the Holy of Holies—where God's presence dwelled—from the rest of the sanctuary. Its tearing signifies not only the end of the Temple's sacrificial efficacy but the end of the spiritual separation that defined humanity's exile since Eden. When Adam and Eve were expelled from the garden, cherubim with flaming swords were set to guard the way back to the tree of life (Gen 3:24). The veil embroidered with cherubim (Exod 26:31) carried this memory forward. Only the high priest could pass through once a year, and only with sacrificial blood. But when Jesus dies, the way into the presence of God is opened perpetually. The division between sacred and profane, between heaven and earth, between God and humanity, is healed in His pierced flesh. "Through Him," writes Paul, "we both have access in one Spirit to the Father" (Eph 2:18). Access to God is no longer mediated by geography, genealogy, or ritual, but by the risen Christ, whose humanity becomes the gateway into divine communion.

John's Gospel makes this theology tangible through the details of the Passion narrative. When Jesus dies, a soldier pierces His side, and blood and water flow forth (John 19:34). The Fathers saw in this not only the sacraments of baptism and Eucharist but the birth of the Church, which comes forth from Christ as Eve came forth from Adam. Cyril of Jerusalem wrote, "From His side flowed blood and water, the symbols of baptism and the mysteries" (*Catechetical Lectures*, 13). Augustine saw in the water and blood the signs of the sacraments that cleanse and nourish. The imagery is priestly, Temple-centred, covenantal: purification and atonement, life and communion, drawn from the very heart of the crucified Son. The Temple's purity rituals pointed forward to this moment; the sacrifices found their meaning in it; the covenant is sealed by it.

Jesus' final words on the cross, "It is finished" (John 19:30), declare not resignation but completion. The Greek term *tetelestai* signifies the fulfillment of a task or the completion of a sacrifice. In the Septuagint, the same verb appears in contexts of sacrificial offering brought to completion. Jesus' death is thus the consummation of His priestly work. The high priest has offered Himself; the victim has been slain; the blood has been poured out; the sanctuary is opened. Nothing further is needed. The sacrifice is perfect because the love that offers it is perfect. Where the blood of bulls and goats signified cleansing, Christ's blood accomplishes it. Where the old covenant rituals could only symbolize access to God, Christ grants the reality.

With the sacrifice completed, a new phase of His priestly ministry begins—not on earth but in heaven. The resurrection is the Father's vindication of the Son's offering, the divine affirmation that the sacrifice has been accepted. Paul writes that Christ "was put to death for our trespasses and raised for our justification" (Rom 4:25). In rising, He does not leave behind His priestly identity; He elevates it. His humanity, now glorified, becomes the permanent bridge between God and the human race. The high priest of old entered the Holy of Holies with trembling, bearing blood not his own. Christ enters "the greater and more perfect tent" (Heb 9:11) with His own blood, carrying not a symbol but the reality of atonement, not for one nation but for the world.

The resurrection also confirms Jesus' claim that His body is the true Temple. "Destroy this temple, and in three days I will raise it up" (John 2:19). When the stone is rolled away and the tomb stands empty, the prophecy is fulfilled. The Temple destroyed by human hands is rebuilt by divine power, and the glory that once filled the sanctuary of stone now fills the risen body of Christ. Ezekiel envisioned a Temple from which living water would flow (Ezek 47:1–12). In the risen Christ, this vision becomes reality, for the water that flowed from His pierced side becomes the spring of eternal life (John 4:14). The presence that dwelled in a building of gold and cedar now dwells in human flesh. The Temple is raised. The glory has returned. God and humanity meet in the risen Christ.

This shift from earthly Temple to heavenly sanctuary redefines the horizon of worship. The disciples no longer gather around altars of stone but around the table where Christ gives His body and blood. The early Church sees in the Eucharist not a reenactment of the Last Supper alone but a participation in the eternal sacrifice Christ presents before the Father. Ignatius of Antioch calls the Eucharist "the medicine of immortality" (*Ephesians*, 20), a phrase that captures both its priestly origin and its transformative power. The Church Fathers will later say that every Eucharist is offered "in heaven," because it is united to Christ's eternal priesthood, not confined to earthly liturgy alone.

The ascension completes this movement, for Christ's departure is not absence but enthronement. The Letter to the Hebrews declares that He has "passed through the heavens" (Heb 4:14) and taken His seat "at the right hand of the Majesty on high" (Heb 1:3). The imagery is drawn from Psalm 110: "Sit at My right hand until I make Your enemies Your footstool" (Ps 110:1). The same psalm proclaims Him "a priest forever according to the order of Melchizedek" (Ps 110:4). Jesus' ascension is His entrance into the true Holy of Holies, the heavenly sanctuary that the earthly Temple only foreshadowed. There He intercedes continually, not by repeated offering but by the abiding presence of His sacrificed and glorified humanity.

The entrance of Christ into the heavenly sanctuary marks the moment when humanity, in His person, crosses the threshold once guarded by the veil. The author of Hebrews uses the language of forerunner: "We have this hope as a sure and steadfast anchor of the soul... where Jesus has gone as a forerunner on our behalf" (Heb 6:19–20). The imagery is profound. A forerunner does not go where others cannot follow; he goes ahead to make the path accessible. The high priest of Israel entered the Holy of Holies alone and left quickly; Christ enters and remains. His presence in heaven is not a solitary privilege but the beginning of humanity's restored communion with God. He bears our nature into the presence of the Father, enthroned in the very life of God, His glorified flesh now the living pathway into the divine mystery.

This is why the ascension is not an epilogue but an essential dimension of His priesthood. On earth He offered the sacrifice; in heaven He presents it. On earth He shed His blood; in heaven the efficacy of that blood unfolds eternally. On earth He reconciled humanity to God; in heaven He intercedes for humanity within God. The high priest in ancient Israel sprinkled blood on the mercy seat; Jesus, in a manner beyond human imagination, presents His own atoning self before the Father. The Letter to the Hebrews declares, "He holds His priesthood permanently, because He continues forever" (Heb 7:24). His intercession is not the repetition of words but the enduring presence of His offered humanity, the human life perfectly united to divine love.

The implications of this priestly intercession stretch across the entire landscape of salvation. Jesus becomes the mediator not of a covenant written on stone but of a covenant written on hearts (Jer 31:33; 2 Cor 3:3). His sacrifice establishes a relationship that does not depend on human achievement or ritual precision but on His own fidelity before the Father. "There is one God, and one mediator between God and men, the man Christ Jesus" (1 Tim 2:5). The humanity He assumed and offered remains the bridge God Himself has placed between heaven and earth. In Him, the exile from Eden is reversed; the guarded path to the Tree of Life is reopened, not through earthly geography but through union with the crucified and risen Son.

The early Church Fathers grasped this mystery with awe. Chrysostom wrote that Christ "took our nature with Him into heaven and gave it a place above the angels" (*Homilies on Hebrews*, 7). Leo the Great proclaimed that "the ascension of Christ is our exaltation, for where the head has gone before in glory, the body is called to follow" (*Sermon 73*). The priesthood of Christ is not merely His work; it becomes ours through participation. Those united to Him enter the presence of the Father not as strangers but as children, their prayer joined to His, their worship elevated through

Him, their lives hidden with Christ in God (Col 3:3).

This participation is already anticipated in the blood and water that flowed from Jesus' side. The Fathers saw in this moment the birth of the Church, for from the crucified Christ emerges the communion that will share in His priestly identity. "You are a chosen race, a royal priesthood, a holy nation" (1 Pet 2:9). Israel's priesthood had been limited to a tribe; Christ's priesthood extends to all who are united to Him through baptism and nourished by His body and blood. The new covenant does not abolish priesthood but expands it, rooting it in Christ's eternal priesthood and making all the faithful participants in the sacrifice that redeems the world.

This expansion, however, does not blur the unique priesthood of Christ. The ordained ministry of the Church derives its power not from human authority but from Christ's own priestly action, made present through the Eucharist. Yet even the priest at the altar stands only as a sacramental sign of the one priest who truly acts. Augustine captured this beautifully: "The whole redeemed city, that is, the congregation and society of the saints, offers sacrifice to God through the great Priest, who offered Himself in His passion for us, that we might be the body of so great a head" (*City of God*, 10.6). Christ is both the one who offers and the one who is offered. The Church participates in the offering; it does not supplement it.

The torn veil therefore signifies not only restored access to God but restored identity. Humanity is no longer defined by distance from the divine presence but by nearness, intimacy, communion. The temple veil guarded the holiness of God from human defilement; Christ's pierced flesh becomes the new veil through which we "enter the sanctuary" (Heb 10:19–20). The imagery is startling: the body once torn on Calvary becomes the pathway into the heart of the Father. The place once barred is now opened, not by human effort but by divine gift. Where fear once governed approach to the Holy of Holies, boldness now reigns, for the one who intercedes is the one who loves us and has joined our nature to His own.

In this mystery we also see the resolution of the longing expressed by the prophets. Ezekiel watched as the glory of the Lord departed from the Temple (Ezek 10:18–19), a devastating sign of judgment. But in the resurrection of Christ, the glory returns—not to a building but to humanity itself. In Him the presence of God dwells bodily (Col 2:9), and through Him the Spirit dwells in all who believe. The new Temple is not made of stone but of living members joined to the risen Christ. The vision of Ezekiel's restored sanctuary finds its fulfillment in the Church, through which the river of living water flows (John 7:37–39). The long exile of God's presence ends in the risen body of Jesus.

This is why the early Christians could speak of Christ as both priest and temple, sacrifice and altar, mediator and sanctuary. He gathers into Himself every symbol, every institution, every sacred gesture of Israel's worship, and reveals their true purpose. The sacrifices were signs; He is the reality. The priesthood was provisional; He is eternal. The veil was a boundary; He is the passage. The Temple was a dwelling place; He is the dwelling of God with humanity.

And yet the fulfillment does not abolish the story that came before. Rather, it casts the entire narrative in its true light. The garden of Gethsemane reveals the heart of priestly obedience; the cross reveals the act of priestly sacrifice; the tomb reveals the birth of a new Temple; the ascension reveals the enthronement of the eternal High Priest. Each moment corresponds to a dimension of Israel's liturgy but surpasses it with divine finality.

Through this lens, the work of Christ becomes the decisive turning point in salvation history. What the priesthood could never accomplish, what the sacrifices could never secure, what the Temple could never manifest, Christ achieves in a single offering of love. The humanity He assumed becomes the bridge between heaven and earth, the altar upon which perfect love is offered, the sanctuary where God and humanity meet. In Him the merciful desire of God to dwell with His people, expressed from Sinai to the prophets, finds its consummation. The veil is torn. The way is opened. The High Priest has entered the sanctuary, and humanity enters with Him.

The paradox at the heart of Christ's priesthood is that the very moment of His sacrificial death becomes the moment of enthronement. In the ancient Temple, the Day of Atonement was the one day when Israel's destiny pivoted upon the actions of a single man. The high priest entered the sanctuary shrouded in incense, bearing the blood that symbolized reconciliation between God and His people. Yet his return from the Holy of Holies was only a temporary sign of peace, for the next year's sins would demand the same ritual again. In Christ, however, the offering culminates not in repeated cycles of sacrifice but in His exaltation at the Father's right hand. When He declares, "It is finished" (John 19:30), He announces the completion of a priestly act whose effects endure forever.

This permanence is what the Letter to the Hebrews stresses with such insistence. The priests of the old covenant "stand daily at their service, offering repeatedly the same sacrifices, which can never take away sins" (Heb 10:11). Christ, by contrast, "offered for all time a single sacrifice for sins" and then "sat down at the right hand of God" (Heb 10:12). The posture itself is theological. A seated priest signifies a work completed. A heavenly throne signifies a priesthood that no death can interrupt. The one who offered His own body on the cross now presents that same glorified body in the heavenly sanctuary, where His intercession takes the form not of repeated petition but of His eternal presence. "He always lives to make intercession for them" (Heb 7:25). The constancy of His priesthood rests upon the constancy of His risen life.

The ancient Temple rites were marked by separation — the people outside, the priests within, the high priest alone behind the veil. Christ reverses this order entirely. In Him, humanity is brought not merely into the outer courts but into the very presence of God. Paul writes, "Through Him we have access in one Spirit to the Father" (Eph 2:18). The access once restricted to a single man for a single moment of the year is now granted continuously to all who are joined to Christ. The tearing of the veil becomes the outward sign of this inward truth: the era of mediation through symbols has given way to mediation through union. The way that was barred since Eden is now opened, not by human striving but by the gift of the Son who restores what Adam lost.

This restored access also transforms the meaning of sacrifice. Under the old covenant, sacrifice was the means by which Israel acknowledged God's holiness and sought forgiveness for sin. But these sacrifices, though commanded by God, were preparatory signs, unable to cleanse the conscience (Heb 9:9). They pointed beyond themselves to a deeper need: reconciliation that touches the root of human estrangement from God. Christ's sacrifice meets this need because it is the offering of a life wholly united to the Father. In Him, obedience is not external observance but perfect filial love. "Father, into Your hands I commit My spirit" (Luke 23:46). The sacrifice of Christ is not the appeasement of a reluctant God but the self-offering of the Son whose love mirrors the Father's own.

This fulfillment also illuminates the ancient prophecy concerning Melchizedek, the mysterious priest-king who offered bread and wine to Abraham (Gen 14:18). Psalm 110 identifies the Messiah as "a priest forever according to the order of Melchizedek" (Ps 110:4). The Letter to the Hebrews interprets this priesthood as one without genealogy, predecessor, or successor — a priesthood grounded not in Levitical descent but in divine appointment (Heb 7:1–3). Christ embodies this priesthood perfectly. He offers not animal sacrifices but bread and wine transformed at the Last Supper into His body and blood. He possesses a priesthood that death cannot interrupt. He blesses not one patriarch but the nations. Melchizedek's fleeting appearance in Genesis becomes a prophetic glimpse of the eternal priesthood that Christ manifestly fulfills.

This priesthood, eternal and unrepeatable, also redefines the nature of worship. In the Temple, worship centred on sacrifice offered by a select group on behalf of the people. In Christ, worship expands beyond sacrificial ritual to embrace the total self-gift of the believer. Paul urges Christians to "present your bodies as a living sacrifice, holy and acceptable to God, which is your spiritual worship" (Rom 12:1). This does not replace the sacrifice of Christ but flows from it. Because the High Priest has offered Himself once for all, His people share in His priestly mission by offering their lives in union with Him. The Eucharist becomes the place where this union is renewed. The Church offers bread and wine, and Christ returns them as His own body and blood. Through this exchange, the faithful are drawn into His sacrifice, not as additional victims but as participants in the love that redeems the world.

Patristic voices echo this truth across centuries. Irenaeus writes that Christ "recapitulates all things in Himself" (*Against Heresies*, 3.18.1), meaning He gathers the entire history of salvation into His person and fulfills its every symbol. Athanasius declares that He "offered Himself on behalf of all" (*On the Incarnation*, 25), becoming the true High Priest whose sacrifice renews creation. Cyril of Alexandria sees the Eucharist as the visible form of this renewal: "We are made one body with Him, for He fills us with His own life" (*Commentary on John*). In each case, the Fathers recognize that Christ's priesthood is not a moment but a mystery: a reality that embraces His incarnation, His earthly ministry, His Passion, His resurrection, His ascension, and His eternal intercession.

The heavenly sanctuary in which Christ now ministers is therefore not a distant realm inaccessible to human experience. It is the very context of Christian worship and prayer. When believers pray "through Christ our Lord," they are not uttering a formula but entering into His priestly mediation. When they celebrate the Eucharist, they do not repeat a sacrifice but participate in the once-for-all sacrifice made eternally present. When they approach the Father with confidence, it is because the Son stands before the Father with human nature glorified. Heavenly worship and earthly worship meet in the risen Christ, who unites the Church to the Father through the Spirit.

This union transforms not only access to God but the understanding of holiness. Under the old covenant, holiness was preserved by separation. The sacred was set apart; the profane was kept at a distance. The Temple, the priesthood, the sacrifices—all spoke of a holiness that could be approached only with caution. In Christ, holiness becomes participatory. God dwells within His people. Their lives become temples of the Spirit (1 Cor 6:19). Their bodies become instruments of righteousness (Rom 6:13). Their daily actions become acts of worship. The holiness once guarded behind the veil now radiates through the Church into the world. The priesthood of Christ extends its reach not by erecting new boundaries but by consecrating humanity itself.

In this way, the redemption Christ accomplishes is not only juridical but ontological. He does not merely secure forgiveness but restores communion. He does not merely remove guilt but renovates the heart. He does not merely grant access but ushers humanity into the divine life. The veil torn in the Temple becomes the emblem of a greater tearing: the rending of every barrier between God and His creation. Through Christ, all creation is summoned into the sanctuary of God's presence.

This transformation of worship and holiness reaches its fullest expression in the mystery of the resurrection, for the risen Christ stands as the living fulfillment of everything the Temple was meant to be. The Temple was the place where heaven touched earth, where God dwelled among His people, where sacrifice was offered and sins forgiven. Jesus, risen from the dead, now embodies this reality in His glorified humanity. When He appears to His disciples and says, "Peace be with you" (John 20:19), He speaks with an authority no priest of the old covenant could ever claim. He breathes upon them and says, "Receive the Holy Spirit" (John 20:22), imparting not ritual purification but divine life. His very body is now the holy space where reconciliation takes place, the new and living Temple in which God and humanity meet without separation.

The risen Christ reveals that the sanctuary is no longer a building of stone but a person. When He invites Thomas to place his hand in His side, He opens the place from which blood and water flowed—the very place where the new covenant was born. The wound becomes a doorway into divine mercy, the torn veil made flesh. Gregory the Great would later write, "The wound in His side was opened so that we might enter and dwell in His heart" (*Homilies on the Gospels*, 26). Resurrection does not erase the marks of sacrifice; it glorifies them. The scars become symbols of victory, signs of a priesthood carried into eternity.

This connection between resurrection and priesthood becomes even more luminous when Christ encounters the disciples on the road to Emmaus. He interprets the Scriptures to them, beginning with Moses and all the prophets, and shows that "it was necessary that the Christ should suffer these things and enter into His glory" (Luke 24:26–27). The necessity lies not in external circumstances but in the logic of divine love: the one who offers Himself as priest and sacrifice must also enter the presence of the Father to complete the work. The recognition of Christ in the breaking of the bread (Luke 24:30–31) reveals that His sacrificial identity is inseparable from His risen presence. The Eucharist becomes the place where the crucified and risen priest continues to feed His people with His own life, a communion that transcends time and space.

The ascension completes the priestly arc of Christ's mission by revealing the final destination of His sacrifice. He does not rise from the dead merely to linger among His disciples but to ascend to the Father, carrying humanity with Him. "He ascended far above all the heavens, that He might fill all things" (Eph 4:10). His ascension is His entry into the heavenly Holy of Holies, the realm to which the earthly sanctuary pointed but could never reach. Hebrews declares that Christ has entered "into heaven itself, now to appear in the presence of God on our behalf" (Heb 9:24). He appears not as a symbol but as a man—glorified, perfected, bearing the wounds of love, presenting to the Father the sacrifice that reconciles the world.

This heavenly ministry is not static but active. Christ "intercedes for us" (Rom 8:34), not by repeating petitions but by being present before the Father as the incarnate expression of divine mercy. His glorified humanity is the eternal reminder that redemption is accomplished. The ascension is not Christ's withdrawal from the world but His elevation above it, enabling Him to pour out the Spirit who unites believers to His priestly life. Through the Spirit, the Church becomes His body, the temple of the living God (1 Cor 3:16; Eph 2:21). What was once confined to a single sanctuary in Jerusalem now expands across the world in countless communities gathered around the Eucharistic table.

This diffusion of divine presence fulfills the prophetic vision of Zechariah, who foresaw a day when "there shall no longer be a trader in the house of the LORD of hosts" (Zech 14:21), a sign that the purity of worship would no longer depend on Temple rites alone. Jesus' cleansing of the Temple anticipates this universalization, but His resurrection and ascension accomplish it. The boundary between sacred and secular dissolves as the Church becomes the new locus of divine activity. The Spirit consecrates not altars of stone but human hearts, making each believer a living sacrifice and each assembly a sanctuary of praise. The holiness once localized now permeates the world.

This shift explains the boldness with which early Christians spoke of Christ's priestly identity. They recognized that His sacrifice fulfilled what the Levitical system could only signify. They understood that His resurrection revealed Him as the new Temple. They proclaimed that His ascension enthroned Him as the eternal High Priest. And they celebrated the Eucharist as the earthly participation in His heavenly offering. For them, Christ's priesthood was not a theological abstraction but the living centre of their worship and the source of their hope.

The torn veil remains the definitive symbol of this new reality. It signifies the end of distance and the beginning of communion. It proclaims that God's desire to dwell with humanity has been fulfilled in Christ. It reveals that holiness is no longer guarded behind layers of ritual but offered freely through the Son. It invites all who believe to step into the presence of the Father with confidence, "holding fast the confession of our hope" (Heb 10:23). The veil torn by God at the moment of Jesus' death becomes the proclamation that death itself has been torn apart, and that life in communion with God has been restored.

In this new covenant, everything finds its centre in Christ. His priesthood is the key to understanding His death, His resurrection, His ascension, and the life of the Church. His sacrifice is the source of the sacraments. His intercession is the strength of prayer. His presence is the heart of worship. His glory is the destiny of humanity. The work of the High Priest is complete and yet ever-present, finished on the cross and everlasting in heaven. The one who offered Himself now draws all who follow Him into the sanctuary of divine love.

The mystery of Christ's priesthood extends beyond the historical events of His earthly life and reaches into the very structure of salvation. Everything that God accomplishes in the world now proceeds through the mediation of the risen High Priest. Creation itself, destined for transfiguration, finds its hope not in the cycles of nature or the achievements of human progress but in the One who stands before the Father bearing glorified humanity. Paul writes that all things were created "through Him and for Him" (Col 1:16), and the same Lord through whom the world was made is the one through whom the world will be redeemed. His priesthood is cosmic in scope. It embraces not only the human race but the entire creation "groaning in travail" (Rom 8:22), awaiting the revelation of the children of God. The One who ascended into heaven carries the destiny of all things in His resurrected flesh.

This cosmic dimension emerges with clarity in the Letter to the Hebrews, where Christ is described as the mediator of a "better covenant" (Heb 8:6), enacted upon "better promises" (Heb 8:6), and sealed by a sacrifice that reaches not merely the earthly sanctuary but the heavenly reality itself. The covenant He mediates does not depend on the fluctuating faithfulness of the people but on His unchanging fidelity. Humanity's union with God no longer rests on the fragile obedience of priests or kings but on the perfect obedience of the Son, whose priestly act flows from the eternal love He shares with the Father. The covenant He inaugurates is unbreakable because its foundation is divine.

This divine stability is what allows the Christian to approach God without fear. The old covenant instilled reverence through distance; the new covenant instils reverence through love. Fear gives way to confidence, not because God is less holy but because the path to His holiness has been made accessible through Christ. The author of Hebrews declares, "Since we have a great high priest who has passed through the heavens, Jesus the Son of God, let us hold fast our confession" (Heb 4:14). The exhortation rests on the certainty that Christ's priesthood is both sympathetic and sovereign. He knows the weakness of humanity because He has assumed it; He overcomes its frailty because He is divine. The Christian stands before God clothed not in personal merit but in the righteousness of the priest who intercedes on behalf of the world.

This confidence reshapes the relationship between prayer and sacrifice.

In the old covenant, prayer accompanied sacrifice; in the new covenant, prayer participates in the eternal sacrifice of Christ. When believers pray, they do so within the priestly mediation of the Son, whose voice never ceases before the Father. Their petitions are joined to His, their thanksgiving united to His self-offering, their praise harmonized with His glory. The liturgy of the Church becomes the earthly manifestation of the heavenly worship described in Revelation, where the Lamb stands as though slain yet reigning from the centre of the throne (Rev 5:6). The Lamb's presence is both crucified and exalted, both priestly and kingly, both humble and triumphant. In Him the worship of heaven and earth converges.

The Eucharist makes this convergence tangible. At every altar, the Church stands at the threshold of the heavenly sanctuary. Bread and wine become the sacramental sign of the new covenant, the gift through which believers receive the life of the risen Christ. The sacrifice made once on Calvary becomes present without being repeated, offered without being multiplied, received without being diminished. The faithful are drawn into the mystery of the priesthood that defines the identity of Christ and shapes the life of His Church. Ignatius of Antioch, writing at the dawn of the second century, called the Eucharist "the flesh of our Savior Jesus Christ" (*Smyrneans*, 7), testifying that the early Church recognized the sacramental participation in the very body once offered on the cross and now glorified in heaven.

This participation carries a moral dimension as well. Those who share in the sacrifice of Christ are called to embody the love revealed upon the cross. The priesthood of the faithful is not a symbolic notion but a vocation to live sacrificially, offering one's life in service, mercy, forgiveness, and fidelity. Paul urges believers to imitate Christ by walking "in love, as Christ loved us and gave Himself up for us, a fragrant offering and sacrifice to God" (Eph 5:2). The moral life becomes an extension of the liturgy, a continual offering in union with the High Priest. Holiness is not separation from the world but consecration within it — a life marked by the presence of the Spirit who conforms the believer to the image of the Son.

This conformity culminates in hope. The High Priest who ascended into heaven will return, not to repeat His sacrifice but to consummate its effects. The resurrected body that entered the divine sanctuary is the first fruits of the new creation, the pledge of what God intends for all who belong to Christ. "When Christ who is your life appears, then you also will appear with Him in glory" (Col 3:4). The torn veil of the Temple prefigures the tearing of the heavens when the Son of Man returns with power. The humanity He has carried into the presence of the Father will be shared in fullness by those who have united themselves to His sacrifice. The priesthood that began in the incarnation and reached its climax on the cross will find its final expression in the glorification of the saints.

Through this vision, the entire sweep of salvation history becomes intelligible. The sacrifices of the old covenant point forward; the sacrifice of Christ fulfills; the worship of the Church participates; the destiny of creation awaits revelation. Christ stands at the centre of this movement, the High Priest whose offering reconciles heaven and earth. His pierced side becomes the fountain of redemption. His risen body becomes the temple of divine glory. His ascended humanity becomes the anchor of hope. All that the Temple signified is gathered into Him. All that the priesthood sought is accomplished in Him. All that sacrifice intended is perfected in Him.

And so the torn veil remains not only a symbol of the past but a summons to the present and a promise for the future. It declares that God has drawn near, that communion has been restored, that the way into the sanctuary is open. It proclaims that the one who offered Himself once for all now lives forever, interceding, sanctifying, feeding, and guiding His people. It invites every believer to enter the holy place with boldness, not through merit but through mercy, not through ritual but through relationship, not through fear but through love. The High Priest has opened the way. The sacrifice has been offered. The covenant has been sealed. The glory has begun.

# 10

# The Servant Suffers: The Passion as Fulfilment of Prophecy

The story of the Passion does not begin in Gethsemane or in the upper room, or even in Bethlehem. Its first contours are drawn centuries earlier in the strange and haunting figure whom Isaiah calls "My servant." The Lord announces, "Behold, My servant shall prosper, He shall be exalted and lifted up, and shall be very high" (Isa 52:13). The language is startling, because the verbs "exalted" and "lifted up" are used elsewhere of the Lord Himself enthroned in glory (Isa 6:1). Yet as the oracle unfolds, this same servant is disfigured beyond human semblance: "His appearance was so marred, beyond human semblance, and His form beyond that of the sons of men" (Isa 52:14). Glory and degradation, exaltation and humiliation, divinity's verbs and humanity's wounds appear intertwined in a single mysterious figure.

The song continues with a confession placed upon the lips of those who once despised him. "Who has believed what we have heard? And to whom has the arm of the LORD been revealed?" (Isa 53:1). The "arm of the LORD" in Isaiah is the symbol of God's saving power (Isa 51:9–10), the same power that once split the sea and rescued Israel from Egypt. Yet this arm appears not in thunder or conquest, but in a figure who "grew up like a young plant, and like a root out of dry ground; He had no form

## THE SERVANT SUFFERS: THE PASSION AS FULFILMENT OF PROPHECY

or comeliness that we should look at Him, and no beauty that we should desire Him" (Isa 53:2). Salvation arrives in unassuming weakness. The servant is not embraced but rejected: "He was despised and rejected by men; a man of sorrows, and acquainted with grief; and as one from whom men hide their faces He was despised, and we esteemed Him not" (Isa 53:3). The very people in need of healing turn away in disgust.

The Gospels present the Passion of Jesus as the moment when this song comes true line by line. Jesus enters His Passion not as a victim of circumstance but as the servant who knowingly walks into the script written long before. He has already identified Himself with this prophecy when He explained His mission: "For the Son of Man also came not to be served but to serve, and to give His life as a ransom for many" (Mark 10:45). The language of service and of giving His life echoes the servant who "poured out His soul to death" and "bore the sin of many" (Isa 53:12). Matthew, commenting on Jesus' healing ministry, already applies Isaiah's words to Him: "This was to fulfil what was spoken by the prophet Isaiah, 'He took our infirmities and bore our diseases'" (Matt 8:17; cf. Isa 53:4). The evangelist does not treat Isaiah 53 as a vague metaphor but as a precise template of Christ's identity and mission.

The core of Isaiah's vision is substitutionary suffering. The confession shifts from "He" to "we," and the pronouns begin to invert: "Surely He has borne our griefs and carried our sorrows" (Isa 53:4). The ones who looked at Him as cursed now realise their mistake. "Yet we esteemed Him stricken, smitten by God, and afflicted" (Isa 53:4). In other words, they believed His suffering was punishment for His own sins. The prophet corrects this misjudgement in the most direct terms: "He was wounded for our transgressions, He was bruised for our iniquities; upon Him was the chastisement that made us whole, and with His stripes we are healed" (Isa 53:5). The Hebrew rhythm drives the point home by repetition; the blows that fall upon the servant are not His but ours. "All we like sheep have gone astray; we have turned every one to his own way; and the LORD has laid on Him the iniquity of us all" (Isa 53:6). The servant suffers not simply with His people, but in their place.

The Passion narratives map themselves consciously onto this pattern. Jesus is bound, mocked, scourged, and disfigured before the people. The soldiers twist together a crown of thorns, place a reed in His hand, and dress Him in a purple robe, then strike Him and spit upon Him, crying, "Hail, King of the Jews!" (Matt 27:29–30). Pilate presents Him with the words, "Behold, the man!" (John 19:5), a figure beaten into near anonymity, the very image of one "from whom men hide their faces" (Isa 53:3). The crowd, stirred by the chief priests and elders, chooses Barabbas and cries, "Let Him be crucified!" (Matt 27:21–23). They interpret His suffering as divine judgment: "He trusts in God; let God deliver Him now, if He desires Him" (Matt 27:43), oblivious to the irony that they themselves fulfil the psalm which says, "He trusts in the LORD; let Him deliver Him, let Him rescue Him, for He delights in Him!" (Ps 22:8).

Silence also marks the servant and reappears with force in the trials of Jesus. Isaiah proclaims, "He was oppressed, and He was afflicted, yet He opened not His mouth; like a lamb that is led to the slaughter, and like a sheep that before its shearers is dumb, so He opened not His mouth" (Isa 53:7). Before the Sanhedrin, Jesus initially remains silent as false witnesses speak against Him (Matt 26:59–63). Before Herod, "He made no answer" (Luke 23:9). Before Pilate, He gives only the briefest of responses, leaving the governor "greatly amazed" (Matt 27:14). The one who had spoken with authority now chooses silence, because the hour for teaching has given way to the hour for offering. The lamb does not argue with the hand that leads Him; He submits, not from weakness but from the strength of obedience.

Isaiah continues, "By oppression and judgment He was taken away; and as for His generation, who considered that He was cut off out of the land of the living, stricken for the transgression of My people?" (Isa 53:8). The language of unjust trial and removal from life frames the servant's death as both judicial and sacrificial. Jesus is "cut off" through a legal process that parodies justice. The leaders seek testimony "that they might put Him to death" (Mark 14:55), yet their witnesses do not agree. Pilate acknowledges, "I find no crime in Him" (John 18:38), but delivers Him to be crucified

## THE SERVANT SUFFERS: THE PASSION AS FULFILMENT OF PROPHECY

under pressure from the crowd. The inscription placed above His head on the cross—"Jesus of Nazareth, the King of the Jews" (John 19:19)—becomes an unintended confession; the one executed as a criminal is in fact the King and Servant promised long before.

Isaiah's detail about the servant's burial finds a striking historical correspondence. "They made His grave with the wicked and with a rich man in His death, although He had done no violence, and there was no deceit in His mouth" (Isa 53:9). Crucified between two criminals (Luke 23:32–33), Jesus dies as one numbered with transgressors (Isa 53:12), yet His body is not discarded like theirs. Joseph of Arimathea, "a rich man" and a respected member of the council (Matt 27:57; Mark 15:43), requests the body from Pilate and lays it in his own new tomb (Matt 27:60). The servant's grave is indeed with both the wicked and the rich. The evangelists are not forcing coincidences; they are bearing witness to the astonishing precision with which Isaiah's paradoxical lines converge upon the facts of Good Friday.

Yet Isaiah's song refuses to end in defeat. "It was the will of the LORD to bruise Him; He has put Him to grief; when He makes Himself an offering for sin, He shall see His offspring, He shall prolong His days; the will of the LORD shall prosper in His hand" (Isa 53:10). The servant who dies as an "offering for sin" lives to see offspring and prolonged days. Death is not the terminus but the threshold. "Out of the anguish of His soul He shall see and be satisfied; by His knowledge shall the righteous one, My servant, make many to be accounted righteous; and He shall bear their iniquities" (Isa 53:11). The resurrection is already sung here in prophetic tones. The righteous servant lives, and in living, communicates righteousness to "many," a phrase Jesus Himself uses at the Last Supper: "This is My blood of the covenant, which is poured out for many for the forgiveness of sins" (Matt 26:28).

The apostles will later anchor their preaching in this very connection. When the Ethiopian official reads Isaiah 53 aloud and asks Philip, "About whom, pray, does the prophet say this, about himself or about someone else?" (Acts 8:34), the evangelist responds by beginning "with this

Scripture" and preaching "the good news of Jesus to him" (Acts 8:35). The question that hovered over Isaiah's servant for centuries—Israel or an individual, prophet or nation, symbol or person—is answered in the crucified and risen Christ. He is the one who embodies Israel, the one righteous sufferer whose obedience heals the disobedience of the many, the servant whose wounds reconcile the world.

Psalm 22 stands alongside Isaiah's Servant Song as the second great prophetic window into the Passion. The psalm begins with the cry that will later shatter the darkness over Golgotha: "My God, my God, why have You forsaken me?" (Ps 22:1). Matthew and Mark record these exact words from the lips of Jesus (Matt 27:46; Mark 15:34), not as a cry of despair but as the deliberate invocation of a psalm that moves from desolation to triumph. The psalmist speaks of being "poured out like water, and all my bones are out of joint; my heart is like wax" (Ps 22:14). Roman crucifixion, which stretched the body's joints and strained the heart, makes these words more than poetic metaphor. "My strength is dried up like a potsherd, and my tongue cleaves to my jaws" (Ps 22:15) evokes the thirst Jesus expresses when He says, "I thirst" (John 19:28), fulfilling Scripture once again.

The psalm continues, "A company of evildoers encircles me; they have pierced my hands and my feet" (Ps 22:16). Though textual debates exist in later Masoretic manuscripts, the Septuagint — the Scriptures of the early Church — preserves the reading *ōryxan* ("they pierced"), a term that uncannily describes the mechanics of crucifixion centuries before the practice was known in Israel. The evangelists do not need to quote this line explicitly; the act of nailing Jesus to the cross embodies it with chilling clarity. Further, the soldiers "divide my garments among them, and for my clothing they cast lots" (Ps 22:18). John writes, "This was to fulfil the Scripture which says, 'They parted my garments among them, and for my clothing they cast lots'" (John 19:24). The evangelist is not drawing a clever parallel but recognizing the Passion as the historical enactment of David's ancient lament.

The mockery Jesus endures beneath the cross also echoes this psalm with extraordinary precision. "All who see me mock me; they make mouths at me, they wag their heads; 'He trusts in the LORD; let Him deliver him; let Him rescue him, for He delights in him!'" (Ps 22:7-8). Matthew records the chief priests, scribes, and elders using almost identical words: "He trusts in God; let God deliver Him now, if He desires Him" (Matt 27:43). The convergence is so exact that the Passion seems as though it unfolds according to a script written in the psalter. Yet this is not theatrical fulfilment but the revelation that David's words were never merely personal lament. The Davidic king, righteous yet persecuted, becomes the prophetic type through whom the Messiah's suffering is foreshadowed.

Psalm 22 does not conclude in death. Its turning point comes with the line, "You have answered me!" (Ps 22:21, LXX), signalling a shift from agony to praise. The psalmist declares, "I will tell of Your name to my brethren; in the midst of the congregation I will praise You" (Ps 22:22). The Letter to the Hebrews applies this directly to the risen Jesus, who "is not ashamed to call them brethren" (Heb 2:11-12), citing the psalm verbatim. The vision expands to the nations: "All the ends of the earth shall remember and turn to the LORD; and all the families of the nations shall worship before Him" (Ps 22:27). The passion of the Messiah blossoms into the missionary horizon of the Church. Death yields to life. Shame yields to proclamation. The suffering of the righteous king becomes the salvation of the world.

Zechariah adds yet another prophetic layer to this tapestry. In a remarkable oracle, the Lord Himself declares, "They shall look upon Me whom they have pierced" (Zech 12:10). The speaker is God, yet the one pierced is also the object of human mourning. The Gospel of John cites this prophecy explicitly at the moment when the soldier thrusts his spear into the side of Christ: "And again another Scripture says, 'They shall look on Him whom they pierced'" (John 19:37). The early Christians saw in this verse not only the physical wounding of Jesus but the theological paradox that the one pierced is both human and divine. The grief that follows — "they shall mourn for Him, as one mourns for an only son" (Zech 12:10) — mirrors the sorrow of the disciples and anticipates the repentance that spreads in the early Church.

Zechariah's prophecies do not stop there. "Strike the shepherd, and the sheep will be scattered" (Zech 13:7). Jesus applies this line to Himself on the night He is arrested, saying, "You will all fall away because of Me this night, for it is written, 'I will strike the shepherd, and the sheep of the flock will be scattered'" (Matt 26:31). The scattering of the disciples is not a collapse of the messianic mission but a necessary element foreseen in Scripture. The shepherd must be struck so that God may gather a purified flock after the resurrection, as Zechariah's oracle continues: "I will turn My hand to the little ones" (Zech 13:7), a gesture fulfilled when the risen Christ restores and recommissions His disciples.

Even within Judaism, long before Christians appealed to these texts, there existed interpretive traditions connecting suffering with the Messiah. The Targum on Isaiah 52–53 refers to "My servant the Messiah" (Targum Jonathan on Isaiah 52:13), and rabbinic literature speaks of a suffering messianic figure known as Messiah ben Joseph, who dies in battle or suffers for Israel's sins (b. *Sukkah* 52a; b. *Sanhedrin* 98b). In *Ruth Rabbah* 5:6, the sufferings described in Isaiah 53 are linked with the Messiah himself. While later rabbis would move toward corporate interpretations of Isaiah 53, these earlier traditions reveal that Jewish expectation was not monolithic; the idea of a suffering messiah was well attested in the centuries surrounding Christ.

The early Christian writers seized upon these convergences with remarkable boldness. Justin Martyr, disputing with the Jew Trypho, insists that "these words, accordingly, refer to Christ" (*Dialogue with Trypho* 13), and later develops a detailed exposition of Isaiah 53 as the key to understanding the crucifixion (*Dialogue* 111–118). Irenaeus argues that Christ "fulfilled the whole economy of His Passion foretold by the prophets" (*Against Heresies* 3.18.1). Origen, responding to Jewish objections, maintains that the specificity of the servant's humiliation, rejection, and exaltation finds no historical candidate other than Jesus (*Contra Celsum* 1.55). Augustine observes that "the Passion of our Lord and Saviour was predicted by the prophets long before it happened" (*City of God* 18.29), affirming the unity of Scripture in revealing Christ.

Beyond Isaiah, the Passion resonates with prophetic motifs scattered throughout the Old Testament. The book of Wisdom portrays the wicked conspiring against the righteous one: "Let us condemn him to a shameful death, for, according to what he says, he will be protected" (Wis 2:20). The parallels to the mockery at the cross are unmistakable. Daniel speaks of an "anointed one" who will be "cut off" (Dan 9:26), a phrase later applied by Christian interpreters to the death of Jesus. The Passover lamb, whose blood spared Israel from judgment (Exod 12), finds its fulfillment in the declaration of John the Baptist: "Behold, the Lamb of God, who takes away the sin of the world!" (John 1:29). Paul will later assert, "Christ, our Passover, has been sacrificed" (1 Cor 5:7), identifying the death of Jesus as the new and definitive exodus.

Taken together, these prophetic strands form a mosaic in which suffering is not incidental to messianic identity but essential. The Messiah is not merely a king or a prophet or a priest; He is the servant who suffers, the lamb who is slain, the shepherd who is struck, the righteous one condemned unjustly, the pierced one mourned by the people, the anointed one cut off for the sake of many. Jesus steps into this mosaic not as a charismatic teacher who met an unfortunate end but as the one whose life aligns with Scripture in a manner that transcends coincidence. The Passion is not a tragedy that befell Him; it is the fulfillment of a divine purpose whispered through the prophets and revealed upon the cross.

The Passion narratives demonstrate that Jesus understood His suffering not as an interruption of His mission but as its fulfilment. Repeatedly in the Gospels He declares that "the Son of Man must suffer many things" (Mark 8:31). The verb "must" (*dei* in Greek) signals divine necessity, not tragic inevitability. It echoes the prophetic logic already embedded in Scripture: the Servant must be wounded, the Shepherd must be struck, the Righteous One must be delivered, because through these wounds the covenant would be renewed. Luke emphasises this after the Resurrection, when Jesus rebukes the disciples on the road to Emmaus: "Was it not necessary that the Christ should suffer these things and enter into His glory?" (Luke

24:26). The necessity arises not from political circumstances but from the Scriptures themselves, for "beginning with Moses and all the prophets, He interpreted to them in all the Scriptures the things concerning Himself" (Luke 24:27).

This hermeneutic of necessity becomes the foundation of apostolic preaching. Peter, on Pentecost, cites Psalm 16 and declares that David foresaw the resurrection of Christ and spoke of Him when he said, "For You will not abandon my soul to Hades, or let Your Holy One see corruption" (Acts 2:27, 31). Later, Peter recounts how "what God foretold by the mouth of all the prophets, that His Christ should suffer, He thus fulfilled" (Acts 3:18). Paul argues in Thessalonica that "it was necessary for the Christ to suffer and to rise from the dead" (Acts 17:3), again grounding his proclamation in Israel's Scriptures. The apostolic witness consistently interprets the Passion not as an unexpected tragedy but as the culmination of the prophetic story.

The voluntary nature of Jesus' suffering intensifies this fulfilment. Isaiah's servant is not dragged unwillingly; he "pours out his soul to death" (Isa 53:12). Jesus speaks in similar terms: "I lay down my life... No one takes it from Me, but I lay it down of My own accord" (John 10:17–18). His prayer in Gethsemane, "Not My will, but Yours, be done" (Luke 22:42), reveals obedience that reverses Adam's rebellion. Where Adam grasped at autonomy and plunged the world into bondage, Christ embraces obedience and restores creation to the Father. Athanasius describes this as the Son's willing descent "even unto death" in order to "destroy death" and "renew humanity" (*On the Incarnation* 20, 25). The Passion is therefore not only foretold but freely embraced; Jesus conforms Himself to Scripture by offering Himself for the sake of the world.

At the trial of Jesus, the prophetic echoes intensify. The false witnesses who accuse Him mirror the imagery of Psalm 27:12: "False witnesses have risen against me." The high priest's rending of his garments contrasts sharply with the seamless garment of Jesus, which the soldiers refuse to tear, casting lots instead (John 19:23–24), fulfilling Psalm 22:18. The silence of Jesus before His accusers evokes both Isaiah's lamb-like submission (Isa 53:7) and Psalm 38:13–14, "I am like a deaf man, I do not hear... like a man who does not open his mouth." Jesus stands at the centre of a liturgical drama in which Scripture becomes incarnate in suffering flesh.

The scourging and mocking further align His experience with the prophetic tradition. Isaiah had spoken of the servant's back being struck and His beard plucked (Isa 50:6). Micah prophesied, "With a rod they strike upon the cheek the ruler of Israel" (Mic 5:1). These humiliations, trivial in their cruelty, are profound in their symbolism: the Messiah bears in His body the rejection of the people He came to save. The purple robe and crown of thorns mock His kingship while unwittingly revealing its true nature. The kingship of Jesus is not secured by violence but revealed in suffering. Augustine later observes, "The crown of thorns signifies the sins of the world, which Christ took upon His head" (*Tractates on John* 117). The mock coronation becomes the paradoxical enthronement of the Servant King.

The crucifixion itself gathers together the prophetic threads into a single event. The piercing of Jesus' hands and feet recalls Psalm 22:16; the offering of vinegar for His thirst echoes Psalm 69:21; His cry, "My God, my God, why have You forsaken Me?" (Mark 15:34), invokes the first line of Psalm 22, drawing the entire psalm into the moment. Even the detail of the passers-by wagging their heads is taken from Psalm 22:7. The soldiers' gambling for His garments fulfills Psalm 22:18. The inscription over His head, "King of the Jews," corresponds to the messianic expectation of Psalm 2:6, "I have set My king on Zion," though in the eyes of Rome it serves as a political accusation.

The Gospel of John adds further prophetic layers. Jesus is crucified at the very hour the Passover lambs were being slaughtered (John 19:14), fulfilling the typology of Exodus 12. Not a bone of His body is broken (John 19:36), in accordance with the Passover regulation, "You shall not break any of its bones" (Exod 12:46; cf. Ps 34:20). When His side is pierced, blood and water flow out (John 19:34), suggesting both sacramental imagery and the fulfilment of Zechariah's oracle, "They shall look on Him whom they pierced" (Zech 12:10). The flow of blood recalls the sin offerings of Leviticus; the flow of water evokes the cleansing streams of Ezekiel's temple vision (Ezek 47:1). The crucified body becomes the true Temple from whose side salvation flows.

The Jewish authorities' reaction to the crucifixion mirrors another prophetic dimension. Wisdom 2:12–20 describes the wicked conspiring against the righteous man "because he is inconvenient to us and opposes our actions." They mock his claim that God will rescue him: "Let us see if his words are true... for if the righteous man is God's son, He will help him" (Wis 2:17–18). These lines find uncanny resonance in the taunts hurled at Jesus: "He trusts in God; let God deliver Him now" (Matt 27:43). The Wisdom literature thus anticipates not only the suffering of the righteous but the psychology of the persecutors, who cannot bear the presence of holiness.

Theological reflection on these convergences is as old as Christianity itself. Irenaeus notes that "the whole economy of His Passion was prefigured by the prophets" (*Against Heresies* 4.6.1). Tertullian argues that the specific details of the crucifixion — the mockery, the piercing, the casting of lots — can only be understood as fulfilments of prophecy (*Against the Jews* 10–13). Cyril of Jerusalem teaches that every blow, every insult, every wound, every drop of blood was foretold "so that you may know that His suffering was voluntary and foreordained" (*Catechetical Lectures* 13.19). The patristic consensus is not imaginative allegory but historical conviction: the events of Good Friday align so closely with Scripture that they disclose the hand of God.

Yet prophecy alone does not explain the Passion. One must also understand the love that animates it. The servant "bears the sin of many" (Isa 53:12), but He does so not merely to fulfil a text but to reconcile humanity to God. Paul expresses this with astonishing clarity: "God shows His love for us in that while we were yet sinners Christ died for us" (Rom 5:8). The cross is the revelation of divine love in its most radical form. Jesus does not die as a martyr, nor as a political revolutionary, nor as a failed prophet. He dies as the Lamb of God, the suffering servant, the righteous man persecuted, the shepherd struck, the atoning sacrifice offered for the world. The Passion is simultaneously the fulfilment of Scripture, the culmination of Israel's story, and the self-giving of divine love.

Even the darkness that falls over the land has prophetic resonance. Amos had announced, "On that day... I will make the sun go down at noon and darken the earth in broad daylight" (Amos 8:9). The cosmic mourning at the death of Jesus reflects not only divine judgment but the gravity of the sacrifice. Creation itself responds to the death of its Creator. Jerome later writes that "the heavens grew dark because the Light of the world was extinguished" (*Commentary on Matthew* 27). The physical phenomenon becomes a cosmic sign of the spiritual reality unveiled upon the cross.

In the final moments, Jesus cries out, "Father, into Your hands I commit My spirit" (Luke 23:46), echoing Psalm 31:5. The servant who suffers in obedience now dies in trust. The one who was despised, rejected, pierced, and crushed places His life into the hands of the Father, confident that death cannot hold Him. Isaiah had foreseen this confidence when he wrote, "He shall see His offspring, He shall prolong His days" (Isa 53:10). Resurrection is the horizon of the Passion, not its denial. The suffering of the servant is the path to His exaltation, for "He shall be exalted and lifted up, and shall be very high" (Isa 52:13). The cross is therefore not the collapse of messianic hope but the throne from which the Servant-King accomplishes salvation.

The cry of Jesus on the cross, far from being a cry of despair, functions as the interpretive key to understanding the entire Passion. When He invokes the opening line of Psalm 22, He draws the psalm into the present moment, revealing that the anguish of the righteous sufferer has reached its climax in Him. The psalm itself moves inexorably toward victory, and Jesus' use of it signals that the apparent abandonment is neither final nor real but part of the salvific pattern wherein God allows the righteous to descend into suffering in order to manifest His power through deliverance. Augustine comments that Christ "took up the voice of our humanity" when He cried those words, expressing not separation within the Trinity but the depth of solidarity with sinners (*Expositions on the Psalms* 22.1). The one who knew no sin voices the anguish of all who do.

This solidarity is central to the prophetic vision of the servant. Isaiah declares, "He was numbered with the transgressors" (Isa 53:12), a line fulfilled literally when Jesus is crucified between two criminals (Luke 23:33). But the theological import goes deeper: the servant enters the condition of sinners not by guilt but by love, standing in their place so that He might bear what they cannot. "He bore the sin of many" (Isa 53:12) implies an act of representation that neither Israel as a nation nor any individual prophet could accomplish. Only one who is without sin can bear sin without being crushed by it. Only one who is divine can give infinite value to the offering. Only one who is fully human can stand in the place of humanity. The servant's identity transcends the categories available before Christ, and the crucifixion reveals the contours of His person.

The Gospels stress repeatedly that Jesus dies as a truly innocent man. Pilate declares, "I find no crime in Him" (John 18:38). The thief on the cross confesses, "This man has done nothing wrong" (Luke 23:41). Even the centurion overseeing the execution proclaims, "Surely this man was righteous" (Luke 23:47). This universal recognition of innocence recalls Isaiah's words, "He had done no violence, and there was no deceit in His mouth" (Isa 53:9). The innocence of the victim is essential to the theology of the Passion. A guilty sufferer could not redeem the guilty. A sinful priest could not offer a perfect sacrifice. The servant's righteousness is the foundation upon which atonement rests.

The voluntary nature of Christ's death is further underscored by His final actions. John records that, after receiving the sour wine, Jesus says, "It is finished," and "bowed His head and gave up His spirit" (John 19:30). The verb "gave up" (*paredōken*) indicates a deliberate handing over of life, not a passive succumbing. This aligns with the prophetic description that "He poured out His soul to death" (Isa 53:12). The servant is not merely overtaken by death but offers Himself to the Father. Cyril of Jerusalem notes that Christ "of His own will endured the Passion" and that His death was "not the triumph of His enemies but the offering of the true High Priest" (*Catechetical Lectures* 13.19). The sacrifice is both priestly and personal, freely embraced for the sake of humanity.

The piercing of Jesus' side by the soldier's spear adds an additional prophetic dimension. John testifies that "one of the soldiers pierced His side with a spear, and at once there came out blood and water" (John 19:34). This action fulfills Zechariah's oracle, "They shall look on Him whom they have pierced" (Zech 12:10). The Fathers saw in the flow of blood and water the sacraments that spring from the heart of the crucified Christ. Augustine writes that the Church was born "from the side of Christ as He slept on the cross" just as Eve was formed from the side of Adam (*Tractates on John* 120.2). The imagery reflects both creation and new creation: the crucified Lord is the new Adam, and humanity is reborn through the water of baptism and the blood of the Eucharist. The prophetic and sacramental converge at the moment of death.

Even the timing of Jesus' death carries typological significance. John emphasises that it occurs during the preparation for Passover (John 19:14), linking Jesus directly to the lambs slain in remembrance of Israel's deliverance from Egypt. Paul later affirms, "Christ, our Passover, has been sacrificed" (1 Cor 5:7). The Passover lamb, whose blood protected Israel from judgment, becomes the paradigm for understanding the crucifixion. The lamb's bones were not to be broken (Exod 12:46), and John notes that Scripture was fulfilled when the soldiers did not break Jesus' legs (John 19:36). The typology is not superficial; it reveals that Jesus' death inaugurates a new exodus, liberating humanity from the bondage of sin just as the first Passover freed Israel from Egypt.

The darkness that covers the land from noon to three (Mark 15:33) evokes Amos's prophecy: "I will make the sun go down at noon and darken the earth in broad daylight" (Amos 8:9). The prophet associates this darkness with judgment upon the land, yet in the Passion the judgment falls not on the guilty but on the innocent one who stands in their place. The cosmic mourning signifies the rupture of creation at the moment when its Creator dies. The earthquake that follows Jesus' death (Matt 27:51) recalls the trembling of Sinai and signals the arrival of a new covenant. The tearing of the temple veil from top to bottom (Matt 27:51) indicates that God Himself opens the way into His presence. Isaiah had foreseen a time when God would "rend the heavens and come down" (Isa 64:1), and in the tearing of the veil the heavens touch the earth at the crucified body of the Son.

The reaction of those present further confirms the prophetic identity of Jesus. The centurion, witnessing the manner of His death, declares, "Truly this man was the Son of God!" (Mark 15:39). This confession comes from a Gentile soldier, not from the religious elite. It anticipates the universal reach of salvation foreseen in Psalm 22, where "all the ends of the earth shall remember and turn to the LORD" (Ps 22:27). The Passion is the moment when Israel's King becomes the Savior of the nations. The righteous one's suffering becomes the proclamation of God's reign.

The burial of Jesus also aligns with prophetic patterns. Isaiah had said, "They made His grave with the wicked and with a rich man in His death" (Isa 53:9). Jesus is executed alongside criminals, yet His body is placed in the new tomb of Joseph of Arimathea, a wealthy disciple (Matt 27:57–60). The combination of shame and honour, rejection and reverence, accords with the paradoxical identity of the servant who is humiliated before men but exalted by God. The Sabbath rest of Jesus' body in the tomb echoes the completion of creation, for the new creation begins in the quiet of Holy Saturday.

Throughout these events, one theme persists: the Messiah's suffering is both voluntary and vicarious. Jesus does not merely endure injustice; He transforms it into atonement. He does not merely fulfil prophecy; He reveals the divine logic that undergirds it. Bernard of Clairvaux would later write that Christ's wounds are "windows of mercy" through which the love of God shines upon the world (*Sermons on the Song of Songs* 61). The Passion discloses that God's response to human sin is not annihilation but self-giving, not condemnation but compassion, not distance but nearness. The servant suffers not because God is powerless, but because divine love chooses the path that saves.

## THE SERVANT SUFFERS: THE PASSION AS FULFILMENT OF PROPHECY

This paradox—power revealed in weakness, victory achieved through suffering—lies at the heart of Christian faith. The prophets spoke of it in riddles and images; the apostles witnessed it in flesh and blood. The cross becomes the axis around which all of Scripture turns. As Paul proclaims, "We preach Christ crucified... the power of God and the wisdom of God" (1 Cor 1:23-24). The Passion is the moment when prophecy becomes history, when the servant becomes the Savior, when death becomes the passage to life.

The cross stands therefore not merely as the place where prophecy is fulfilled but as the locus where God interprets Himself to the world. Long before Golgotha, the prophets had grappled with the paradox of a God who is infinitely just yet infinitely merciful. How could He forgive without compromising justice? How could He punish without extinguishing mercy? Isaiah's servant song offers an answer that seems impossible until Christ appears: justice is satisfied because sin truly receives its due in the suffering of the servant; mercy is manifested because the servant freely takes upon himself the burden of the guilty. "The LORD has laid on Him the iniquity of us all" (Isa 53:6). This is not a transfer that occurs by legal fiction but by the mysterious solidarity the servant assumes with sinners.

Paul's theology echoes this prophetic vision: "For our sake He made Him to be sin who knew no sin, so that in Him we might become the righteousness of God" (2 Cor 5:21). The righteousness of the servant becomes the righteousness of the many; the sin of the many is borne by the one righteous servant. The crucifixion is not the defeat of God's justice but its perfect accomplishment, for justice and mercy converge in the person of the Son. Athanasius describes this convergence as the moment when Christ "offered up His body on behalf of all" to "destroy death" and "renew humanity" (*On the Incarnation* 8, 20). The servant's suffering is the very means by which God heals what sin has wounded.

This healing extends not only to individuals but to the entire people of God. Isaiah proclaims, "By His stripes we are healed" (Isa 53:5), a verse later echoed by Peter: "By His wounds you have been healed" (1 Pet 2:24). Peter situates this healing within the context of Christ's exemplary suffering:

"Christ also suffered for you, leaving you an example, that you should follow in His steps" (1 Pet 2:21). The cross becomes both the instrument of redemption and the pattern of discipleship. The servant not only saves; He teaches by His suffering what it means to love unto the end.

This theological pattern was already anticipated in the Wisdom literature. The Book of Wisdom portrays the righteous man who is condemned because of his fidelity to God: "He professes to have knowledge of God... Let us see if his words are true, and let us test what will happen at the end of his life" (Wis 2:13, 17). The wicked mock him precisely because he trusts in God: "For if the righteous man is God's son, He will help him" (Wis 2:18). The line is a perfect prelude to the taunts of the chief priests at the crucifixion: "He trusts in God; let God deliver Him now" (Matt 27:43). The Wisdom text concludes with the wicked's fatal miscalculation: "They did not know the secret purposes of God, nor hope for the wages of holiness" (Wis 2:22). The Passion becomes the unveiling of that secret: God saves by suffering with and for His people.

The story deepens when these prophetic texts are placed within the wider framework of Israel's sacrificial system. The servant is described as an "offering for sin" (Isa 53:10), invoking the Levitical categories of atonement. The sin offering involved the transfer of guilt onto a spotless victim, whose blood was then offered to reconcile the people to God (Lev 4; 16). Yet these sacrifices were never ultimate; they pointed toward a deeper reality. The Letter to the Hebrews explains, "It is impossible that the blood of bulls and goats should take away sins" (Heb 10:4). Only a perfect offering — divinely appointed and freely given — could effect true reconciliation.

Jesus becomes that offering not simply by dying but by uniting His death to the will of the Father. "Lo, I have come to do Your will, O God" (Heb 10:7), hearkening back to Psalm 40, which emphasizes obedience over ritual sacrifice. The servant's obedience is the new form of sacrifice, fulfilling the prophetic critique voiced centuries earlier: "I desire mercy, and not sacrifice" (Hos 6:6). Jesus repeats this line during His ministry (Matt 9:13; 12:7), positioning Himself as the culmination of the prophetic

## THE SERVANT SUFFERS: THE PASSION AS FULFILMENT OF PROPHECY

tradition that sought not ritual precision but a transformation of the heart. The cross is the moment where obedience reaches its supreme expression.

The Passion, when viewed through this lens, becomes the intersection of priesthood and prophecy. Jesus acts as both priest and victim. He offers Himself, as Hebrews declares, "through the eternal Spirit" (Heb 9:14), aligning His human will perfectly with the divine purpose. The prophets envisioned a future in which God would purify His people and establish a new covenant; Jesus speaks those very words at the Last Supper: "This is My blood of the covenant, which is poured out for many for the forgiveness of sins" (Matt 26:28). The suffering servant becomes the mediator of this covenant, offering not the blood of animals but His own.

The role of the servant also illuminates the dimension of vicarious suffering that runs through Israel's history. Moses once offered himself on behalf of the people: "Blot me out of Your book; only forgive their sin" (Exod 32:32). David intercedes for Israel, saying, "It is I who have sinned... but these sheep, what have they done?" (2 Sam 24:17). The prophets often suffer rejection for the sake of their mission. Yet none of these figures can truly take away sin, for they are themselves sinners. The servant, however, is righteous, spotless, innocent. He bears sin not as one who shares in guilt but as one who stands in solidarity with the guilty. He is the fulfilment, not the repetition, of Israel's intercessory tradition.

This theme of solidarity extends beyond the Jewish people to the Gentiles. Isaiah envisions the servant as a light to the nations (Isa 49:6), and the Passion becomes the moment when this vision begins to unfold. The presence of the Roman centurion at the cross, confessing Jesus as Son of God, is the first fruits of this global recognition. The nations who once remained in darkness now look upon the pierced one and find salvation. The servant's suffering becomes the universal invitation to enter the covenant family of God.

The unity of Scripture becomes especially clear in the Passion's chronology. Each detail, from the betrayal for thirty pieces of silver (Zech 11:12–13; Matt 26:15) to the striking of the shepherd (Zech 13:7; Matt 26:31) to the casting of lots (Ps 22:18; John 19:24), conforms not to the expectations of the disciples but to the hidden script of the prophets. The motive force behind these events is not political machination or human cunning but divine purpose. As Peter later declares, Jesus was "delivered up according to the definite plan and foreknowledge of God" (Acts 2:23). Foreknowledge does not negate human agency; it reveals that God's providence encompasses human choices without being constrained by them.

This providence shines most clearly in the paradox of the cross. The one who is mocked as king is in fact the King. The one who is despised as a criminal is the Holy One of Israel. The one who seems abandoned is fulfilling the deepest meaning of Abraham's prophetic words: "God Himself will provide the lamb" (Gen 22:8). The Passion becomes the moment when God provides what humanity could never supply: a perfect sacrifice born of perfect love. Bernard of Clairvaux writes that the cross is "the supreme demonstration of charity," where Christ reveals the depth of divine compassion (*Sermon 1 on the Song of Songs*). The servant suffers not because God delights in suffering but because humanity needs healing, and love chooses the path that heals.

The prophetic fulfilment embedded in the Passion therefore reveals the shape of salvation. Redemption comes not through worldly power but through humility. Victory comes not through domination but through self-giving. The Messiah does not escape suffering; He transforms it into the means of redemption. Isaiah foresaw this when he proclaimed that the servant "shall sprinkle many nations" (Isa 52:15), a priestly image of atonement applied not to Israel alone but to the entire world. The sprinkling of nations corresponds to the blood poured out for many, the covenant sealed for all time.

The Passion reaches its interpretive summit when viewed through the lens of the new covenant promised by Jeremiah. "Behold, the days are coming, says the LORD, when I will make a new covenant... I will put My law within them, and I will write it upon their hearts" (Jer 31:31, 33). The covenant requires not only divine initiative but sacrificial sealing, for covenants in Israel's Scriptures are ratified in blood. When Jesus lifts the cup at the Last Supper and says, "This is My blood of the covenant, which is poured out for many for the forgiveness of sins" (Matt 26:28), He consciously unites His impending death with Jeremiah's promise. The servant who suffers becomes the mediator who establishes the new covenant through His own blood, fulfilling the pattern hinted at in Exodus 24:8: "Behold the blood of the covenant which the LORD has made with you."

The atoning significance of the servant's death unfolds even more profoundly when considered alongside the Day of Atonement rituals described in Leviticus 16. The high priest enters the Holy of Holies with blood to make atonement for the people, yet this ritual must be repeated every year. Hebrews interprets this repetition as a sign of insufficiency: "The law has but a shadow of the good things to come" (Heb 10:1). Christ, however, "entered once for all into the Holy Place... by means of His own blood, thus securing an eternal redemption" (Heb 9:12). The suffering servant thus becomes the eternal high priest, and His self-offering accomplishes what the Levitical system could only anticipate.

This fulfillment reconfigures the meaning of sacrifice itself. Sacrifice is no longer merely the offering of something external to oneself; it becomes the total self-offering of the Son to the Father on behalf of the world. "He humbled Himself and became obedient unto death, even death on a cross" (Phil 2:8). The cross is the altar where love is perfected, and obedience becomes the source of life for humanity. Gregory of Nazianzus captures this mystery when he writes that Christ "accepts our sufferings as His own, for He loves humanity with a love that cannot be measured" (*Oration 45*). The servant does not die because God demands death; He dies because love demands restoration, and only a love stronger than death can accomplish it.

The Passion also reveals the divine strategy against evil. From the earliest pages of Scripture, the serpent stands as the deceiver, the accuser, the one who inflicts death upon humanity. Genesis 3:15 speaks of enmity between the serpent and the woman, between the serpent's seed and her seed; the promise concludes that the seed of the woman "shall bruise your head, and you shall bruise his heel." On the cross, the bruising of the heel becomes the bruising of the head. Christ suffers, but in suffering He crushes the dominion of sin and death. Paul interprets the cross as the moment when God "disarmed the principalities and powers and made a public spectacle of them, triumphing over them in Him" (Col 2:15). The Passion is therefore both sacrifice and victory, humiliation and conquest.

This victory, however, is hidden beneath the appearance of defeat. Isaiah had anticipated this paradox: "We esteemed Him stricken, smitten by God, and afflicted" (Isa 53:4). The bystanders at the cross interpret His suffering as divine rejection, not realizing that He is fulfilling the divine plan. "He saved others; He cannot save Himself" (Matt 27:42) becomes the unwitting confession of the very truth they deny. He cannot save Himself if He is to save others. The inability is not physical but moral: the mission of the servant is love unto the end, and love refuses self-preservation when the salvation of the beloved is at stake.

The Gospels portray this love with an intimacy that transcends words. Jesus speaks to the women of Jerusalem, warning them with compassion (Luke 23:28). He forgives His executioners: "Father, forgive them; for they know not what they do" (Luke 23:34). He promises the repentant thief, "Today you will be with Me in Paradise" (Luke 23:43). He entrusts His mother to the beloved disciple: "Behold your mother" (John 19:27). These gestures reflect not only the tenderness of His humanity but the character of the servant described in Isaiah: "A bruised reed He will not break, and a dimly burning wick He will not quench" (Isa 42:3). Even while dying, He upholds the weak, consoles the sorrowful, forgives the guilty, and gathers the lost. The Passion is not simply the enactment of prophecy but the revelation of a heart that loves without limit.

This love continues to reveal itself even in the silence of death. When Jesus breathes His last, Mark writes that He "uttered a loud cry and breathed His last" (Mark 15:37). The centurion, witnessing the manner of His death, confesses, "Truly this man was the Son of God!" (Mark 15:39). The confession is extraordinary: a Gentile soldier, hardened by violence, becomes the first human witness in Mark's Gospel to declare Jesus' divine

## THE SERVANT SUFFERS: THE PASSION AS FULFILMENT OF PROPHECY

sonship. This moment fulfills the universal horizon of Isaiah's prophecy: "So shall He startle many nations; kings shall shut their mouths because of Him" (Isa 52:15). The Passion thus becomes the moment when the identity of Jesus is unveiled to the nations, and the mission of the servant expands beyond the boundaries of Israel.

The descent into death also fulfills the prophetic symbolism of Jonah, whom Jesus Himself references: "For as Jonah was three days and three nights in the belly of the whale, so will the Son of Man be three days and three nights in the heart of the earth" (Matt 12:40). Jonah's descent foreshadows Christ's entrance into the realm of the dead, not as one swallowed by judgment but as one who overturns its power. The righteous servant enters Sheol to liberate those held captive by death, fulfilling the cry of the psalmist, "You do not give me up to Sheol" (Ps 16:10), a text Peter applies directly to Christ (Acts 2:27, 31).

The prophetic fulfillment continues even in the burial. Isaiah's paradox—"with a rich man in His death" (Isa 53:9)—is realised when Joseph of Arimathea, a wealthy disciple, buries Jesus in his own unused tomb. The detail is both historical and theological. The servant's humiliation is complete, yet God grants Him honour in death. The tomb becomes the threshold of glory, for in three days the prophecy of Isaiah will reach its final crescendo: "He shall prolong His days; the will of the LORD shall prosper in His hand" (Isa 53:10). Resurrection is already woven into the servant's song. The suffering one becomes the exalted one. The pierced one becomes the life-giver. The servant becomes the Savior.

The resurrection does not negate the Passion but reveals its hidden meaning. Isaiah had said, "Out of the anguish of His soul He shall see and be satisfied" (Isa 53:11). The satisfaction is not the relief of suffering escaped but the joy of redemption accomplished. The servant "shall see His offspring" (Isa 53:10), a prophecy fulfilled when the risen Christ calls His disciples "brothers" (Matt 28:10) and appears among them, breathing peace and commissioning them for mission (John 20:21–22). The life that emerges from death is the sign that the sacrifice has been accepted. In the resurrection, God vindicates the servant, affirming His righteousness and declaring that His suffering has truly borne the sins of many.

The resurrection also completes the prophetic paradox first introduced in Isaiah 52:13: "He shall be exalted and lifted up, and shall be very high." The verbs used — "exalted," "lifted up" (*rum, nasa*) — appear elsewhere only for God Himself (Isa 6:1). The servant therefore shares in the divine exaltation, a reality unfolded in the ascension, where Christ is seated at the right hand of the Father (Ps 110:1; Heb 1:3). The one who descended into suffering now ascends in glory, and His exaltation confirms the divine identity hinted at throughout the prophets. The suffering servant is not merely the representative of Israel; He is the incarnate Word who enters the depths of human misery to raise humanity into the life of God.

The prophetic fulfillment reaches its climax when the risen Christ interprets the Scriptures to His disciples. He opens their minds to understand that "everything written about Me in the law of Moses and the prophets and the psalms must be fulfilled" (Luke 24:44). The necessity of fulfilment (*dei*) reveals that the Passion is not a late Christian re-reading imposed upon the text but the divinely intended meaning of Scripture from the beginning. Christ stands as the key to the entire canon, the one in whom promises, symbols, and sacrifices find their true significance. The servant songs, the psalms of lament, the prophecies of the pierced one, the imagery of the lamb, the righteous sufferer of Wisdom — all converge in Him.

The early Church fathers grasped this unity with profound insight. Justin Martyr argued that the Passion fulfilled "all that was spoken by the prophets, especially those in Isaiah 53" (*Dialogue with Trypho* 111). Origen declared that the suffering servant "prefigures the passion of Christ and the salvation that comes through Him" (*Homilies on Isaiah*). Augustine insisted that "our Lord's passion was foretold by so many clear prophecies that the blind alone failed to see it" (*City of God* 18.29). Cyril of Alexandria taught that Christ's suffering "was the medicine for the world, the healing of our nature, the means by which corruption was destroyed" (*Commentary on John*). Across the early centuries, the Passion is never treated as accidental, tragic, or merely exemplary. It is the fulfilment of the divine plan revealed in Scripture.

The central mystery of the Passion, however, is not simply predictive fulfillment but redemptive transformation. The servant does not suffer merely to match the prophetic script; He suffers to reconcile God and humanity. The violent rejection He endures becomes the means of peace: "Upon Him was the chastisement that made us whole" (Isa 53:5). The wounds inflicted by human sin become the channels of divine mercy: "With His stripes we are healed" (Isa 53:5). The death He dies is the death of death itself, for in rising He breaks the curse that held humanity captive. The Passion is therefore not a concession to evil but its defeat. As Chrysostom proclaims, "The cross is the throne of Christ, the place where He conquered not by force but by love" (*Homilies on John* 85).

In this victory, the vocation of Israel comes to fruition. The servant is Israel and more than Israel; He embodies the nation's calling to be a light to the nations (Isa 49:6) while achieving what the nation alone could not. He is the faithful Israelite whose obedience heals the disobedience of all. He is the righteous one whose suffering brings redemption to the many. He is the covenant in person, the sacrifice made once for all, the priest and the victim, the shepherd and the lamb. The Passion reveals the identity of the true Israel in the body of the crucified and risen Messiah.

Because of this, the cross becomes the interpretive centre of the entire biblical narrative. Everything before it leads toward it; everything after it flows from it. Abraham's ram caught in the thicket, the Passover lamb slain in Egypt, the bronze serpent lifted in the wilderness, the suffering prophet Jeremiah, the lamenting psalmists, the pierced figure of Zechariah — each is a shadow cast by the cross before the dawn of its reality. And once the cross is erected, its light stretches backward across the Scriptures, illuminating what had remained hidden, and forward across the world, drawing all nations toward the suffering servant lifted up for their salvation (John 12:32).

The Passion therefore establishes the Messiah's identity not only as king, prophet, and priest but as the suffering servant whose love reaches its consummation in sacrifice. The cross is not a contradiction of messianic hope but its fulfilment. The Messiah must suffer, not because God is cruel, but because only a suffering Messiah can heal a suffering world. Only a pierced heart can open the way for sinners to return. Only a broken body can become the bread of life. Only a crucified king can reveal a kingdom not of domination but of self-giving love.

Thus the chapter ends where prophecy itself ends: in the triumph of the servant who suffers and rises. "Therefore I will divide Him a portion with the great" (Isa 53:12). The servant who bore the iniquity of many receives the inheritance that Adam forfeited and bestows it upon those united to Him. The Passion is the unveiling of God's love in its deepest form. It is the hinge of history, the fulfillment of prophecy, the heart of the Gospel, and the place where the Messiah reveals Himself as the Redeemer of the world.

# 11

# The Son of Man Enthroned: Resurrection, Ascension, and Dominion

Jesus' preferred self-designation, the title He carries from the beginning of His public ministry to the threshold of His death, is the mysterious and charged phrase "the Son of Man." It appears repeatedly in the Gospels, not as a casual expression of humility but as a deliberate self-revelation. The density of its scriptural associations gives it a force that the modern reader often misses. In the ancient world, and especially within the imagination shaped by Israel's Scriptures, the phrase "son of man" could function at the level of ordinary speech — meaning simply a human being — yet this is not how Jesus uses it. His own words reveal a title that gathers authority, judgment, suffering, and heavenly exaltation into a single identity. When He says, "The Son of Man has authority on earth to forgive sins" (Mark 2:10), He claims a prerogative belonging to God alone. When He says, "The Son of Man is lord even of the sabbath" (Mark 2:28), He places Himself above the covenantal sign given at Sinai. When He teaches that "the Son of Man must suffer many things" (Mark 8:31), He joins this exalted figure to the path of humiliation foretold by the prophets. These moments are not scattered remarks but steps in a revelation moving toward a climax.

This expectation reaches its summit in the apocalyptic imagination of Israel's later Scriptures, especially in the vision recorded in Daniel. The prophet describes a heavenly scene in which thrones are set, the Ancient of Days takes His seat, and judgment begins. Into this scene comes a figure unlike any other: "I saw in the night visions, and behold, with the clouds of heaven there came one like a son of man, and he came to the Ancient of Days and was presented before him. And to him was given dominion and glory and kingdom, that all peoples, nations, and languages should serve him; his dominion is an everlasting dominion, which shall not pass away, and his kingdom one that shall not be destroyed" (Dan 7:13–14). The vision moves with majestic clarity: the figure rides the clouds — an action associated exclusively with God in the Old Testament (cf. Ps 104:3: "He makes the clouds his chariot"; Isa 19:1: "Behold, the LORD is riding on a swift cloud"). He approaches the Ancient of Days rather than being summoned for judgement. He receives not merely a task or symbolic authority but everlasting dominion. And he is served (*pelach* in Aramaic), a verb used in Daniel only for the worship offered to God. This figure is human in appearance yet divine in status.

Second Temple Judaism recognized the mystery of this figure and attempted to interpret him. The *Similitudes of Enoch* present a portrait of a pre-existent heavenly figure: "At that hour that Son of Man was named in the presence of the Lord of Spirits… Before the sun and the signs were created, before the stars of heaven were made, his name was named" (1 Enoch 48:2–3). Later the text affirms: "The kings and the mighty shall perish… For the Son of Man was concealed… and the Most High preserved him in the presence of His power" (1 Enoch 62:5–7). This is no ordinary human being; he is a heavenly redeemer whose dominion includes judgment of the nations. In *4 Ezra* the imagery intensifies: "I saw, and behold, a wind arose from the sea and stirred up all its waves. And I looked, and behold, this man flew with the clouds of heaven… And when he saw the onrush of the approaching multitude, he neither lifted his hand nor held a spear, nor any weapon of war; but I saw only how he sent forth from his mouth something like a stream of fire" (4 Ezra 13:1–4, 9–10). The ancient Jewish imagination understood Daniel's figure to be an eschatological agent of God, endowed with authority that transcended human categories.

When Jesus uses the title "Son of Man," He taps directly into this apocalyptic reservoir. The Gospels give no hint that His hearers regarded the phrase as harmless. Rather, His repeated use of it forces a choice: either He is a blasphemer claiming divine prerogatives, or He is the figure Daniel saw, the one to whom the Ancient of Days grants everlasting dominion. The tension breaks open fully at His trial. Confronted by the high priest and commanded to declare His identity, Jesus speaks the decisive words: "I am; and you will see the Son of Man seated at the right hand of Power, and coming with the clouds of heaven" (Mark 14:62). This is the moment when all veiled hints become explicit. The reference merges Daniel 7 with Psalm 110:1 — "Sit at my right hand, till I make your enemies your footstool" — the psalm most frequently cited in the New Testament to express Christ's exaltation. The reaction of the high priest reveals the magnitude of Jesus' claim: "And the high priest tore his garments, and said, 'Why do we still need witnesses? You have heard his blasphemy'" (Mark 14:63–64). The charge is not misunderstanding but blasphemy, because Jesus identifies Himself as the one who will be enthroned beside God and come with divine authority.

The early Church Fathers recognized the significance of this moment with absolute clarity. Justin Martyr declared to Trypho the Jew: "There is, and was, and is to be, another God and Lord subject to the Maker of all things... this one is called Angel because He announces to mankind whatsoever the Maker of all things — above whom there is no other God — wishes to announce to them... He is the one seen by Daniel as the Son of Man coming on the clouds" (*Dialogue with Trypho* 56). Irenaeus likewise identifies Jesus directly with Daniel's vision: "The Son of Man, who received from the Ancient of Days the everlasting kingdom, is He who is Himself the everlasting King" (*Against Heresies* 4.20.6). Hippolytus, in the earliest surviving Christian commentary on Daniel, writes: "He who will come forth as judge is the same who came once in humility. The one like a Son of Man who comes with the clouds is Christ" (*Commentary on Daniel* 2.7). The Fathers treat the connection between Jesus and Daniel

7 not as subtle exegesis but as the heart of the Church's proclamation.

This identity, however, requires vindication. Jesus does not merely claim to be the Son of Man; He lives in such a way that His claim becomes either madness or revelation. His crucifixion appears at first glance to dismantle all expectation, for Daniel's Son of Man is enthroned, victorious, and glorious, not humiliated and condemned. Yet Jesus Himself teaches that the path to glory passes through suffering: "Was it not necessary that the Christ should suffer these things and enter into his glory?" (Luke 24:26). The word "necessary" (*dei*) conveys divine purpose rather than tragic inevitability. The suffering of the Son of Man completes the pattern set by the prophets. And the resurrection reveals that His humiliation is the path to exaltation, for "God raised him up, having loosed the pangs of death, because it was not possible for him to be held by it" (Acts 2:24). The impossibility is metaphysical: death cannot hold the one whose very identity is life.

The resurrection functions therefore as God's own testimony to the truth of Jesus' claim. Paul expresses it with lapidary clarity: Jesus was "designated Son of God in power according to the Spirit of holiness by his resurrection from the dead" (Rom 1:4). The resurrection is not a reversal of failure but the divine confirmation of identity. The one whom the Sanhedrin judged as a blasphemer is vindicated by God as His Beloved. Peter proclaims this reversal on the day of Pentecost with boldness impossible before: "Let all the house of Israel therefore know assuredly that God has made him both Lord and Christ, this Jesus whom you crucified" (Acts 2:36). The resurrection becomes the moment in which Jesus' messianic and divine identity is publicly revealed. Every title that Jesus claimed in His earthly ministry — Son of Man, Son of God, Lord of the Sabbath, Judge of the nations — now becomes manifest truth.

The resurrection appearances underscore the continuity and transformation of Jesus' risen humanity. He stands among His disciples and says, "Peace be with you" (John 20:19), the greeting of divine reconciliation. He invites Thomas to "put your finger here, and see my hands" (John 20:27), preserving in His glorified body the marks of His passion, signs that the enthroned Son of Man is the crucified servant of Isaiah. He eats with His disciples, speaks with them, teaches them, and opens the Scriptures to them. On the road to Emmaus, He interprets "in all the scriptures the things concerning himself" (Luke 24:27), showing that His suffering and glory were written not in isolated verses but woven throughout the whole canon. Augustine comments on this scene with luminous simplicity: "He walked with them in the way, and He Himself was the way... He interpreted to them what was obscure in Scripture, for He was the key that opened what was closed" (*Sermon 235*). The risen Christ thus appears not only as living Lord but as the living exegesis of prophecy.

This prophetic fulfillment moves into even sharper focus when the risen Jesus delivers the most sweeping claim of authority found anywhere in the Gospels: "All authority in heaven and on earth has been given to me" (Matt 28:18). This declaration resonates with Daniel 7:14, where the Son of Man is given "dominion and glory and kingdom." The authority is universal, extending over the entire created order. The resurrection is therefore not merely the victory of life over death but the moment at which the dominion of the Son of Man becomes manifest. Athanasius, contemplating the scope of this claim, writes: "The Word took to Himself a body that He might reign in it over all created things, and in it subdue the enemy" (*On the Incarnation* 9). The resurrection reveals the enthroned Lord whose dominion is rooted in His humanity as well as His divinity.

Yet the movement of resurrection is incomplete without ascension. The Scriptures do not treat ascension as a postscript to salvation but as the climactic moment foreseen by Daniel. The prophet does not say that the Son of Man comes *from* the Ancient of Days but that he comes *to* Him: "He came to the Ancient of Days and was presented before him" (Dan 7:13). This is not the Second Coming but the ascension. When Jesus is "lifted up, and a cloud took him out of their sight" (Acts 1:9), He is enacting Daniel's vision. The cloud is not meteorological detail but theophanic symbol; the same cloud that overshadows Sinai, fills the tabernacle, and surrounds the glory of God now receives the risen Christ. Cyril of Jerusalem captures this mystery: "He was taken up by a cloud, not as one caught up unwillingly, but as one seated upon a royal chariot" (*Catechetical Lectures* 4.13).

The ascension therefore is enthronement. It is the moment when the Son of Man receives the dominion promised in Daniel's vision. The New Testament witnesses to this truth with a consistency that reveals its centrality. Peter, again quoting Psalm 110, declares: "For David did not ascend into the heavens; but he himself says, 'The Lord said to my Lord, Sit at my right hand'" (Acts 2:34). The contrast is decisive: David, the greatest of Israel's kings, did not ascend; Jesus did. This distinction marks the inauguration of a new phase in the messianic reign. Paul confirms the same truth when he writes that God "raised him from the dead and made him sit at his right hand in the heavenly places, far above all rule and authority and power and dominion" (Eph 1:20–21). The vocabulary of elevation — "far above all rule and authority" — echoes Daniel's language of everlasting dominion. Christ's enthronement is cosmic.

Hebrews, with its extraordinary theological clarity, presents the enthronement as both priestly and royal: "After making purification for sins, he sat down at the right hand of the Majesty on high" (Heb 1:3). The phrase "sat down" bears profound significance. No priest of the old covenant ever sat in the sanctuary, for his work was never finished. But Christ sits, because His offering is complete and His reign has begun. Chrysostom comments: "He sits because all is now accomplished; He rules because the kingdom is His; He is at the right hand because He is equal to the Father" (*Homilies on Hebrews* 2). In the ascension, therefore, the Son of Man becomes the King-Priest whose dominion fulfills both Daniel's vision and Psalm 110's decree.

The enthronement is not merely symbolic. The early Church speaks of it as a real and active kingship exercised from heaven. The Book of Revelation, likely the earliest Christian text outside Paul to reflect explicitly on Christ's heavenly reign, depicts Him as "the ruler of the kings of the earth" (Rev 1:5). John sees "one like a son of man" (Rev 1:13), clothed in garments of priestly and royal dignity, walking among the lampstands and holding the stars in His right hand. The imagery draws directly from Daniel 7 and transfers its authority to the risen Christ. He is the one who "opens and no one shall shut, who shuts and no one opens" (Rev 3:7), echoing Isaiah 22's language of Davidic authority. He is the Lamb standing as though slain yet reigning at the centre of divine worship, receiving the adoration of "every creature in heaven and on earth and under the earth and in the sea" (Rev 5:13). The universal worship confirms the divinity of the Son of Man and the reality of His enthronement.

This heavenly dominion of the Son of Man becomes the central confession of the early Christian proclamation, not a later theological development but the very foundation of the Gospel as the apostles preached it. When Peter and John stand before the Sanhedrin, the same court that condemned Jesus, they declare that God has exalted Him "at his right hand as Leader and Savior" (Acts 5:31). The word "Leader" (*archēgos*) implies founder, prince, and ruler — one who opens a path and exercises authority as the head of a new order. Stephen, at the moment of his martyrdom, sees "the heavens opened, and the Son of Man standing at the right hand of God" (Acts 7:56). The vision confirms that the one who once stood before this same council now stands in divine glory, bearing witness to His martyr in turn. This is the earliest recorded Christian vision of the exalted Christ, and it identifies Him explicitly as the Son of Man of Daniel, enthroned and active.

Paul's letters reinforce this conviction in language that leaves no ambiguity. He speaks of Christ as the one "who is seated at the right hand of God, who indeed intercedes for us" (Rom 8:34). The Son of Man is not a passive symbol but a living mediator, exercising dominion through intercession. When Paul says, "He must reign until he has put all his enemies under his feet" (1 Cor 15:25), he echoes Psalm 110:1, interpreting the enthronement of Christ as a reign already begun, moving toward the final subjection of death. He describes Christ as the one "through whom are all things and through whom we exist" (1 Cor 8:6), applying to Jesus the creative power attributed exclusively to God in Jewish monotheism. And in a hymn that likely predates Paul himself, he writes: "Therefore God has highly exalted him and bestowed on him the name which is above every name, that at the name of Jesus every knee should bow... and every tongue confess that Jesus Christ is Lord" (Phil 2:9–11). Here Paul applies Isaiah 45:23 — a passage in which Yahweh swears by His own name that every knee will bow to Him — directly to Jesus. This is enthronement in its highest form: participation in the divine identity.

The patristic tradition receives these apostolic convictions and articulates them with increasing clarity. Ignatius of Antioch, writing at the dawn of the second century, describes Jesus Christ as "our God" (*Letter to the Ephesians* 18) and insists that His suffering and resurrection reveal His true identity as the divine Son who reigns. Irenaeus develops the theme of dominion by connecting the Son of Man to the restoration of Adam's lost kingship: "The Word of God… became what we are, that He might bring us to be even what He is Himself" (*Against Heresies* 5. Preface). For Irenaeus, the Son of Man's enthronement is not merely His triumph but humanity's elevation in Him. Origen interprets Daniel 7 in Christological terms: "The Son of Man coming on the clouds is the Word of God coming with the glory of His divinity" (*Commentary on Matthew* 14). Athanasius sees the enthronement as the proof of Christ's divinity: "Who is seated at the right hand of the Father but the Son? For this is proper to Him who is one in essence with the Father" (*Against the Arians* 3.33). The Fathers understand Daniel 7 as a window into the eternal relationship between the Father and the Son, a relationship revealed and enacted in salvation history.

The ascended Son of Man exercises this dominion in ways that shape the Church's mission and identity. He pours out the Holy Spirit at Pentecost, fulfilling Joel's prophecy and inaugurating the age of the Church. Peter explains the event by appealing once again to the enthronement: "Being therefore exalted at the right hand of God… he has poured out this which you see and hear" (Acts 2:33). The Spirit's descent is the royal action of the enthroned Messiah. Christ reigns by giving His own life to His people. He distributes gifts, raises up apostles, empowers witness, and strengthens martyrs. The Book of Revelation depicts Him walking among the lampstands, tending the churches, correcting, consoling, and commanding. His dominion is not distant sovereignty but intimate governance. The King is not remote; He is present in the midst of His people.

This presence is not only spiritual but sacramental. The enthroned Christ, who once offered Himself upon the cross, continues to make that offering present in the Eucharist. The early liturgies address Him directly: "We lift them up to the Lord." The dialogue presupposes the one who reigns. The Church prays to Him, worships Him, and receives His Body and Blood as the gift of His enthroned humanity. The Son of Man who ascends is the same Son of Man who feeds His people with heavenly bread. This sacramental dimension of His dominion was clear to Cyril of Alexandria, who wrote: "Though He is in heaven with the Father, He is present with us in the mystery, giving Himself to those who are worthy" (*Commentary on John* 4). The throne of heaven and the altar of earth become united in the priestly kingship of Christ.

This dominion extends also to judgment, for the Son of Man is not only king and priest but judge of all the earth. Jesus had predicted this role during His earthly ministry: "The Son of Man is going to come with his angels in the glory of his Father, and then he will repay every man for what he has done" (Matt 16:27). The judgment envisioned by Daniel — where thrones are set and books are opened — is entrusted to the Son of Man. Yet the enthroned Christ exercises judgment even now, guiding the course of history. He opens the seals in Revelation, reveals the destiny of nations, and shepherds the Church through persecution. The crucified and risen Son of Man governs the unfolding of the world's story with the authority given Him by the Father. Basil the Great, reflecting on this mystery, writes: "He who sits with the Father on the same throne presides over all creation, judging with righteousness and mercy" (*On the Holy Spirit* 8).

The universal scope of Christ's dominion does not eclipse His humanity but reveals its exalted destiny. The Son of Man reigns as man. His enthroned humanity is the pledge of humanity's future. The dominion Daniel foresaw, the glory that transcends all kingdoms, is exercised in the very nature that He assumed from the Virgin. This is why the ascension is theologically indispensable: humanity has entered heaven in the person of Christ. Athanasius exults in this truth when he writes: "The humanity of Christ has been taken up into the Godhead, not to vanish but to be glorified, that we might be raised with Him" (*Against the Arians* 3.34). The exaltation of Jesus is the exaltation of human nature, the beginning of the new creation.

The enthronement of Christ as the Son of Man thus initiates a kingdom that is present yet awaiting consummation. His dominion is real, active, and universal, but it unfolds according to the wisdom of God rather than the spectacle of earthly power. Jesus had prepared His disciples for this paradox when He taught, "The kingdom of God is in the midst of you" (Luke 17:21), and when He likened the kingdom to seed that grows slowly, imperceptibly (Mark 4:26–29). The Son of Man reigns, yet the fullness of His reign is still awaited. This tension reflects the very structure of Daniel's vision, in which the kingdom is given to the Son of Man and then, through Him, to "the saints of the Most High" (Dan 7:18). The enthronement is immediate, but the sharing of dominion with the saints unfolds through history.

The early Church understood itself as the community that participates in this royal dominion. Peter calls the baptized "a royal priesthood" (1 Pet 2:9), echoing Exodus 19:6 and extending the privilege of Christ's royal priesthood to His people. Paul teaches that believers are already raised with Christ and seated with Him "in the heavenly places" (Eph 2:6). The enthroned Son of Man draws His people into His own exalted life. This participation is not metaphorical but mystical, rooted in the union established by baptism and nourished in the Eucharist. The dominion of the Son of Man becomes the destiny of those who belong to Him. As Irenaeus writes, "If the Head is in heaven, the members must follow; for where the Head is, there the body shall be also" (*Against Heresies* 5. Preface).

The ascended Christ exercises His dominion also through the Church's mission. Before ascending, He commanded, "Go therefore and make disciples of all nations... And behold, I am with you always, to the close of the age" (Matt 28:19–20). The mission flows directly from His authority: "All authority in heaven and on earth has been given to me. Go therefore..." (Matt 28:18–19). Evangelization is not an optional activity but the necessary outworking of Christ's enthronement. The Son of Man gathers the nations not by force but by witness, not by coercion but by the transforming power of grace. The book of Acts portrays this mission as the visible extension of His invisible reign, driven by the Spirit whom He pours out from the throne. When Paul preaches in Athens that God "has fixed a day on which he will judge the world in righteousness by a man whom he has appointed, and of this he has given assurance to all men by raising him from the dead" (Acts 17:31), he proclaims both the authority of the Son of Man and the universal scope of His kingship.

This dominion has a cosmic dimension that Paul articulates with unprecedented boldness. In Colossians, he writes: "He is the image of the invisible God, the first-born of all creation; for in him all things were created, in heaven and on earth... all things were created through him and for him" (Col 1:15–16). The Son of Man does not merely rule over the nations; He reigns over the cosmos. His enthroned humanity becomes the point at which creation is gathered, renewed, and directed toward its final purpose. This is why Paul can declare that Christ "must reign until he has put all his enemies under his feet" (1 Cor 15:25). The phrase "must reign" is not a prediction but a theological necessity. The dominion given by the Ancient of Days to the Son of Man requires the subjugation of every force opposed to God — sin, evil, suffering, and finally death itself.

The victory over death, however, is not completed at the cross or even at the resurrection but will manifest fully at the end of time. Paul explains: "The last enemy to be destroyed is death" (1 Cor 15:26). Christ's resurrection is the first fruits; the general resurrection will be the harvest. The enthroned Christ rules over a world still awaiting its final transformation. His dominion is both already and not yet, present in its authority but awaiting completion in glory. This tension reflects the vision of Daniel, in which the Son of Man receives dominion immediately, yet the saints receive the kingdom progressively. The dominion begins with the Messiah and extends outward until all creation is renewed.

The Book of Revelation portrays this unfolding dominion in scenes that draw heavily from Daniel's imagery. John sees the Son of Man walking among the lampstands (Rev 1:13), holding the seven stars, His face shining like the sun. He sees the Lamb on the throne, receiving the worship of the elders and the angels. He hears every creature praising "Him who sits upon the throne and the Lamb" (Rev 5:13). These scenes are not visions of the future alone but revelations of the present heavenly reality. The enthroned Son of Man governs history, directs the Church, judges the nations, and manifests His dominion in acts of mercy and judgment. As Gregory the Great explains, "In His ascension He did not abandon us; in His government He is never absent, for He rules all things by His power" (*Homilies on the Gospels* 29).

The practical consequence of Christ's enthronement is the assurance given to His disciples amid persecution. The Son of Man reigns above all earthly powers, and no suffering can overturn His victory. Stephen sees Him standing at the right hand of God not to remain seated in indifference but to rise in solidarity with His martyr. John's vision of the glorified Son of Man comes to believers in exile. The letters to the seven churches address communities facing internal struggles and external threats. Christ's dominion is not abstract theology but the living source of courage, hope, and perseverance. Persecution does not negate His reign; it becomes the arena in which His power is revealed through weakness. Chrysostom, preaching in the face of imperial opposition, reminds his hearers: "No one can harm the man who has Christ for his King. For if He reigns in heaven, what can earth do against Him?" (*Homilies on Matthew* 4).

This kingship also recasts the shape of Christian discipleship. To follow the Son of Man is to share in His pattern of suffering and glory. Jesus had predicted: "If any man would come after me, let him deny himself and take up his cross and follow me" (Mark 8:34). The path of the enthroned King is the path of the suffering servant. His dominion is exercised through self-giving love, and His disciples participate in that dominion by imitating His humility. The authority of the kingdom is not coercive but sacrificial; it conquers not by violence but by truth and mercy. The enthroned Son of Man has been given all authority, yet He uses that authority to forgive, to heal, and to save. His rule reflects the character of God — not domination but communion, not tyranny but love.

The final dimension of Christ's dominion is eschatological. The enthroned Son of Man will appear again, not to receive authority but to manifest the authority already given Him. Jesus Himself foretold this moment: "Then they will see the Son of Man coming in clouds with great power and glory" (Mark 13:26). This second coming is the unveiling of His kingship before all nations. Daniel foresaw not only the enthronement but the final judgment, when the Son of Man executes justice and establishes the eternal kingdom. Revelation echoes this: "Behold, he is coming with the clouds, and every eye will see him" (Rev 1:7). The enthroned Christ will return, and His return will consummate the dominion given Him by the Ancient of Days.

The return of the Son of Man will not establish a new kingdom but reveal the fullness of the kingdom He already possesses. The nations will behold what has been true since the ascension: that "all authority in heaven and on earth" belongs to Him (Matt 28:18). His coming will not elevate Him to the throne; it will unveil the throne before the eyes of the world. The clouds that once concealed Him in His ascent (Acts 1:9) will be the vehicle of His revelation when He returns. The imagery is identical to Daniel's vision: "with the clouds of heaven there came one like a son of man" (Dan 7:13). The Second Coming is the visible manifestation of the enthroned Christ. What Stephen saw in his martyrdom — the Son of Man at the right hand of God — will be seen by all creation.

In the meantime, His dominion continues to shape the course of history, even when that dominion seems hidden. The kingdoms of this world rise and fall, but the kingdom of the Son of Man remains unshaken. His authority is not political in the worldly sense; it is cosmic and moral, extending to the depths of human hearts and the heights of angelic realms. Paul writes that Christ has been exalted "far above all rule and authority and power and dominion" (Eph 1:21), naming the angelic and demonic hierarchies recognized in Jewish apocalyptic thought. The dominion of the Son of Man is not limited to human affairs but governs the entire spiritual order. His resurrection announces the defeat of death; His ascension announces the subjugation of all powers; His enthronement announces the arrival of the age to come.

The early Christians understood this cosmic dimension intimately. Their confession "Jesus is Lord" was not a private devotion but a public declaration challenging every competing authority — imperial, spiritual, or cultural. The title *Kyrios*, drawn from the Greek translation of the divine name, proclaimed that the Son of Man shared in the very sovereignty of Yahweh. When Paul writes that at the name of Jesus "every knee should bow, in heaven and on earth and under the earth" (Phil 2:10), he describes a worship that bridges the entire cosmos. The Son of Man enthroned beside the Father receives homage not only from believers but from angels, heavenly powers, and the saints who have departed this life. The dominion of Christ unites heaven and earth in a single liturgy.

This union of heaven and earth is expressed most profoundly in the Eucharist, where the worship of the Church participates in the worship of the heavenly sanctuary. The liturgy of the early Church reflects this understanding. The *Didache* speaks of the Church being gathered "from the ends of the earth into Your kingdom," echoing Daniel's vision of the nations brought under the dominion of the Son of Man. The ancient anaphoras invoke Christ directly as the one who reigns from the right hand of the Father and who will come again in glory. The Church's worship is an act of allegiance to the enthroned King. As Chrysostom taught his congregation: "When you see the Lord sacrificed and laid upon the altar... think that a choir of angels surrounds Him, standing by in awe because of the great mystery" (*Homilies on the Hebrews* 17). The Eucharist becomes the earthly enactment of the heavenly reality revealed in Daniel's vision.

The dominion of the Son of Man also shapes Christian hope. Because He reigns, believers can endure trials, persecution, and suffering without despair. Jesus Himself prepared His disciples for this by saying, "In the world you have tribulation; but be of good cheer, I have overcome the world" (John 16:33). The victory of the Son of Man over the world is not merely future but present, rooted in His resurrection and enthronement. The martyrs of the early Church understood their suffering as participation in Christ's dominion. Ignatius of Antioch, on his way to martyrdom, wrote: "Now I begin to be a disciple. Let fire and cross, encounters with beasts... come upon me, so that I may attain to Jesus Christ" (*Letter to the Romans* 5). He saw his suffering through the lens of Christ's kingship — not defeat but victory through union with the enthroned Lord.

The exaltation of Christ also provides the framework for understanding the resurrection of the dead. Paul explains that Christ is "the first fruits of those who have fallen asleep" (1 Cor 15:20), meaning that His resurrection inaugurates the age of resurrection for all humanity. The Son of Man, who reigns in glorified humanity, draws all humanity into His glory. Daniel had foreseen this: "Many of those who sleep in the dust of the earth shall awake" (Dan 12:2). The resurrection of the Son of Man is the first act of this great renewal. The enthroned humanity of Christ becomes the source of the resurrection life promised to all who belong to Him. As Athanasius writes with triumphant clarity, "His resurrection is the promise of our resurrection, for as He rose in His body, so shall we rise" (*On the Incarnation* 56). The dominion of the Son of Man therefore extends not only over the present world but over the world to come.

There is also a profoundly personal dimension to Christ's dominion. The Son of Man reigns not merely over nations and angels but over the human heart. His authority confronts every person with a choice: to enter His kingdom or to resist His rule. Jesus expresses this truth when He says, "He who is not with me is against me" (Matt 12:30). The kingdom is not neutral territory. The enthronement of the Son of Man demands allegiance, repentance, and faith. To follow Him is to enter into life; to reject Him is to remain in darkness. The dominion of Christ is both gift and judgment. It offers salvation to all who receive Him, and it exposes the futility of every rival claim to sovereignty.

This personal dimension is inseparable from the communal. The enthroned Christ forms a people who live under His rule and manifest His reign in the world. The early Christians described the Church as the "colony of heaven" (Phil 3:20), a community whose politics, worship, and ethics are shaped by the kingship of Christ. Their refusal to worship Caesar was not political rebellion but theological fidelity: only the Son of Man receives worship. Only He shares the throne of God. Only His dominion is eternal. This conviction sustained the Church through centuries of persecution and remains the foundation of Christian identity.

The world, however, often fails to perceive this dominion. The reign of the Son of Man is hidden beneath the fragility of the Church, the weakness of its members, and the apparent triumph of evil. Yet this hiddenness is part of the divine plan. Just as the Messiah's identity was concealed in humility before being revealed in glory, so the dominion of Christ operates through what appears weak and insignificant. Paul describes this paradox when he writes, "We have this treasure in earthen vessels, to show that the transcendent power belongs to God and not to us" (2 Cor 4:7). The kingdom grows like seed in the ground, unnoticed until the harvest. The enthroned Christ governs history through grace rather than spectacle, through holiness rather than force, through the quiet triumph of the saints rather than the noise of earthly power.

The dominion of the Son of Man reaches its fullest expression not only in His reign over the cosmos but in His victory over death and His promise to renew all creation. The New Testament consistently links His enthronement to the restoration of the world, for the one seated at the right hand of the Father is the same one through whom "all things were made" (John 1:3). The authority He receives from the Ancient of Days is the authority to complete the work of creation by bringing it into the freedom and glory intended from the beginning. Paul captures this breathtaking vision when he writes: "The creation itself will be set free from its bondage to decay… For in this hope we were saved" (Rom 8:21, 24). The dominion of the Son of Man is therefore eschatological in scope. It encompasses not only human salvation but the transformation of the entire created order.

The Book of Revelation offers a glimpse of this consummation through symbols drawn from Daniel's visions. John sees a new heaven and a new earth, and he hears a voice declaring: "Behold, the dwelling of God is with men" (Rev 21:3). The enthronement of Christ makes possible the union of God and creation. The Lamb, once slain, now enthroned, presides over the renewal of all things. Daniel foresaw a kingdom "that shall not be destroyed" (Dan 7:14), and Revelation shows its everlasting form: a city filled with the glory of God, with no need of sun or moon, "for the glory of God is its light, and its lamp is the Lamb" (Rev 21:23). The lamp is the Son of Man, whose risen humanity radiates the divine light that transforms creation.

This eschatological vision is not separate from the present reign of Christ but grows out of it. The ascended Lord governs the unfolding of salvation history, guiding the Church toward its final destiny. His reign is both hidden and revealed: hidden in the weakness of the saints, revealed in the sacraments, hidden in the apparent triumph of evil, revealed in every act of grace. The tension between what is already accomplished and what is not yet fulfilled marks the entire Christian experience. As Augustine writes, "The Church progresses on this pilgrimage amid the persecutions of the world and the consolations of God" (*City of God* 18.51). The enthroned Christ accompanies His people in this tension, assuring them that His dominion will ultimately triumph.

The confidence of the Church rests not on human strength but on the victory of the Son of Man. When Jesus declares, "I am with you always, to the close of the age" (Matt 28:20), He speaks not as a distant ruler but as the enthroned King who fills all things with His presence. His reign is not postponed until the end of time; it is operative now, shaping the lives of believers and the destiny of nations. The early Christians were unafraid to face suffering, persecution, and even death because they knew that their lives were held in the hands of the One who reigns. Cyprian expresses this confidence during a time of plague and turmoil: "We do not leave the world in fear but in faith, knowing that Christ reigns and calls us to Himself" (*On Mortality* 13). The dominion of the Son of Man transforms the Christian attitude toward life and death.

This transformation includes the moral and spiritual dimensions of discipleship. To acknowledge Christ as the enthroned Son of Man is to submit one's life to His authority. His teachings within the Gospels are not merely wise sayings but royal decrees from the King of the kingdom. His commandments direct the life of His subjects. His example reveals the pattern of the kingdom. The Sermon on the Mount becomes the constitution of the new covenant people. The Beatitudes reflect the character of the King. To be poor in spirit, meek, merciful, pure in heart, and persecuted for righteousness is to embody the life of the kingdom. The enthroned Christ forms His people according to His own image. As Gregory of Nyssa observes, "The goal of the Christian life is the imitation of God, but this is possible only because God first became man" (*On the Beatitudes*, Prologue). The enthroned Son of Man reveals what humanity is meant to become.

The dominion of Christ also defines the Church's relationship to earthly powers. The early Christians respected civil authority, recognizing its role in maintaining order, yet they refused to grant it ultimate allegiance. Their loyalty belonged to Christ alone. This was not political rebellion but theological fidelity. When the apostles declare, "We must obey God rather than men" (Acts 5:29), they articulate the fundamental principle of Christian political theology: no earthly power can claim the allegiance owed to the Son of Man. His kingdom is not of this world (John 18:36), yet it confronts the world with a higher authority. This confrontation is peaceful, rooted in truth, not violence. The martyrs suffered not because they sought conflict but because they refused to worship any other lord. Their witness becomes an extension of Christ's own dominion, manifesting His reign through their fidelity.

The universality of Christ's dominion also includes the gathering of the nations into the new covenant. Jesus' command to make disciples of "all nations" (Matt 28:19) fulfills the promise to Abraham that "all the families of the earth shall be blessed" (Gen 12:3). The Son of Man inherits not only Israel but the world. Psalm 2 anticipates this: "Ask of me, and I will make the nations your heritage, and the ends of the earth your possession" (Ps 2:8). The ascended Christ exercises this inheritance through the mission of the Church. Every conversion, every act of charity, every proclamation of the Gospel becomes a sign of His dominion. Augustine captures this expansive vision: "The kingdom of Christ grows not by conquering lands but by conquering hearts" (*Expositions on the Psalms* 2). The reign of Christ spreads through the transformation of humanity from within.

Yet the spread of this kingdom faces opposition. The powers of this world resist the dominion of Christ, just as the beasts in Daniel's vision opposed the Son of Man. The struggle between the kingdom of God and the kingdoms of the world continues throughout history. The Church is the arena where this conflict becomes visible. It experiences both triumphs and failures, sanctity and sin, unity and division. But the outcome is assured, for "the kingdom and the dominion and the greatness of the kingdoms under the whole heaven shall be given to the saints of the Most High" (Dan 7:27). The triumph of Christ becomes the triumph of His people. Gregory the Great writes, "We shall reign with Him because we suffer with Him; for no one comes to the kingdom without sharing in the cross" (*Moralia* 31.22). The path to glory leads through suffering, just as it did for the Son of Man.

This promise of shared dominion gives hope to the weary and courage to the faithful. Christ's enthronement is the guarantee that their labour is not in vain. Every act of charity, every moment of fidelity, every hidden sacrifice participates in the reign of the Son of Man. The struggles of the present world cannot overturn the victory of Christ. The Church waits not in uncertainty but in hope, confident that the one who sits on the throne will bring His work to completion. As Paul affirms, "He who began a good work in you will bring it to completion at the day of Jesus Christ" (Phil 1:6). The dominion of the Son of Man ensures that history moves toward fulfillment, not futility.

The certainty of Christ's dominion invites the Christian not into complacency but into vigilance. The Son of Man who reigns also calls His disciples to remain watchful, for His return will be sudden and unmistakable. "Watch therefore, for you do not know on what day your Lord is coming" (Matt 24:42). The enthroned King will appear in glory, and the hidden sovereignty of the present age will become the manifest sovereignty of the age to come. The faithful servant who lives under His authority now will rejoice when He appears; the one who ignores His dominion will be taken by surprise. Jesus' parables of judgment—of the wise and foolish virgins, the talents, the sheep and goats—draw their force from His identity as the Son of Man. He is not only the ruler but the judge. He inspects the hearts of His servants, discerns their fidelity, and assigns their place in the kingdom. His judgments are not arbitrary but expressions of divine justice and mercy.

This eschatological dimension of Christ's dominion also clarifies the nature of Christian hope. Hope is not wishful thinking but steadfast trust in the promises God has fulfilled in Christ. The resurrection demonstrates God's fidelity to His word; the ascension reveals the destiny of humanity; the outpouring of the Spirit confirms the nearness of the kingdom; and the promise of Christ's return anchors the believer's longing for justice and renewal. Augustine captures this interplay of fulfillment and expectation when he writes, "We are saved in hope; but hope that is seen is not hope. What we hope for is not yet seen, but we believe because He who promised is faithful" (*Enchiridion* 8). The enthroned Son of Man stands as the guarantee of this hope. His resurrected and glorified humanity is the pledge that creation itself will be renewed.

In this light, the dominion of Christ becomes the interpretive key for all human history. The rise and fall of empires, the suffering of the just, the apparent triumph of wickedness, the persistence of faith—all find their meaning within the reign of the Son of Man. Daniel's vision is therefore not merely a prediction but a theology of history. The beasts represent the violent and oppressive structures of earthly kingdoms; the Son of Man represents the divine purpose that overcomes them. The ascended Christ is the living fulfillment of this vision. His dominion relativizes every earthly power, exposes their limits, and reveals their transience. The only kingdom that endures is His. As John Chrysostom declares, "All kingdoms are shattered; His alone remains unshaken. For He who established it is God" (*Homilies on Matthew* 4). The dominion of Christ is the axis of history.

This dominion also illuminates the mystery of suffering. The Son of Man who reigns is the Son of Man who suffered. His glorified wounds reveal that suffering is not erased but transfigured. The cross becomes the throne; the wounds become the insignia of victory. The saints who suffer for His sake share in this pattern. Their suffering is not meaningless but participates in the work of the kingdom. Paul expresses this profound truth when he writes, "If we suffer with him, we shall also be glorified with him" (Rom 8:17). The dominion of Christ makes Christian suffering intelligible. It is the pathway to glory, the means by which the believer is conformed to the image of the Son of Man.

In this way, the reign of Christ also exposes the illusions of worldly power. Earthly rulers imagine their authority to be absolute, yet their kingdoms crumble. Nations rise and fall, yet none endure. The dominion of Christ is not threatened by human rebellion, nor is it advanced by human strength. It grows through grace, humility, and truth. The martyrs accomplish more by their deaths than conquerors by their armies. The saints transform more through their prayers than emperors through their laws. The power of the kingdom is the power of divine love, exercised through the enthroned humanity of Christ. As Gregory of Nazianzus proclaims, "His power is not of this world, for He reigns by conquering through humility and subduing through love" (*Oration 37*). The kingdom of the Son of Man reveals the futility of worldly ambition and the enduring value of holiness.

The dominion of Christ is therefore inseparable from the call to holiness. To acknowledge His kingship is to order one's life according to His will. Holiness is not a private virtue but participation in the reign of the Son of Man. The saints are those who allow the dominion of Christ to reshape their desires, purify their loves, and direct their actions. Their lives become signs of the kingdom. Their charity reveals the mercy of the King; their courage reveals His strength; their purity reveals His beauty; their perseverance reveals His stability. The enthroned Christ reigns through them, manifesting His dominion in the world. The kingdom becomes visible wherever holiness takes root.

The final revelation of Christ's dominion will bring all things to completion. Paul describes this moment with solemn grandeur: "Then comes the end, when he delivers the kingdom to God the Father after destroying every rule and every authority and power... that God may be everything to every one" (1 Cor 15:24, 28). The Son of Man, enthroned and exalted, will bring history to its consummation by restoring all things to the Father. His dominion is not a rival to the Father's sovereignty but its perfect expression. The Son reigns in obedience to the Father; the Father reigns through the Son. The final act of the kingdom is the revelation of the mutual glory of Father and Son, united in the Spirit.

This return of the kingdom to the Father does not diminish Christ's humanity but glorifies it. The Son of Man hands over a redeemed creation; He offers to the Father His own perfected humanity and the humanity of all who belong to Him. The throne He shares remains forever, for His priesthood is eternal. The saints will reign with Him, not as independent rulers but as participants in His divine-human kingship. The kingdom will endure because the King endures. His dominion will have no end.

In the end, the Son of Man enthroned is the fulfillment of all prophecy, the revelation of God's plan, the centre of history, the hope of humanity, and the destiny of creation. Daniel's vision becomes reality in the risen and ascended Christ. The clouds have received Him, the Ancient of Days has exalted Him, the nations are being gathered to Him, and He will come again in glory. The kingdom has begun; the King reigns; and the world moves toward the moment when every eye shall behold the Son of Man, and every tongue shall confess that Jesus Christ is Lord, to the glory of God the Father.

# 12

# The Question of Authority

From the moment Jesus steps into the waters of the Jordan to the moment He ascends in glory, the story that unfolds cannot be understood merely as the biography of a remarkable rabbi or a gifted prophet. By the time we reach the end of His earthly ministry, history itself has begun to bend around Him. The patterns formed in Israel's Scriptures—the royal promises given to David, the prophetic expectation of a new Moses, the priestly longing for a perfect sacrifice, the suffering foreseen in Isaiah, and the heavenly enthronement envisioned by Daniel—have all converged in a single life. Part II has traced this convergence step by step, moving from promise to fulfillment, from whisper to proclamation, from shadow to the radiant clarity of the risen Christ. Yet even this is not the whole story. The deeds of Jesus reveal the Messiah promised from ancient days, but His deeds alone cannot fully disclose His identity. The greatest mysteries of His person are unveiled not only in what He *does*, but in what He *says*.

The movement of Part II has shown that Jesus fulfils the messianic promises in ways that surpass every expectation. As the Son of David, He embodies kingship not through conquest but compassion, not through force but through healing and deliverance. He restores sight to the blind, frees the oppressed from demonic tyranny, speaks of a kingdom that heals rather than dominates, and enters Jerusalem not on a warhorse but on a donkey, fulfilling Zechariah's vision of a gentle king. His royal authority is unmistakable, yet it is exercised in a manner that reveals the heart of God rather than the ambitions of men. This kingship reaches its paradoxical climax on the cross, where the true King reigns by offering His life for His people.

In Him also the prophetic hopes take on flesh. Jesus emerges as the new Moses who leads a new exodus—not from political slavery but from sin and death. On the mountain He speaks with the authority of the Lawgiver who once thundered from Sinai, declaring, "You have heard that it was said... but I say to you," revealing a law that penetrates beyond actions into the hidden chambers of the heart. In His miracles He reenacts the signs of the exodus—stilling the storm, multiplying bread in the wilderness, casting out demons with a word—each act a declaration that the God who once descended upon Mount Sinai now walks among His people in human form. At the Transfiguration He stands between Moses and Elijah, not as a participant in their revelation but as its fulfillment, the radiant centre toward which the Law and the Prophets have always pointed.

The priestly dimension of His mission shines forth in His approach to the Temple and in the mysteries of the Last Supper. He acts with the authority of one who is not merely reforming Israel's worship but bringing it to its ordained completion. He calls His body the true Temple, offers bread and wine as His own Body and Blood, and declares a new covenant sealed through His sacrifice. The tearing of the Temple veil at His death is more than a sign of judgment; it is the revelation that the barrier between God and humanity has been removed. In His risen Body, humanity enters the sanctuary once closed, and through His ascension He carries that humanity into the presence of the Father. The earthly priesthood finds its perfection in the heavenly High Priest who offers Himself once for all.

The path of the Suffering Servant runs through all of this. In every rejection, every misunderstanding, every betrayal, the words of Isaiah echo: "He was despised and rejected by men; a man of sorrows, and acquainted with grief." The Passion narratives reveal that Jesus did not stumble accidentally into suffering but embraced it knowingly as the vocation given Him by the Father. Every detail corresponds to prophetic expectation—His silence before accusers, His wounds, His bearing the sins of many, His offering of Himself as a ransom. The cross does not interrupt the messianic story; it completes it.

And when He rises, the vision of Daniel finally stands unveiled. The Son of Man receives dominion, glory, and kingship, ascending on the clouds to the Ancient of Days. The resurrection is God's public declaration that Jesus' claims are true, His sacrifice accepted, His identity vindicated. The ascension is His enthronement, the moment in which the kingdom promised by the prophets becomes a living and active reality. The early Church proclaims this truth without hesitation: the crucified Jesus is both Lord and Messiah, the One through whom the world was made and the One through whom the world will be judged. The dominion He receives is not metaphorical but universal, extending over angels and nations, over history and the human heart.

This is where Part II leaves us: standing before a Messiah who fulfils every promise of Israel's Scriptures in deeds that reveal divine authority, divine compassion, and divine purpose. Yet even with all this, the deepest question presses forward: *What does Jesus say about Himself?* For a figure who fulfils prophecy so completely, it is not enough to examine what others said about Him—David, Moses, Isaiah, Daniel, the evangelists, the apostles. The Messiah, if He truly stands at the centre of God's plan, must reveal His own identity. Prophecy can tell us who to expect; fulfillment can show us what He does; but only His own voice can unveil the mystery of who He *is*.

Part III turns to this question with the seriousness it deserves. For Jesus does not speak with the voice of a mere prophet repeating divine oracles. He does not introduce His teachings with the familiar formula of the prophets—"Thus says the Lord." Instead, He speaks in the first person, as the One who possesses authority in Himself. "You have heard that it was said... but I say to you." He forgives sins not in God's name but on His own authority: "Your sins are forgiven." He declares Himself greater than the Temple, greater than Jonah, greater than Solomon. He commands the winds and the sea as their Creator. He identifies Himself with the divine

Wisdom through whom the world was made. He accepts worship that would be idolatrous if offered to any other. And in the Gospel of John, He utters words that echo the very name revealed to Moses at the burning bush—"Before Abraham was, I AM."

These sayings cannot be dismissed as later embellishments or poetic exaggerations. They are the core of the Gospel tradition, the words that provoked both faith and fury, devotion and accusations of blasphemy. When Jesus speaks, He speaks as one who knows that His identity surpasses kingship, prophecy, and priesthood. These roles reveal aspects of who He is, but they do not exhaust the mystery. At the heart of His mission lies a claim far greater: that He stands not only as the fulfilment of messianic prophecy but as the self-revelation of Israel's God. His words do not merely clarify Scripture; they complete it. His voice does not merely echo the prophets; it transcends them.

Thus the shift from Part II to Part III marks a deepening of the book's argument. In Part II we have watched the Messiah act; in Part III we will listen to Him speak. In Part II we saw prophecy fulfilled; in Part III we will witness prophecy interpreted by the One who authored it. In Part II we followed the earthly journey of the Son of David, the new Moses, the High Priest, the Suffering Servant, the enthroned Son of Man; in Part III we will encounter the One who claims equality with the Father, who reveals the divine name, who interprets the Scriptures as their origin and end, and who declares that life itself flows from believing in Him.

The journey now moves from fulfillment to revelation, from history to identity. The Messiah has acted; now the Messiah will speak. And in His words, everything concealed from the beginning of the world—everything toward which the Scriptures have been moving—will be made manifest.

# III

# THE MESSIAH IN HIS OWN WORDS

# 13

# Before Abraham Was, I AM: Jesus' Divine Self-Revelation

The mystery of Jesus' identity does not emerge slowly or accidentally. It presses itself upon the reader from the moment He begins to speak. The prophets had long prepared Israel for a Messiah anointed with the Spirit, a king in David's line, a prophet like Moses, a priest whose sacrifice would reconcile humanity to God, a Servant who would suffer and a Son of Man who would reign. Yet when Jesus finally enters history, His words do something no prophet or king had ever dared. He does not simply point to God. He speaks with the voice of God. He does not describe the divine name; He utters it. He does not merely interpret the law; He authoritatively deepens it. He does not avoid worship; He receives it. And those who heard Him understood the weight of His words with perfect clarity, for they accused Him of the one crime that only a claim to divinity could invite: blasphemy.

Everything turns here. If Jesus had only fulfilled external messianic expectations—royal lineage, prophetic power, priestly action—then one might argue He belonged among the great anointed figures of Israel's past. But when He begins to say, "I AM," the boundaries shift. The question is no longer whether He is the Messiah. The question becomes what kind of Messiah He is. For the Messiah promised by the prophets is not simply an exalted king or eschatological deliverer, but the very presence of God returning to His people. Isaiah had declared, "Say to the cities of Judah, 'Behold your God!'" (Isa 40:9), and Ezekiel had promised that the LORD Himself would come to shepherd His flock (Ezek 34:11–15). Jesus, in the Gospel of John, stands within this prophetic horizon and speaks in a manner that collapses all intermediary categories. He claims what belongs to God alone.

It begins unmistakably in John's Gospel with the divine formula: *egō eimi*—"I AM." When Jesus declares, "Before Abraham was, I AM" (John 8:58), He does not reach for a poetic metaphor. He invokes the Name revealed to Moses in the burning bush, where God said, "I AM WHO I AM" (Exod 3:14). The Greek of the Septuagint renders this as *egō eimi ho ōn*—"I am the One who is." Jesus does not use the fuller phrase, but He lifts the heart of the divine self-identification and places it upon His own lips. Augustine comments on this with absolute clarity: "He did not say, 'Before Abraham was, I was,' but 'I AM,' for in divinity there is no past or future but eternal present." Cyril of Alexandria likewise insists that Christ "appropriates to Himself the divine Name, revealing His natural and eternal being." The reaction of Jesus' opponents confirms the claim. They do not misunderstand Him. They try to stone Him because they understand Him perfectly.

But this is only one moment in a larger pattern. John's Gospel structures its entire narrative around a series of "I AM" declarations that echo the self-revelation of God in Isaiah 40–55, where the LORD repeatedly proclaims, "I AM He" (Isa 43:10), "I, I am the LORD, and besides me there is no saviour" (Isa 43:11), and "I am the first and I am the last" (Isa 44:6). When Jesus says, "I am the light of the world" (John 8:12), He echoes the LORD who is Israel's light (Isa 60:19). When He says, "I am the good shepherd" (John 10:11), He steps directly into the role Ezekiel had said belonged to God alone (Ezek 34:11–16). When He says, "I am the resurrection and the life" (John 11:25), He claims not merely to mediate divine power but to possess it. And when He says, "I am the way, and the truth, and the life" (John 14:6), He does not describe a path; He offers Himself as the living access to the Father.

Second Temple Judaism did not lack exalted figures—angels, the heavenly Son of Man, the pre-existent Wisdom of God—but the consistent witness of these traditions is that whatever mediator one imagines, the Name belongs to God alone. Scholars like Larry Hurtado and Richard Bauckham have shown, through exhaustive analysis, that early Christian worship emerges from the shock of this self-identification. Jesus speaks in ways that place Him within the exclusive identity of the God of Israel. He is not appended to God's identity; He is internal to it. And because He speaks this way, His earliest followers worship Him in ways that Second Temple Jews reserved only for the LORD.

Echoes of Sinai heighten this. In the Sermon on the Mount, Jesus speaks with an authority that transcends Moses. Over and over He says, "You have heard... but I say to you" (Matt 5:21–22, 27–28, 31–32, 33–34). He does not interpret the law as prophets did. He extends it with a divine immediacy. When He claims, "The Son of Man is lord even of the Sabbath" (Mark 2:28), He places Himself above the divine command given in Exodus 20. No prophet in Israel's history had ever positioned himself over the Sabbath. No sage had ever declared mastery over the Mosaic covenant. Yet Jesus speaks as if He is the One who established it. The early Fathers saw this instantly. Origen writes that Christ "speaks as the Lawgiver Himself, not as one who interprets another." Augustine notes that Christ teaches from the mountain "as God had from Sinai, but with greater authority because He perfects what He gave."

His actions align with His words. When He forgives sins, He exercises the unique prerogative of God. In Capernaum, He looks at the paralytic and says, "Your sins are forgiven" (Mark 2:5). The scribes respond exactly as Torah would require: "Who can forgive sins but God alone?" Jesus heals the man precisely to prove the authority of His word. In Luke's account, the same scene ends with the crowd overwhelmed, asking, "Who is this who even forgives sins?" (Luke 7:49). Forgiveness in Scripture is the sovereign action of God—"The LORD, the LORD... forgiving iniquity and transgression and sin" (Exod 34:6–7). The Psalms treat forgiveness as something no creature can bestow. Yet Jesus grants it without appeal, hesitation, or invocation. Hilary of Poitiers summarises the scene: "He forgives with the power of His nature, not with borrowed authority."

Even the Sabbath controversies serve as moments of self-disclosure. When He heals on the Sabbath and declares His authority over it, He transforms the day from external observance to a sign of His own divine rest. His relationship to the Sabbath is not that of a reformer but of its originator. And when He says something greater than the Temple is here (Matt 12:6), He positions His own body as the locus of divine presence. The Temple was the meeting place of God and man. Jesus claims to be that meeting place personally.

What finally crystallises this divine identity is worship. Worship in Israel is the litmus test of divinity. "You shall worship no other god," the LORD had commanded (Exod 34:14). Isaiah declares that God will not share His glory with another (Isa 42:8). Yet Jesus receives worship repeatedly. After He calms the sea, the disciples worship Him, saying, "Truly you are the Son of God" (Matt 14:33). After the resurrection, "they came up and took hold of his feet and worshiped him" (Matt 28:9). The man born blind, healed by Jesus, responds with the simple confession, "Lord, I believe," and "he worshiped him" (John 9:38). Thomas, touching His risen wounds, goes further than any disciple had dared: "My Lord and my God" (John 20:28). Jesus does not rebuke him. He accepts the title.

Gregory of Nazianzus states the obvious conclusion: "If He were not God, He would be a blasphemer in accepting worship. If He is worshipped rightly, He is God by nature." Athanasius affirms the same point: "The apostles did not fall into idolatry, for the One they adored was God." The early Christians worshipped Jesus because His own words left them no alternative. He acted like God, spoke like God, forgave like God, commanded like God, and received honour like God.

Jesus' critics understood these claims with a clarity that modern readers sometimes lack. The Gospels do not depict confused opponents who misheard Him or misread His intentions. They present leaders who grasped His meaning with lucid precision. John records, "This was why the Jews sought all the more to kill him, because... he was even calling God his own Father, making himself equal with God" (John 5:18). Later, when Jesus declares, "I and the Father are one" (John 10:30), His opponents respond, "It is not for a good work that we stone you but for blasphemy, because you, being a man, make yourself God" (John 10:33). The charge mirrors Leviticus 24:16: one who blasphemes the Name should be put to death. They do not misunderstand Him. They recognize that His words imply equality with the God of Israel. The Gospel writers preserve these reactions because they illuminate precisely what His self-revelation meant.

The climax occurs at His trial before the Sanhedrin. When the High Priest confronts Him directly—"Tell us if you are the Christ, the Son of God" (Matt 26:63)—Jesus answers with the most audacious conflation of prophecy in all Scripture: "You will see the Son of Man seated at the right hand of Power and coming on the clouds of heaven" (Matt 26:64). He merges Daniel's vision of the exalted Son of Man (Dan 7:13–14) with Psalm 110's oracle of divine enthronement at God's right hand. No first-century Jew could have missed the implication. The High Priest tears his garments and cries, "He has uttered blasphemy!" (Matt 26:65). Tearing one's robes was a formal response to hearing the divine name profaned. Yet Jesus had not spoken the name Yahweh. He had done something more provocative. He had placed Himself within the very imagery Israel reserved for God alone—riding the clouds, seated in the heavenly court, sharing the authority of the Most High. Tertullian explains that Christ "claimed what Daniel had seen concerning the Son of Man, which belonged to no mere mortal but to one equal with God." The trial scene is therefore not a misunderstanding but a confrontation between Jesus' divine self-revelation and a leadership unwilling to accept its implications.

His claim to pre-existence strengthens the pattern. When He prays, "Father, glorify me in your own presence with the glory which I had with you before the world was made" (John 17:5), He speaks from a horizon no human creature occupies. The glory He describes is not bestowed but shared eternally. John opens his Gospel with this same truth: "In the beginning was the Word, and the Word was with God, and the Word was

God... All things were made through him" (John 1:1–3). The evangelist does not say the Word was created first or exalted later. He places the Word at the origin, alongside the Father, as co-eternal and co-creator. Irenaeus appeals to this as proof that Christ is the visible manifestation of the invisible God, the One who walked with Adam, spoke with Abraham, and wrestled with Jacob. The early Church never entertained the possibility that Jesus' divinity was a later invention. They saw in His own words the revelation of a divine person who had stepped into history.

Even Jewish literature outside Scripture helps illuminate the weight of these claims. Wisdom is depicted as present with God before creation. The Book of Wisdom says, "She is a breath of the power of God... though she is but one, she can do all things" (Wis 7:25, 27). Sirach calls Wisdom "the first-born of creation" (Sir 24:9). Proverbs 8 personifies Wisdom beside God as He forms the world. These texts provided conceptual frameworks within Judaism for divine participation in creation without compromising monotheism. Jesus surpasses these by identifying Himself not as a created or personified attribute of God but as the eternal Word who shares the divine nature.

Daniel's heavenly Son of Man also shaped messianic expectation. This figure receives "dominion and glory and kingdom, that all peoples, nations, and languages should serve him" (Dan 7:14). The term "serve" in Aramaic (*pelach*) is used in Daniel exclusively for the worship of God. No angel or prophet receives such service. The Son of Man rides the clouds, an activity reserved in Scripture for God alone (Ps 68:4; Isa 19:1). When Jesus claims this identity, He claims divine prerogatives grounded in Scripture, not in mythology or political aspiration.

The Gospel of Matthew testifies that even the demons recognized His divine authority. The Gadarene demoniacs cry out, "What have you to do with us, O Son of God? Have you come here to torment us before the time?" (Matt 8:29). Their question presupposes that He holds eschatological authority, the power to judge spiritual beings, a role Isaiah and Daniel ascribe to God alone. The narrative assumes that Jesus occupies the divine position in the cosmic order.

## BEFORE ABRAHAM WAS, I AM: JESUS' DIVINE SELF-REVELATION

This convergence—His authority over Torah, His rewriting of Sabbath, His forgiveness of sins, His acceptance of worship, His claim to pre-existence, His identification with the divine Name, the recognition of His enemies, the confession of His disciples, and the testimony of demon spirits—forms an unbroken chain. Each strand reinforces the others. Jesus does not merely perform wonders; prophets had done that. He does not merely teach wisdom; rabbis had done that. He does not merely speak with authority; kings had done that. He speaks and acts with a divine immediacy that no creature could replicate.

Wherever He stands, He stands as the place where God meets His people. He is the new Temple, not built by hands. He is the new Sinai, where the law is perfected. He is the new burning bush, aflame with divine light yet not consumed. He is the new ladder of Jacob, on whom angels ascend and descend (John 1:51). The Apostles did not invent these images. Jesus gave them the interpretive keys in His own speech.

The weight of Jesus' claims becomes most striking when placed against the backdrop of Israel's uncompromising monotheism. The Shema declares, "Hear, O Israel: The LORD our God, the LORD is one" (Deut 6:4), a creed recited morning and evening by every faithful Jew. The prophets proclaim again and again that there is no god besides the LORD (Isa 45:5). Every attempt in Israel's history to elevate a human figure to divine status is condemned as idolatry. Israel's identity itself is bound to the exclusive worship of the one true God. Yet within the heart of this monotheistic world, Jesus stands and speaks words that force a rethinking not of God's oneness but of the way that oneness is lived and revealed.

This is why early Christian worship astonished the ancient world. They prayed to Jesus, sang hymns to Him, invoked His name in baptism, called upon Him in danger, and offered doxologies through Him. Pliny the Younger, writing around AD 112, describes Christians as gathering before dawn "to sing a hymn to Christ as to a god." This is decades before Nicea, centuries before complex Trinitarian dogma. The devotion emerges directly from Jesus' own self-revelation. Larry Hurtado, summarising decades of research into early Christian worship, repeatedly notes that there is no precedent within Judaism for such treatment of a human figure. The only explanation for this sudden shift is the shock of Jesus' words and the force of His resurrection.

Even Jesus' metaphors carry divine resonance. When He calls Himself the good shepherd, He is not reaching for a comforting pastoral image. Ezekiel 34 promises that the LORD Himself will shepherd His people, rescuing the lost, binding the injured, strengthening the weak. When He claims this identity, He absorbs into Himself the divine prerogative to gather, judge, and save. When He declares Himself the light of the world, He reflects the opening of Genesis, where God speaks light into darkness, and the vision of Isaiah 60, where God Himself becomes Israel's everlasting light. When He claims to be the bread of life, He evokes the manna that came from God alone, not from Moses (John 6:32). In each instance, the point is the same: Jesus steps into the roles that Scripture reserves for God.

The response of the disciples deepens this revelation. They do not simply admire Him. They entrust their entire worldview to His self-disclosure. John calls Him "the Word" who was with God and was God (John 1:1). Paul writes that in Him "the whole fullness of deity dwells bodily" (Col 2:9). He speaks of Christ as existing "in the form of God" but accepting the path of humility "to the point of death, even death on a cross," after which God "highly exalted him" (Phil 2:6–9). Scholars rightly see in this an early Christian hymnic confession, one that predates Paul's letter and reflects the worship of the first generation of believers. It is impossible to imagine any Jew singing such words about a mere human messiah. The language belongs in the sphere of divine identity.

Thomas' confession after the resurrection marks the climax of disciple recognition. Confronted with the risen Jesus, he exclaims, "My Lord and my God!" (John 20:28). These words echo the Psalms, where the psalmist calls upon the LORD as "my God and my Lord" (Ps 35:23). Jesus receives the confession without hesitation. Augustine emphasizes the significance: "If He were not God, He would have corrected Thomas; if He accepts the title, He is true God." This scene is not an anomaly. It is the natural conclusion of the entire Gospel.

Even Jesus' authority over life and death reveals His divine identity. When He stands before the tomb of Lazarus and says, "Lazarus, come out," He commands with a voice that reaches the dead. In the Hebrew Scriptures, only God speaks to the dead and they rise (Deut 32:39; 1 Sam 2:6). When He says, "The hour is coming when the dead will hear the voice of the Son of God, and those who hear will live" (John 5:25), He attributes to Himself the power of resurrection. That same chapter contains one of the most powerful declarations of His equality with the Father: "Whatever the Father does, the Son does likewise" (John 5:19). No prophet, no angel, no anointed king would ever dare to speak this way. The works of God—judgment, resurrection, creation—are His own.

His authority to judge the world is equally decisive. The prophets attribute the final judgment to God alone. Isaiah declares that the LORD is judge of all the earth (Isa 33:22). Joel proclaims that God will gather the nations for judgment (Joel 3:12). Yet Jesus states, "The Father judges no one, but has given all judgment to the Son" (John 5:22). And later, "When the Son of Man comes in his glory... he will separate people one from another as a shepherd separates the sheep from the goats" (Matt 25:31–32). He does not merely participate in divine judgment. He executes it. By placing Himself on the judgment seat of God, He steps fully into the identity of the LORD who judges the earth.

The authority He claims over angels confirms this. Angels minister before the throne of God. They do not obey the commands of men. Yet Jesus speaks of sending forth His angels (Matt 13:41) and returning "with his angels in the glory of his Father" (Matt 16:27). He treats the heavenly hosts as His own. In the Hebrew Bible, YHWH is "the LORD of Hosts," the commander of the angelic armies. Jesus speaks within that same horizon, assuming a role no creature could accept.

In the Gospel of John, His unity with the Father is expressed with breathtaking intimacy. "I and the Father are one," He declares (John 10:30). "He who has seen me has seen the Father" (John 14:9). These are not metaphorical expressions of moral unity or spiritual harmony.

They are ontological statements. Cyril of Alexandria says that Christ "reveals that the Father is in Him by nature, and He in the Father, showing the consubstantiality of their being." Athanasius reads these words as the final and irrefutable testimony of the Son's divinity: "For if the Son were a creature, He could not be one with the Father in essence or operation."

The earliest Christian devotion emerges precisely because this divine identity is both revealed and vindicated in the resurrection. His claims would have been blasphemous if He had died and remained in the tomb. The resurrection functions as God's own affirmation of Jesus' divine identity. Paul says that He "was declared to be Son of God in power... by his resurrection from the dead" (Rom 1:4). The apostles preach the resurrection as the moment when God publicly enthrones Jesus as Lord and Messiah (Acts 2:36). In the Book of Revelation, John sees Him shining with the glory reserved for God alone, saying, "I am the first and the last, and the living one" (Rev 1:17–18), echoing Isaiah's declarations of God's eternal nature.

The divine self-revelation of Jesus reaches its most penetrating depth in the way He places Himself within the story of Israel's God. He does not simply announce the kingdom of God; He embodies it. He does not merely call disciples; He summons them with a voice that echoes God's calling of Abraham, Moses, and the prophets. "Follow me" is not an invitation to a rabbinic circle; it is a command spoken with the same sovereign immediacy with which the LORD called Samuel or sent Isaiah. In each encounter, His authority is not derivative. It flows from His very identity. When He says, "You did not choose me, but I chose you" (John 15:16), He speaks with the initiative that only the Creator possesses.

This divine initiative becomes even clearer in His promise of eternal life. In the Hebrew Scriptures, only God bestows life everlasting. Psalm 36 declares, "With you is the fountain of life" (Ps 36:9). Daniel speaks of the resurrection as the work of God who raises the dead to everlasting life (Dan 12:2). Yet Jesus repeatedly attributes eternal life to His own voice and power. "My sheep hear my voice... I give them eternal life, and they shall never perish" (John 10:27–28). Augustine comments that Jesus does not say, "I will ask the Father to give them life," but rather "I give," revealing His divine prerogative. No prophet ever used such language. Moses mediated a covenant that promised blessings; he did not claim to grant eternal life. Elijah raised the dead by prayer; he did not act as the source of life itself. Jesus stands in a different order.

This is why so many of His words cannot be reduced to moral instruction. They reveal His ontology. When He says, "The Son gives life to whom he will" (John 5:21), He speaks with the same sovereign will attributed to the LORD in Deuteronomy: "I kill and I make alive" (Deut 32:39). When He says, "No one knows the Son except the Father, and no one knows the Father except the Son and anyone to whom the Son chooses to reveal him" (Matt 11:27), He stands at the centre of an exclusive knowledge that no merely human figure could claim. This mutual knowledge between Father and Son is eternal, immediate, and perfect. Origen explains that this saying "opens to us the mystery of His divine origin, for none can know the Father except one who shares His nature." Cyril argues that the text reveals an ontological intimacy in which the Son's knowledge is not learned but natural, "for He is Light from Light."

The same divine prerogative appears in His authority over nature. When Jesus calms the storm with a word (Mark 4:39), the disciples are filled with fear, asking, "Who then is this, that even wind and sea obey him?" (Mark 4:41). The narrative recalls Psalm 107, where the LORD stills the storm and hushes the waves. In the Old Testament, control over nature is a signature of divinity. Job hears God ask, "Who shut in the sea?" (Job 38:8). The psalmist proclaims, "The sea is His, for He made it" (Ps 95:5). Jesus' mastery over creation, executed by His own command, reveals that the authority of the Creator resides in Him.

His authority extends to the realm of the demonic. Throughout the Gospels, the demons recognize His identity before the crowds do. "I know who you are—the Holy One of God" (Mark 1:24). The unclean spirits fall before Him, not as before a prophet, but as before the One whose presence signals their inevitable defeat. When He sends them out, He does not pray for their removal. He commands them directly. In ancient Judaism, exorcism typically relied on invoking the name of God. Jesus invokes no name. He speaks with immediate authority, and the demons obey. The crowds marvel, saying, "He commands even the unclean spirits, and they obey him" (Mark 1:27). Chrysostom notes the distinction: "The prophets cast out demons by calling upon God; Christ casts them out as Lord."

All of this coalesces in the climactic statements where Jesus appropriates the divine prerogatives of judgment. He speaks of Himself as the One who will sit upon the throne of glory, before whom all nations will be gathered (Matt 25:31–32). The verb He uses for the gathering of nations echoes Joel's prophecy of the LORD summoning the nations to the Valley of Jehoshaphat for judgment (Joel 3:12). In Isaiah, it is the LORD who comes with reward and recompense (Isa 40:10). In the Psalms, judgment belongs to God alone. Yet Jesus describes the final judgment as His own act, executed by His authority. He is not a messenger delivering God's verdict. He is the Judge.

In John 12:48, He declares that His word will judge humanity on the last day. No prophet ever claimed that his own words possessed eschatological authority. The prophets said, "Thus says the LORD." Jesus says, "Truly, truly, I say to you." The formula is His own. The authority is His own. Basil the Great remarks that Jesus' repeated "Amen, amen" signals not an appeal to a higher authority but an assertion of His own divine truthfulness.

Even His teaching about prayer reveals His divine consciousness. Prophets prayed to God. Teachers instructed others how to pray. Jesus tells His disciples to pray in His name (John 14:13–14), promising that whatever they ask the Father in His name will be granted. In Jewish tradition, to invoke the name of God was to call upon His presence and power. Jesus allows His own name to function this way, revealing that He shares the divine identity that sanctifies the name invoked in prayer.

This divine identity is also revealed in His claim to send the Spirit. In Joel's prophecy, it is God who pours out the Spirit (Joel 2:28). In Ezekiel, it is the LORD who says, "I will put my Spirit within you" (Ezek 36:27). Yet Jesus declares that He Himself will send the Spirit (John 15:26; 16:7). He breathes upon His disciples and says, "Receive the Holy Spirit" (John

20:22), an act that echoes the divine breath in Genesis 2:7. Athanasius comments that the Son "breathes the Spirit as one who possesses the fullness of deity."

Every thread of Jesus' self-revelation leads to the same conclusion: His words place Him in the very identity of the God of Israel. His actions confirm it. His resurrection vindicates it. The worship of the early Church seals it. The entire narrative of the Gospels is shaped around the unveiling of a divine person walking among His people—not a prophet pointing to God, but God Himself speaking through a human voice, looking through human eyes, loving with a human heart.

The divine identity Jesus claims becomes even clearer when He speaks of His relationship to the Father. No prophet, sage, or rabbi in Israel ever approached God with the intimacy Jesus reveals. He does not speak of the Father as one speaks of a distant sovereign, nor as one speaks of a master whose will must be discerned. He speaks of the Father as the One with whom He shares life itself. "As the Father has life in himself, so he has granted the Son also to have life in himself" (John 5:26). The expression "life in himself" describes the divine attribute of self-existence, the unborrowed, uncreated life that belongs only to God. The Father possessing life in Himself is a given of Jewish monotheism. For Jesus to claim that He also possesses life in Himself is to claim equality with the divine essence. The Fathers read this as a statement of shared nature, not delegated power. Cyril of Alexandria writes that Christ possesses "life in Himself, being by nature God, Light from Light, living with the Father an eternal life."

His prayers reveal this same intimacy. When He lifts His eyes to heaven and speaks of the glory He shared with the Father "before the world was made" (John 17:5), He does not express aspiration but remembrance. He speaks from within an eternal communion that precedes the creation of time. The prayer of John 17 opens a window into the intra-divine life, revealing a relationship of mutual glorification: "All mine are yours, and yours are mine" (John 17:10). No creature could speak these words. A creature can belong to God, but cannot say that what belongs to God belongs to him. Athanasius used these lines against the Arians precisely because they express a unity of nature, not a unity of will alone. Only one who shares the divine essence can claim such mutual possession.

Jesus also reveals His divine identity in His authority to reveal the Father. In Deuteronomy, Moses says that no one can see God and live (Deut 5:24; Exod 33:20). The prophets experienced visions of God's glory, but even Isaiah, seeing the Lord "high and lifted up" (Isa 6:1), understood that he was glimpsing only a mediated manifestation. Yet Jesus declares, "He who has seen me has seen the Father" (John 14:9). This is not metaphor. It is the foundation of Christian revelation: the invisible God has made Himself visible in the face of Christ. As Gregory of Nyssa puts it, the Son is "the radiance of the Father's glory, manifesting in Himself the entire nature of the Father." To see Christ is to behold God incarnate.

This is why the early Church never presented Jesus as a holy man elevated to divine dignity. They proclaimed Him as the eternal Son made flesh, the one who was with the Father from the beginning. When John says, "The Word became flesh and dwelt among us" (John 1:14), he does not mean that a divine being appeared in human disguise. He means that the eternal Word, who was God and with God, entered into human nature without ceasing to be divine. The language echoes the tabernacle imagery of Exodus, where God pitched His tent among His people. Now the Word tabernacles in human flesh. The glory seen in the cloud of the wilderness is now revealed in the humanity of Jesus.

This revelation continues through His authority to impart the Spirit. When He promises the Spirit, He does not speak as a prophet announcing a future gift from God. He speaks as the sender of the Spirit. "When the Counsellor comes, whom I shall send to you from the Father, even the Spirit of truth" (John 15:26). Later, He declares that if He does not go away, the Spirit will not come, "but if I go, I will send him to you" (John 16:7). Only God sends the Spirit. Joel's promise—"I will pour out my Spirit on all flesh" (Joel 2:28)—belongs to the LORD alone. Yet Jesus appropriates this prerogative, acting as the source of the Spirit's mission. When He breathes on the disciples and says, "Receive the Holy Spirit" (John 20:22),

He reenacts the divine breath of Genesis 2:7. The Fathers recognized that this is divine action. Basil writes that the Spirit proceeds from the Father "through the Son," indicating that Christ is the divine mediator of the Spirit's mission.

Everything Jesus says about His authority to command, to forgive, to give life, to judge, and to send the Spirit rests upon a deeper truth: He knows Himself to be the Son in the most absolute sense. His sonship is not metaphorical, symbolic, or merely messianic. It is ontological. He is Son by nature, not adoption. When He speaks of the Father as "my Father," He does so in a unique and exclusive way. He distinguishes His relationship from that of His disciples. "I am ascending to my Father and your Father, to my God and your God" (John 20:17). He does not say "our Father" in a shared sense. He differentiates between His natural sonship and their adoptive one. Augustine comments that by this distinction, Jesus reveals the structure of divine filiation: He is Son by nature; we are sons by grace.

This unique divine sonship appears in passages where He claims absolute unity with the Father's work "My Father is working still, and I am working" (John 5:17). In Jewish tradition, God alone continues to work on the Sabbath by sustaining creation. When Jesus includes Himself in this divine activity, He asserts equality with the divine operation. This is why His opponents respond by seeking to kill Him (John 5:18). They encounter not a reformer of Torah but one who claims the prerogatives of the Creator. The healing of the man at the pool of Bethesda becomes the stage for the revelation of His consubstantiality with the Father. The Fathers repeatedly highlight this. Hilary of Poitiers writes that Christ "claims for Himself the same continuous activity in which the Father is engaged, for He is one with Him in nature."

Even the way Jesus speaks of His obedience reveals divinity. He submits to the Father not as a creature submits to its maker, but as one divine person offers loving obedience to another. His obedience is the manifestation of eternal love, not the sign of inferiority. "I always do what is pleasing to Him" (John 8:29) expresses the harmony of will that exists within the Trinity. The submission He embodies in Gethsemane—"Not my will, but yours be done" (Luke 22:42)—reveals the perfect human obedience of His assumed nature, not a conflict within the divine essence. Cyril of Alexandria explains that in the Incarnation, the Word assumed a human will, and the harmony between the divine and human wills in Christ displays both the fullness of His humanity and the integrity of His divinity.

The culmination of all these themes appears when Jesus declares that He is "the way, the truth, and the life" (John 14:6). He does not claim to show the way, or speak the truth, or grant life. He claims to be these things in His very person. Truth in Scripture is a divine attribute: "The LORD is the true God" (Jer 10:10). Life is a divine prerogative. The way to God is God's own revelation. By placing Himself within these categories, Jesus identifies Himself with the very attributes of God.

His identification with divine truth appears again when He declares, "Before Abraham was, I AM" (John 8:58). This statement is not simply the centrepiece of His self-revelation; it is its apex. Here the veil between heaven and earth grows thin. He does not claim a prophetic role bestowed in time. He claims a mode of existence that transcends time. Abraham belongs to the past; Jesus speaks from eternity. The verb He chooses—*I AM*—is the present tense of divine being. The crowd reacts by taking up stones, for they know exactly what He has done. He has placed Himself within the divine Name revealed in Exodus 3:14, where God says to Moses, "I AM WHO I AM." Augustine writes, "By this He revealed that though He appeared as man, He remained God, for He assumed humanity without losing divinity." Cyril of Alexandria likewise insists that in this moment, Christ "appropriates to Himself the divine mode of being," expressing eternal presence rather than temporal origin.

The response of His opponents confirms the meaning. When Jesus says, "I and the Father are one" (John 10:30), they again take up stones, saying, "You, being a man, make yourself God" (John 10:33). The charge is not that He speaks dangerously or arrogantly but that He speaks divinely. In Israel's tradition, to claim equality with God is blasphemy unless the claim is true. Yet Jesus never retracts His words. He never softens His claims. He never clarifies them in a way that would place Him safely in the category of prophet or sage. Instead, He intensifies them by revealing the works that accompany His identity—works that only God can do.

His authority to raise the dead stands at the centre of these works. When He calls Lazarus from the tomb, the evangelist emphasizes that Jesus speaks as one who commands death itself. "Lazarus, come out!" (John 11:43). In the Hebrew Scriptures, the LORD says, "I kill and I make alive" (Deut 32:39). Hannah declares, "The LORD kills and brings to life" (1 Sam 2:6). The power of life and death is never delegated to angels or prophets; it belongs to God alone. Jesus therefore steps into the divine role not by symbolic gesture but by sovereign command. He speaks and the dead obey. This is why He says earlier, "The hour is coming, and now is, when the dead will hear the voice of the Son of God, and those who hear will live" (John 5:25). He attributes to His own voice the power Isaiah and Ezekiel ascribe to God.

His authority to judge the world deepens this revelation. Judgment in Scripture belongs to God alone. Abraham calls the LORD "the Judge of all the earth" (Gen 18:25). The Psalms describe the LORD coming to judge the world with righteousness (Ps 96:13). Yet Jesus repeatedly places Himself at the centre of the final judgment. He says, "The Father judges no one but has given all judgment to the Son" (John 5:22). He describes the Son of Man coming in glory with His angels and sitting on His glorious throne to separate the nations (Matt 25:31–32). This is the language of divine kingship. Jesus does not say He will announce God's judgment. He says He will execute it. Athanasius argues that this is decisive: "The One who judges all things must be God, for judgment belongs to none but God." If Jesus were not divine, this claim would be intolerable. The fact that He speaks it so plainly reveals the truth of His identity.

Even His authority over angels is telling. In Scripture, the angels serve before the throne of God. They are "mighty ones who do his word" (Ps 103:20). No prophet in Israel commands angels. Yet Jesus speaks of sending them. "The Son of Man will send his angels" (Matt 13:41). He speaks of returning with His angels in the glory of His Father (Matt 16:27). This is the prerogative of the LORD of Hosts, the God who commands the armies of heaven. Jesus assumes this authority as naturally as He walks upon the sea.

His authority to reveal the Father penetrates deeper still. In ancient Judaism, prophets revealed messages from God, but no prophet ever claimed to reveal God Himself by His own essence. Jesus does. "No one knows the Father except the Son and anyone to whom the Son chooses to reveal him" (Matt 11:27). This mutual knowledge is not experiential but essential. The Son knows the Father because He shares the Father's nature. Gregory of Nazianzus writes that this mutual knowledge "belongs to those who are alike in essence and united by nature."

This is why the Incarnation must be understood not as a descent of a divine messenger but as the entrance of the eternal Word into human nature. John's declaration—"The Word became flesh and dwelt among us" (John 1:14)—is not a metaphor. It is a metaphysical statement. The eternal Word, who is God and is with God from the beginning, has taken on human nature. The glory that Moses glimpsed through a cleft in the rock, the glory that filled the tabernacle and later the Temple, is now veiled in the humanity of Christ. The Fathers never tire of this image. Irenaeus says that in Jesus "the invisible becomes visible, the incomprehensible is grasped, the impassible suffers, and the Word becomes man." Gregory of Nyssa speaks of Christ as "the radiant mirror of the Father's glory."

This divine self-revelation is also displayed in Jesus' acceptance of worship. In every instance in Scripture where a creature is mistakenly worshiped—whether an angel or a prophet—the creature rebukes the act. When John bows before an angel in Revelation, the angel responds, "You must not do that! Worship God!" (Rev 22:9). Yet when Jesus is worshiped, He receives the act without hesitation. After He walks on water and calms the storm, "those in the boat worshiped him, saying, 'Truly you are the Son of God'" (Matt 14:33). After the resurrection, "they came up and took hold of his feet and worshiped him" (Matt 28:9). When Thomas touches His wounds, he exclaims, "My Lord and my God!" (John 20:28). Jesus does not correct him. He receives the confession because it speaks the truth about His identity. Gregory of Nazianzus summarizes the point succinctly: "If

Christ were not God, the apostles would be idolaters; if He is worshipped rightly, He is God by nature."

The cumulative weight of Jesus' words and deeds forms a portrait that cannot be reduced to a merely human messiah. He takes upon Himself the Name of God, receives the worship of God, exercises the authority of God, and reveals the presence of God. He does everything the Scriptures say only God can do. And He does these things not as one who has been granted temporary authority but as one who possesses them by nature. He speaks, acts, and loves as God made visible.

The more closely one attends to the pattern of Jesus' speech and action, the more irresistible the conclusion becomes. He does not fit into Israel's categories of prophet, priest, or king—not because He fails to meet them, but because He fills them to overflowing. The prophets spoke in God's name; Jesus speaks in His own. The priests mediated atonement with blood not their own; Jesus offers Himself. The kings of Israel sat upon David's throne; Jesus sits at the right hand of the Father. Every role that Scripture opens, He inhabits with a fullness that stretches beyond human measure. Every image that Scripture offers, He transforms from within. He is not the continuation of Israel's story so much as its centre, the point at which every thread converges into a single, incandescent revelation: Emmanuel—God with us.

This is why His presence generates division even before His cross does. Those who heard Him recognized that His words were weighted with divine authority. They were pierced or offended, enlightened or enraged, not because He broke the law, but because He spoke as its Author. He healed with a touch, forgave with a word, commanded nature with ease, judged with perfect discernment, and restored with tenderness. He revealed the Father because He shared the Father's being. He promised the Spirit because the Spirit proceeds from the Father through Him. He called the weary to Himself, saying, "Come to me... and I will give you rest" (Matt 11:28), echoing the promise of God in Jeremiah: "You will find rest for your souls" (Jer 6:16). In Jesus, the divine voice becomes audible, the divine compassion tangible, the divine glory visible.

This is why the earliest Christian proclamation did not begin with metaphysics but with memory—with the astonished recollection of what they had seen and heard. No one had ever spoken this way. No one had ever acted this way. The fishermen who followed Him were not schooled in philosophical distinctions or theological speculation. They knew the God of Israel from the Scriptures read in the synagogue, from the psalms sung in their childhood, from the feasts that shaped their lives. Yet in Jesus they encountered the very radiance of that God. When they fell at His feet, when they clung to His risen body, when they cried out "Lord," they were not engaging in poetic exaggeration. They were responding to the One whose identity had unveiled itself in word and deed.

Everything Jesus reveals about Himself converges upon a single, inescapable truth: the Messiah of Israel is God in the flesh. Not a second god beside the LORD, not a human raised to divine dignity, not a heavenly mediator distinct from the One God, but the eternal Son, consubstantial with the Father, incarnate for our salvation. This is the heart of the Gospel, the reason the Church worships Him, the reason baptism is given in His name, and the reason His death and resurrection stand at the centre of history.

And yet, the greatest mystery of His self-revelation is not merely that He claims the divine Name, but that He wields it in humility. "The Word became flesh and dwelt among us" (John 1:14) is not only a statement of divine incarnation but of divine condescension. The One who spoke to Moses from the burning bush now speaks through human lips. The One who thundered from Sinai now teaches with a human voice. The One whose glory filled the Temple now walks the dusty roads of Galilee with unassuming gentleness. He does not overwhelm by power; He persuades by love. He does not conquer by force; He draws by truth. Cyril of Jerusalem writes that in Christ, "God stoops to humanity that humanity might be lifted to God."

The culmination of His divine self-revelation is not found in a throne room but on a cross. There, in apparent defeat, His Glory shines brightest. For it is at Golgotha that the divine identity He has unveiled becomes the divine gift He offers. He gives His life as the true Paschal Lamb, the priest offering Himself, the Shepherd laying down His life for the sheep, the Bridegroom embracing His bride through the outpouring of His blood. The cross is not the contradiction of His divinity but its revelation. "When you have lifted up the Son of Man," He says, "then you will know that I AM" (John 8:28). The crucifixion becomes the burning bush of the new covenant—flaming with divine love, yet not consumed.

When He rises, His divine identity stands vindicated. When He ascends, His equality with the Father is openly displayed. When He pours out the Spirit, His lordship over creation is sealed. And when the apostles go forth in His name, healing, teaching, and baptizing, they proclaim not a memory of a great teacher but the living presence of the Lord who reigns at the right hand of God.

# 14

# In All the Scriptures: Jesus as the Key to Prophecy

The first act of Jesus' public ministry is not a miracle or a parable but an interpretation. He stands in the synagogue of Nazareth, takes the scroll of Isaiah, finds the place where the prophet proclaims, "The Spirit of the Lord is upon me, because he has anointed me to preach good news to the poor… to proclaim release to the captives and recovering of sight to the blind, to set at liberty those who are oppressed, to proclaim the acceptable year of the Lord" (Luke 4:18–19; Isa 61:1–2), and having read it, He rolls up the scroll and says, "Today this scripture has been fulfilled in your hearing" (Luke 4:21). With that single word—*today*—He reveals that the Scriptures are not archives of ancient longing but a living witness unfolding in His presence. He does not treat prophecy as a prediction waiting to be matched with an event. He treats it as a revelation whose meaning is unveiled in His person. The one who speaks is the one of whom the prophet spoke. The voice that proclaimed the mission of the anointed one in Isaiah now speaks the same mission in Nazareth because the Spirit who inspired Isaiah rests upon Him.

Even the way He reads Isaiah 61 contains revelation. He stops before the phrase "the day of vengeance of our God" (Isa 61:2). The omission is deliberate. He reveals the divine timetable—not by altering prophecy, but by unveiling its fulfillment in stages. Cyril of Alexandria notes that Christ "reads what pertains to His present economy and withholds what pertains to His glorious return," showing that He is not merely quoting Scripture but interpreting its divine intention. In that moment, Jesus stands not as a commentator on Scripture but as the one to whom Scripture bears witness. Prophecy is not external to Him. It arises from Him. It reaches toward Him. Its meaning is disclosed in His presence.

This becomes even more evident on the road to Emmaus. After the crucifixion, when the disciples walk in sorrow and confusion, Jesus draws near and rebukes them for their slowness of heart to believe "all that the prophets had spoken" (Luke 24:25). Then Luke writes the most important hermeneutical sentence in the New Testament: "Beginning with Moses and all the prophets, he interpreted to them in all the Scriptures the things concerning himself" (24:27). The resurrected Christ does not offer scattered proof texts but reveals the unity of the biblical narrative. Everything written—law, prophets, psalms, histories, wisdom—speaks of Him. He is the thread that binds Genesis to Malachi, the inner logic that turns Israel's diverse literature into a single revelation.

The Fathers return to this scene endlessly. Origen says, "If you understand the Scriptures, you will find everywhere the Word of God speaking of Himself." Augustine writes, "In the Old Testament the New lies hidden; in the New the Old is made manifest." The unity they describe is not an artificial Christian overlay but the very pattern Jesus reveals. He does not treat the Scriptures as a fragmented anthology. He treats them as a single testimony, a symphony whose melodies anticipate and resolve in Him.

When Jesus later appears to His disciples in Jerusalem, He presses the point further. "These are my words which I spoke to you… that everything written about me in the law of Moses, the prophets, and the psalms must be fulfilled" (Luke 24:44). Then Luke writes, "He opened their minds to understand the Scriptures" (24:45). This opening is not intellectual but spiritual—the unveiling of the divine intention that threads through every text. The Scriptures speak because the Word who inspired them stands before them. The voice that once thundered from Sinai now interprets what He Himself gave. The author explains His own book. Every prophecy is illuminated by the presence of the One who fulfills it.

This Christocentric reading is evident throughout His ministry. When He speaks of Jonah, He reveals its typology: "For as Jonah was three days and three nights in the belly of the whale, so will the Son of Man be three days and three nights in the heart of the earth" (Matt 12:40). The story of Jonah is not merely a moral warning but a prophetic sign of resurrection. When He speaks of the bronze serpent raised by Moses, saying, "So must the Son of Man be lifted up" (John 3:14), He reveals the typological depth hidden in Israel's wilderness history. The serpent was a sign of judgment lifted up for healing; the cross will be the place where judgment and healing converge through the exaltation of the Son.

He reads the Psalms the same way. On the cross He cries out, "My God, my God, why have you forsaken me?" (Ps 22:1; Matt 27:46). He does not quote this to express despair. He invokes the entire psalm, which begins in desolation and ends in vindication, proclaiming that the afflicted one will be delivered and the nations will worship the LORD. He identifies Himself as the righteous sufferer of the Psalms whose agony becomes the means of salvation. He cites Psalm 110 to reveal His exalted identity. When He asks, "How is it then that David, inspired by the Spirit, calls him Lord... If David thus calls him Lord, how is he his son?" (Matt 22:43–45), He unveils that the Messiah is not a merely human descendant but the Lord who sits at God's right hand. The Psalm itself says, "The LORD says to my lord: 'Sit at my right hand'" (Ps 110:1). Jesus interprets this not as poetry but as revelation of His divine status.

He draws from Daniel with similar clarity. When He stands before the Sanhedrin and says, "You will see the Son of Man seated at the right hand of Power and coming on the clouds of heaven" (Matt 26:64), He identifies Himself as the heavenly figure of Daniel 7:13–14. This is not typology but direct identification. Daniel saw "one like a son of man" coming with the clouds to receive everlasting dominion. Jesus declares that vision to be His own destiny. His hearers understand this as a divine claim, for cloud-riding is an activity reserved for God in the Hebrew Scriptures (Ps 68:4; Isa 19:1). The prophecy is no longer a distant hope but a present unveiling.

The same pattern appears when Jesus interprets the destruction and restoration of the Temple. When He says, "Destroy this temple, and in three days I will raise it up" (John 2:19), the evangelist explains that "He spoke of the temple of his body" (2:21). This is more than metaphor. Jesus reveals that the Temple itself was a prophecy, and its meaning is fulfilled in His incarnate presence. The Temple was where God dwelt among His people; now God dwells bodily in Him. The sacrifices offered there foreshadow the one sacrifice He will make. The priesthood mediated God's holiness; He embodies it. Thus the Temple's significance is not abolished but consummated. Origen captures this with precision when he calls Christ "the true Temple, the place of God's dwelling among men." Cyril of Jerusalem echoes the same truth, teaching that "what the Temple signified, Christ accomplished."

Even His parables carry prophetic force. When He speaks of the vineyard in Isaiah 5 and applies it to Himself as the beloved Son sent by the owner (Matt 21:33–39), He reveals that Israel's history holds a typological pattern culminating in the rejection of the Son. The parable is not merely moral instruction but the unveiling of prophetic drama. The vineyard is Israel, the servants are the prophets, and the Son is the Messiah whose rejection fulfills the Scriptures. Jesus thus interprets the Old Testament narrative as a unified story moving toward a climactic confrontation with God's own Son.

This Christ-centred reading becomes the foundation of apostolic preaching. When Peter stands before the crowds at Pentecost, he interprets Joel's promise—"I will pour out my spirit on all flesh" (Joel 2:28)—as fulfilled in the resurrection and exaltation of Jesus. He cites Psalm 16 to show that David foresaw the resurrection: "For you will not abandon my soul to Hades, or let your Holy One see corruption" (Ps 16:10). Peter argues that David "foresaw and spoke of the resurrection of the Christ" (Acts 2:31). He then invokes Psalm 110 to proclaim that Jesus has been enthroned at the right hand of God: "The LORD said to my Lord, 'Sit at my right hand'" (Ps 110:1). Peter concludes, "Let all the house of Israel therefore know assuredly that God has made him both Lord and Christ" (Acts 2:36). This is not clever proof-texting. It is the hermeneutic Jesus Himself had given—Scripture understood through the lens of the crucified and risen Messiah.

The same hermeneutic shapes Stephen's final testimony. In Acts 7, he recounts Israel's entire history—not as a disconnected sequence of events but as a typological foreshadowing of Christ. Joseph prefigures the righteous one rejected by his brothers. Moses prefigures the deliverer spurned by the people he comes to save. The Tabernacle and the Temple foreshadow God's presence culminating in Christ. Stephen quotes Moses' words, "God will raise up for you a prophet from your brethren as he raised me up" (Acts 7:37; Deut 18:15), and reveals their fulfillment in Jesus. His speech is the Emmaus lesson expanded: the entire story points to the Righteous One.

Philip's encounter with the Ethiopian eunuch offers the most explicit example. The eunuch is reading Isaiah 53—"He was led as a sheep to the slaughter" (Isa 53:7). He asks Philip, "About whom does the prophet say this?" Philip begins "with this scripture and told him the good news of Jesus" (Acts 8:35). Isaiah's Suffering Servant is not a nation or a collective metaphor but a prophecy of Christ's atoning death. The early Christians did not invent this reading; they received it from Jesus, who had said that the Son of Man must "suffer many things... and be killed, and on the third day be raised" (Luke 9:22). He had explained to the disciples on the Emmaus road that it was "necessary that the Christ should suffer these things and enter into his glory" (Luke 24:26). The apostles therefore read Isaiah not as isolated poetry but as prophecy fulfilled in the crucified Messiah.

This Christological reading is deeply rooted in Jewish interpretive traditions. Second Temple Judaism recognized that Scripture had layers of meaning and that many texts pointed beyond themselves. The Targums often insert messianic themes into passages where the Hebrew text is more veiled. Targum Isaiah 9 reads, "His name has been called from before the Ancient of Days, Wonderful Counsellor, Mighty God," a striking witness to Jewish messianic expectation. The Psalms of Solomon, written a century before Christ, speak of a Davidic king who will purge Jerusalem, gather the nations, and judge with righteousness. Other Jewish writings, like 4 Ezra and 1 Enoch, anticipate a heavenly figure who embodies divine wisdom and executes God's final judgment. These traditions show that Jewish readers expected Scripture to contain deeper, sometimes hidden, revelations about the Messiah. Jesus steps into this world and claims that He is the meaning toward which it all points.

Modern scholars observe that Jesus' hermeneutic cannot be explained merely as rabbinic interpretation. He does not cite competing schools. He does not appeal to tradition. He reveals Scripture's meaning with the authority of the One who authored it. This is why Luke writes that He "opened their minds to understand the Scriptures" (Luke 24:45). The divine author unveils the divine intention. Richard Bauckham notes that the earliest Christian exegesis places Jesus within the unique identity of God, and N.T. Wright argues that the resurrection forced the disciples to reread Israel's entire history in the light of Christ. But this rereading begins not with the apostles but with Jesus Himself. He does not interpret Scripture the way a scholar interprets a text. He interprets it the way an author reveals His work.

The unity Jesus reveals in Scripture becomes unmistakable when He declares that Moses himself wrote of Him. "If you believed Moses, you would believe me, for he wrote of me" (John 5:46). This is not a general affirmation of prophetic anticipation. It is a claim that the Torah—the foundational revelation of Israel—finds its true meaning in Him. Moses spoke of the creation of the world, of the covenant with Abraham, of the deliverance from Egypt, of the giving of the Law, of the building of the Tabernacle, and of the wandering of Israel, yet Jesus insists that all of this bears witness to His identity. The rabbis often spoke of "the secrets of the Torah" and the hidden things waiting to be revealed. Jesus now unveils that secret: the Torah is a portrait of the Messiah, drawn in shadows and symbols, awaiting its substance in Him.

When He speaks of the serpent lifted up in the wilderness, He reveals that the bronze image foreshadowed the cross (John 3:14). When He speaks of the manna, He declares, "I am the bread of life" (John 6:35), identifying Himself as the divine sustenance Israel received in figure. When He offers living water in John 7, He draws from the rock in the wilderness, of which Paul later says, "The Rock was Christ" (1 Cor 10:4). Jesus interprets these events not as disconnected miracles but as prophetic signs of His own mission. Irenaeus captures the heart of it: "In every age, the Word of God was revealing the things that pertained to Himself."

Even the sacrificial system bears this Christocentric meaning. When Jesus institutes the Eucharist, saying, "This is my body which is given for you... this cup is the new covenant in my blood" (Luke 22:19–20), He reveals that the sacrifices of Leviticus, the blood of the covenant at Sinai, and the Day of Atonement rituals all pointed to the offering of His own life. The Lamb of Passover was not a random symbol. It anticipated "the Lamb of God, who takes away the sin of the world" (John 1:29). The sprinkled blood that sealed the covenant in Exodus 24 foreshadowed the blood poured out for many. The high priest entering the Holy of Holies once a year prefigured the true High Priest entering the heavenly sanctuary by His own blood. Jesus does not dismantle the sacrificial system; He reveals its fulfillment. The shadows dissolve as the reality arrives.

This is why the apostles preach with such confidence. They are not inventing a new religion; they are reading Scripture through the mind of Christ. When Peter stands before the crowds after healing the lame man and says that God has fulfilled what "He foretold by the mouth of all the prophets, that his Christ should suffer" (Acts 3:18), he is echoing the Emmaus lesson. He cites Moses' promise of a prophet like himself (Deut 18:15) and says that Jesus is the one Moses spoke of. He invokes Abraham and the covenant promise that through his seed all families of the earth would be blessed (Gen 22:18), and declares that Jesus is that seed (Acts 3:25–26). Peter reads the entire Old Testament as a network of promises converging upon Christ.

## IN ALL THE SCRIPTURES: JESUS AS THE KEY TO PROPHECY

Paul follows the same pattern. In the synagogue of Pisidian Antioch, he interprets Psalm 2—"You are my Son, today I have begotten you" (Ps 2:7)—as fulfilled in the resurrection of Jesus (Acts 13:33). He interprets the promise made to David of "the holy and sure blessings" (Isa 55:3) as finding their meaning in Christ's eternal kingship (Acts 13:34). He turns to Psalm 16—"You will not let your Holy One see corruption" (Ps 16:10)—and argues that David spoke of Christ, not of himself, since David died and was buried. Paul's hermeneutic is not speculative. It arises from the same interpretive horizon Jesus gave the disciples: Scripture speaks of Christ both directly and typologically, in prophecy and in pattern, in promise and in prefigurement.

Philip's encounter with the Ethiopian eunuch stands as the clearest sign of this hermeneutic in action. The eunuch reads from Isaiah 53—"Like a sheep he was led to the slaughter" (Isa 53:7)—and asks, "About whom, I ask you, does the prophet say this?" Philip "began with this scripture and told him the good news of Jesus" (Acts 8:34–35). The apostolic answer is definitive: Isaiah's Suffering Servant is Jesus. Early Christians read the Servant Songs not as vague symbolic poetry but as the revelation of the Messiah's atoning mission. When Jesus taught that the Son of Man must suffer and be rejected and killed (Mark 8:31), He was not imposing a new meaning on Isaiah. He was unveiling the meaning Isaiah had carried all along.

This way of reading Scripture has roots in Jewish interpretive traditions. The Targums often paraphrase biblical texts with explicit messianic references. Targum Isaiah 9 speaks of the Messiah whose name is "from before the Ancient of Days." Targum Jonathan on Genesis 49 interprets the royal sceptre of Judah as belonging to the Messiah. In these translations, the Messiah is embedded in the text even where the Hebrew is more subtle. Jesus steps into this world of layered interpretation and reveals that He is the fulfillment of every layer—literal, symbolic, typological, and eschatological. The apostles embrace this because they have seen the risen Lord, and His resurrection transforms the way Scripture must be read.

The resurrection itself becomes the hermeneutical key. When Jesus rises on the third day, He fulfills not only His own predictions but the patterns embedded in Scripture. The third day becomes a marker of divine intervention. Hosea had declared, "On the third day he will raise us up, that we may live before him" (Hos 6:2). Jonah's three days in the fish becomes a sign. The offering of Isaac on the third day becomes a foreshadowing of resurrection (Gen 22:4). These patterns are not coincidences but prophetic architecture pointing toward Christ. As modern scholars note, the early Christians recognized in the resurrection the unveiling of Scripture's hidden unity. The Christ-event did not alter the meaning of Scripture; it revealed it.

The deepest truth of Jesus' interpretation of Scripture is that He does not stand outside the text. He stands within it as its centre. When He says, "It is they that bear witness to me" (John 5:39), He is not offering a method but revealing an identity. The Scriptures bear witness to Him because He is the Word through whom they were spoken. He is the Wisdom who shaped creation, the voice who called Abraham, the presence who guided Moses, the glory who filled the Temple, the promise who sustained the prophets. He is the key because He is the Author. He interprets because He is the meaning. The Law finds its fulfillment in His teaching, the prophets in His suffering and glory, the Psalms in His kingship and lament, the Temple in His body, and Israel's entire story in His death and resurrection.

The Christ who interprets Scripture does so not by rearranging its meaning but by revealing its heart. Every prophecy, every symbol, every narrative thread converges upon the reality made visible in Him. The promises to Abraham find their fulfillment in the One through whom all nations will be blessed. The exodus becomes the template for the liberation He accomplishes. The wilderness manna anticipates the bread that gives eternal life. The water from the rock foreshadows the Spirit He pours out. The Davidic kingdom foreshadows His everlasting reign. The Temple prefigures His own body. The sacrifices anticipate His offering. The prophets announce His suffering and glory. Scripture is not a scattered mosaic requiring clever assembly; it is a single story whose centre is Christ, and the moment He rises, the story becomes intelligible.

This is why the early Christians read even the creation narratives in the light of Christ. John declares, "All things were made through him" (John 1:3). Paul affirms that "in him all things were created, in heaven and on earth, visible and invisible" (Col 1:16). The Word who speaks creation into existence is the same Word who walks with the disciples after the resurrection. Thus the wisdom literature of Israel, which personifies divine Wisdom as present before creation, finds its fulfillment in the eternal Son. Proverbs says, "When he established the heavens, I was there" (Prov 8:27). Early Christians recognized in this a foreshadowing of the pre-existent Christ. Athanasius saw in Wisdom's eternal presence a testimony to the Son's divine nature, not as a metaphor or creaturely attribute but as the eternal radiance of the Father.

The same unity appears when Jesus speaks of the Scriptures as testifying to Him. He says to the religious leaders, "You search the scriptures because you think that in them you have eternal life; and it is they that bear witness to me" (John 5:39). The issue is not their devotion but their blindness. They approach Scripture as if eternal life were found in the text itself, rather than in the One to whom the text points. The Scriptures bear witness because they are shaped by the Word who will one day take flesh. The Law contains shadows of the realities Christ embodies. The prophets contain anticipations of the glory Christ reveals. The Psalms contain the voice Christ Himself will pray. To search Scripture without encountering Christ is to read a book whose meaning remains veiled.

The veil is removed through the resurrection. When Christ rises, He not only conquers death; He illuminates Scripture. His suffering and glory reveal the logic of God's saving plan. The disciples, who once struggled to understand, find that their hearts burn within them when He opens the Scriptures (Luke 24:32). This burning is not emotional fervour but the awakening of spiritual sight. The entire tradition of Christian biblical interpretation begins here—in the moment when Christ opens the Scriptures and reveals Himself as their fulfillment.

This Christic centre explains the apostolic pattern we see in the New Testament epistles. Paul does not argue that Christ fulfils prophecy in isolated ways. He argues that Christ is the telos—"Christ is the end of the law" (Rom 10:4)—the goal to which the Law was always directing Israel. He interprets Adam as a type of Christ: "For as in Adam all die, so also in Christ shall all be made alive" (1 Cor 15:22). He interprets the exodus event typologically: Israel was "baptized into Moses in the cloud and in the sea" (1 Cor 10:2), a foreshadowing of baptism into Christ. He interprets the festivals as shadows whose substance is in Christ (Col 2:17). Paul's hermeneutic is not innovation but inheritance. He reads Scripture the way Jesus taught him to read it.

The Letter to the Hebrews extends this even further. It reads the entire sacrificial system, the priesthood, the Temple, and the covenant through the lens of Christ's priestly work. The author says that the Law contains "but a shadow of the good things to come instead of the true form of these realities" (Heb 10:1). Christ's offering is the reality; the sacrifices are the shadows. The high priest entering the Holy of Holies each year anticipates Christ entering the heavenly sanctuary "by his own blood, thus securing an eternal redemption" (Heb 9:12). Melchizedek becomes a figure pointing toward Christ's eternal priesthood. The writer is not forcing connections; he is unveiling the meaning embedded in Scripture from the beginning. This is the Emmaus hermeneutic in its most mature form.

The early Christians also inherited Jesus' use of typology. Noah's ark, Peter says, prefigures baptism (1 Pet 3:20–21). The flood becomes not merely a story of judgment but a type of salvation through water. The exodus becomes the pattern for redemption. The Passover lamb becomes the image of Christ's sacrifice: "Christ, our paschal lamb, has been sacrificed" (1 Cor 5:7). The wilderness rock becomes the sign of Christ's presence. These readings are not arbitrary. They are rooted in Jesus' own hermeneutic, which sees the events of Israel's history as signs pointing forward to Him.

The tradition of reading Scripture this way unfolds in the Fathers with magnificent richness. Justin Martyr argues that the Law contains "types of the Christ who was to come." Irenaeus teaches that the Son "recapitulates" all things, gathering the fragments of prophecy into their fulfillment.

## IN ALL THE SCRIPTURES: JESUS AS THE KEY TO PROPHECY

Augustine sees in Scripture a divine pedagogy leading to Christ as its teacher and goal. For them, Christ is not on the margins of Scripture but at its core. To read Scripture without Christ is to miss its meaning; to read Scripture with Christ is to behold its glory.

The more deeply one enters this Christ-centred reading, the clearer it becomes that Jesus is not merely the fulfiller of prophecy; He is the principle by which prophecy becomes intelligible. Without Him, Israel's Scriptures remain an unfinished story, a sequence of anticipations awaiting resolution. With Him, the story finds its unity. The patterns come into focus. The promises gain coherence. What seemed fragmented becomes whole. This explains why the earliest Christian writers insisted that the prophets spoke with one voice, because the Spirit of Christ was in them. Peter says that the prophets were "inquiring what person or time the Spirit of Christ within them was indicating" (1 Pet 1:11). Christ is not retroactively inserted into their words; He was the One inspiring them.

This truth also explains Jesus' relationship to the Psalms. He prays them as His own words because they ultimately speak of Him. When He cites Psalm 22 on the cross—"My God, my God, why hast thou forsaken me?"—He is not merely expressing anguish. He is revealing that David's lament reaches its fullest expression in the suffering of the Messiah. The psalm's later lines—"they have pierced my hands and feet," "they divide my garments among them"—find literal fulfillment in His Passion. Yet the psalm moves toward triumph, ending with the proclamation that "all the ends of the earth shall remember and turn to the LORD." The pattern of suffering moving into glory is the pattern of Christ's mission. The early Christians recognized in the Psalms not only prophetic statements but the inner life of the Messiah laid bare before His appearance.

Jesus extends this interpretive unity even to the figure of Jonah. He says, "Just as Jonah was three days and three nights in the belly of the whale, so will the Son of Man be three days and three nights in the heart of the earth" (Matt 12:40). Jonah becomes a sign not because of his righteousness but because of God's mercy and power manifested through him. The reluctant prophet, swallowed and returned to life, becomes an image of death and resurrection. Jesus declares that this sign reaches its fulfillment in Him, the One who willingly enters death and rises with authority to judge the nations. The Ninevites, who repented at Jonah's preaching, become witnesses against a generation that refuses to acknowledge one greater than Jonah.

In the same way, Jesus interprets the wisdom of Solomon as pointing beyond itself. He says, "Behold, something greater than Solomon is here" (Matt 12:42). If Solomon stands for the height of Israel's wisdom tradition, Jesus claims to surpass that height. This is not self-aggrandizement. It is revelation. The One who speaks is Wisdom incarnate, the eternal Word through whom the world was made. The Queen of Sheba travelled to behold Solomon's wisdom; all nations will come to Christ, in whom "are hid all the treasures of wisdom and knowledge" (Col 2:3). Solomon's splendour foreshadows a glory that cannot fade because it is divine.

Thus Jesus reads kingship, prophecy, wisdom, priesthood, sacrifice, covenant, and judgment as threads woven together in Him. Every office in Israel's life finds its completion in His person. Every symbol finds its substance. Every promise finds its yes. This is why Paul can say, "For all the promises of God find their Yes in him" (2 Cor 1:20). Christ is not the final piece of a puzzle; He is the image into which all the pieces were shaped from the beginning.

This Christic unity is not imposed upon Scripture; it is perceived through the illumination of the Spirit. The same Spirit who inspired the prophets reveals to the disciples the meaning of what they wrote. This is why Paul says that the gospel "was promised beforehand through his prophets in the holy Scriptures" (Rom 1:2). He sees the gospel not as new information but as the unveiling of what was present all along. When the veil is lifted, the unity of Scripture emerges with breathtaking clarity. The Law becomes preparation, the Prophets become proclamation, the Writings become meditation on the mystery soon to be revealed.

The Jewish tradition itself contains the seeds of this unity. The rabbis spoke of the "closed" and "open" meanings of Scripture, the peshat and the deeper sod. They recognized that God, who is unchanging, does not waste words; every detail carries significance. Midrashic interpretation sought to uncover the links between stories, symbols, and themes. Jesus does not reject this tradition; He perfects it. He reveals that the deeper meaning of Scripture is not an idea or principle but a person. The sod of Scripture is the Messiah Himself.

This is why the early Church fathers so confidently proclaimed that Christ is the key to Scripture. Ignatius of Antioch called the cross "the eternal mystery that was kept hidden from the ruler of this age." Irenaeus said that Christ "brings herein all things, both visible and invisible," and that apart from Him "we could not know the Father." Origen wrote that the Scriptures are like a house filled with locked rooms, and Christ holds the key that opens them. Augustine insisted that the Old Testament is revealed in the New, and the New is concealed in the Old. For the Fathers, Christ is not an interpreter standing above Scripture; He is the incarnate meaning of Scripture, the one who makes the story whole.

The more the apostles preach Christ from the Scriptures, the more evident it becomes that this is not a method they devised but a revelation they received. They do not scour the Old Testament looking for scattered predictions to match with isolated events in Jesus' life. They proclaim that the entire narrative, in its breadth and depth, has always been moving toward Him. This is why the earliest Christian proclamation reads the Scriptures not in fragments but in patterns. Adam anticipates Christ. Noah prefigures deliverance through water. Abraham reveals the promise of universal blessing through one seed. Isaac foreshadows the beloved Son placed on the altar. Joseph anticipates the righteous sufferer who is vindicated and becomes the means of life for many. Moses anticipates the liberator who mediates covenant. David anticipates the king whose reign will never end. The prophets anticipate the suffering and glorified Servant. The apocalyptic visions anticipate the Son of Man who receives everlasting dominion. These are not isolated hints. They are the contours of a single story shaped by God to lead His people to the Messiah.

This story reaches its decisive illumination when the risen Christ breathes the Spirit upon the apostles, opening their minds to understand what had been veiled. The same breath that animated creation now animates their understanding. The prophets had spoken under the Spirit's inspiration; the apostles now hear under the Spirit's illumination. The two movements are inseparable. The Scripture that was written through the Word is now interpreted by the Word made flesh. The soil that produced the prophetic voice is the same soil in which the apostolic proclamation takes root. This is why Christian interpretation is always more than an intellectual exercise; it is an act of faith, a participation in the life of the Spirit who reveals Christ.

This Christic illumination extends even to the apocalyptic visions of Daniel and Zechariah. What once appeared cryptic now stands in the clarity of fulfillment. The one "like a son of man" who approaches the Ancient of Days receives His dominion through the resurrection and ascension of Christ. The pierced one of Zechariah becomes manifest on the cross. The shepherd struck becomes the crucified Messiah. The nations streaming to the mountain of the Lord become the nations entering the Church. The prophets did not foresee only events; they foresaw the shape of salvation. Jesus reveals that shape by revealing Himself.

All of this converges in the simple but profound claim made by Jesus in Luke's Gospel: "Everything written about me in the law of Moses and the prophets and the psalms must be fulfilled" (Luke 24:44). The phrase "law, prophets, and psalms" encompasses the entire canon of Israel's Scriptures. Jesus does not isolate specific prophecies; He declares that the entire Scripture speaks of Him. The Law anticipates Him; the Prophets proclaim Him; the Psalms sing of Him. The unity of Scripture is grounded in the unity of God's saving plan, and that plan finds its centre in Christ.

This unity is not merely historical. It becomes the foundation of Christian worship. When the Church gathers, it listens to the Scriptures not as ancient relics but as the living voice of the Spirit revealing Christ. The readings from the Torah, the prophets, and the psalms are proclaimed precisely because they speak of Him. The Gospel is proclaimed because it reveals Him directly. The Eucharist is celebrated as the climax of this revelation, where the Word who spoke in Scripture becomes present in sacrament. The liturgy becomes the place where Scripture's Christ-centred meaning is made visible and tangible. The same Christ who walked with the disciples to Emmaus now walks with His Church, breaking open the Scriptures and breaking the bread so that eyes may be opened.

The Fathers insist again and again that Scripture can only be truly understood through this Christic lens. Athanasius teaches that without Christ, the Old Testament remains a closed book; with Him, it becomes a radiant testimony of God's wisdom. Chrysostom proclaims that the prophets "spoke not of themselves but of Christ who was to come." Cyril of Alexandria argues that the unity of Scripture arises from the unity of the Word who speaks in both Testaments. Augustine summarizes the entire Christian hermeneutic with the words, "The New Testament lies hidden in the Old, and the Old is unveiled in the New." These are not rhetorical statements. They express the living conviction that Christ is the meaning of Scripture, and Scripture is the revelation of Christ.

The deepest beauty of this Christ-centred reading is that it is both vast and intimate. It reveals a divine architecture spanning centuries, covenants, nations, and prophets. Yet it also reveals a God who speaks personally, who bends history toward redemption, who enters His creation to fulfill His word. The Scriptures are not a human attempt to describe God; they are God's unfolding promise to reveal Himself. Every page participates in that revelation. Every story carries a thread of the divine tapestry. Every symbol casts a shadow of the reality to come. When Christ appears, the shadows turn toward the light.

Thus Jesus does not merely interpret Scripture; He brings Scripture to completion. He is the faithful Israel who keeps the covenant, the true Temple where God dwells, the final Prophet who speaks God's word, the eternal King who reigns in justice, the great High Priest who offers Himself, the Lamb whose blood redeems, the Wisdom who orders creation, the Word who speaks life, and the Lord who fulfills all things. He is the centre toward which every line of Scripture bends, the horizon toward which every prophecy looks, and the light by which every mystery becomes clear.

The unity revealed in this Christ-centred reading is not an abstraction but a living reality. Scripture does not merely point toward Christ in theory; it forms hearts capable of recognizing Him. The disciples on the Emmaus road embody this. They walk in sorrow, unable to see the meaning of the events that have unfolded. They know the facts. They know the Scriptures. Yet the meaning eludes them until the risen Christ walks with them, opens the Scriptures, and breaks the bread. Only then do they say, "Did not our hearts burn within us while he talked to us on the road, while he opened to us the Scriptures?" (Luke 24:32). The burning of their hearts is the birth of Christian understanding. It is the moment when the veil is removed and Scripture becomes a living encounter with the One who fulfills it.

That pattern continues in every generation. Understanding the Scriptures is not primarily an intellectual achievement but a grace. The book becomes luminous when the One who inspired it breathes His light upon the reader. This is why the Church reads Scripture in the Spirit. The same Spirit who overshadowed Mary, who descended upon Jesus at His baptism, who drove Him into the wilderness, who raised Him from the dead, and who was poured out at Pentecost, is the Spirit who opens the Scriptures to believers. The written word and the living Word are united through the Spirit, forming a single revelation of God's saving love.

This is also why Scripture cannot be approached as a neutral document. It is covenantal. It demands faith. It shapes a people. The same God who revealed Himself to Abraham, who delivered Israel from Egypt, who spoke through the prophets, and who took flesh in the fullness of time, speaks still through these sacred writings. The Christ who rose and reigns continues to reveal Himself through the text He fulfills. The Scriptures, read in the light of Christ, become the place where the believer encounters the living God. They are not merely words about Him; they are His words to His people.

The early Church grasped this with instinctive certainty. When they proclaimed Christ from the Scriptures, they were not performing clever exegesis. They were continuing the revelation given to them by the risen Lord. They understood that the Messiah is not an isolated figure but the culmination of Israel's entire story. They understood that the Law, the Prophets, and the Writings all converge in Him because He is the Word through whom they came to be. They understood that the resurrection is not a detached miracle but the unveiling of Scripture's deepest promise—that God would act decisively to redeem His people and renew creation.

This is why the apostles preach with such authority. They do not hesitate to declare that Christ is the fulfillment of Moses, the wisdom of Solomon, the true Davidic king, the suffering Servant, the Son of Man, and the priest of the new covenant. They see in His life, death, and resurrection the realization of what Israel had long awaited. The scattered threads of prophecy are drawn together in Him. The shadows of the old covenant yield to the light of the new. The promises whispered in ages past find their yes and amen in the One who is both the Son of David and the Lord of David, both the prophet like Moses and the Word of God, both the Servant who suffers and the Son of Man enthroned.

The Fathers took up this apostolic vision and carried it forward, reading Scripture with the mind of Christ. Justin Martyr saw Christ in the burning bush. Irenaeus saw Him in the recapitulation of Adam's story. Tertullian saw Him in the suffering Servant. Origen saw Him in the mysteries concealed beneath the literal sense. Augustine saw Him in the unity of the Testaments. Cyril saw Him in every prophetic image. Their interpretations differ in style but not in substance. They read Scripture with the certainty that Christ is its centre, its meaning, its fulfillment, and its radiant light.

This Christ-centred reading does not diminish the Old Testament; it reveals its glory. It shows the reader that Israel's Scriptures contain a depth that only God Himself could weave—a story of promise, patience, judgment, mercy, exile, return, sacrifice, glory, and hope. It shows that the God of Israel is faithful, that His word does not return void, and that His promises find consummation in ways that surpass expectation. It shows that the Messiah is not an addendum or interruption but the flowering of a seed planted at the beginning of the world.

To read Scripture with Christ at the centre is to discover that every page is animated by divine purpose. It is to hear the voice that spoke to Moses in the bush, that whispered to Elijah on the mountain, that strengthened the psalmist in distress, that guided the prophets through persecution, and that rose from the grave. It is to encounter the One who was promised, who has come, who has risen, and who will come again.

It is to find, in the Scriptures of Israel, not a closed book but an open door.

# 15

# Vindicated on the Third Day: Resurrection as Fulfilment and Revelation

From the beginning of Israel's story, the question of life beyond death lingered like a distant horizon—present, hinted at, but not yet fully revealed. The patriarchs walked with God, yet the Scriptures speak of them going down to Sheol, the shadowed realm where praise was muted and hope was dim. The Psalms cry from its depths—"For in death there is no remembrance of thee; in Sheol who can give thee praise?" (Ps 6:5). The Hebrew imagination did not begin with philosophical speculation about immortality. It began with covenant: the God who chose Abraham, who swore by His own name, who binds Himself to His people with promises that reach beyond the fragility of flesh. If God is faithful, then His faithfulness must outlast the grave. If His covenant is everlasting, then death cannot be the final master over those who belong to Him.

That conviction grows slowly, like dawn rising over the hills. By the time Israel endures exile and return, a clearer hope begins to appear. Daniel sees a vision of the end: "many of those who sleep in the dust of the earth shall awake, some to everlasting life, and some to shame and everlasting contempt" (Dan 12:2). This is no metaphor. It is the bold declaration that

Israel's God will act with creative power once more, drawing life out of dust just as He did in the beginning. The martyrs of the Maccabean revolt proclaim the same confidence with striking clarity. One tortured brother declares to his captors, "The King of the universe will raise us up to an everlasting renewal of life" (2 Macc 7:9). Another stretches forth his hands and says, "I got these from Heaven, and because of His laws I disdain them, and from Him I hope to get them back again" (2 Macc 7:11). Their words reveal a faith that the Creator is not defeated by death, and that obedience to His covenant opens the path to resurrection.

Even the wisdom tradition begins to discern this hope. The Book of Wisdom proclaims that "the souls of the righteous are in the hand of God… they are at peace" (Wis 3:1–3), and speaks of the righteous shining and running "like sparks through the stubble" (Wis 3:7). Apocalyptic writings amplify this vision with breathtaking imagery. First Enoch describes the dead awaiting vindication in chambers prepared by God. The Dead Sea Scrolls contain the remarkable text 4Q521, which announces that in the days of the Messiah, the dead will be raised. None of this is foreign to Jewish expectation. Rather, it forms a tapestry of hope that the God who created the world will also re-create it.

Yet all these expectations share a crucial feature: they concern the end of time. Resurrection was not imagined as something occurring within history. It belonged to the great day of the Lord, when judgment would be executed, the wicked cast down, and the righteous exalted. It was cosmic, final, climactic. No Jewish group imagined that one solitary man would rise bodily in the middle of history while the world continued on as before. When Martha speaks to Jesus of her brother's death, she expresses the standard belief of her time: "I know that he will rise again in the resurrection at the last day" (John 11:24). Resurrection was future. Resurrection was collective. Resurrection was eschatological.

This is the world into which Jesus begins to speak of His own rising. He does not speak vaguely or symbolically. He predicts His death and resurrection with sober specificity. "The Son of Man must suffer many things… and be killed, and on the third day be raised" (Mark 8:31). He repeats it: "They will kill him; and after he is killed, he will rise on the third day" (Mark 9:31). And again: "They will mock him and spit upon him, and scourge him, and kill him; and after three days he will rise" (Mark 10:34). These predictions are not mere prophecies of vindication. They are declarations that God's eschatological act—the act reserved for the end of the world—will break into the middle of history.

Jesus ties this rising to the deep patterns of Scripture. He gives Jonah as a sign: "For as Jonah was three days and three nights in the belly of the whale, so will the Son of Man be three days and three nights in the heart of the earth" (Matt 12:40). He interprets the Temple in the same light: "Destroy this temple, and in three days I will raise it up" (John 2:19). The evangelist clarifies: "He spoke of the temple of his body" (2:21). Jesus is not merely foretelling His return to life; He is revealing that His resurrection will be the moment when the true Temple is unveiled—the meeting place of God and man, raised in indestructible glory.

The "third day" emerges not simply as a chronological detail but as a biblical motif. Hosea had proclaimed, "After two days he will revive us; on the third day he will raise us up" (Hos 6:2). Abraham had lifted his eyes on the third day and seen the place where he would offer Isaac—the son who is delivered from death by divine intervention (Gen 22:4). The deliverance of Israel in Esther unfolds on the third day (Est 5:1). Jonah emerges from the deep on the third day. Again and again, the third day becomes the day of divine action, the day when God intervenes, the day when despair turns to deliverance.

The early Christians saw this with luminous clarity. Irenaeus, writing in the second century, draws together these threads and sees in them a divine pattern pointing toward the resurrection of Christ. Origen speaks of the third day as the day of revelation, the moment when the hidden things of God come to light. Augustine sees Psalm 16—which declares, "For thou wilt not abandon my soul to Sheol, or let thy holy one see corruption" (Ps 16:10)—as the prophetic announcement that the Messiah would rise before His body could decay. The resurrection is not an anomaly inserted into the story of Israel; it is the climax toward which the story had been bending.

Yet when the resurrection arrives, it does not come as an idea or an interpretation. It comes as a fact. A stone rolled away. Burial cloths lying where a body had been. A tomb that no longer held the dead but testified to the living. All four Gospels, with striking simplicity, describe the empty tomb as the first sign of the new creation breaking into the old. Mary Magdalene arrives "while it was still dark" (John 20:1), echoing the creation darkness before the first light. The women come and find the stone moved, not by human hands but by divine action. The angel announces not a vision, not a metaphor, not a spiritual awakening, but a historical reality: "He is not here; for he has risen" (Matt 28:6).

The earliest objections to this proclamation are themselves testimony to the empty tomb. Matthew records that the chief priests spread the report that "His disciples came by night and stole him away" (Matt 28:13). Such a claim makes sense only if the tomb was known to be empty. The opponents of Christianity never argued that Jesus' body remained where it had been laid. They argued instead about what *happened* to it. That debate, fierce and immediate, is the clearest sign that something had occurred that demanded explanation.

The Gospel narratives about the empty tomb bear the marks of authenticity. Women are the first witnesses—Mary Magdalene above all. In a culture where female testimony held little legal weight, inventing such origins would have been counterproductive. The accounts lack the legendary embellishments typical of later Christian imagination. They retain the awkwardness and surprise of eyewitness memory. The disciples do not expect the resurrection; they are bewildered by it. The tomb is not accompanied by dazzling theological reflection. It is simply empty. Modern scholars note that this starkness—the combination of early attestation, independent sources, and counterproductive details—belongs to history, not legend. The empty tomb stands at the foundation of Christian faith not because the Church preferred it that way, but because it confronted the Church before it had any chance to imagine alternatives.

This is the dawn of the resurrection. Not yet the appearances. Not yet the encounters that will change the world. For now, the world stands before a tomb that no longer contains a dead Messiah. The God of Israel has acted. The third day has arrived. Creation stirs with new life. And history itself begins to turn toward its fulfillment.

Yet the empty tomb, astonishing as it is, does not by itself create faith. It creates questions, wonder, confusion, fear. The decisive movement from bewilderment to proclamation happens only when the risen Jesus appears to His followers. The earliest witness we possess comes not from the Gospels but from Paul, who delivers what is almost universally recognized as a pre-Pauline creed—something he received from the earliest community within a few years of the resurrection itself. "For I delivered to you as of first importance what I also received," he writes, "that Christ died for our sins in accordance with the scriptures, that he was buried, that he was raised on the third day in accordance with the scriptures, and that he appeared to Cephas, then to the twelve" (1 Cor 15:3–5). He continues with an extraordinary litany: Christ appeared to more than five hundred brothers at once, most of whom were still alive when Paul wrote; He appeared to James; then to all the apostles; and "last of all... he appeared also to me" (1 Cor 15:6–8).

This is not poetry. It is testimony. It is the voice of a community convinced that what they had seen—and whom they had seen—was no mere resuscitation, no vision induced by grief, no spiritual metaphor. They saw Him alive. They touched Him. They ate with Him. They heard Him speak in the ways only He spoke. They recognized Him not merely by sight but by presence, by the authority that had once calmed storms and now overcame death itself. Jesus appears not as a ghost nor as a disembodied spirit, but as the same Jesus who died, now transformed in glory. He stands among them and says, "See my hands and my feet, that it is I myself; handle me, and see" (Luke 24:39). He takes fish and eats it before them, not because He needs food but because they need assurance.

The Gospel of John preserves some of the most intimate moments between the risen Christ and His disciples. Mary Magdalene, weeping outside the tomb, mistakes Him for the gardener until He speaks her name—"Mary" (John 20:16). That single word becomes the turning point of her life. It is not a vision she follows in ecstasy; it is a voice she knows. When Jesus appears to Thomas, He invites him to "put your finger here, and see my hands" (John 20:27). Thomas responds not with astonishment alone but with worship: "My Lord and my God!" (20:28). The risen Christ receives this confession, not correcting it, not softening it, but accepting the adoration reserved for Israel's God. In that moment, the resurrection reveals not only the triumph of the Messiah but the identity of the One who stands before them.

These encounters are marked by sobriety rather than spectacle. There are no grand displays of celestial power. No thunder, no cosmic signs. Instead, the risen Jesus walks with disciples on the road, breaks bread at a table, stands on a shore at dawn and prepares breakfast. These are the quiet acts of the same Lord who once healed, taught, forgave, and fed His people. The familiarity of the scenes underscores the reality of His risen presence. The extraordinary arrives clothed in the ordinary, revealing that the new creation is not the abolishment of the old but its transformation.

From the beginning, the Church insisted that these appearances were bodily, tangible, and historical. Ignatius of Antioch, writing in the early second century, declares of Christ: "He was truly nailed in the flesh for our sakes... He truly suffered, as He also truly raised Himself" (Ign. Smyrn. 2). Justin Martyr emphasizes that the apostles saw Him after His resurrection and handled Him as one alive. Irenaeus insists that He rose "in the same flesh in which He suffered, showing the prints of the nails" (Against Heresies 5.7). Tertullian mocks those who reduce the resurrection to spiritual metaphor, arguing that a metaphor cannot eat broiled fish. The early Christian conviction is unanimous: the resurrection was not an idea; it was an encounter with the living Lord.

The historical force of these appearances cannot be overstated. A group of frightened, scattered disciples—many of whom had fled in fear—were transformed practically overnight into bold proclaimers willing to suffer and die for the truth of what they had seen. The shift in their belief is unparalleled in religious history. First-century Jews did not expect an individual to rise from the dead in the middle of time, nor did they expect the Messiah to be crucified, let alone raised. Something happened that rewrote their expectations, reshaped their understanding, and redefined their mission. They encountered Him.

The resurrection also reveals the pattern of Scripture in a way that nothing else could. When Jesus opens the minds of the disciples on the road to Emmaus, He does so not by presenting new information but by showing how the Scriptures already bore witness to Him. He says that it was "necessary that the Christ should suffer these things and enter into his glory" (Luke 24:26). The necessity arises from the divine plan woven into the Law, the Prophets, and the Psalms. The suffering of the Servant in Isaiah, the pierced figure of Zechariah, the righteous man vindicated in the Psalms—all converge in the resurrection as their fulfillment. Psalm 16, which declares that God will not allow His holy one to see corruption, takes on its full meaning only when the Messiah rises before His body can decay. As Peter proclaims, David "foresaw and spoke of the resurrection of the Christ" (Acts 2:31).

The resurrection is therefore both fulfillment and revelation. It fulfills the Scriptures because it accomplishes what the prophets envisioned. It reveals the Scriptures because it shows their inner unity. It fulfills the covenant because it proves God's fidelity to His promises. It reveals the covenant because it shows that God's intentions run deeper than Israel imagined. It fulfills the identity of Jesus as Messiah because it vindicates His mission. It reveals His identity as Son of God because only God can conquer death from within.

But the resurrection does not merely confirm what came before; it inaugurates what will come after. When Jesus rises from the dead on the first day of the week, the evangelists are not merely telling time. They are announcing new creation. John's Gospel begins with "In the beginning," echoing Genesis. It reaches its climax when the new Adam rises in a garden on the first day, reversing the curse of the first Adam. Paul says, "If anyone is in Christ, he is a new creation" (2 Cor 5:17), meaning that the resurrection is not only Christ's transformation but the beginning of ours.

The world itself begins again.

The resurrection is God's definitive declaration that the age to come has broken into the present world. Israel had long awaited the day when God would act with creative power, when He would vindicate the righteous, overthrow death, and renew all things. That hope was projected into the future, toward the last day. Yet when Christ rises, the last day intrudes into time. The hinge of history swings open, and the future begins to reshape the present. The resurrection is not only the reversal of death; it is the arrival of the kingdom. The apostles proclaim it not simply as a miracle but as the inauguration of God's reign in the person of the risen Lord. Peter announces that God has made Jesus "both Lord and Christ" (Acts 2:36). Paul proclaims that He is "declared to be the Son of God in power… by his resurrection from the dead" (Rom 1:4). The resurrection is the moment when Jesus' claims—His authority, His identity, His mission—are ratified by God Himself.

Yet this vindication is not merely forensic; it is relational and covenantal. The God who promised to redeem His people has acted with faithfulness that surpasses expectation. He does not merely restore life; He reveals the life He intends for humanity. The risen Christ does not return to the life He had before. He enters a new mode of existence, transfigured, glorified, and rendered imperishable. Paul calls Him "the first fruits of those who have fallen asleep" (1 Cor 15:20). In Israel's liturgy, the offering of first fruits signalled the arrival of harvest—the beginning of a greater abundance. If Christ is the first fruits, then resurrection is not an exception but a beginning. What has occurred in Him will occur in all who belong to Him, and eventually in creation itself. The resurrection is therefore both personal and cosmic. It reveals who Jesus is, and it reveals what humanity is destined to become.

This is why Paul speaks of Christ as the new Adam. "For as in Adam all die, so also in Christ shall all be made alive" (1 Cor 15:22). Adam's story sets the trajectory of the human race toward death; Christ's story redirects it toward life. The first Adam returns to dust; the last Adam rises from the dust with a glorified body, never to die again. The resurrection thus becomes the axis upon which human destiny turns. Gregory of Nyssa captures this with profound simplicity: "The resurrection is the re-creation of our nature." The defeat of death is not merely the reversal of a curse; it is the restoration of the human vocation. Humanity was created for communion with God, and communion requires life stronger than death. Christ rises to grant that life, not as a private reward but as a gift for all who will enter His new creation.

The resurrection also fulfills the deepest rituals and longings of Israel. The Temple, with its sacrifices and priestly ministry, pointed forward to a moment when sin would be dealt with decisively. Isaiah spoke of a Servant who would be "pierced for our transgressions" and who, after making "himself an offering for sin," would nevertheless "see his offspring" and "prolong his days" (Isa 53:5, 10). The resurrection is the divine confirmation that this sacrifice has been accepted. Death does not hold the One who has offered Himself in perfect obedience and love. He rises bearing wounds that do not bleed because they have completed their work. He is the Lamb standing as though slain—alive and yet marked by the love that conquered death.

The resurrection vindicates His teaching as well. Jesus had spoken with an authority unlike that of any prophet or sage. He forgave sins. He redefined the Sabbath. He claimed the authority to judge the world. He spoke of God as His Father in a unique and intimate way. Such claims demanded divine confirmation. If He had remained in the tomb, His words would have been reduced to the aspirations of a noble teacher betrayed by circumstances. But when He rises, His authority is sealed with divine affirmation. "All authority in heaven and on earth has been given to me" (Matt 28:18) is not poetic flourish; it is the declaration of the enthroned Son of Man of Daniel's vision, who receives dominion from the Ancient of Days. Resurrection is enthronement. Ascension is coronation. The empty tomb is the first sign that the kingdom has come in power.

The resurrection also transforms Israel's Scriptures from a closed narrative to an open revelation. Prophecy becomes transparent, typology luminous, covenantal patterns fulfilled. The psalmist's cry, "The stone which the builders rejected has become the cornerstone" (Ps 118:22), finds startling realization in Christ's triumph over rejection. The righteous sufferer of Psalm 22, who is mocked, pierced, and surrounded by enemies, becomes the risen Lord who proclaims God's glory "in the midst of the congregation." Jonah's emergence from the depths becomes more than an allegory; it becomes a divine sign that anticipates Christ's rising from the realm of death. Hosea's third-day promise becomes a key to understanding why the Messiah rises when He does. The resurrection casts a retroactive light across the whole of Scripture, revealing its unity and purpose with a clarity that had remained hidden until the tomb was emptied.

Yet perhaps the most astonishing dimension of the resurrection is the intimacy with which Jesus engages His disciples afterward. He appears not merely to instruct but to console, to restore, to send. Peter, who had denied Him three times, is given three invitations to love and three commissions to shepherd. The disciples who hid in fear are breathed upon with the Holy Spirit. Those who doubted are granted sight. Those who despaired are granted joy. Jesus rises not to dazzle but to draw near. He is not distant in glory but present in mercy. He reveals that the God who conquers death is the God who calls His friends by name.

The resurrection is therefore not only historical verification of messianic identity but also the revelation of the heart of God. It shows that divine power expresses itself as fidelity, that divine glory expresses itself as love, and that divine victory expresses itself as communion. Christ rises not to escape the world but to redeem it. He rises not to abandon His people but to dwell with them in ways more intimate than before. He rises so that the new creation may begin in Him and spread outward through those who belong to Him.

The resurrection accomplishes what no earthly revolution, no covenant renewal, no prophetic reform could ever achieve: it inaugurates a humanity that death cannot touch. Every covenant in Israel's history fought against death—Abraham's child born from a barren womb, the Passover lamb sparing Israel's firstborn, the Day of Atonement purging the sins that bring death, the promises of the prophets pointing toward a restored people. Yet in every age, death still claimed its due. Saints died. Prophets died. Kings died. Even the righteous went down to Sheol with the same silence that awaited sinners. The resurrection of Christ breaks this pattern not by postponing death, not by explaining it, but by overrunning it from within. Death encounters the Son of God and cannot contain Him.

Athanasius expresses this with crystalline simplicity: "It was by surrendering to death the body which He had taken, as an offering and sacrifice free from every stain, that He forthwith abolished death for His human brethren." Death is undone not from afar but through intimate confrontation. The immortal becomes mortal in order to touch death in its depths, and when divine life enters the grave, the grave collapses. Chrysostom captures this triumph in the exultant cry: "He destroyed death by death." The paradox is not poetic exaggeration; it is metaphysical truth. Death, whose power lies in the corruption of flesh and the separation of soul, is disarmed when incorruptible life enters its domain. It cannot cling to Him because there is nothing in Him that belongs to it.

But the resurrection is not only victory over death; it is revelation of what resurrected life is. The risen Christ is not a return to the conditions of earthly existence. He is not a revived corpse or a resuscitated mortal. He is the same Jesus, recognizable in voice and gesture, yet changed in a way that reveals the future of humanity. His body is glorified, no longer bound by the limitations of space and decay, yet still marked by wounds—the wounds that become, paradoxically, the signs of healing. When He invites Thomas to touch His side, He is not appealing to mere empirical verification. He is revealing that the love which suffered has become the love which glorifies. The wounds remain not as scars of defeat but as the permanent testimony of divine mercy.

Paul speaks of the resurrection body as "spiritual," meaning not immaterial but Spirit-filled, permeated by the divine presence, transfigured by the glory of God. "It is sown a natural body," he says, "it is raised a spiritual body" (1 Cor 15:44). The contrast is not between physical and non-physical but between mortality and immortality, weakness and power, corruption and incorruption. The resurrection is the unveiling of humanity as God intended it to be: radiant with divine life, capable of communion unbroken by sin or suffering, alive with a permanence that reflects the eternity of its Maker. Gregory of Nazianzus describes the risen Christ as the pattern of renewed creation, saying, "What is not assumed is not healed." Christ assumes our mortal nature fully so that He might heal it fully, raising it into glory.

This glory radiates outward into the mission entrusted to His disciples. When Jesus appears to them after His resurrection, He does not merely display His victory; He commissions them to proclaim it. "As the Father has sent me, even so I send you" (John 20:21). The resurrection is not a private vindication but a public proclamation. It is the foundation of the Church's identity. Without it, the disciples would have returned to Galilee defeated, their hopes extinguished. With it, they become heralds of the kingdom, witnesses of the One who conquered death. The Church is not built on teachings alone, nor on memories of a holy man, but on the living presence of Christ, who continues to act, to guide, to shepherd His people.

In the resurrection, Scripture also finds its clarity. The stories of Israel, once rich yet enigmatic, become luminous. The suffering righteous one in Isaiah 53, who is "cut off out of the land of the living" yet who "shall see his offspring" and "prolong his days," now stands revealed in Christ. The vindication promised in Isaiah's Servant Songs is no longer a metaphor but an event. The pierced figure of Zechariah, upon whom Israel will look and mourn, is now the crucified and risen Lord. The Psalms, with their cries of anguish and songs of deliverance, unfold their deepest meaning in Him who prayed them in Gethsemane and fulfilled them on Easter morning. Augustine says that the Psalms are the voice of Christ "singing in the members of His Body." They foreshadowed His Passion and now proclaim His triumph.

The resurrection also reveals the identity of Jesus in a way that no miracle, no teaching, no parable had yet achieved. His authority, which astonished the crowds; His forgiveness of sins, which scandalized the scribes; His claim to judge the nations; His declaration of unity with the

Father; His "I AM" sayings that echoed the divine name—all these come to rest upon the foundation of the resurrection. If He had remained in the tomb, His claims would have collapsed into tragic overreach. But when He rises, the Father vindicates every word He spoke. The resurrection becomes the divine seal upon His identity. As Paul says, He is "designated Son of God in power… by his resurrection from the dead" (Rom 1:4). What He claimed during His earthly ministry is now confirmed in heavenly glory.

This is why the resurrection is inseparable from exaltation. Jesus does not merely return to life; He takes His place at the right hand of the Father. The one raised from the grave is the one enthroned as Lord. The resurrection and ascension form a single movement, the raising up of the Son of Man in fulfillment of Daniel's vision. The one who comes "with the clouds of heaven" to receive dominion is the risen Jesus, whose kingdom shall not be destroyed. The early Christians proclaimed this with boldness. Peter declares that "God has highly exalted Him" (Acts 2:33). Paul proclaims that every knee shall bow to Him (Phil 2:10). John beholds Him in Revelation as "the firstborn of the dead, and the ruler of kings on earth" (Rev 1:5).

Thus the resurrection is not an appendix to the gospel; it is the heart of it. It transforms the cross from tragedy into triumph. It transforms the disciples from fugitives into witnesses. It transforms death from a prison into a passage. It transforms Scripture from promise into fulfillment. It transforms humanity from dust-bound mortality into a destiny of glory. It is the moment when time divides, when hope is reborn, when creation stirs with new life.

The resurrection is also the moment when the Church learns to see the world through the eyes of God. Until this point, even the disciples interpreted reality through the lens of death. Death defined the limits of hope, the trajectory of every story, the meaning of every human life. It was the boundary no wisdom could cross, the silence no prophet could break. But when the risen Christ stands among them, death ceases to be the horizon of existence. Something larger—infinitely larger—has entered the world. The disciples behold not only a man restored to life but the unveiling of the age to come. In His risen body, the future has arrived. Eternal life is no longer a distant promise but a present reality, embodied in the One who stands before them and speaks peace into their fear.

This is why the resurrection becomes the heart of the Church's proclamation from the very beginning. When Peter preaches to the crowds at Pentecost, he does not begin with moral exhortation or philosophical reasoning. He begins with the resurrection. He cites the words of David: "For thou wilt not abandon my soul to Hades, nor let thy Holy One see corruption" (Ps 16:10), and declares that David spoke of Christ. "This Jesus God raised up," he says, "and of that we are all witnesses" (Acts 2:32). The resurrection is the divine act that confirms Jesus as Messiah and Lord. Without it, the cross would be the defeat of a righteous man; with it, the cross becomes the very means by which death is conquered and salvation accomplished.

Paul's proclamation follows the same pattern. He writes to the Corinthians that if Christ has not been raised, then "your faith is futile and you are still in your sins" (1 Cor 15:17). These are not rhetorical words but theological truth. The resurrection is not merely the ratification of Christ's identity; it is the revelation of the efficacy of His sacrifice. If death holds Him, sin still reigns. If death is broken, sin is forgiven. The resurrection is the Father's declaration that Christ's offering has been accepted, that His blood has accomplished what the blood of bulls and goats could never achieve. This is why Hebrews speaks of Christ entering "into heaven itself, now to appear in the presence of God on our behalf" (Heb 9:24). The risen Christ carries not only His glorified humanity but the reconciliation of His people into the presence of the Father.

The resurrection also reorients the Church's understanding of time itself. The Jews of Jesus' day expected resurrection at the end of history. Yet in Jesus, that end arrives within history, transforming the present age from within. Paul speaks of Christians as those "on whom the end of the ages has come" (1 Cor 10:11), not meaning that history has concluded but that the decisive act of God has already taken place. The age to come overlaps with the present age. The future has broken in upon the now. The resurrection is the hinge upon which this cosmic transition turns.

Because of this, the resurrection shapes Christian identity. Believers are not merely forgiven; they are participants in the life of the risen Christ. Paul says, "If we have been united with him in a death like his, we shall certainly be united with him in a resurrection like his" (Rom 6:5). The union is not metaphorical. Baptism plunges the believer into Christ's death so that he may rise into Christ's life. The Christian vocation is therefore resurrection-shaped. It involves not only dying to sin but living in the power of new creation. The risen Christ becomes the pattern of Christian existence, the source of Christian hope, and the destiny of Christian humanity.

This new creation reality extends beyond individuals and touches the whole cosmos. Paul speaks in Romans 8 of creation groaning, "waiting with eager longing for the revealing of the sons of God" (Rom 8:19). Creation itself is enslaved to decay, not by its own will, but by the consequences of human sin. Yet creation awaits redemption because creation's fate is bound to humanity's. When Christ rises, He becomes the firstborn not only from the dead but of the new creation. His glorified body is the first instance of the world to come. What God has done in Him, God intends for the whole universe. Gregory of Nyssa sees this when he writes that in the resurrection Christ begins "the restoration of the nature," meaning that His rising is the seed from which the renewal of all things will grow.

The early Christians perceived this cosmic dimension instinctively. They gathered on the first day of the week, the day after the Sabbath, to celebrate the Eucharist. This was not merely practical scheduling. It was theological. The first day is the day of creation, when God said, "Let there be light." It is also the day of new creation, when the true Light rose from the grave. Sunday becomes the weekly proclamation that the world has begun again. The Church lives in the rhythm of resurrection. Its worship, its sacraments, its morality, its mission—everything flows from the belief that Jesus Christ has conquered death and initiated the restoration of all things.

The resurrection also reveals the truth about judgment. Jesus had said that the Father "has given him authority to execute judgment, because he is the Son of Man" (John 5:27). This authority is now exercised through His risen humanity. The one who judges the world is the one who has borne its sins, entered its death, and risen as its hope. Judgment is no longer the threat of a distant deity but the illumination of human life in the presence of the risen Lord. It is the encounter with truth and love in their highest expression. For those who belong to Him, judgment becomes liberation, the unveiling of their true identity in Christ. For those who resist Him, judgment reveals the tragedy of rejecting the one hope of life.

Yet even in judgment, the resurrection reveals mercy. The risen Christ bears wounds. They are not erased by glory; they are transformed by it. These wounds are the perpetual sign that divine judgment is inseparable from divine love. The hands that will judge the living and the dead are the hands pierced for their salvation. The side that once opened to pour forth blood and water remains open as the fountain of new life. The resurrection reveals not only the justice of God but the tenderness of His compassion.

All of this—the victory over death, the vindication of Jesus, the fulfillment of Scripture, the dawn of new creation, the transformation of humanity, the reordering of time, the illumination of judgment—converges in the simple, astonishing truth proclaimed throughout the New Testament: "Christ is risen." Not metaphorically. Not spiritually. Not symbolically. He is risen in the body, risen in glory, risen as Lord, risen as the firstborn of the dead, risen as the beginning of the world that will never end.

The resurrection also reveals the depth of God's fidelity to His covenant. Israel knew a God who acts in history, who rescues the oppressed, who judges the wicked, who raises up deliverers and restores His people. Yet even the greatest acts of salvation in the Old Testament—Egypt's defeat, the return from exile, the restoration of the Temple—remained partial, provisional, shadows of a greater deliverance yet to come. Death still claimed Abraham. It claimed David. It claimed the prophets. It claimed the righteous and the wicked alike. The promises of God were magnificent, yet their fulfillment required something that no human power could achieve. Only God could conquer death. Only God could raise the dead. Only God could transform the curse of mortality into the path of eternal life. When Christ rises, God declares His covenant irrevocable. What He promised to the fathers—blessing, life, restoration, communion—He now accomplishes in the One who is both Son of David and Son of God.

This fidelity is not only revealed to Israel but extended to the nations. The resurrection enlarges the covenant horizon. Isaiah had spoken of a Servant who would be "a light to the nations, that my salvation may reach to the end of the earth" (Isa 49:6). The risen Christ fulfills this word not merely by revealing the light but by becoming the light in which all humanity may walk. The nations are not spectators of Israel's redemption; they are participants in it. The resurrection transforms the covenant from a particular history into a universal hope. This is why the Church, from the earliest days, proclaims Christ not only in Jerusalem but in Samaria, Antioch, Rome, and beyond. The risen Lord is not the Messiah of one people alone; He is the Savior of the world.

Yet this universal mission begins in the intimacy of resurrection encounters. Jesus does not ascend immediately but remains with His disciples for forty days, teaching them about the kingdom of God. He breaks bread with them. He opens Scripture to them. He breathes peace upon them. These gestures reveal the character of the kingdom He inaugurates. It is not a kingdom of coercion but of communion, not a kingdom of domination but of transformation. The risen Lord draws near in gentleness, forming a people whose lives mirror His own self-giving love. When He tells Mary Magdalene, "Go to my brethren and say to them, I am ascending to my Father and your Father" (John 20:17), He reveals that His resurrection opens a new relationship with God. The Father of Jesus becomes the Father of His disciples. His resurrection is their adoption.

This intimacy becomes the foundation of Christian sacraments. The risen Christ who broke bread at Emmaus continues to break bread in the Eucharist, giving Himself as the sustenance of new creation. The Christ who breathed the Spirit upon His apostles continues to bestow the Spirit in baptism and confirmation. The Christ who forgave Peter continues to forgive sinners through the ministry of reconciliation. The resurrection is not a past event that fades into memory; it is the living power that animates the Church's life. Every sacrament flows from the risen Christ. Every grace participates in His victory. Every Christian life is shaped by His resurrection.

The resurrection also reveals the meaning of suffering. Before it, suffering seemed like the universal contradiction of God's promise: the righteous afflicted, the innocent crushed, the faithful betrayed. With the resurrection, suffering becomes the seed of glory. Christ's own Passion—the humiliation, the rejection, the torture, the death—is transformed into the path by which He enters His kingdom. His wounds are glorified, not erased. His sorrow becomes the wellspring of joy. His obedience unto death becomes the revelation of divine love. The resurrection does not minimize the horror of the cross; it reveals its purpose. It shows that God brings life out of death, redemption out of suffering, victory out of defeat.

This transformation extends to the believer. Paul says, "I have been crucified with Christ; it is no longer I who live, but Christ who lives in me" (Gal 2:20). To belong to Christ is to share in His death so as to share in His life. The Christian is not spared suffering but given the means to transform it. Suffering becomes participation in the redemptive work of Christ, a sharing in His Passion that leads to a share in His resurrection. This is why Paul can speak of knowing "the power of his resurrection" and sharing "his sufferings" (Phil 3:10). The two truths—suffering and resurrection—cannot be separated. The one leads to the other because both are held together in the crucified and risen Lord.

The resurrection thus becomes the interpretive key not only of Scripture but of human life. Without it, existence appears as a cycle of striving, failing, aging, and dying. With it, existence becomes pilgrimage toward glory. The resurrection reveals that God has not abandoned His creation to decay. He intends to heal it, renew it, and draw it into communion with Himself. The world is not drifting toward dissolution but moving toward transformation. The risen Christ is the sign, the guarantee, the first fruit of that transformation. In Him we see not only who God is but what humanity is destined to be.

This is why the resurrection becomes the Christian hope. It is not optimism or sentiment. It is not the denial of suffering or the escape from death. It is confidence grounded in the event that redefined history. "If the Spirit of him who raised Jesus from the dead dwells in you," Paul writes, "he who raised Christ Jesus from the dead will give life to your mortal bodies also" (Rom 8:11). The same Spirit who raised Jesus will raise those who belong to Him. This is not wish but promise. Not imagination but revelation. Not myth but covenant.

The resurrection is the anchor of Christian faith because it is the revelation of God's final word: that death does not have the last word. Life does. Love does. The faithfulness of God does. In the resurrection, the covenant reaches its climax, the Scriptures find their fulfillment, the disciples receive their mission, and the world begins its renewal. The Messiah is vindicated. Humanity is restored. Creation is set on a path toward glory.

The resurrection also reveals the horizon toward which all prophecy has been moving. Israel awaited not only a king, a prophet, or a priest, but the moment when God Himself would act to restore His people. The prophets spoke of a day when God would swallow up death forever, when He would wipe away tears, when He would renew creation. These hopes were not poetic abstractions; they were anchored in the conviction that the God who made the world would not abandon it. Yet the specifics of how He would accomplish this remained veiled. The resurrection removes the veil. It shows that God's definitive act of salvation is not merely an intervention but an incarnation. The One who rises is not a distant deliverer but the very Word who took flesh, dwelt among His people, and entered death on their behalf. The risen Christ is the fulfillment of prophecy because He is the fulfillment of God's own presence among His people.

The resurrection also vindicates the identity Jesus revealed in His words. He had spoken of Himself as the Son who shares the Father's authority, the judge of the living and the dead, the Lord of the Sabbath, the giver of life, the One with the power to forgive sins. These were not claims that could remain in suspense. They demanded a divine verdict. The resurrection is that verdict. It is the Father's confirmation that the one who taught, healed, forgave, and suffered is indeed the One He claimed to be. The resurrection is not merely proof of immortality; it is proof of divinity. "Before Abraham was, I AM" (John 8:58) stands or falls on the resurrection. When Christ rises, the divine name He spoke is sealed with divine action. His identity is vindicated because His mission is fulfilled.

This is why the resurrection becomes the means by which the Church reads the future as well as the past. What happened in Christ becomes the pattern for what will happen in the world. Paul describes Christ as "the firstborn from the dead" (Col 1:18) and "the first fruits" (1 Cor 15:20) of the resurrection that awaits humanity. These are agricultural metaphors, yet they carry cosmic meaning. The first fruits reveal the nature of the coming harvest. The resurrection of Jesus is not a different kind of event than the resurrection of humanity; it is the same kind of event, occurring earlier in Him because He is the Messiah, the head of the new creation. The glory that shines in His risen body is the glory promised to those who belong to Him. The world that begins again in Him will one day be renewed in its entirety. What God has done in Christ, He intends for creation itself.

This truth lies at the heart of Christian hope. Death, which once appeared as the final enemy, becomes the defeated foe awaiting its ultimate destruction. Paul calls death "the last enemy to be destroyed" (1 Cor 15:26), not because its power remains untouched, but because its defeat has already begun in Christ. The resurrection is the pledge that death's reign is ending. The Christian does not hope for escape from the world but for the renewal of the world. The promise of resurrection means that God loves the world He created—not as an idea but as a reality destined for glory. The body is not a shell to be discarded but a temple to be raised. Creation is not a prison to be fled but a sanctuary to be transformed. The resurrection affirms that God's purposes for creation are good, enduring, and victorious.

This is why the resurrection transforms even grief. Christians mourn, yet not as those without hope. They grieve with the knowledge that Christ has gone before them into death and emerged triumphant. They bury their dead in the confidence that what has been sown in weakness will be raised in power, that what has been sown in dishonour will be raised in glory, that what has been sown a natural body will be raised a spiritual body. The grave becomes not a wall but a doorway, not an end but a beginning. The resurrection does not trivialize loss; it transfigures it. It reveals that love is stronger than death because God is stronger than death, and love belongs to Him.

In this light, the resurrection becomes the final and decisive answer to the question of the Messiah. Without it, Jesus remains an extraordinary teacher whose life ended in tragedy. Without it, His death becomes a symbol of suffering but not a source of salvation. Without it, His claims about the kingdom, about the Father, about Himself, dissolve into the silence of the tomb. But with the resurrection—everything changes. His death becomes the sacrifice that reconciles. His cross becomes the throne of the true king. His words become the revelation of God's own voice. His wounds become the fountain of the world's healing. His body becomes the beginning of new creation. The resurrection is not an appendage to the gospel but its heart. It is the moment when the Messiah is revealed, the Scriptures are fulfilled, the covenant is ratified, the Church is born, and the world begins to be made new.

This is why the earliest Christians, facing persecution, ridicule, and death, held to the resurrection with unshakable certainty. They had seen the Lord. They had touched Him. They had eaten with Him. They had watched Him ascend and had received His Spirit. Their faith was not built on speculation but on encounter. Their hope was not grounded in myth but in reality. Their courage was not drawn from philosophy but from the risen Christ who promised, "I am with you always" (Matt 28:20). The resurrection became the centre of their identity because it revealed the centre of God's plan: that humanity is destined not for despair but for glory, not for corruption but for in corruption, not for death but for eternal life in communion with Him.

In the risen Christ, Israel's hope stands fulfilled. In Him, God's promises stand confirmed. In Him, creation's destiny stands revealed. He is the vindicated Messiah, the conqueror of death, the firstborn of the new creation, the radiance of the Father's glory, the living heart of Scripture's prophecy and humanity's redemption. The resurrection proclaims, once and for all, that the God of Israel has acted decisively and forever, and that His Messiah reigns.

# 16

# A Sword That Divides

The moment Jesus speaks His own name into Israel's hearing, the story crosses a threshold from expectation into judgment. The prophets had spoken in fragments, announcing what God would do when He returned to His people. Jesus does not announce that return as imminent; He speaks as the One in whom it has already arrived. The divine Name once revealed to Moses from the fire now passes the lips of a Galilean teacher, not as quotation but as self-identification. Authority over sin, Sabbath, and Temple is not claimed by appeal to higher sanction but exercised as native right. Worship is neither deflected nor corrected. Scripture is not revised but gathered, drawn inward, and brought to rest in a single human life. Revelation, at this point, has reached its fullness.

The resurrection seals this fullness with divine finality. It is not merely a miracle granted to a righteous man, nor a symbol of hope granted to grieving disciples. It is God's public verdict on Jesus' identity. The God who raised Him thereby confirms that the claims spoken in His earthly ministry were not presumption but truth. The resurrection is thus not an appendix to the messianic claim but its decisive confirmation. If Jesus had spoken falsely, the grave would have silenced Him. Instead, the grave yields. Scripture, read backward from Easter morning, does not dissolve into allegory; it sharpens. What Moses hinted, what David sang, what Isaiah saw dimly, now stands embodied and vindicated.

Yet Scripture has always taught that the fullness of revelation does not produce uniform recognition. When God speaks with clarity, division follows. Isaiah was warned from the outset that his prophetic mission would harden as much as it healed: eyes would see yet not perceive, ears would hear yet not understand. Jesus does not distance Himself from this pattern; He claims it. He speaks openly of a people whose hearts have grown dull, not because the message is obscure, but because judgment accompanies revelation. John states the consequence without qualification: many could not believe, because the word of Isaiah was being fulfilled in them. Paul later names the same reality as hardness, a veil lying over the reading of Moses when Christ is not seen.

This hardness is not sociological confusion or cultural inertia. It is covenantal judgment. Israel had been given the Law, the promises, the worship, and the prophets. The coming of the Messiah does not reset this history; it brings it to account. Jesus' ministry unfolds as a final visitation, a moment of decision in which acceptance and refusal carry irreversible weight. His lament over Jerusalem is not sentimental grief but prophetic announcement. He weeps precisely because judgment is now inevitable. The city that stones the prophets will soon fall, and Jesus names the reason with precision: the time of visitation was not recognized.

The Temple stands at the centre of this reckoning. Jesus prophesies its destruction repeatedly, not as a speculative warning but as an inevitable consequence. Not one stone will remain upon another. The house will be left desolate. These words echo Jeremiah's warnings before the first Temple fell, placing Jesus unmistakably within the prophetic tradition of covenant judgment. When Jerusalem is destroyed in AD 70, the event does not stand apart from Jesus' ministry; it stands within it as fulfillment. The God who once withdrew His glory from Solomon's Temple now allows the second Temple to fall after the true dwelling of His presence has been rejected.

This judgment does not negate Israel's Scriptures; it confirms their logic. Election has always carried responsibility, and responsibility has always carried consequence. Israel's history already bore the scars of exile and return. The rejection of the Messiah stands within that same tragic continuity. The God of Israel is faithful, but His faithfulness is not permissive. He warns before He judges, and He judges in order to preserve the truth of His covenant. Hardness, in this light, is not arbitrary punishment but the exposure of a refusal already present.

At the same time, Scripture refuses the conclusion that judgment exhausts God's purpose. The same apostle who speaks of hardness with anguish insists that it is partial and ordered toward a mystery not yet complete. God has not rejected His people. The covenant made with the patriarchs has not been revoked. Judgment does not erase election; it disciplines it. A remnant remains, and the promises continue to press forward toward a future still held within God's faithfulness. Severity and mercy stand together, not as competing impulses, but as aspects of the same divine holiness.

What emerges at this point is not resolution but conflict. Revelation has been given. Judgment has followed. The messianic claim now stands exposed in history, and the objections rise not from ignorance but from covenant loyalty. Questions of genealogy, suffering, Torah, kingship, and national restoration do not arise from pagan scepticism. They arise from Scripture itself, read with seriousness and fear of error. Israel does not reject Jesus because it has abandoned the Law, but because it seeks to defend it. The scandal lies precisely here: that the Messiah fulfills the Scriptures in a way that overturns settled expectation without violating covenant truth.

The story therefore moves from proclamation to contest. The issue is no longer whether Jesus has revealed Himself, but whether Israel's objections can stand before the full witness of Scripture. The battlefield is now clearly drawn. Revelation has spoken. Judgment has fallen. The objections must be named, weighed, and answered from within the same sacred texts that first gave birth to hope.

The objections that arise at this point do not belong to the margins of Israel's faith; they emerge from its centre. They are shaped by centuries of covenantal discipline, by a people trained to test spirits, weigh claims, and guard the holiness of the Name. Israel had learned, through bitter experience, that false deliverers multiply in times of suffering. Fidelity demanded discernment. Any claim that the God who spoke at Sinai had now acted definitively in a single human life had to withstand the full pressure of Scripture, tradition, and national memory. The resistance to Jesus therefore cannot be reduced to ignorance or malice. It is the resistance of a people who know that God is holy and that His promises are not to be handled lightly.

Genealogy becomes a fault line because the promises were not abstract. The Messiah was to arise from David's house, anchored in Israel's flesh-and-blood history. Claims of descent mattered because covenant fidelity had always moved through lineage. Suffering becomes an even sharper offense. The Law spoke of blessing for obedience and curse for disobedience, and Israel's collective memory had been formed by exile as punishment for covenant failure. A Messiah executed by Gentile power, displayed publicly under the sign of curse, appeared to contradict the very grammar of redemption. Kingship itself posed another stumbling block. The prophets spoke of peace, justice, and restoration, yet Rome remained in power and Israel's wounds remained open. A kingdom that announced itself without immediate political deliverance seemed incomplete, even suspect.

Torah observance sharpened the conflict further. Israel's vocation among the nations depended upon fidelity to the Law. Sabbath, purity, and boundary markers were not arbitrary regulations but signs of belonging to the covenant. Jesus' authority over Sabbath, His freedom in relation to purity laws, and His association with sinners did not look, at first glance, like fulfillment but transgression. Even when His teaching intensified the Law rather than relaxed it, the manner in which He spoke—"but I say to you"—placed Him in a position no prophet had occupied. The question was unavoidable: by what authority does He speak in God's place?

These objections are not evasions; they are serious theological claims. Scripture itself had taught Israel to expect fidelity, holiness, and visible blessing. To accept Jesus required a reconfiguration of expectation so profound that it felt, to many, like betrayal rather than obedience. The cross, in particular, condensed every objection into a single scandal. The Messiah was expected to defeat Israel's enemies, not submit to them. The servant songs of Isaiah had spoken of suffering, but how that suffering related to kingship remained unresolved. To many, the crucifixion did not illuminate Scripture; it contradicted it.

And yet Scripture itself insists that this contradiction belongs to God's way of acting. Joseph is rejected by his brothers before becoming the instrument of their salvation. Moses is opposed by his own people before leading them out of bondage. David is hunted before he is enthroned. The prophets are persecuted before they are vindicated. The pattern is not incidental; it is constitutive. God's chosen servants pass through rejection before recognition, humiliation before glory. What distinguishes Jesus is not the pattern itself but its depth. The suffering borne by the Messiah is not only representative; it is redemptive. The rejection He endures is not merely human resistance; it becomes the place where judgment and mercy meet.

This pattern does not excuse hardness of heart; it exposes it. Scripture never portrays rejection as neutral. Those who resist God's servants are held accountable, even when their resistance arises from fear of error. The same Scriptures that explain why rejection occurs also declare its cost. Jerusalem's fall is not an abstraction. It is the concrete consequence of refusing God's visitation. Yet judgment does not exhaust the story. The prophets had already taught that judgment purifies rather than annihilates, that exile precedes restoration, and that God preserves a remnant through whom His promises endure.

Here the argument turns decisively. The revelation given in Jesus is complete. The resurrection has rendered God's verdict. Judgment has fallen, as foretold. What remains is not speculation but discernment. The objections must now be examined not sentimentally but scripturally. They must be allowed their full force, and then measured against the whole counsel of God. Christianity does not evade these objections; it enters them. It does not dismiss Israel's expectations; it argues that those expectations find their true coherence only in the Messiah who suffered, rose, and reigns.

The conflict that now unfolds is therefore not between faith and unbelief in the abstract, but between competing readings of Israel's own Scriptures. The question is not whether God is faithful, but how His faithfulness is revealed. The coming chapters will stand within this contested space, taking each objection seriously and answering it from within the covenant logic that first gave rise to hope. The Messiah has been revealed and rejected. The reasons for that rejection must now be faced, not to diminish Israel's story, but to show that the one who was refused is the very one Israel's God promised from the beginning.

# IV

# THE MESSIAH REJECTED AND RECOGNISED

# 17

# The Messianic Hope of Second Temple Judaism

The world into which Jesus was born was not religiously neutral, nor was it spiritually complacent. It was charged with memory, burdened by history, and animated by expectation. Israel in the centuries before Christ lived with the accumulated weight of promises that had not yet found their fulfilment. The exile had ended, yet restoration remained incomplete. The Temple stood again in Jerusalem, but the glory that once filled it had not returned in the way the prophets had envisioned. Foreign powers still ruled the land promised to Abraham, and the people of the covenant continued to live under the shadow of empires not their own. This unresolved condition created a spiritual tension that pressed relentlessly toward the future. The Scriptures had spoken of deliverance, kingship, renewal, and divine intervention. History, however, seemed to hesitate, as though waiting for a decisive act of God that had not yet arrived.

Second Temple Judaism emerged within this tension. The period stretching from the Persian restoration through Greek domination and into Roman occupation was not merely a political backdrop; it was a crucible in which Israel's messianic hope was refined, intensified, and diversified. Under Persian rule, the return from exile brought hope tempered by disappointment. The rebuilt Temple lacked the splendour of Solomon's, and the Davidic monarchy was not restored. Prophetic voices such as Haggai and Zechariah spoke of future glory, yet the present remained marked by fragility and dependence. The covenant had been renewed, but its promises seemed suspended between memory and anticipation.

Greek domination deepened this unease. Hellenisation confronted Israel with a cultural and philosophical world alien to its covenantal identity. The crisis reached its breaking point under Antiochus IV Epiphanes, whose desecration of the Temple provoked the Maccabean revolt. This period seared into Israel's consciousness the conviction that fidelity to the law and loyalty to God might demand resistance, suffering, and even martyrdom. Texts such as Daniel, written or received anew in this context, interpreted history apocalyptically, portraying the rise and fall of empires as part of a divine drama moving inexorably toward God's final intervention. The kingdom of God was no longer imagined simply as a restored monarchy but as a dominion that would shatter the kingdoms of the world and endure forever (Dan 2:44; 7:13–14).

Roman occupation intensified these hopes further. Rome's presence was both stabilising and humiliating. It allowed the Temple cult to function, yet it stripped Israel of sovereignty. Kingship existed only as parody, embodied in client rulers such as Herod the Great, whose reign was marked by brutality and insecurity rather than covenant fidelity. Taxes were paid to Caesar, Roman standards entered the land, and crucifixions lined the roads as grim reminders of imperial power. Against this backdrop, messianic expectation was not an abstract doctrine but a lived longing. To ask about the Messiah was to ask about the meaning of Israel's suffering and the faithfulness of God to His promises.

Scripture was the engine that drove this expectation. The Hebrew Scriptures were not read as relics of a closed past but as living words whose full meaning was still unfolding. Prophetic texts were revisited, reinterpreted, and applied to new circumstances. Daniel's visions were read alongside Isaiah's promises of a renewed creation and the Psalms' proclamations of divine kingship. The Scriptures formed a coherent narrative in which Israel's present distress was understood as a prelude to divine action. The messianic hope of this period was therefore profoundly textual. It arose not from speculation but from sustained engagement with the words that Israel believed God Himself had spoken.

This scriptural engagement did not produce uniform conclusions. On the contrary, the richness of the biblical witness generated a plurality of expectations. The prophets spoke of a Davidic ruler who would establish justice and peace (Isa 11:1–9; Jer 23:5–6). The Psalms celebrated a king who was called God's son and promised dominion over the nations (Ps 2; 72; 110). Deuteronomy held out the promise of a prophet like Moses who would speak with divine authority (Deut 18:15–19). Apocalyptic texts envisioned a heavenly figure, "one like a son of man," who would receive everlasting dominion from God Himself (Dan 7:13–14). These images were not mutually exclusive within Scripture, but neither were they easily harmonised.

As a result, messianic hope in Second Temple Judaism became diversified rather than diluted. Different communities emphasised different strands of the biblical witness, often shaped by their own historical experiences and theological priorities. Some looked primarily for a royal Messiah, a son of David who would restore Israel's sovereignty and defeat her enemies. Others anticipated a priestly figure who would purify worship, renew the covenant, and restore the holiness of the Temple. Still others focused on a prophetic redeemer, a teacher endowed with divine wisdom who would reveal God's will with clarity and authority. Apocalyptic circles, drawing on Daniel and related literature, expected a transcendent agent of divine judgment who would bring history itself to its appointed end.

The Dead Sea Scrolls provide a striking window into this diversity. The Qumran community, shaped by a profound dissatisfaction with the Jerusalem priesthood, anticipated not one but two Messiahs: a priestly Messiah of Aaron and a royal Messiah of Israel. Their writings reflect a conviction that the fullness of God's plan required both purification and kingship, both cultic renewal and political restoration. Elsewhere, texts such as the Psalms of Solomon portray a fervently Davidic hope, envisioning a righteous king who would purge Jerusalem of foreign influence and rule in accordance with God's law. Apocalyptic literature like 1 Enoch develops the figure of the Son of Man as a pre-existent, heavenly agent of judgment and salvation, further expanding the range of messianic imagination.

What unites these varied expectations is not uniformity but intensity. Israel was waiting. The question was not whether God would act, but how and through whom. The Messiah was expected to be recognisably rooted in Israel's Scriptures, yet capable of addressing the unprecedented challenges of the present. This combination of fidelity and anticipation created an environment in which recognition and rejection of a messianic claimant were both possible, even likely. A figure who embodied one strand of expectation while redefining another could attract devotion from some and opposition from others, all within the shared framework of covenant faithfulness.

By the first century, then, messianic hope had become both focused and fractured. It was focused in its conviction that God's promises were nearing fulfilment, fractured in its interpretations of what that fulfilment would entail. Jesus of Nazareth would enter precisely this world: a world saturated with Scripture, shaped by suffering, and alive with expectation. Understanding this context does not resolve the question of His identity, but it clarifies why His appearance would provoke such sharply divided responses. Recognition and rejection emerge not as anomalies but as the natural outcome of a hope that was at once unified in longing and divided in vision.

Expectation did not remain an abstract idea within this world; it organised lives, shaped communities, and determined how Scripture itself was read. The Second Temple period witnessed not merely an increase in messianic language, but a sharpening of interpretive habits that sought to discern where history stood within God's unfolding plan. Scripture was approached as a map of the present and a key to the future. Passages that once spoke broadly of God's kingship or Israel's vocation were now read with heightened specificity. Timelines were calculated, symbols decoded, and prophecies aligned with contemporary events. The sense that Israel was living on the edge of fulfilment intensified the urgency with which the sacred texts were studied.

This urgency was particularly evident in apocalyptic interpretation. Daniel's visions of successive empires, culminating in divine intervention, were no longer confined to the distant past. They were read as living commentary on Persian, Greek, and Roman rule. The "fourth kingdom" was identified, debated, feared. The Son of Man figure, who receives dominion from the Ancient of Days, became a focal point of hope for those who believed that God's answer to imperial domination would be decisive and cosmic rather than incremental. In these readings, messianic expectation expanded beyond national restoration toward the renewal of creation itself. Judgment and salvation were bound together. God would not merely rescue Israel; He would set the world right.

Alongside apocalyptic readings, the covenantal and legal traditions of Israel also generated messianic hope. Deuteronomy's promise of a prophet like Moses was not forgotten. In a period marked by disputed authority and competing interpretations of the law, the prospect of a divinely authorised teacher carried immense weight. Such a figure would not only interpret Torah correctly but embody it, restoring unity to a fractured people. This expectation was not speculative. It emerged from the recognition that Israel's fidelity to the covenant had been repeatedly compromised, and that only divine initiative could heal the breach. The Messiah, in this sense, was expected to be an agent of internal renewal as much as external deliverance.

The Temple occupied a central place in this hope. Even when political power was lost, the Temple remained the heart of Israel's religious life, the visible sign that God dwelt among His people. Its rituals structured time, its sacrifices addressed sin, and its festivals rehearsed Israel's foundational story. Yet the Temple also became a site of anxiety. Prophetic critiques of corrupt worship were reread with fresh intensity. Questions arose about the legitimacy of the priesthood, the adequacy of sacrifice, and the permanence of the Temple itself. Some groups withdrew in protest, seeking purity apart from Jerusalem. Others clung more fiercely to the cult, convinced that restoration depended on fidelity to its rites. In both cases, messianic hope was intertwined with the fate of the Temple. A restored Israel required purified worship; a purified Temple required divine intervention.

The diversity of expectations did not imply relativism or confusion. It reflected the breadth of Scripture itself. The Hebrew Bible does not present a single, flat portrait of redemption. It speaks through narrative, law, poetry, prophecy, and vision. Each genre contributes to Israel's understanding of God's purposes, and each leaves room for anticipation. The Messiah, therefore, was never expected to be a simplistic figure. He would have to stand at the intersection of multiple roles: king and servant, prophet and priest, judge and healer. The difficulty lay not in recognising these roles individually, but in imagining how they might be unified.

Later Jewish reflection would articulate this difficulty through the distinction between Messiah ben David and Messiah ben Joseph. Although these formulations crystallise in rabbinic literature after the destruction of the Temple, they give voice to an earlier problem already implicit in the Scriptures. Some texts speak of a victorious, reigning Messiah; others of a suffering, rejected figure. Rather than forcing these strands together, later tradition separated them into two messianic roles. One would suffer and die; the other would triumph and reign. This conceptual move acknowledges the tension without resolving it. It preserves the integrity of the texts, even as it postpones their unification.

The existence of such interpretive strategies underscores a crucial point: Jewish difficulty with a suffering Messiah did not arise from ignorance of Scripture, but from fidelity to it. The problem was not that Isaiah 53 or Psalm 22 were unknown, but that their integration into a single messianic identity posed a theological challenge. The expectation of suffering was present, but it was not easily reconciled with expectations of sovereignty and glory. The Messiah was awaited as the one who would heal Israel's wounds, not as one who would bear them. That suffering might be redemptive rather than disqualifying was an insight that required a hermeneutical key not yet possessed.

Sectarian life in this period further shaped how messianic hope was lived. The Pharisees, committed to the study and observance of Torah, emphasised covenant fidelity and anticipated a future in which obedience would be vindicated. The Sadducees, aligned with the Temple establishment, focused on cultic continuity and stability, showing less interest in apocalyptic speculation. The Essenes withdrew from what they perceived as a corrupted society, awaiting divine intervention that would vindicate their purity and expose the wicked. Zealot movements, though diverse, tended toward a more immediate and political understanding of deliverance, viewing armed resistance as participation in God's plan.

Each of these groups drew upon Scripture, yet each read it through a distinct lens. Their differences did not negate the messianic hope; they testified to its vitality. Israel was not indifferent to the future. She was actively interpreting it. The Messiah was not a marginal figure in this world; he was the centre of gravity around which theology, politics, and worship revolved. To speak of messianic hope in Second Temple Judaism is therefore to speak of a living, contested, and deeply serious engagement with God's promises.

This context is essential for understanding what follows. When Jesus appears, proclaiming the kingdom of God, healing the sick, forgiving sins, and challenging established authorities, He does not step into a vacuum. He enters a field already charged with expectation. His words and deeds inevitably evoke scriptural associations. They resonate with some hopes and disrupt others. Recognition and resistance emerge not as accidents but as responses shaped by Scripture itself. The messianic hope of Second Temple Judaism was sufficiently rich to make faith in Jesus possible, and sufficiently complex to make rejection intelligible.

Yet for all its diversity, this world of expectation shared a common conviction: God had not finished with Israel. The covenant was not a relic of the past but a living promise pressing toward fulfilment. This conviction sustained Israel through domination and disappointment, and it shaped how messianic claims were evaluated. Any figure who aspired to be taken seriously as the Messiah would be measured against Scripture, history, and the lived hopes of the people. Signs mattered. Lineage mattered. Fidelity to the law mattered. So did the capacity to interpret Israel's suffering in a way that honoured both divine justice and divine mercy. The Messiah would not merely resolve political problems; he would have to make sense of Israel's story itself.

This is why messianic movements in the Second Temple period often rose and fell quickly. Josephus records several figures who claimed or were claimed to be agents of divine deliverance. Their followers were drawn by promises of liberation, signs, or prophetic authority, yet their movements collapsed when Roman power reasserted itself or when the leaders themselves were killed. The failure of these claimants reinforced a sobering lesson: enthusiasm was not fulfilment, and zeal was not proof. Israel learned, painfully, that the Messiah could not be identified merely by resistance to Rome or by the ability to gather a following. Authentic messianic identity had to be deeper, more enduring, and more faithful to the whole counsel of Scripture.

At the same time, the Scriptures themselves resisted reduction to a single expectation. The same texts that spoke of victory also spoke of purification; the same prophets who envisioned restored sovereignty also warned of judgment beginning with God's own people. Israel's Scriptures insisted that salvation would come through righteousness as well as power, through repentance as well as deliverance. This insistence created a tension that no political programme could resolve. The Messiah would have to address the root of Israel's problem, not only its symptoms. Foreign domination was grievous, but it was not the deepest wound. Sin, covenant infidelity, and the fractured heart of the people remained unresolved. Any hope for lasting restoration had to confront these realities.

This recognition explains why messianic expectation often carried a moral and spiritual dimension alongside its political aspirations. The anticipated king was expected to judge with righteousness, to defend the poor, to establish justice not by force alone but by fidelity to God's law. The prophetic hope was inseparable from the call to repentance. Israel's longing for deliverance was intertwined with a longing for renewal. The Messiah was awaited not only as a conqueror but as a healer, not only as a ruler but as a shepherd who would gather the scattered and restore the lost. These images, drawn from Scripture, resisted simplistic interpretation. They demanded a figure who could hold together authority and compassion, judgment and mercy.

It is within this layered and contested world that the question of recognition must be understood. To recognise the Messiah was not merely to accept a claim; it was to perceive in a person the convergence of Scripture's many threads. Recognition required a particular kind of sight, one trained by Scripture yet open to surprise. Those who looked only for political liberation could miss a Messiah who spoke of inner transformation. Those who expected immediate triumph could stumble over a path that led through suffering. Conversely, those attentive to the deeper currents of Scripture—its emphasis on humility, obedience, and trust in God's timing—might discern fulfilment where others saw failure.

Rejection, then, cannot be explained simply as blindness or malice. It arises from the same seriousness that makes recognition possible. Fidelity to Scripture can lead in different directions when interpretive emphases diverge. A Messiah who fulfilled the promises in a way that overturned dominant expectations would inevitably divide opinion. The more intensely Israel hoped, the sharper the division would become. The stakes were too high for indifference. Acceptance and opposition were both forms of engagement, both rooted in a desire to honour God's covenant.

This dynamic becomes even clearer when one considers the role of suffering in Israel's self-understanding. National suffering had long been interpreted through the lens of covenant discipline and prophetic warning. Exile, oppression, and loss were not merely political misfortunes; they were theological events. God was purifying His people, calling them back to fidelity. Yet the idea that the Messiah himself might suffer—voluntarily, redemptively, and decisively—remained difficult to integrate. Suffering was expected to end with the Messiah's arrival, not to mark his mission. The notion that suffering could be the means of salvation rather than its obstacle was present in Scripture but not easily foregrounded in popular expectation.

Thus the stage is set for the drama that follows. The messianic hope of Second Temple Judaism was genuine, scriptural, and intense. It was also complex, contested, and unfinished. When Jesus of Nazareth appears in this world, proclaiming the kingdom of God and acting with an authority that evokes Israel's deepest hopes, the question of his identity cannot be separated from this context. Recognition and rejection emerge as responses conditioned by Scripture, shaped by history, and driven by longing. To understand why Jesus is both embraced and opposed, one must first understand the world that was waiting for him—a world that hoped for the Messiah with all the seriousness of a people who believed that God's promises were worth staking everything upon.

And yet, even as Israel waited with seriousness and intensity, there remained a fundamental ambiguity at the heart of expectation. The Scriptures promised that God would act decisively, but they did not specify the manner or the timetable of that action with the clarity later readers often desire. Prophetic language was rich, symbolic, and deliberately open-ended. Images of restoration, judgment, and renewal overlapped without being systematised. The same prophetic corpus could speak of imminent deliverance and distant hope, of divine intervention within history and of transformation beyond history. This ambiguity did not weaken messianic hope; it sustained it. It allowed each generation to see its own struggles reflected in the sacred texts and to await God's answer anew.

This openness, however, also meant that messianic expectation was vulnerable to disappointment. When anticipated deliverance did not materialise in expected forms, interpretations had to adjust. Some responded by intensifying apocalyptic hope, projecting fulfilment beyond the present age. Others recalibrated expectations inward, emphasising fidelity to Torah and communal holiness while awaiting God's timing. Still others sought immediate action, believing that faithfulness demanded participation in God's impending victory. The diversity of responses reveals a people deeply engaged with the question of God's faithfulness, wrestling with the tension between promise and experience rather than abandoning either.

Within this environment, Scripture functioned not only as authority but as conversation partner. Interpretive practices such as midrash and pesher reflect a conviction that the meaning of the text unfolded alongside history. The Word of God was not static; it addressed the present moment. This conviction explains why messianic claims were tested not merely against isolated proof texts but against the perceived trajectory of Scripture as a whole. The Messiah had to make sense of Israel's past and illuminate its future. He had to stand in continuity with the covenant and yet open it toward something new. Expectation was therefore dynamic, oriented toward discernment rather than mere anticipation.

The unresolved nature of messianic hope also sharpened Israel's awareness of divine transcendence. God's promises were trusted precisely because they could not be engineered or predicted. Deliverance would come not through human planning but through God's initiative. This conviction fostered a posture of waiting that was both hopeful and wary. Claims of fulfilment were scrutinised carefully, not out of scepticism alone but out of reverence for the magnitude of what was expected. The Messiah was not merely another leader; he was the hinge upon which history itself would turn. To accept such a figure prematurely would be to risk idolatry; to reject him unjustly would be to resist God.

This reverence helps explain the seriousness with which messianic claims were debated. Disagreement did not imply indifference. On the contrary, it reflected the conviction that the stakes were ultimate. The Messiah would not simply improve Israel's circumstances; he would reveal God's will for the world. Recognition required humility and openness to divine surprise; rejection often stemmed from a desire to protect the covenant from distortion. Both responses were animated by concern for God's honour, even when they led in divergent directions.

By the time Jesus appears in the narrative of history, this world of expectation has reached a critical intensity. Hope has not faded; it has matured. The Scriptures have been read and reread, the promises rehearsed and refined. The categories are in place, yet they strain under their own weight. The longing for a king, a prophet, a priest, and a redeemer presses toward a figure capable of embodying all these roles without collapsing into any one of them. The messianic hope of Second Temple Judaism, for all its diversity, converges on a single question: how will God finally act to vindicate His covenant and heal His people?

# 18

# Objections to Jesus: Genealogy, Suffering, Torah, and Kingship

The expectation of Israel's Messiah was never casual, and it was never abstract. It was covenantal, historical, and fiercely guarded. The promises spoken to Abraham and sworn to David were not metaphors but anchors of identity, rehearsed in prayer, encoded in Scripture, and defended through centuries of conquest, exile, and survival. When messianic hope intensified in the final centuries before Jesus, it did so under the pressure of foreign rule and theological crisis. The Messiah was not expected to emerge ambiguously. He was expected to *fit*—to stand recognisably within the contours of Israel's Scriptures, lineage, and hope. It is within this framework that the first and most immediate objections to Jesus arose.

Central among these was the question of lineage. The Messiah was expected to be a son of David, not symbolically but genealogically. God's promise in 2 Samuel 7 had set the terms decisively: "I will raise up your offspring after you... and I will establish the throne of his kingdom for ever" (2 Sam 7:12–13). Psalm 89 wrestles with this same promise in the face of apparent collapse, insisting that God's covenant with David could not fail even when history suggested otherwise: "I will not violate my covenant... His line shall endure forever, his throne as long as the sun before me" (Ps 89:34–36). Messianic expectation, therefore, was inseparable from verifiable descent.

The Gospels themselves attest that this expectation shaped popular reaction to Jesus. In Jerusalem, the crowd objects plainly: "Has not the Scripture said that the Christ comes from the offspring of David, and comes from Bethlehem, the village where David was?" (John 7:42). The objection is not hostile; it is scriptural. Jesus' association with Galilee, with Nazareth in particular, immediately raised doubts about His legitimacy. Even His miracles did not dissolve this concern. Signs could provoke wonder, but they could not override the covenantal logic that governed messianic recognition.

Matthew and Luke both present genealogies, yet their very existence highlights the problem rather than eliminating it. Matthew opens his Gospel with a formal claim: "The book of the genealogy of Jesus Christ, the son of David, the son of Abraham" (Matt 1:1). Luke traces Jesus' ancestry differently, extending it beyond David to Adam (Luke 3:23–38). For later Christian theology, these genealogies would be read sacramentally and theologically. For many Jews of the first century, however, they invited scrutiny. Lineage was not established by theological assertion but by public record and communal memory. After the destruction of Jerusalem in 70 AD, such records were largely lost, intensifying suspicion toward claims that could no longer be externally verified.

The difficulty was sharpened further by Christian proclamation of Jesus' birth. Claims surrounding His conception—however central they would become to Christian faith—introduced tension into Jewish categories of descent. Legal fatherhood carried weight, but biological descent remained the ordinary measure of tribal and dynastic continuity. From within Jewish expectation, these claims complicated rather than clarified Jesus' messianic profile.

Jesus Himself appears aware of this tension and refuses to ground His authority primarily in genealogy. When questioned about Davidic descent, He turns the argument back upon His interlocutors by citing Psalm 110: "How can they say that the Christ is David's son? For David himself says in the Book of Psalms, 'The Lord said to my Lord, Sit at my right hand'"

(Luke 20:41-42). The question destabilises purely genealogical reasoning without abolishing it. Yet for many, this destabilisation did not resolve doubt; it intensified it. If messianic identity could not be securely anchored in lineage, what safeguards remained against false claimants?

Alongside genealogical concern stood an even more formidable obstacle: the manner of Jesus' death. No expectation weighed more heavily against Him than the cross. Deuteronomy's judgment was explicit and unambiguous: "If a man has committed a crime punishable by death and he is put to death, and you hang him on a tree... he who is hanged is accursed by God" (Deut 21:22-23). This text was not marginal. It was embedded in Israel's moral imagination, shaping how execution and divine judgment were interpreted. Roman crucifixion, designed to humiliate and terrorise, appeared to enact precisely the curse the Torah described.

The apostle Paul would later acknowledge the force of this objection without softening it: "We preach Christ crucified, a stumbling block to Jews" (1 Cor 1:23). The Greek term *skandalon* does not suggest mild difficulty but a barrier that causes collapse. From within Jewish categories, a crucified Messiah appeared not paradoxical but disqualified. Even Isaiah's Servant Songs, which speak of suffering and rejection, had not prepared Israel for a Messiah publicly executed by pagan authorities as a criminal.

Paul himself articulates the problem starkly: "Christ redeemed us from the curse of the law, having become a curse for us—for it is written, 'Cursed be everyone who hangs on a tree'" (Gal 3:13). The logic here presupposes the objection. Jesus' death did not merely appear cursed; according to the Torah, it was cursed. Without the Resurrection, the cross would have functioned as final refutation.

The Gospels preserve the reality that even Jesus' closest followers struggled with this logic. When He predicts His suffering and death, Peter rebukes Him, prompting Jesus' severe response: "You are not on the side of God, but of men" (Mark 8:33). The resistance is not ignorance of Scripture but adherence to an interpretive framework in which suffering could not belong to messianic vocation. If the disciples faltered here, it is hardly surprising that many others could not cross this threshold.

These objections—genealogical and cruciform—did not arise from indifference or hostility to Scripture. They arose from fidelity to it. Israel had learned, through bitter experience, the danger of false messiahs and misplaced hope. Josephus records the devastation wrought by messianic pretenders whose promises ended in slaughter and ruin (*Jewish War* 2.259–263). Against this backdrop, caution was not faithlessness but survival.

Yet the Gospel narratives insist that something more than caution was at work as Jesus' ministry progressed. Signs accumulated. Authority manifested itself not only in teaching but in healing, exorcism, and command over nature. Still, resistance hardened, particularly among leaders charged with guarding Israel's spiritual life. Jesus' lament over Jerusalem captures the tragedy in covenantal language: "O Jerusalem, Jerusalem... How often would I have gathered your children together... and you would not!" (Luke 13:34). The refusal is no longer framed as confusion but as will.

This tension—between intelligible objection and culpable resistance—defines the fault line that runs through Israel's response to Jesus. It is a tension that cannot yet be resolved, only traced. The Messiah stands before His people bearing promises they know and fulfilling them in ways they do not expect. Recognition and rejection emerge side by side, not because Scripture is unclear, but because its fulfilment arrives through suffering, judgment, and divine action that overturn settled assumptions.

If lineage and death formed the first barriers to recognition, the question of kingship pressed no less forcefully upon Israel's conscience. The Messiah was expected not merely to possess David's bloodline but to enact David's vocation: to shepherd Israel, establish justice, and restore the nation under God's rule. Royal psalms had given this hope its vocabulary. Psalm 2 proclaimed a king installed by God Himself, before whom the nations would tremble: "Ask of me, and I will make the nations your heritage, and the ends of the earth your possession" (Ps 2:8). Psalm 72 envisioned a reign marked by visible justice and peace, where the king would "defend the cause of the poor of the people" and "crush the oppressor" (Ps 72:4). These texts were not read privately or allegorically; they shaped public expectation.

Second Temple literature confirms how concretely these hopes were held. The *Psalms of Solomon*, composed in the aftermath of Roman intrusion, pray for a son of David who will "drive out the sinners from the inheritance" and "destroy the unlawful nations with the word of his mouth" (Pss. Sol. 17:22–23). The Messiah here is a figure of purification and political reversal, restoring Jerusalem and reasserting Israel's sovereignty. Such expectations did not arise from nationalist fantasy but from covenantal logic: if God is faithful, His people must ultimately be vindicated in history.

Against this backdrop, Jesus' ministry generated both attraction and disorientation. He announced the kingdom of God, yet refused to define it in political terms. He healed the sick and cast out demons, signs traditionally associated with divine visitation, yet declined every attempt to make Him king by force. John records the crowd's reaction after the multiplication of the loaves: "Perceiving then that they were about to come and take him by force to make him king, Jesus withdrew again to the mountain by himself" (John 6:15). The withdrawal itself was a statement. Whatever kingship Jesus claimed, it would not conform to popular expectation.

Even after the Resurrection, the disciples reveal how deeply political restoration had shaped their hopes. As Jesus prepares to ascend, they ask, "Lord, will you at this time restore the kingdom to Israel?" (Acts 1:6). The question is not rebuked as illegitimate; it is deferred. For many who did not share the apostolic experience of Easter, the deferral appeared indistinguishable from failure. Rome remained. The Temple stood under foreign oversight. The nations were not judged. If the Messiah had come, why did the world look unchanged?

Jesus Himself confronts this tension by turning prophetic judgment inward. As He approaches Jerusalem, He weeps over the city and interprets its future in theological terms: "Would that you, even you, had known on this day the things that make for peace! But now they are hidden from your eyes" (Luke 19:42). The consequence is devastating and explicit: "They will not leave one stone upon another in you, because you did not know the time of your visitation" (Luke 19:44). The failure is not merely political miscalculation; it is failure to recognise divine presence.

The destruction of Jerusalem in 70 AD would etch these words into Jewish memory with searing clarity. Yet before that catastrophe, Jesus' warnings already functioned as prophetic indictment. Like Jeremiah before the fall of the first Temple, He announced judgment not as divine abandonment but as covenant consequence. The leaders' confidence in the Temple as an inviolable guarantee echoed precisely the error Jeremiah condemned: "Do not trust in these deceptive words: 'This is the temple of the Lord'" (Jer 7:4). Jesus' symbolic actions in the Temple—overturning tables, halting commerce—signalled that judgment was imminent and that access to God could no longer be secured through inherited structures alone.

This claim cut to the heart of another objection: Jesus' relationship to Torah and tradition. Fidelity to the law was not ancillary to Jewish identity; it was constitutive. Deuteronomy warned Israel explicitly against prophets who would lead the people astray, even if accompanied by signs: "You shall not listen to the words of that prophet... for the Lord your God is testing you" (Deut 13:3). Discernment required suspicion, not enthusiasm. Any figure who appeared to relativise the Torah invited alarm.

Jesus' teaching repeatedly touched these nerves. His actions on the Sabbath, His association with sinners, and His pronouncements regarding purity provoked controversy because they appeared to bypass established interpretive authority. When questioned about Sabbath observance, He replies not with appeal to precedent but with sovereign declaration: "The Son of Man is lord of the Sabbath" (Mark 2:28). The claim is staggering. Authority over the Sabbath implied authority over one of the Torah's central signs of covenant fidelity.

Conflicts over tradition intensified the rupture. In disputing practices of ritual washing, Jesus accuses certain Pharisees of "making void the word of God by your tradition that you have handed down" (Mark 7:13). The accusation does not reject tradition as such; it indicts a use of tradition that shields the heart from obedience. Yet from the perspective of those entrusted with preserving Israel's way of life under occupation, such critique threatened the fragile boundary between faithfulness and assimilation.

John's Gospel preserves the escalation vividly. After healing on the Sabbath, Jesus defends His action by asserting unique divine intimacy: "My Father is working still, and I am working" (John 5:17). The response is immediate: "This was why the Jews were seeking all the more to kill him, because… he was even calling God his own Father, making himself equal with God" (John 5:18). The issue is no longer merely halakhic disagreement but perceived blasphemy.

Jesus addresses this resistance with a mixture of appeal and judgment. "You search the Scriptures, because you think that in them you have eternal life; and it is they that bear witness about me, yet you refuse to come to me that you may have life" (John 5:39–40). The charge is severe. Scripture itself is not rejected; it is studied. The failure lies in refusal—*ouk thelete*—a will that resists the testimony Scripture offers when it confronts the reader with an unexpected fulfilment. Jesus intensifies the accusation by locating the resistance not in ignorance but in misplaced allegiance: "I know that you do not have the love of God within you… How can you believe, when you receive glory from one another and do not seek the glory that comes from the only God?" (John 5:42–44). The critique penetrates beyond interpretive disagreement into the moral economy of recognition.

This distinction between ignorance and culpability becomes explicit in the episode of the man born blind. After healing him, Jesus confronts the Pharisees who interrogate the miracle. Their insistence on juridical categories leads them to deny the sign rather than reassess their framework. Jesus' judgment is precise: "If you were blind, you would have no guilt; but now that you say, 'We see,' your guilt remains" (John 9:41). Blindness acknowledged invites mercy; blindness denied becomes guilt. Here resistance has crossed a threshold.

The Gospels thus present opposition to Jesus as a dynamic process. Initial objections—genealogical, political, legal—are intelligible within Israel's covenantal horizon. Yet as Jesus' ministry unfolds, as teaching is accompanied by authority and signs, objection hardens into refusal. The prophetic register sharpens accordingly. In Matthew's Gospel, Jesus delivers His woes against the scribes and Pharisees not as an outsider attacking Judaism, but as Israel's prophet announcing covenant judgment: "You shut the kingdom of heaven in people's faces. For you neither enter yourselves nor allow those who would enter to go in" (Matt 23:13). The language recalls Isaiah's indictment of leaders who mislead the people and Ezekiel's condemnation of shepherds who feed themselves rather than the flock.

These woes culminate in a lament that fuses compassion and judgment: "O Jerusalem, Jerusalem, the city that kills the prophets and stones those who are sent to it!" (Matt 23:37). The charge situates Jesus squarely within Israel's prophetic tradition. Rejection of the Messiah is not an isolated failure but the climax of a recurring pattern—resistance to God's messengers precisely when their word threatens established security.

The destruction of Jerusalem would later be read by Christians as confirmation of Jesus' prophetic authority, yet the Gospels present it first as warning. "Your house is left to you desolate" (Matt 23:38) echoes Jeremiah's temple sermon, where false confidence in sacred space masked impending judgment. Jesus' prophecy does not annul God's covenant; it exposes the cost of refusing its fulfilment.

At the same time, the New Testament refuses to universalise this judgment across Israel as a whole. Acts records thousands of Jews embracing the Gospel in Jerusalem itself. Paul, once a persecutor, becomes its most ardent witness. The divided response remains. In his letter to the Romans, Paul wrestles with this mystery without flattening it. He affirms Israel's privileges—"the adoption, the glory, the covenants, the giving of the law" (Rom 9:4)—while acknowledging a hardening that is neither total nor final. "A hardening has come upon part of Israel, until the full number of the Gentiles comes in" (Rom 11:25). Judgment and mercy intertwine.

Chapter 15 thus stands at the intersection of covenant fidelity and prophetic indictment. The objections raised against Jesus are not straw men; they arise from Scripture, history, and responsibility. Yet the Gospels insist that responsibility cuts both ways. To guard the covenant is not the same as to recognise its fulfilment. When resistance persists in the face of revelation, objection becomes refusal, and refusal invites judgment.

The question that presses upon the reader at this point is unavoidable and unresolved. If the Messiah was not meant to triumph as expected—if suffering, rejection, and apparent defeat belong to God's design—where was this written? How could Israel's Scriptures themselves prepare for a Messiah who would be cursed, rejected, and yet vindicated by God? That question hangs unanswered, demanding a return to the prophets with new seriousness, and it opens the way to the deeper logic that follows.

The consolidation of resistance to Jesus did not end with His death. It intensified in the decades that followed, shaped decisively by the catastrophe of 70 AD. The destruction of the Temple was not only a political and military trauma; it was a theological earthquake. For centuries, Israel's worship, identity, and hope had revolved around the sanctuary where heaven and earth were believed to meet. When that centre was violently removed, Judaism faced a crisis not unlike the one that followed the Babylonian exile. Once again, the question arose: how does the covenant endure when its visible heart has been torn out?

In the wake of this devastation, competing interpretations of Israel's future hardened into distinct paths. The Jesus movement proclaimed that the destruction of the Temple confirmed what Jesus Himself had announced—that a new mode of access to God had been inaugurated through His death and resurrection. Rabbinic Judaism, by contrast, undertook the urgent task of preserving Israel's identity through Torah, prayer, and communal discipline. This divergence was not merely sociological. It was theological. The claims made about Jesus could no longer be treated as one interpretive option among others; they now threatened to redefine Israel's story at the moment of its deepest vulnerability.

This post-70 context helps explain why objections to Jesus sharpened into polemic. Earlier disputes had centred on interpretation—on lineage, authority, and expectation. After the Temple's fall, the stakes rose dramatically. To accept Jesus as Messiah now appeared to many not only mistaken but dangerous. If Jesus had been rejected and executed, and if Jerusalem had fallen anyway, what evidence remained that He stood at the centre of God's saving purpose? The logic could easily invert: perhaps the catastrophe itself proved that messianic claims surrounding Jesus had been false, that Israel had suffered precisely because it had been led astray by dangerous hopes.

Rabbinic literature from later centuries preserves echoes of this polemical memory. While these texts must be handled with care, they reveal how Jesus came to be situated within Jewish discourse as a troubling figure whose legacy had to be decisively contained. The Mishnah's brief references to heresy and the boundaries of Israel's faith reflect a community intent on survival and coherence. In this setting, rejection of Jesus was no longer simply an interpretive judgment; it became a matter of covenantal preservation.

Yet the New Testament insists that this hardening did not occur in a vacuum. Paul frames it within a theology of divine providence that refuses both triumphalism and despair. "Did they stumble so as to fall? By no means!" he asks (Rom 11:11). Israel's resistance, however grave, does not annul God's promises. Instead, Paul discerns a mysterious economy in which rejection and acceptance serve a wider purpose: through Israel's stumbling, the Gospel reaches the nations, provoking Israel itself to jealousy and, ultimately, renewal.

This perspective does not soften the seriousness of resistance. Paul speaks of "severity" as well as kindness (Rom 11:22). Hardening is real, judgment is real, and consequences unfold in history. Yet none of this authorises contempt. Israel remains "beloved for the sake of the patriarchs" (Rom 11:28). The covenant is neither revoked nor replaced. The tension remains unresolved, suspended between judgment pronounced and mercy promised.

The early Church Fathers wrestled with this same tension, often in dialogue with Jewish interlocutors who pressed the objections preserved in Scripture and tradition. Justin Martyr's *Dialogue with Trypho* records sustained debate over lineage, suffering, and the curse of the cross. Trypho does not deny that Scripture speaks of a Messiah; he denies that the Messiah could have suffered in such a way. Justin acknowledges the scandal without evasion, admitting that the claim appears offensive before arguing that it is precisely what the prophets foretold. The exchange reveals how deeply rooted the objections were, and how central they remained to Jewish-Christian disagreement well into the second century.

Origen, writing a generation later, notes that Jewish critics continued to view Jesus' death as decisive evidence against His claims. In *Contra Celsum*, he preserves their reasoning in order to answer it: a true Messiah, they argued, would not have been abandoned to such a fate. Origen does not dismiss the force of this logic; he insists that it can only be overturned by the Resurrection. Without it, the objections would stand. With it, Scripture itself must be reread.

The persistence of these debates underscores a central truth: the rejection of Jesus was not an accident of misunderstanding that faded with time. It was a sustained theological judgment shaped by Scripture, history, and trauma. Jesus' own condemnations of blindness and hypocrisy do not negate this complexity; they intensify it. They reveal that resistance to fulfilment can coexist with devotion to tradition, and that zeal for God can become an obstacle when it hardens into self-certainty.

This is why the Gospels frame Jesus' polemic not as ethnic denunciation but as prophetic confrontation. His language mirrors Isaiah's commission to a people who will "hear and hear, but not understand" (Isa 6:9), a passage the evangelists repeatedly invoke. The blindness He names is judicial, the consequence of persistent refusal. Yet even here, judgment is never the final word. Isaiah's vision ends not in annihilation but in the promise of a holy seed remaining in the stump (Isa 6:13).

By the end of this chapter, the reader stands within this unresolved field of tension. The objections to Jesus are coherent, historically grounded, and weighty. His condemnations are equally clear, severe, and prophetic. Israel's rejection is neither total nor inexplicable, neither excusable nor final. The question that now presses forward is sharper than before. If suffering, rejection, and apparent defeat belong within the messianic vocation, then Scripture itself must disclose a pattern deeper than kingship alone—a pattern in which glory emerges only through abasement, and vindication follows obedience unto death.

The depth of this tension becomes clearer when one considers how messianic expectation functioned not only as future hope but as interpretive lens. Israel did not read its Scriptures neutrally; it read them through patterns established by its history. Deliverance had come before through strength displayed in public acts—through plagues, parted seas, shattered armies. Even when the prophets spoke of suffering, that suffering was typically understood as preparatory, the birth pangs that preceded visible restoration. What was without precedent was the notion that suffering itself could *constitute* the Messiah's mission rather than merely accompany it.

This is why the figure of the suffering righteous one, though present in Israel's Scriptures, did not naturally resolve into messianic identity. Psalms such as Psalm 22 gave voice to the anguish of the innocent, yet they ended in vindication within the same lifetime. Isaiah's Servant bore griefs and carried sorrows, but the identity of this Servant remained debated. Corporate readings that understood the Servant as Israel itself were widespread and plausible, especially in light of the nation's experience of exile and humiliation. To identify this figure decisively with the Messiah required a hermeneutical leap that many were unwilling—or unable—to make without an unmistakable act of God.

The Gospels themselves acknowledge this difficulty. After His Resurrection, Jesus rebukes the disciples on the road to Emmaus not for ignorance of Scripture, but for slowness of heart: "Was it not necessary that the Christ should suffer these things and enter into his glory?" (Luke 24:26). The rebuke presupposes that the necessity was not obvious beforehand. Only in retrospect does the pattern cohere. Before Easter, the prophetic strands lay side by side without synthesis; after Easter, they converge.

For those who did not share this retrospective illumination, the objections remained formidable. The Messiah was expected to vindicate Israel, not to be rejected by it. Yet Jesus' ministry unfolded as a steady inversion of this expectation. He was opposed by those most invested in preserving Israel's religious life, while sinners, outsiders, and the marginal responded with faith. This reversal itself functioned as a sign, yet it was a sign that cut against instinct rather than confirming it.

Jesus interprets this reversal through the language of judgment and mercy. In the parable of the wicked tenants, He portrays Israel's leaders as those who reject the servants sent by the landowner and finally kill his son (Mark 12:1–12). The parable is not an abstract moral tale; it is a transparent interpretation of Israel's history and of Jesus' own fate. The leaders perceive this, and "they were seeking to arrest him, but feared the people, for they perceived that he had told the parable against them" (Mark 12:12). Recognition here does not lead to repentance but to entrenchment.

This pattern reveals why Jesus' condemnations are so severe. They are not reactions to misunderstanding but responses to refusal. When Jesus speaks of blindness, He does so in the context of those who claim sight. "If you were blind, you would have no guilt; but now that you say, 'We see,' your guilt remains" (John 9:41). The issue is not the absence of revelation but resistance to it. The leaders' confidence in their interpretive authority becomes the very means by which they exclude the possibility that God might act beyond their control.

At the same time, Jesus' judgments never collapse into rejection of Israel as a whole. His lament over Jerusalem is filled with grief, not triumph: "How often would I have gathered your children together as a hen gathers her brood under her wings, and you were not willing" (Matt 23:37). Judgment here is framed as the consequence of refusal, not as divine delight in punishment. The covenantal language of gathering and visitation underscores that the offer was real, the rejection tragic.

The New Testament's insistence on this tragic dimension is crucial. It refuses to narrate Israel's rejection as simple failure or as total apostasy.

Acts records again and again that the Gospel is preached "to the Jew first" (Rom 1:16), that synagogues are the initial locus of proclamation, and that division, not uniform rejection, follows. Some believe, others oppose, and the community fractures along lines that cut through families and cities. This is not the story of an entire people turning away from God, but of a people divided at the moment of fulfilment.

Paul's own anguish testifies to the unresolved nature of this division. "I have great sorrow and unceasing anguish in my heart," he writes, "for I could wish that I myself were accursed and cut off from Christ for the sake of my brothers" (Rom 9:2–3). Such language would be incoherent if Israel's rejection were merely reasonable misunderstanding or, conversely, total infidelity. It reflects a mystery that resists reduction: a people chosen by God, encountering their Messiah, and yet largely failing to recognise Him.

This unresolved mystery prepares the ground for the argument that must follow. The objections surveyed in this chapter—genealogical, cruciform, political, legal—do not dissolve on their own. They demand an answer that does not bypass Scripture but plunges more deeply into it. If the Messiah truly had to suffer, then the logic of suffering must be shown to belong to God's plan from the beginning. Only then can the scandal of the cross be understood not as contradiction but as fulfilment.

The persistence of these objections forces a deeper question about the nature of revelation itself. Israel's Scriptures were not delivered as abstract propositions but as a living history in which God disclosed His will through events as much as through words. Recognition of God's action therefore required more than textual literacy; it required discernment of the moment in which God was acting. Jesus names this failure with striking clarity when He rebukes the crowds: "You know how to interpret the appearance of earth and sky, but why do you not know how to interpret the present time?" (Luke 12:56). The charge is not ignorance of Scripture but inability—or unwillingness—to perceive fulfilment when it stands before them.

This inability was not evenly distributed. The Gospels repeatedly distinguish between the people at large and the leaders who claimed interpretive authority. Many among the crowds respond with astonishment and faith, while opposition crystallises among those whose status depended upon maintaining existing structures of authority. This distinction sharpens Jesus' warnings. "The scribes and the Pharisees sit on Moses' seat," He acknowledges, affirming their legitimate role (Matt 23:2). Yet He immediately condemns the manner in which that authority is exercised: "They preach, but do not practice… They bind heavy burdens, hard to bear, and lay them on men's shoulders" (Matt 23:3–4). The problem is not Torah itself, but a mode of guardianship that transforms the law into a barrier rather than a path.

The critique reaches its climax in Jesus' denunciation of hypocrisy, a charge that strikes at the heart of religious self-understanding. "Woe to you, scribes and Pharisees, hypocrites! For you cleanse the outside of the cup and of the plate, but inside they are full of extortion and rapacity" (Matt 23:25). The language is deliberately prophetic, echoing Isaiah's condemnation of worship divorced from justice (Isa 1:11–17). Jesus stands firmly within this tradition, exposing a disjunction between outward fidelity and inward resistance. Such exposure inevitably provokes hostility, for it threatens not only beliefs but identities.

This hostility culminates in the decision to eliminate Jesus as a destabilising presence. John's Gospel situates this decision explicitly within a calculus of preservation: "If we let him go on thus, everyone will believe in him, and the Romans will come and destroy both our holy place and our nation" (John 11:48). The concern is not frivolous. Recent history had shown how swiftly Roman power could annihilate perceived threats. Yet the irony is devastating. In seeking to preserve the nation by rejecting Jesus, the leaders enact the very judgment they fear. Caiaphas' unwitting prophecy—"It is better for you that one man should die for the people, and that the whole nation should not perish" (John 11:50)—reveals how political prudence and theological blindness can converge.

Here the boundary between intelligible objection and culpable resistance is crossed decisively. The leaders are no longer weighing scriptural claims;

they are suppressing a threat. The calculus is pragmatic rather than theological. Jesus' subsequent arrest, trial, and execution are not the result of confusion but of choice. The Gospels are unambiguous on this point. "This is the judgment," Jesus declares, "that the light has come into the world, and men loved darkness rather than light" (John 3:19). Judgment, in this sense, is not imposed externally but emerges from response.

Yet even at this point, the narrative refuses to erase complexity. Jesus' prayer from the cross—"Father, forgive them; for they know not what they do" (Luke 23:34)—introduces a note of mercy that resists total condemnation. Ignorance and culpability coexist. Some act in blindness; others exploit it. The prayer does not deny guilt; it opens the possibility of forgiveness. Indeed, Acts records that many priests later become obedient to the faith (Acts 6:7), suggesting that resistance was neither uniform nor irreversible.

Theologically, this coexistence of judgment and mercy shapes the New Testament's understanding of Israel's fate. The fall of Jerusalem is interpreted as real judgment, fulfilling Jesus' warnings. Yet it is never narrated as the cancellation of God's covenant. Paul insists that Israel's stumbling serves a wider purpose without exhausting God's intention. "As regards the gospel they are enemies for your sake, but as regards election they are beloved for the sake of their forefathers" (Rom 11:28). The dialectic is unresolved, deliberately so.

This unresolved tension guards against two opposite errors. It prevents the minimisation of Israel's responsibility in rejecting Jesus, and it prevents the demonisation of Israel as a whole. The Gospels allow neither sentimental neutrality nor total condemnation. They present a people encountering their Messiah and responding in divided ways—some with faith, others with fear, some with repentance, others with hardened resistance. Jesus' severe words belong to this drama, not as blanket denunciation, but as prophetic judgment directed at those who obstruct recognition of God's work.

By this point, the reader is confronted with the full weight of the problem. Scripture testifies both to legitimate messianic expectations that Jesus did not visibly satisfy and to a prophetic indictment of those who refused Him. Neither dimension can be erased without distorting the Gospel witness. The objections stand. The judgments stand. The mystery deepens. The question that now presses cannot be postponed any longer: if the Messiah was always destined to suffer, to be rejected, and to bring salvation through apparent defeat, where is this necessity inscribed in Israel's Scriptures themselves?

The force of this question exposes the limits of expectation shaped solely by precedent. Israel's history had trained its imagination to recognise God's saving action when it manifested as deliverance from visible oppression. Yet the same history also bore witness to a recurring refusal to hear when God's word unsettled established security. The prophets had long warned that Israel's greatest danger did not lie in foreign armies but in hearts resistant to correction. Isaiah's commission—to speak to a people who would hear without understanding—was not an anomaly but a pattern repeated across generations. Jesus stands consciously within this prophetic trajectory, identifying His own rejection as the culmination of a long history of resistance.

This continuity explains why Jesus interprets opposition to His mission as more than personal hostility. "Woe to you," He declares, "for you build the tombs of the prophets whom your fathers killed" (Luke 11:47). The charge is not genealogical guilt but spiritual imitation. Honouring the prophets of the past while rejecting the prophetic word in the present reveals a disposition that preserves memory while resisting encounter. In this sense, the rejection of Jesus is not a break from Israel's story but an intensification of its internal conflict.

The accusation reaches its sharpest form when Jesus identifies the leaders' resistance as a barrier placed before others. "You have taken away the key of knowledge; you did not enter yourselves, and you hindered those who were entering" (Luke 11:52). Knowledge here is not information but access—participation in God's unfolding purpose. To block that access is to incur judgment precisely because it prevents others from recognising what God is doing. This is why Jesus' condemnations are directed so specifically at those who claim interpretive authority. Their blindness carries communal consequences.

At the same time, Jesus' own ministry complicates any simplistic assignment of blame. He consistently engages the Scriptures, reasons from them, and appeals to their witness. "If you believed Moses, you would believe me, for he wrote of me" (John 5:46). The claim is staggering. Moses, the lawgiver whose authority undergirded Israel's identity, is said to testify to Jesus. Yet the claim is immediately paired with recognition of resistance: "But if you do not believe his writings, how will you believe my words?" (John 5:47). The problem is not the absence of testimony but the refusal to trust it when it leads beyond established categories.

This refusal becomes particularly acute when messianic hope intersects with suffering. The expectation that God's chosen one would triumph through power was deeply ingrained, reinforced by narratives of conquest and restoration. To suggest that God would accomplish salvation through apparent defeat was not merely counterintuitive; it threatened to undermine confidence in God's fidelity. If the Messiah could be rejected, humiliated, and executed, what assurance remained that God's promises were reliable? The objection was theological, not emotional.

Yet it is precisely here that Jesus locates the heart of the matter. In confronting the disciples' inability to accept His passion predictions, He names their resistance as misunderstanding of God's ways: "You are not on the side of God, but of men" (Mark 8:33). The contrast does not pit piety against impiety, but divine logic against human expectation. What appears as failure from one angle reveals obedience from another. This inversion destabilises not only messianic expectation but the criteria by which faithfulness itself is measured.

The early Christian proclamation recognises this destabilisation openly. Peter's speech in Acts does not minimise Israel's responsibility: "You denied the Holy and Righteous One… and killed the Author of life" (Acts 3:14–15). Yet it immediately introduces mercy: "Now, brethren, I know that you acted in ignorance, as did also your rulers" (Acts 3:17). Ignorance does not erase guilt, but it opens the door to repentance. The invitation follows without delay: "Repent therefore, and turn again, that your sins may be blotted out" (Acts 3:19). The Gospel confronts without despairing.

This dual note—judgment without annihilation, accusation without final condemnation—pervades the apostolic witness. It resists the temptation to flatten Israel's response into a single moral verdict. Instead, it narrates a people encountering God's decisive act and responding in divided ways. Some recognise fulfilment; others resist it. Some repent; others entrench themselves. The divisions intensify, not because the message is unclear, but because it demands a reconfiguration of hope itself.

By this stage, the reader is positioned at the edge of a decisive hermeneutical shift. The objections catalogued throughout this chapter are not easily dismissed, nor are the judgments pronounced by Jesus easily softened. Both belong to the same reality. Israel's Scriptures have produced expectations that Jesus both fulfils and overturns. Recognition requires more than textual agreement; it requires conversion of imagination. Rejection, when it persists in the face of revelation, becomes culpable blindness.

The chapter therefore ends where it must: not with resolution, but with demand. If the Messiah was always destined to suffer, to be rejected, and to bring salvation through obedience unto death, then this destiny must be traced within the Scriptures themselves. The logic of suffering cannot be imposed from outside; it must be shown to arise from within Israel's own story. Only then can the scandal of the cross be understood as fulfilment rather than contradiction.

The full weight of Israel's response to Jesus, then, cannot be borne by any single explanation. It cannot be reduced to ignorance, nor can it be dismissed as obstinacy alone. The Scriptures, the Gospels, and the apostolic witness together insist on a more demanding account. Israel encountered her Messiah at the precise moment when messianic hope had reached its most intense articulation, and that encounter exposed the limits of expectation formed without precedent for suffering obedience. The objections that arose were grounded in Scripture and covenantal logic; the resistance that followed, however, revealed how easily fidelity can harden into refusal when fulfilment arrives in an unexpected form.

Jesus' own words press this judgment home with prophetic severity. He does not accuse His opponents of lacking religious seriousness, but of misdirecting it. "You tithe mint and dill and cumin," He says, "and have neglected the weightier matters of the law: justice and mercy and faith" (Matt 23:23). The accusation cuts deeply, because it identifies not lawlessness but imbalance—an adherence to precision that eclipses discernment. In this light, rejection of Jesus is not portrayed as atheism or indifference, but as a tragic misalignment of zeal and perception.

The fall of Jerusalem stands as the historical echo of this misalignment. Jesus' prediction is not vague or symbolic. It is concrete and devastating: siege, destruction, desolation. When it comes to pass, the event confirms that judgment has entered history, not as arbitrary punishment, but as consequence of a failure to recognise divine visitation. Yet even here, the narrative resists finality. Judgment is real, but it is not the last word. The prophets had always spoken of judgment as purgative, not annihilative. The stump remains; the holy seed endures.

Paul's wrestling in Romans gives voice to this unresolved hope. He refuses both triumphalism and despair. Israel's resistance has opened the way for the nations, yet this very opening is ordered toward Israel's eventual restoration. "For God has consigned all men to disobedience, that he may have mercy upon all" (Rom 11:32). Mercy, not exclusion, frames the final horizon. The mystery is not that Israel failed while the Church succeeded, but that God's faithfulness operates through rejection and acceptance alike, weaving judgment and mercy into a single economy.

Chapter 15 therefore leaves the reader deliberately unsettled. The objections to Jesus remain formidable. The condemnations pronounced by Jesus remain uncompromising. Neither can be dissolved without violence to the biblical witness. Israel's Scriptures have generated expectations that Jesus does not meet in the manner anticipated, and yet Jesus claims those same Scriptures as testimony to Himself. The tension is not accidental; it is revelatory. It forces a question that cannot be avoided and cannot be answered superficially.

If the Messiah was always destined to suffer, to be rejected by His own, and to bring salvation through apparent defeat, then this destiny must be inscribed within the prophetic imagination of Israel itself. It must be shown not as an afterthought imposed by disappointment, but as a pattern woven into the story from the beginning. Only then can the cross cease to be a contradiction and become a disclosure. Only then can rejection be understood not as the negation of messianic hope, but as the dark passage through which that hope is fulfilled.

The Scriptures must now be read again—this time with attention to the figures who suffer before they reign, to the servants who bear the sins of others, and to the pattern by which God brings life out of death. The logic of suffering has not yet been demonstrated. It awaits recovery in the prophets themselves. That task now stands before us.

# 19

# The Christian Response: Why the Messiah Had to Suffer

The question that now presses upon Israel's Scriptures is not whether suffering *can* be reconciled with messianic hope, but whether suffering belongs to the very grammar by which God acts in history. If rejection were proof against divine election, then Israel's own story would unravel at its centre. From the beginning, God's chosen instruments are marked not first by triumph but by abasement, not by immediate vindication but by descent into obscurity and loss. The Scriptures do not treat this pattern as incidental. They present it as revelatory.

Joseph's story establishes the pattern with unmistakable clarity. Chosen through dreams, marked out within his family, Joseph is betrayed by his brothers, stripped of his robe, and cast into a pit before being sold into slavery (Gen 37:23–28). His descent continues in Egypt, where false accusation leads to imprisonment (Gen 39:20). Yet the text is careful to insist that "the Lord was with Joseph" even in confinement (Gen 39:21). Vindication comes not by escape but through patient endurance, culminating in exaltation at Pharaoh's right hand: "You shall be over my house… only as regards the throne will I be greater than you" (Gen 41:40). Joseph himself interprets the logic of the narrative with theological sobriety: "You meant evil against me; but God meant it for good, to bring it about that many people should be kept alive" (Gen 50:20). Election, betrayal, suffering, and exaltation belong to a single providential design.

Moses' vocation unfolds according to the same grammar. Though raised within Pharaoh's household, he is rejected by his own people at the first attempt to intervene: "Who made you a prince and a judge over us?" (Exod 2:14). This rejection drives him into exile, where decades of obscurity precede his call. Only after rejection and displacement does God reveal Himself from the burning bush and send Moses back as deliverer (Exod 3:1–12). The pattern is not accidental. Israel's redeemer must first share Israel's marginalisation. Deliverance emerges from suffering endured, not power seized.

David's story intensifies the pattern further. Anointed by Samuel while Saul still reigns, David immediately becomes a target rather than a king. Saul's hostility forces him into flight, betrayal, and near-death experiences, despite David's repeated refusal to grasp the throne by violence. "I will not put forth my hand against my lord, for he is the Lord's anointed" (1 Sam 24:6). David's kingship is forged through obedience and restraint under persecution. Only after years of rejection does vindication arrive, and even then it is marked by loss. The Psalms David composes during this period do not romanticise suffering; they voice abandonment, injustice, and appeal to God's righteousness. "My God, my God, why hast thou forsaken me?" (Ps 22:1). The cry is not rhetorical. It assumes innocence and covenantal trust even as suffering persists.

These narratives establish a principle that cannot be ignored: God's chosen ones are not recognised by immediate success. They are often recognised by contradiction. The Scriptures themselves teach Israel to expect that divine election provokes resistance before it produces restoration. When messianic expectation emerges, it does so within this inherited logic.

The Psalms sharpen this logic by giving voice to the suffering of the righteous as a theological category. Psalm 22 describes not generic distress but the humiliation of one who trusts God and yet is scorned: "All who see me mock at me, they make mouths at me, they wag their heads; 'He trusted in the Lord; let him deliver him'" (Ps 22:7–8). The mockery presumes covenantal logic: if God is faithful, rescue should be visible. The psalm refuses to resolve the tension quickly. Only after prolonged abandonment does vindication emerge, expanding outward into universal praise: "All the ends of the earth shall remember and turn to the Lord" (Ps 22:27). Suffering precedes glory not as an aberration but as its path.

Psalm 69 intensifies the theme, binding suffering explicitly to zeal for God's house: "Zeal for thy house has consumed me, and the insults of those who insult thee have fallen on me" (Ps 69:9). Here suffering is not the result of sin but of fidelity. Reproach is borne precisely because the sufferer stands within God's purposes. Psalm 118 adds the decisive metaphor: "The stone which the builders rejected has become the head of the corner" (Ps 118:22). Rejection is not merely compatible with election; it becomes the means by which God reveals His choice.

Second Temple literature echoes this pattern, confirming that it was not alien to Jewish thought. The *Wisdom of Solomon* portrays the righteous one as persecuted precisely because his life exposes the wicked: "Let us condemn him to a shameful death, for, according to what he says, he will be protected" (Wis 2:20). The text presents suffering as the consequence of righteousness, not its negation. Vindication, however, lies beyond the immediate horizon, reserved for God's judgment.

Isaiah's Servant Songs bring this pattern to its theological climax. The Servant is introduced with exalted promise—"Behold, my servant shall prosper, he shall be exalted and lifted up" (Isa 52:13)—yet the path to exaltation passes through disfigurement and rejection: "His appearance was so marred, beyond human semblance" (Isa 52:14). Isaiah 53 refuses to soften the scandal. The Servant is "despised and rejected by men; a man of sorrows, and acquainted with grief" (Isa 53:3). His suffering is not incidental; it is purposeful and vicarious: "He was wounded for our transgressions... and with his stripes we are healed" (Isa 53:5). Death does not terminate his mission. After offering his life as an offering for sin, "he shall see his offspring; he shall prolong his days" (Isa 53:10). Vindication follows suffering as divine necessity.

## THE CHRISTIAN RESPONSE: WHY THE MESSIAH HAD TO SUFFER

The logic Isaiah presents cannot be assimilated into a purely triumphalist messianism. Kings themselves are said to be astonished because expectations are overturned: "Kings shall shut their mouths because of him" (Isa 52:15). Astonishment implies reversal. What was not anticipated is revealed as essential.

Zechariah deepens the mystery by uniting divine action with suffering in startling language. "They shall look on me whom they have pierced, and they shall mourn for him" (Zech 12:10). The pierced one is not a distant agent but bound to God's own presence. Mourning follows recognition, not conquest. Zechariah's struck shepherd motif intensifies this dynamic: "Strike the shepherd, that the sheep may be scattered" (Zech 13:7). Dispersion precedes restoration. Judgment becomes the instrument of purification.

Daniel's vision of the Son of Man resolves the paradox not by erasing suffering but by situating exaltation after persecution. The saints are oppressed before dominion is granted; the Son of Man receives authority only after the beasts have exercised their violence (Dan 7:21–22). Vindication is judicial, not immediate. Glory follows endurance.

When Jesus asks on the road to Emmaus, "Was it not necessary that the Christ should suffer these things and enter into his glory?" (Luke 24:26), He is not inventing a new logic. He is naming what Scripture had been saying all along. Necessity arises not from disappointment but from pattern. The Messiah stands where Joseph stood, where Moses stood, where David stood, where the righteous sufferer and the Servant stood. Suffering is not the contradiction of messianic identity. It is its confirmation.

The necessity of the Messiah's suffering, once seen within this scriptural pattern, reveals itself not as an embarrassment to be explained away but as a theological coherence demanding recognition. Israel's Scriptures do not merely tolerate suffering within God's purposes; they insist upon it as the crucible through which obedience is perfected and divine vindication disclosed. This insistence reaches its sharpest articulation in the prophetic imagination, where suffering becomes the very means by which covenant fidelity is restored.

Isaiah's Servant Songs resist every attempt to marginalise this logic. The Servant is not an unfortunate victim caught in historical turbulence; he is a chosen instrument whose mission is defined by suffering. Isaiah speaks with unsettling clarity: "It was the will of the Lord to crush him; he has put him to grief" (Isa 53:10). The verb is unambiguous. Suffering is not merely foreseen; it is embraced within God's redemptive will. Yet the purpose of this crushing is not annihilation but healing. The Servant bears sin, intercedes for transgressors, and brings justification to many (Isa 53:11–12). The pattern established earlier—suffering before exaltation—is here intensified into substitution. The Servant suffers not only *before* others but *for* them.

This vicarious dimension addresses directly the scandal articulated in Deuteronomy's curse. If the Messiah is cursed by God, how can He be God's chosen? Isaiah's answer is not denial but transformation. The curse is borne intentionally and transferred: "The Lord has laid on him the iniquity of us all" (Isa 53:6). What appears as divine rejection is revealed as divine agency. Judgment falls, but it falls upon the Servant so that restoration might follow for the people. The logic does not soften the curse; it reassigns it.

The Psalms reinforce this reconfiguration of suffering by binding innocence and obedience to affliction endured. Psalm 69 speaks of reproach suffered "for thy sake" (Ps 69:7). The sufferer is not distant from God; he is consumed by zeal for God's house. This zeal provokes hostility precisely because it exposes false security. When the psalmist cries, "Let not those who hope in thee be put to shame because of me" (Ps 69:6), he articulates a fear that fidelity itself may become a stumbling block for others. This fear resonates deeply with the messianic vocation as it unfolds in the Gospels.

Psalm 118 completes the picture by naming rejection as the mechanism of divine selection. "The stone which the builders rejected has become the head of the corner" (Ps 118:22). The builders are not pagans or outsiders; they are those entrusted with construction. Rejection occurs within the house itself. Yet God's response is not replacement but reversal. What is cast aside becomes foundational. The psalm immediately attributes this reversal to God's sovereign action: "This is the Lord's doing; it is marvellous in our eyes" (Ps 118:23). The logic is not human ingenuity but divine paradox.

Second Temple texts confirm that such paradoxes were not foreign to Jewish reflection, even if they were not universally applied to the Messiah. The *Wisdom of Solomon* presents the righteous one as condemned precisely because his life indicts the wicked: "He professes to have knowledge of God, and calls himself a child of the Lord... Let us see if his words are true" (Wis 2:13,17). The mockery mirrors Psalm 22 and anticipates the logic of vindication beyond death. "The righteous man will stand with great confidence in the presence of those who have afflicted him" (Wis 5:1). Suffering gives way to eschatological reversal.

This eschatological horizon is essential. Without it, suffering remains contradiction. With it, suffering becomes preparation. Daniel's vision situates vindication beyond immediate history. The saints are "given into [the beast's] hand for a time, times, and half a time" (Dan 7:25), yet judgment is rendered, and "the kingdom and the dominion... shall be given to the people of the saints of the Most High" (Dan 7:27). The Son of Man's exaltation emerges not in isolation but as the culmination of suffering endured by the faithful. Dominion follows endurance.

This pattern exposes the inadequacy of expectations that demand visible triumph as the criterion of divine favour. The Messiah's mission cannot be judged solely by immediate outcomes. The Scriptures repeatedly locate God's decisive action within apparent failure. Resurrection faith does not invent this logic; it reveals it.

Jesus' own teaching aligns with this scriptural insistence. When He speaks of the grain of wheat that must fall into the earth and die in order to bear fruit (John 12:24), He articulates a principle already embedded in Israel's story. Life emerges from death; fruitfulness follows loss. The metaphor is not illustrative only of Jesus' fate but of the divine economy itself. Those who cling to life will lose it; those who lose life for God's sake will find it (Matt 16:25). The Messiah embodies what Israel's Scriptures have long proclaimed.

The apostolic proclamation consistently appeals to this necessity. Peter declares that Jesus was "delivered up according to the definite plan and foreknowledge of God" (Acts 2:23). The cross is neither accident nor contingency. It is plan. Yet Peter immediately charges his hearers with responsibility: "you crucified and killed" (Acts 2:23). Divine necessity and human culpability intersect. Suffering is necessary; rejection remains blameworthy. The paradox is not resolved by choosing one over the other.

When the apostles proclaim the Resurrection, they do not erase the scandal of the cross; they reinterpret it. The Resurrection does not cancel suffering but vindicates it. Only because God has acted does the necessity of suffering become intelligible. Without vindication, the logic collapses. With it, Scripture itself demands re-reading.

The Messiah's suffering, then, is not a concession to disappointment but the fulfilment of a pattern that runs through Israel's history, worship, and prophecy. The necessity lies not in hindsight but in coherence. A Messiah who does not suffer would fracture the story God has been telling all along.

The coherence of this pattern becomes unmistakable when the prophetic texts are allowed to interpret one another rather than being isolated into competing portraits. What earlier chapters exposed as tension—the suffering Servant and the reigning Son of Man—now resolves itself as a single trajectory viewed from different angles. Scripture does not offer alternative messianic options; it unfolds a single vocation whose fullness can only be grasped when humiliation and exaltation are read together.

Daniel's vision of the Son of Man has often been treated as the decisive counterweight to suffering. Yet the vision itself embeds exaltation within persecution. Daniel watches as the beasts exercise violent dominion, and he observes that "the horn made war with the saints, and prevailed over them" (Dan 7:21). The Son of Man does not interrupt this violence immediately. Vindication arrives only when "the Ancient of Days came, and judgment was given for the saints of the Most High" (Dan 7:22). Dominion is conferred after endurance, not before it. The Son of

## THE CHRISTIAN RESPONSE: WHY THE MESSIAH HAD TO SUFFER

Man's exaltation presupposes the suffering of the saints with whom he is identified. Glory emerges as judicial reversal, not as pre-emptive triumph.

This structure clarifies why Jesus repeatedly unites the title "Son of Man" with predictions of suffering. "The Son of Man must suffer many things and be rejected" (Mark 8:31). The verb *dei*—"must"—signals necessity rather than possibility. Jesus is not forecasting an unfortunate outcome; He is articulating destiny grounded in Scripture. When He declares before the Sanhedrin, "You will see the Son of Man seated at the right hand of Power, and coming with the clouds of heaven" (Mark 14:62), He fuses Daniel's vision with His imminent condemnation. Exaltation and rejection are not sequential accidents; they belong to a single revelation.

Zechariah's pierced one provides the connective tissue between Servant suffering and Son of Man vindication. "They shall look on me whom they have pierced" (Zech 12:10). The text resists reduction. The pierced figure is bound to divine identity, and recognition comes through mourning rather than conquest. The following oracle intensifies the cost: "Strike the shepherd, that the sheep may be scattered" (Zech 13:7). Scattering precedes gathering; loss precedes restoration. Zechariah refuses any messianism that bypasses judgment.

These prophetic patterns reframe the objection that suffering disqualifies messianic identity. On the contrary, Scripture presents suffering as the condition of faithful mediation. The Servant bears sin, the righteous sufferer is vindicated, the shepherd is struck, the saints are oppressed, and only then does dominion emerge. The Messiah stands at the intersection of these figures, not as an exception but as their fulfilment.

The logic extends even to the covenant itself. Jeremiah's promise of a new covenant does not arise from triumph but from failure. "They broke my covenant, though I was their husband" (Jer 31:32). Restoration follows rupture. The law is written on the heart only after the old structures prove inadequate. Ezekiel's promise of renewal likewise emerges from exile and death: "I will put my Spirit within you, and you shall live" (Ezek 37:14). Resurrection imagery saturates covenant renewal. Life comes out of death because God's faithfulness operates through judgment.

This covenantal logic exposes the inadequacy of objections grounded solely in visible success. Israel's own Scriptures locate divine action precisely where human expectation falters. The Messiah's suffering is therefore not an anomaly but a concentrated expression of a long-established pattern. Rejection becomes the crucible in which obedience is revealed. Vindication follows not as compensation but as confirmation.

The apostles insist on this necessity with remarkable unanimity. Peter proclaims that "all the prophets who have spoken... foretold these days" (Acts 3:24). Paul declares that the Gospel he received accords with Scripture: Christ "died for our sins in accordance with the Scriptures" and "was raised on the third day in accordance with the Scriptures" (1 Cor 15:3–4). The appeal is not to innovation but to continuity. The suffering Messiah is not discovered after the fact; He is recognised as the one Scripture has been preparing all along.

The road to Emmaus narrative crystallises this recognition. Jesus does not begin with Himself and work backward. He begins "with Moses and all the prophets" and interprets "the things concerning himself" (Luke 24:27). The necessity of suffering emerges from the totality of Scripture read as a unified witness. Hearts burn not because expectations are affirmed, but because coherence is revealed. The Scriptures do not change; the readers do.

By this stage, the claim becomes unavoidable. A Messiah who bypasses suffering would stand outside the logic of Israel's own story. Such a figure might satisfy immediate longing for power, but he would fracture the narrative through which God has consistently acted. The suffering Messiah does not solve the scandal of rejection by eliminating it. He transforms it into revelation.

Once this scriptural logic is grasped, the charge that a suffering Messiah represents a theological improvisation collapses. What had appeared to be a contradiction now reveals itself as convergence. Israel's Scriptures do not scatter suffering across disparate figures accidentally; they concentrate it progressively, drawing the lines tighter until they meet in a single vocation. The Messiah stands where Israel's story itself converges.

This convergence becomes especially clear when the role of mediation is considered. Moses suffers rejection before he becomes redeemer. David endures persecution before enthronement. The prophets bear hostility precisely because they speak God's word. In each case, suffering accompanies the task of standing between God and the people. The mediator absorbs resistance in order to bring restoration. Isaiah's Servant intensifies this mediatorial role beyond precedent. He does not merely suffer alongside the people; he suffers in their place. "He bore the sin of many, and made intercession for the transgressors" (Isa 53:12). The Servant's suffering is priestly as well as prophetic. It accomplishes what proclamation alone cannot.

This priestly dimension resolves another objection raised in earlier chapters: the problem of curse. Deuteronomy's warning that one hanged on a tree is cursed does not evaporate in Isaiah's vision; it is redirected. The Servant bears curse as intercession. He is not cursed because he is rejected by God; he is rejected because he bears what belongs to others. The logic anticipates the later apostolic formulation without depending upon it. Isaiah's Servant already inhabits the paradox of being stricken by God while acting in obedience to God's will. The contradiction dissolves only when suffering is understood as vocation.

The Psalms of lament reinforce this priestly logic by giving the righteous sufferer a representative voice. The psalmist cries not merely for personal vindication but for the vindication of God's name. "Let not those who hope in thee be put to shame through me, O Lord God of hosts" (Ps 69:6). Suffering borne in fidelity becomes a public test of God's righteousness. Vindication, therefore, is not optional. It is demanded by God's own faithfulness. When vindication comes, it extends beyond the individual to encompass the community. "The humble shall see it and be glad" (Ps 69:32). Representation replaces isolation.

This representative suffering explains why messianic rejection functions as revelation rather than refutation. The Messiah does not stand apart from Israel's failures; he gathers them into himself. Hosea had spoken of Israel as God's son called out of Egypt (Hos 11:1), yet the son proved disobedient. The Messiah recapitulates this filial identity, walking the same path without deviation. Where Israel faltered, he remains faithful. The path is marked not by triumph but by obedience under pressure. Suffering becomes the measure of fidelity.

Daniel's vision, read through this lens, sharpens rather than softens the necessity of suffering. The Son of Man's exaltation is not detached from the fate of the saints; it is bound to it. Authority is given after endurance, and dominion follows judgment. The vision does not offer an escape from history but its transfiguration. God's rule is revealed precisely when human power exhausts itself. The beasts reign briefly; the saints inherit permanently. The Son of Man embodies this reversal.

This reversal exposes the inadequacy of objections rooted in immediacy. A Messiah who conforms to expectations of instant deliverance would short-circuit the narrative through which God has been forming His people. Scripture trains Israel to recognise God's action not by spectacle alone but by fidelity tested through suffering. The Messiah stands within this training, not above it. His suffering does not negate messianic hope; it fulfils it.

The apostles recognise this fulfilment not as innovation but as discovery. Peter insists that what occurred in Jerusalem unfolded "according to the definite plan and foreknowledge of God" (Acts 2:23). Paul speaks of the mystery "hidden for ages" but now revealed (Col 1:26). The mystery is not that suffering occurs, but that suffering redeems. The Messiah does not merely endure rejection; he transforms it into the instrument of restoration.

At this point, the logic of necessity stands fully exposed. The Messiah must suffer because the story God has been telling from the beginning demands it. Election provokes resistance. Mediation absorbs hostility. Vindication follows obedience. Glory emerges through abasement. These are not isolated themes; they form a coherent pattern that converges in the Messiah.

The question posed at the end of the previous chapter has now received its answer. Scripture itself requires a suffering Messiah. The objection that suffering disqualifies messianic identity has been overturned not by appeal to later theology but by the internal logic of Israel's own witness. What remains is not doubt but decision: whether to accept that God's ways consistently confound human expectation, or to insist that fulfilment must conform to prior assumptions.

This decision is never merely intellectual. The recognition of a suffering Messiah requires not only rereading Scripture but relinquishing the criteria by which power, success, and divine favour are ordinarily measured. Israel's Scriptures had long prepared for such a relinquishment, even as they resisted it. The prophets repeatedly warned that God's ways would overturn expectation, that deliverance would arrive through judgment, and that life would emerge from death. The Messiah embodies this reversal in its most concentrated form.

The figure of the righteous sufferer stands at the heart of this preparation. Wisdom literature does not treat suffering as accidental to righteousness but as its testing ground. "The souls of the righteous are in the hand of God," declares the *Wisdom of Solomon*, "and no torment will ever touch them" (Wis 3:1). Yet this assurance is spoken precisely in the context of their apparent destruction. The righteous are "thought to have died," their departure "considered a disaster" (Wis 3:2–3). Vindication lies beyond immediate perception. This eschatological horizon reshapes the meaning of suffering itself. What appears as defeat becomes the seed of life when measured by God's judgment rather than human sight.

This horizon is indispensable for understanding why Scripture insists that suffering precedes glory. Without it, suffering remains scandal. With it, suffering becomes passage. The prophets consistently locate renewal beyond catastrophe. Ezekiel's valley of dry bones does not deny death; it traverses it. "Our bones are dried up, and our hope is lost," the people lament (Ezek 37:11). God responds not by disputing the diagnosis but by transforming it: "I will open your graves, and raise you from your graves, O my people" (Ezek 37:12). Resurrection imagery becomes the grammar of restoration. The Messiah's path mirrors this movement from apparent annihilation to divine re-creation.

The necessity of suffering also clarifies the meaning of obedience. Scripture does not define obedience as success but as faithfulness under trial. Abraham's willingness to offer Isaac, though not culminating in death, establishes obedience as surrender to God's promise beyond comprehension (Gen 22:1–18). The promise is secured not through grasping but through relinquishing. The Messiah embodies this obedience not symbolically but existentially. He entrusts himself to God in the very moment when divine promise seems most obscured.

This obedience exposes the deepest root of messianic resistance. The objection to a suffering Messiah is not only that such a figure appears cursed or defeated, but that he undermines the logic of self-justification. If God saves through suffering obedience, then human systems of merit, control, and security are revealed as insufficient. The Messiah becomes not merely a deliverer but a judge of hearts. Recognition demands repentance, not merely assent.

The Gospels preserve this dynamic in Jesus' encounters with those who struggle to accept His path. When James and John ask for places of honour, Jesus responds not with rebuke alone but with a question that reframes glory itself: "Are you able to drink the cup that I drink?" (Mark 10:38). The cup signifies suffering accepted in obedience. Glory follows, but it follows the cup. The structure mirrors Isaiah's Servant and Daniel's Son of Man alike. Authority is given to those who endure.

The apostolic witness confirms that this pattern does not end with Jesus; it extends to those who belong to Him. Peter exhorts believers not to be surprised at suffering, but to recognise it as participation in Christ's path: "Rejoice insofar as you share Christ's sufferings, that you may also rejoice and be glad when his glory is revealed" (1 Pet 4:13). Participation in suffering becomes participation in glory. The Messiah's vocation sets the template for the people formed in His image.

This participatory dimension reinforces the necessity of suffering within messianic identity. The Messiah does not suffer in isolation; He inaugurates a way of being in covenant with God that passes through death to life. Israel's Scriptures had prepared for this by narrating a people formed through exile, loss, and return. The Messiah gathers this history into Himself, fulfilling it not by bypassing its darkest chapters but by inhabiting them fully.

At this point, the objections catalogued in the previous chapter are transformed from barriers into signposts. The cross, once the ultimate scandal, becomes the decisive disclosure of God's fidelity. The curse borne becomes the means of blessing. The rejection endured becomes the foundation of reconciliation. Scripture itself demands this inversion. Without it, the story remains incomplete.

The suffering Messiah, therefore, does not represent a departure from Israel's hope but its unveiling. What had been hinted through narrative, lament, and prophecy now stands revealed as necessity. God's chosen one must suffer because God's way of saving has always moved through obedience tested by loss. The Messiah's path is the culmination of Israel's long education in trust.

Seen in this light, the scandal of a suffering Messiah gives way to a more unsettling realisation: the Scriptures do not merely *permit* such a Messiah, they *form Israel to recognise Him*. The difficulty lies not in the texts themselves but in the resistance of the human heart to the kind of salvation God enacts. From the beginning, Israel is taught that God's strength is disclosed through weakness, His fidelity through apparent absence, His victory through surrender. The Messiah stands at the centre of this pedagogy.

This pedagogical dimension explains why recognition of the Messiah is repeatedly portrayed as a matter of sight rather than information. Isaiah laments a people who hear but do not understand, who see but do not perceive (Isa 6:9–10). The problem is not lack of revelation but incapacity to receive it. The suffering Servant intensifies this incapacity because He contradicts the expectations formed by power. "We esteemed him stricken, smitten by God, and afflicted" (Isa 53:4). The verb *esteemed* reveals perception shaped by assumption. What looks like divine rejection is misread because the logic of redemptive suffering has not yet been grasped.

Zechariah's oracle captures this moment of reversal with painful clarity.

Mourning comes *after* recognition: "They shall look on him whom they have pierced, and they shall mourn for him" (Zech 12:10). The text assumes that recognition arrives through grief rather than triumph. Acceptance follows repentance. The Messiah is recognised not when He conforms to expectation, but when expectation is shattered.

This sequence aligns with Israel's broader covenantal rhythm. Repentance precedes restoration. Exile comes before return. Judgment clears the ground for renewal. The Messiah stands within this rhythm, embodying it personally. His suffering is not merely representative; it is pedagogical. It teaches Israel how God saves.

The New Testament writers are acutely aware of this pedagogical function. Paul describes the cross as a "stumbling block to Jews" (1 Cor 1:23), yet he immediately insists that it is "the power of God and the wisdom of God" (1 Cor 1:24). Wisdom here does not mean cleverness; it means fidelity to God's way of acting. The cross reveals a divine wisdom that subverts human criteria of strength and success. It unmasks the limits of human judgment.

Paul's insistence that Christ was "obedient unto death, even death on a cross" (Phil 2:8) situates suffering squarely within obedience. Exaltation follows, but only after obedience has been tested to its limit. This is not a detour from messianic vocation; it is its fulfilment. The Messiah does not merely teach obedience; He enacts it.

The logic extends backward into Israel's worship. The sacrificial system itself presupposes that life is restored through offering. Blood is poured out not as spectacle but as mediation. The Day of Atonement dramatizes the truth that reconciliation requires passage through death-like symbolism before restoration is declared (Lev 16). The Messiah's suffering gathers this liturgical grammar into a single, definitive act. The offering is not repeated because the obedience is complete.

This liturgical dimension underscores why suffering cannot be excised from messianic identity without dismantling the covenant itself. The Messiah stands as priest, victim, and mediator. His suffering is not merely endured; it is offered. The Scriptures had prepared Israel for such an offering through ritual, prophecy, and narrative. Recognition requires seeing these strands together.

At this point, the force of necessity presses with full weight. The Messiah must suffer because God's covenantal dealings have always unfolded through loss that leads to life. The attempt to imagine a Messiah who reigns without suffering does not elevate hope; it diminishes it by severing it from the story God has told. Scripture resists such abstraction. It insists on history, obedience, and cost.

The remaining question is not whether the suffering Messiah fits the Scriptures, but whether one is willing to accept the kind of God those Scriptures reveal. A God who saves through suffering overturns every instinct for control. He demands trust rather than calculation, repentance rather than reassurance. The Messiah embodies this demand, confronting every reader with a decision that is at once theological and existential.

When the Scriptures are allowed to speak in this full register, the question that once appeared decisive—*how could the Messiah suffer?*—is transformed into a more searching one: *how could he not?* To remove suffering from the messianic vocation would be to rupture the inner logic by which God has revealed Himself from the beginning. The Messiah does not interrupt Israel's story; He brings it to coherence.

From Joseph to Moses, from David to the prophets, from the righteous sufferer of the Psalms to the Servant of Isaiah, God's chosen agents are recognised not by immediate vindication but by obedience endured under contradiction. The Scriptures train Israel to expect that God's decisive work will pass through humiliation before it emerges in glory. This training is not accidental. It forms a people capable of recognising salvation when it arrives in unexpected form.

The suffering Messiah, therefore, stands not as a theological problem to be solved but as the culmination of divine pedagogy. He gathers into Himself Israel's long history of election and rejection, promise and exile, obedience and failure. Where Israel faltered, He remains faithful. Where Israel bore the weight of judgment, He bears it fully. Where Israel hoped for restoration, He enacts it through obedience unto death.

This is why the Resurrection does not negate the necessity of suffering but confirms it. Vindication does not erase the cross; it reveals its meaning. The risen Messiah remains the crucified one. Glory does not overwrite obedience; it ratifies it. The marks of suffering become the signs of authority because they testify to a faithfulness that endured without compromise.

At this point, the objections catalogued earlier in the book no longer carry the same force. The curse borne is revealed as the means of blessing. The rejection endured is disclosed as the foundation of reconciliation. The apparent failure becomes the instrument of renewal. Scripture itself insists upon this inversion. To deny it is not to preserve fidelity to Israel's hope, but to truncate it.

The Messiah's suffering is not a concession to historical circumstance. It is the necessary form of divine love within a broken world. God does not redeem from a distance. He enters into the depths of human rejection, absorbs its violence, and transforms it from within. The Messiah's path exposes the cost of covenant fidelity and reveals the extent of God's commitment to His people.

This recognition presses a final decision upon the reader. The question is no longer whether the Scriptures *allow* for a suffering Messiah, but whether one is willing to accept a God who saves in this way. Such a God overturns every instinct for domination and control. He calls not for admiration alone, but for repentance, trust, and participation.

Israel's Scriptures had been preparing for this moment all along. The suffering Messiah does not stand outside their witness. He stands at its centre. To recognise Him is not to abandon the hope of Israel, but to see that hope fulfilled in a way deeper, more demanding, and more glorious than expectation had imagined.

# 20

# Israel and the Church: The Mystery of God's Faithfulness

Paul begins where any faithful account must begin: not with theory, not with triumph, but with anguish. He swears an oath that strains language to its limit. "I am speaking the truth in Christ, I am not lying; my conscience bears me witness in the Holy Spirit, that I have great sorrow and unceasing anguish in my heart" (Rom 9:1–2). The weight of the sentence is deliberate. Paul does not permit himself the comfort of abstraction. The question of Israel and the Messiah is not an academic puzzle but a wound that does not close. Any theology that speaks lightly here has already departed from the apostolic mind.

The cause of this anguish is not uncertainty about Israel's status but the opposite. Paul rehearses Israel's privileges with solemn insistence, as though to forbid any later attempt to diminish them. "They are Israelites, and to them belong the adoption, the glory, the covenants, the giving of the law, the worship, and the promises; to them belong the patriarchs, and of their race, according to the flesh, is the Christ" (Rom 9:4–5). Nothing is revoked. Nothing is spiritualised away. The Messiah Himself is bound irrevocably to Israel "according to the flesh." Paul's sorrow arises precisely because Israel remains elect. If Israel had been discarded, grief would give way to explanation. Instead, grief remains because covenant remains.

This opening establishes the moral atmosphere of the entire chapter. Paul does not speak as a Gentile judge surveying Israel from a distance. He speaks as an Israelite for Israel, bearing within himself the tension of promise and non-recognition. John Chrysostom captures this posture with clarity: Paul "does not merely lament, but burns; not for strangers, but for his own people, whose dignity he sets forth before accusing their unbelief" (*Homilies on Romans*, on Rom 9). Love precedes judgment, and grief precedes argument.

From this grief Paul articulates the governing axiom that will carry the entire discussion: "It is not as though the word of God has failed" (Rom 9:6). The sentence is stark. Failure is the category he refuses above all others. Israel's present non-recognition of Jesus cannot be interpreted as divine collapse or covenantal nullification. God's fidelity does not rise or fall with immediate human response. To concede failure here would be to indict God Himself.

Paul grounds this claim not in novelty but in Israel's own Scriptures. Election, he insists, has never unfolded as a flat or automatic process. "Not all who are descended from Israel belong to Israel" (Rom 9:6). The statement is not a rejection of Israel but an internal distinction already present within her history. Isaac is chosen over Ishmael; Jacob over Esau, "though they were not yet born and had done nothing either good or bad" (Rom 9:11). Paul presses the point relentlessly: election precedes merit, response, or comprehension. "I will have mercy on whom I have mercy, and I will have compassion on whom I have compassion" (Exod 33:19, cited in Rom 9:15). Mercy is not a reaction to human success; it is the ground upon which all history stands.

This appeal to divine freedom does not dissolve responsibility, nor does it excuse unbelief. It establishes the framework within which unbelief must be interpreted. Israel's story has always included resistance under revelation. Isaiah was commissioned to speak to a people who would hear without understanding and see without perceiving (Isa 6:9–10). Revelation, Scripture insists, does not guarantee recognition. On the contrary, it intensifies the drama of response.

Origen, commenting on this passage, insists that Paul's argument does not diminish Israel but deepens the mystery of God's dealings with her. God permits resistance, Origen writes, "not in order to destroy those who resist, but in order to reveal the riches of His mercy toward all" (*Commentary on Romans*, on Rom 9). Resistance itself is drawn, unwillingly, into God's providential economy.

Paul therefore refuses two simplifications at once. He refuses the claim that Israel's unbelief proves God's promise false, and he refuses the claim that unbelief is inconsequential. The tension is real because covenant is real. Israel's privileges remain intact, and Israel's stumbling will therefore be treated with full seriousness. The Messiah has not come to annul election but to expose its depth.

This opening also establishes the tone with which modern objections must be addressed. When contemporary rabbinic Judaism insists that the Messiah must accomplish all restoration in a single historical act, Paul's response is already implicit. Scripture itself does not measure fidelity by immediacy. Israel's own history bears witness to promises given long before fulfilment is visible. Abraham receives the promise before Isaac is born; David is anointed long before he reigns; exile intervenes between covenant and restoration. Delay is not failure. It is the ordinary medium of God's faithfulness.

Augustine presses this point with sober restraint. God's promises, he insists, "are not undone by delay, nor exhausted by one moment in time; they stand because God stands" (cf. *Against Two Letters of the Pelagians*, drawing on Romans). Covenant fidelity belongs to God's character, not to human timetables.

Thus the chapter begins where it must: with grief that refuses despair, with election that refuses erasure, and with fidelity that refuses the category of failure. The Messiah stands within this tension, not as its negation but as its decisive revelation. Israel's story is not closed by Christ; it is brought into its most searching moment. The question that now presses is not whether God has been faithful, but how that faithfulness is unfolding in time.

If the word of God has not failed, then Israel's present condition must be read not as refutation but as revelation. Paul moves immediately to the most difficult territory without softening the force of his claims. Israel, he says, pursued the law as a way of righteousness and did not attain it, "because they did not pursue it through faith, but as if it were based on works" (Rom 9:32). The result is not ambiguity but collision. "They stumbled over the stumbling stone" (Rom 9:32), a phrase Paul anchors deliberately in Isaiah: "Behold, I am laying in Zion a stone that will make men stumble, and a rock that will make them fall" (Isa 8:14; Isa 28:16, cited in Rom 9:33). The stumbling is not accidental. The stone is laid by God Himself.

This language permits no sentimental reading of Israel's non-recognition of the Messiah. Scripture names it a stumble, not merely an alternative interpretation. Paul intensifies the claim in the following chapter: "My heart's desire and prayer to God for them is that they may be saved" (Rom 10:1). Prayer for salvation presupposes danger. He does not accuse Israel of malice, but he does diagnose a profound disorder: "They have a zeal for God, but it is not according to knowledge" (Rom 10:2). Zeal, which elsewhere Scripture praises, here becomes tragically misdirected. The problem is not indifference but misrecognition.

Paul identifies the nerve of the conflict with uncompromising clarity. "Christ is the end of the law, that everyone who has faith may be justified" (Rom 10:4). The Greek *telos* does not mean abolition but fulfilment, goal, completion. The law reaches its purpose in the Messiah. Israel's stumbling, therefore, is not over a foreign object but over the very fulfilment of her own Scriptures. The seriousness of the moment lies precisely here. To miss the Messiah is not to abandon the covenant, but to fail to recognise where the covenant has been leading.

The gravity of this failure is not Paul's invention. Jesus Himself speaks of Israel's resistance in language that echoes the prophets. He laments a people who refuse to see and hear, who honour God with their lips while their hearts remain far from Him. He names the leaders of His time blind guides, warns of hardness of heart, and foretells judgment upon Jerusalem "because you did not know the time of your visitation." These sayings do not contradict Paul's posture of anguish; they intensify it. Love speaks truth because the stakes are real.

The apostolic preaching in Acts preserves this balance with remarkable consistency. Peter declares to the men of Israel that they "killed the Author of life" (Acts 3:15), language that leaves no room for neutrality. Yet he immediately adds, "I know that you acted in ignorance, as did also your rulers" (Acts 3:17), and follows this with a summons to repentance so that sins may be blotted out and times of refreshing may come from the presence of the Lord (Acts 3:19). Responsibility and mercy are held together without dilution. Ignorance explains; it does not excuse. Repentance remains possible because God's purpose has not been exhausted.

Paul presses this diagnosis further by invoking the category of hardening. "What Israel sought it did not obtain, but the elect obtained it. The rest were hardened" (Rom 11:7). He again turns to Scripture, citing Isaiah and the Psalms: "God gave them a spirit of stupor, eyes that should not see and ears that should not hear" (Isa 29:10; Ps 69:22–23, cited in Rom 11:8–10). This language is severe, and Paul does not apologise for it. Israel's resistance is not merely sociological or historical; it participates in a judicial mystery already attested in the prophets.

John Chrysostom refuses to blunt this severity, even as he guards against arrogance. Commenting on Romans 11, he warns Gentile believers that Israel's hardening is "both a punishment and a medicine," a judgment that chastens and a providence that restrains pride (*Homilies on Romans*, on Rom 11). Hardening is real, but it is not identical with abandonment. It belongs within God's governance rather than outside it.

This is the point at which any honest theology must resist diplomatic evasions. Israel's non-recognition of the Messiah is not morally neutral. Scripture itself speaks of stumbling, ignorance, blindness, and hardening. To deny this is to contradict both Jesus and the apostles. Yet Scripture is equally insistent that this condition does not exhaust Israel's identity. Judgment and mercy are not rivals in God's economy; they are successive movements within it.

Here the modern rabbinic objection begins to show its fragility. The claim that the Messiah must accomplish all restoration in a single historical act assumes that Scripture equates fulfilment with immediacy. Paul's argument moves in the opposite direction. Revelation intensifies responsibility, but it does not collapse history. Israel's stumble is serious precisely because God's purposes are still at work. If the story were finished, judgment would be final. Instead, Paul insists that it is not.

Origen makes this point with precision. Reflecting on Israel's hardening, he writes that God "permits blindness for a time, so that grace may come to the nations and, through that grace, provoke Israel to return" (*Commentary on Romans*, on Rom 11). Time itself becomes an instrument of mercy. Delay is not evidence of failure; it is the space in which God's patience operates.

Thus the chapter advances without softening its claims. Israel has stumbled over the Messiah. The stumbling is grave. Scripture names it as such. Yet the presence of judgment itself testifies that covenantal relationship remains intact. God disciplines those He has not abandoned. The word of God has not failed, and Israel's story has not reached its end.

If Israel's stumbling is real and grave, it must now be asked whether it is final. Paul frames the question with deliberate force, as though anticipating the conclusion some readers are eager to draw. "Did they stumble so as to fall?" (Rom 11:11). The Greek verb presses the issue toward irreversibility. His answer is immediate and emphatic: "By no means." The denial is categorical. Whatever Israel's present condition may be, it cannot be interpreted as terminal. To do so would be to misunderstand the way God acts in history.

Paul's reasoning at this point is not sentimental but strategic. He does not minimise Israel's trespass; he assigns it a place within a larger providence. "Through their trespass salvation has come to the Gentiles, so as to make Israel jealous" (Rom 11:11). The sentence refuses simplification. Israel's rejection is neither praised nor ignored. It becomes, paradoxically, an instrument through which mercy is extended beyond Israel's borders and, ultimately, back toward Israel herself. Rejection functions within God's economy without being endorsed by it.

Paul sharpens the paradox further. "If their trespass means riches for the world, and if their failure means riches for the Gentiles, how much more will their full inclusion mean!" (Rom 11:12). The logic is unmistakable. Israel's future restoration is not an afterthought but a climactic hope. The phrase "how much more" introduces an eschatological escalation. Present mercy anticipates greater mercy still to come. The story moves forward, not in circles.

This forward movement exposes the inadequacy of the claim that messianic fulfilment must occur all at once or else be invalid. Paul's argument presupposes temporal sequencing. Mercy unfolds in stages. Israel's stumble opens a door; Israel's return will open it wider. Scripture itself refuses to compress God's purposes into a single moment. Fulfilment, in Paul's account, is dynamic rather than instantaneous.

The prophets had already prepared for such dynamism. Isaiah speaks of a Redeemer who comes to Zion while transgression remains an active reality, and of a covenant that endures "from this time forth and for evermore" (Isa 59:20–21). The Redeemer's coming does not erase history; it redirects it. Zechariah likewise envisions recognition following rejection: "They shall look on him whom they have pierced, and they shall mourn" (Zech 12:10). Mourning presupposes prior refusal. Restoration unfolds through repentance, not erasure.

Paul draws these prophetic threads together when he introduces the decisive temporal marker: "A hardening has come upon part of Israel, until the full number of the Gentiles come in" (Rom 11:25). The word *until* carries immense theological weight. It establishes sequence without speculation. Hardening is partial, not total; temporal, not eternal; purposeful, not arbitrary. Scripture itself authorises this structure. The Messiah's work unfolds within it.

This temporal structure directly challenges the modern rabbinic assertion that a Messiah who does not complete all restoration in a single act cannot be the Messiah. Paul's argument presupposes precisely the opposite.

The Messiah's coming inaugurates a process whose consummation lies ahead. Delay is not deficiency. It is fidelity to the pattern God has already revealed.

Augustine articulates this with sober clarity. Reflecting on Romans 11, he insists that Israel's unbelief "does not abolish the promises, but suspends their fulfilment, so that mercy may be shown first to the nations and afterward to Israel" (cf. *Against Two Letters of the Pelagians*, drawing on Rom 11). Suspension is not negation. Time itself becomes the medium of mercy.

Paul intensifies the hope by casting Israel's future in resurrection language. "If their rejection means the reconciliation of the world, what will their acceptance mean but life from the dead?" (Rom 11:15). The phrase resists reduction. Israel's restoration is not merely administrative or sociological; it is eschatological. It belongs to the same order of divine action as resurrection itself. The Messiah's work, therefore, is not exhausted by His first coming. It continues toward a horizon Scripture itself announces.

This horizon preserves both gravity and hope. Israel's stumble remains a tragedy; it is never relativised into harmless difference. Yet tragedy is not the final word. Scripture refuses despair because God refuses abandonment. Israel's election endures, Israel's discipline remains real, and Israel's future remains promised. The Messiah stands at the centre of this unfolding economy, not as the terminus of God's patience, but as its decisive revelation.

The logic of the chapter now presses toward its central image, one that will make replacement theology impossible and arrogance indefensible. Mercy has unfolded through Israel's stumble, but it has not severed the root from which mercy flows. That image must now be allowed to speak with its full force.

Paul now turns from argument to image, not to soften his claims but to render them unmistakable. "If some of the branches were broken off, and you, a wild olive shoot, were grafted in their place to share the richness of the olive tree, do not boast over the branches" (Rom 11:17–18).

The metaphor is deliberately unsettling. The Gentiles are not a new tree planted beside Israel; they are an unnatural graft inserted into Israel's own life. The root remains prior, sustaining, and indispensable. "It is not you that support the root, but the root that supports you" (Rom 11:18). Paul leaves no conceptual space for replacement.

The olive tree carries covenantal density. Israel is not described as a failed project replaced by a superior species. She remains the cultivated tree whose life flows from promises given to the patriarchs. The Gentiles participate only by grace, not by right. The image does not permit triumphalism, because participation itself is contingent. "They were broken off because of their unbelief, but you stand fast only through faith" (Rom 11:20). Faith, not ethnicity, secures participation, yet ethnicity remains the historical bearer of the promises. The tension is intentional and irreducible.

Paul's warning intensifies rather than relaxes. "Do not become proud, but stand in awe" (Rom 11:20). Awe, not analysis, is the appropriate posture. Gentile believers are reminded that the same God who did not spare the natural branches will not spare arrogance. "Note then the kindness and the severity of God" (Rom 11:22). Mercy and judgment are not competing attributes; they are coordinated expressions of divine fidelity. Kindness without severity degenerates into sentiment. Severity without kindness collapses into despair.

This image dismantles supersessionism at its root. The Church does not replace Israel; she lives from Israel. Any theology that treats Israel as obsolete contradicts the apostolic witness at its most basic level. John Chrysostom presses this point with pastoral urgency. Commenting on the olive tree, he warns Gentile Christians that "if God spared not the branches which were natural, much less will He spare those who are grafted in, should they fall into pride" (*Homilies on Romans*, on Rom 11). The image humbles even as it instructs.

At the same time, the metaphor refuses relativism. Broken branches are not praised for their breakage. Unbelief remains destructive. Yet Paul insists that even broken branches are not beyond restoration. "God has the power to graft them in again" (Rom 11:23). The possibility of re-grafting is not speculative optimism; it is grounded in God's creative power. The natural branches belong to the tree by origin. Their restoration is not alien to God's design but consonant with it.

Paul presses the logic further to ensure it cannot be misunderstood. "If you have been cut from what is by nature a wild olive tree and grafted, contrary to nature, into a cultivated olive tree, how much more will these, the natural branches, be grafted back into their own olive tree" (Rom 11:24). The phrase "how much more" echoes earlier statements of future hope. Restoration is not only possible; it is fitting. The covenantal order itself leans toward it.

This image also exposes the inadequacy of claims that Christianity annuls Judaism or renders Israel irrelevant. The Church's identity is parasitic in the holy sense: life received, not seized. Israel's present unbelief does not erase her role as bearer of the promises. Nor does Gentile faith confer superiority. Everything rests on mercy.

The Church's own teaching has repeatedly returned to this Pauline image to guard against distortion. The Catechism affirms without ambiguity that "the Jewish faith, unlike other non-Christian religions, is already a response to God's revelation in the Old Covenant" and that the Jewish people remain dear to God "for the sake of the fathers" (CCC 839–840). These statements do not soften the necessity of Christ; they honour the irrevocable gifts that precede Him historically and converge in Him theologically.

*Nostra Aetate* speaks in the same register, confessing that the Church "cannot forget that she received the revelation of the Old Testament through the people with whom God in His inexpressible mercy concluded the Ancient Covenant," and affirming that God "does not repent of the gifts He makes nor of the calls He issues" (*Nostra Aetate* 4, echoing Rom 11:29). The document does not invent this vision; it receives it directly from Paul.

The olive tree, therefore, becomes the interpretive key for the entire question. Israel remains the root-bearing people. The Church remains a graft sustained by mercy. Judgment is real; restoration remains possible;

arrogance is forbidden. The Messiah stands at the centre of this tree not as a substitute for Israel, but as the fulfilment toward which Israel's life has always tended.

The argument now reaches its most daring claim. Paul moves from image to promise, from warning to hope, from partial hardening to a future horizon that cannot be dismissed. The logic of mercy presses onward.

Paul now names the mystery explicitly, as though to prevent both despair and presumption from claiming the final word. "Lest you be wise in your own conceits," he writes, "I want you to understand this mystery" (Rom 11:25). The warning is not incidental. Wisdom, untethered from humility, becomes blindness. The mystery he unveils is not a secret to be mastered but a truth to be received with reverence. "A hardening has come upon part of Israel, until the full number of the Gentiles come in" (Rom 11:25). Every term is carefully bounded. The hardening is partial, not total. It is temporal, not eternal. It has a divinely appointed limit.

The presence of the word *until* forbids the claim that Israel's present condition exhausts her destiny. Scripture itself introduces sequence into redemption. History is not flattened into a single moment of fulfilment. God's purposes unfold according to an order that transcends human expectation. The Messiah's coming inaugurates what God Himself will bring to completion. Any insistence that fulfilment must be immediate stands corrected by the apostolic witness.

Paul grounds this future hope not in speculation but in prophecy. "And so all Israel will be saved; as it is written, 'The Deliverer will come from Zion, he will banish ungodliness from Jacob'; 'and this will be my covenant with them when I take away their sins'" (Rom 11:26–27, citing Isa 59:20–21 and Isa 27:9). The citation is decisive. Paul does not abandon the prophets; he interprets them. Israel's salvation remains covenantal, messianic, and eschatological. The Deliverer does not cease to be the Messiah because recognition unfolds over time.

This future horizon directly challenges the modern rabbinic claim that a Messiah who does not complete all expected outcomes in a single historical act cannot be authentic. Paul's argument rests on the opposite assumption. Scripture itself anticipates delay, resistance, repentance, and restoration. The prophets speak repeatedly of recognition following rejection. Zechariah's vision of mourning over the pierced one presupposes prior refusal (Zech 12:10). Daniel's vision of the Son of Man unfolds within a prolonged struggle before dominion is fully manifest (Dan 7:21–27). The pattern is not foreign to Israel's Scriptures; it is woven into them.

Origen interprets Paul's words with striking restraint. He insists that Israel's future salvation does not bypass Christ but returns to Him. "They will not be saved apart from the Deliverer," he writes, "but by turning to Him whom they once did not recognise" (*Commentary on Romans*, on Rom 11). Restoration, in this reading, is not an alternative covenant but the unveiling of the covenant's true centre.

Paul safeguards this hope from misinterpretation by returning once more to the theme of election. "As regards the gospel they are enemies of God, for your sake; but as regards election they are beloved for the sake of their forefathers" (Rom 11:28). The tension is deliberate. Enmity and belovedness coexist without cancellation. The gospel confronts unbelief; election preserves promise. Neither truth erases the other. The Messiah intensifies the paradox rather than resolving it prematurely.

The reason this paradox can be sustained without contradiction lies in God's character. "For the gifts and the call of God are irrevocable" (Rom 11:29). The sentence is as absolute as language allows. God does not revoke what He has given. Covenant is not a temporary arrangement subject to revision. Israel's election, therefore, cannot be annulled by her disobedience any more than the Gentiles' salvation can be claimed as entitlement.

Augustine insists that this irrevocability excludes both despair and arrogance. Reflecting on Romans 11, he writes that God "permits unbelief without abandoning His promise, so that mercy may be shown to all, and boasting may be excluded" (drawing on Rom 11:29–32). Mercy, not merit, governs the entire economy.

Paul draws the argument to its sharpest theological point. "Just as you were once disobedient to God but now have received mercy because of their disobedience, so they too have now been disobedient in order that by the mercy shown to you they also may receive mercy" (Rom 11:30–31). Disobedience itself becomes the occasion for mercy, without being justified by it. God "has consigned all men to disobedience, that he may have mercy upon all" (Rom 11:32). The sentence does not erase moral distinctions; it situates them within a mercy that precedes and surpasses them.

Here the chapter's central claim stands exposed. Israel's present non-recognition is neither excused nor final. It belongs within a providential economy aimed at universal mercy. The Messiah's work is not frustrated by resistance; it incorporates it without endorsing it. History becomes the stage on which mercy displays its patience.

The only remaining question is how such a mystery can be spoken of without distortion. Paul's answer is not further argument but worship. The logic of mercy now gives way to praise.

At this point Paul refuses to say more in the mode of explanation. The argument has reached its limit, not because it is weak, but because it has succeeded. What remains cannot be resolved by analysis without being betrayed. The only faithful response to a mercy this deep is adoration. "O the depth of the riches and wisdom and knowledge of God! How unsearchable are his judgments and how inscrutable his ways!" (Rom 11:33). The doxology is not an ornament appended to theology; it is theology's proper end. When reasoning has carried the mind as far as revelation permits, praise alone remains.

The form of the doxology matters. Paul does not praise God in general terms, but precisely as the One whose ways overturn human expectations. "For who has known the mind of the Lord, or who has been his counsellor?" (Rom 11:34). The question silences both accusation and control. God does not submit His covenantal decisions to human arbitration. Neither Israel nor the Gentiles dictate the terms of mercy. Redemption unfolds according to a wisdom that precedes history and sustains it from within.

This closing movement guards against a final distortion that often accompanies discussions of Israel and the Church: the temptation to mastery. Systems that claim to explain exactly how and when Israel will turn risk replacing awe with calculation. Paul refuses such closure. He confesses mystery without embarrassment. The future of Israel belongs to God not because it is unknowable, but because it is holy ground.

John Chrysostom underscores this posture with pastoral urgency. He warns that when Paul ends in praise, he is teaching the Church how to think rightly about Israel: "Where understanding fails, worship must take over, lest inquiry become arrogance" (*Homilies on Romans*, on Rom 11). Theology that does not culminate in humility has misunderstood its subject.

This humility also preserves the seriousness of Israel's present condition. The doxology does not negate the reality of stumbling, hardening, or judgment. It situates them within a horizon that only God fully comprehends. Mercy does not trivialise sin; it overcomes it. Judgment does not cancel promise; it disciplines it. The Messiah stands at the centre of this convergence as both the stone over which Israel stumbled and the cornerstone upon which God builds His house.

The Church's magisterial teaching consistently echoes this Pauline restraint. The Catechism affirms that "the Jews are still beloved by God, for the sake of the patriarchs," while simultaneously confessing Christ as the fulfilment of the promises made to Israel (CCC 839–840). These affirmations are not contradictory because they arise from the same mystery Paul proclaims. The Church does not resolve the tension by choosing one truth over the other. She holds both because Scripture holds both.

*Nostra Aetate* likewise concludes not with a timetable but with reverence. It calls Christians to remember their shared patrimony with Israel and to reject contempt, precisely because God's covenantal fidelity transcends human calculation (*Nostra Aetate* 4). The document does not soften the gospel; it safeguards it from arrogance. The Messiah remains the centre of salvation history, and Israel remains inseparable from that history.

Paul's doxology therefore functions as a boundary as much as a culmination. It marks the point beyond which speculation becomes presumption. The future reconciliation of Israel is promised, but not scheduled. Its mode is hinted at, but not diagrammed. The Church waits, not as a judge but as a beneficiary of mercy, aware that she herself stands only by grace.

The last line of the doxology gathers everything into a single confession. "For from him and through him and to him are all things. To him be glory for ever. Amen" (Rom 11:36). Origin, means, and end converge in God alone. Israel's election, the Church's calling, the Messiah's work, and history's consummation all flow from this source and return to it. The chapter ends not with resolution, but with surrender.

One movement remains. Paul's praise leaves the reader standing before a future still open, still charged with promise, still governed by mercy. The final word must therefore return to hope—not optimism, not presumption, but the hope born of God's irrevocable faithfulness.

Hope, as Paul leaves it to us, is not a strategy for managing uncertainty but a confession rooted in God's character. The chapter cannot end with Israel solved, the Church secured, or history domesticated. It ends with God trusted. The Messiah's work has revealed enough to bind faith, but not so much as to exhaust mystery. Israel's story remains open because God's fidelity remains active.

This openness does not relativise truth. The Messiah has come. Jesus of Nazareth is not one claimant among many but the fulfilment of Israel's Scriptures, the *telos* toward which law, prophecy, kingship, priesthood, and suffering all converge. Israel's non-recognition of Him is real and grave, named by Scripture itself as stumbling and hardening. Yet Scripture is equally insistent that this condition does not nullify covenantal election. The same God who judges unbelief preserves promise. To deny either truth is to fracture the apostolic witness.

Paul's final vision therefore forbids two equal and opposite errors. It forbids contempt, which treats Israel as discarded once the Church appears. It also forbids indifference, which treats Israel's rejection of the Messiah as theologically inconsequential. The Church stands between these errors only by remaining tethered to Scripture. Israel remains beloved; Israel remains accountable. Mercy remains available; recognition remains necessary. The Messiah remains the centre toward which all must turn.

The rabbinic insistence that messianic fulfilment must be immediate collapses under this weight. Scripture itself refuses such compression. God's redemptive acts unfold through promise, delay, judgment, repentance, and restoration. Abraham waits. David suffers before reigning. Israel endures exile before return. The Messiah Himself passes through rejection, death, and resurrection before exaltation. Staged fulfilment is not a Christian repair; it is a biblical pattern. Paul's "until" stands as an inspired rebuke to any attempt to force God's fidelity into human timetables.

The Church's posture in the meantime is neither triumphal nor anxious. She proclaims Christ without dilution and waits without despair. She recognises that her own existence is bound to Israel's root and sustained by mercy alone. Every Eucharist, every confession of Christ as Lord, every proclamation of the Scriptures testifies to a covenant that has not failed and a promise that has not been exhausted.

Origen captures the final posture with austere clarity. Israel's future, he insists, is not a curiosity for speculation but a summons to humility. "Let the Gentiles fear, lest they too be cut off," he writes, "and let Israel hope, for God is able to graft them in again" (*Commentary on Romans*, on Rom 11). Fear and hope are not opposites here; they are the twin fruits of mercy rightly received.

Augustine echoes the same restraint. The Church does not stand as judge over Israel, nor does she abandon the confession that salvation comes through Christ alone. She waits, he says, "trusting not in her own insight but in the mercy of God, who has enclosed all in disobedience that He may have mercy upon all" (drawing on Rom 11:32). The Church's confidence lies not in prediction but in promise.

The story has not ended. God has not finished. The final word belongs, as it always has, to mercy.

# 21

# The Promise Still Unfinished

From the moment the Messiah was recognised and resisted, the story entered a new tension. Israel's hope did not collapse, yet neither did it settle. The Scriptures had spoken, history had moved, and a figure had appeared who gathered the promises into Himself — yet the world itself remained unresolved. Forgiveness had been proclaimed, the kingdom announced, the sick healed, the dead raised, and still the deeper ache of creation endured. The Messiah had come, and yet the promise continued to reach forward, as though history itself were holding its breath.

Part IV has traced this tension to its roots. Israel's messianic hope emerged not from abstraction but from lived covenantal experience: exile and return, worship and waiting, suffering and fidelity. The diversity of expectation that developed during the Second Temple period did not represent fragmentation of faith, but the stretching of hope under pressure. Kingship, priesthood, prophecy, suffering, glory — these strands did not compete so much as converge, each insisting that God's redemption would be total. The Messiah would not merely correct Israel's past; He would heal the world.

When Jesus of Nazareth entered this world of expectation, He did not stand outside it. He spoke its language, fulfilled its signs, and acted within its symbols. His ministry resonated unmistakably with Israel's Scriptures. He proclaimed the kingdom of God with an authority that recalled Sinai.

He healed with the compassion Isaiah foresaw. He forgave sins as though the Temple's deepest meaning were embodied in His own person. Many recognised in Him the figure toward whom Israel's hope had been leaning. Others hesitated, not from indifference, but from fidelity to Scripture as they understood it. The very magnitude of the promise sharpened the crisis.

The objections that arose were therefore not superficial. They touched the nerve of Israel's faith. The Messiah was expected to restore, to reign, to gather, to judge, and to renew. Suffering, rejection, and execution appeared not merely unexpected, but disqualifying. Deuteronomy's curse, the persistence of foreign domination, the collapse of the Temple — these realities pressed hard against any claim that redemption had arrived. If the Messiah had come, why did the world remain unhealed? Why did history continue to groan?

Christian proclamation did not answer these questions by diminishing Israel's hope. It answered them by refusing to compress fulfilment into a single historical moment. The suffering of the Messiah was not interpreted as a contradiction of Scripture, but as a disclosure of its deeper pattern. His resurrection was proclaimed not as the conclusion of the story, but as its turning point. From the beginning, the Church spoke in two tenses at once: what had been accomplished and what remained. Redemption had begun, yet restoration awaited its hour.

This refusal to close the story prematurely is not an evasion. It is an act of fidelity to Scripture itself. Israel's sacred history had already revealed that God's decisive acts unfold across time. The promise to Abraham did not culminate in his lifetime. The exodus did not end with liberation alone, but opened a long wilderness journey. The covenant at Sinai did not secure immediate faithfulness. The kingdom established under David did not prevent exile. Each act of God opened a future it did not immediately complete. Fulfilment, in the biblical imagination, is rarely instantaneous.

Seen within this pattern, the unresolved hopes surrounding the Messiah are not anomalies. They are indicators of sequence. Recognition and rejection belong to one horizon. Completion belongs to another. The

Messiah has acted decisively within history, yet history itself remains the arena in which God's purposes continue to unfold. Scripture has never allowed redemption to terminate in partial healing. It presses relentlessly toward consummation.

This forward pressure also preserves the mystery of Israel's vocation. The covenant spoken to Abraham, sworn to David, proclaimed by the prophets, and carried through exile was never exhausted by a single generation's response. Scripture speaks instead of delay, of remnant, of mercy unfolding across time. The coming of the Messiah does not cancel this story; it intensifies it. Israel's hope is not closed by fulfilment; it is carried forward by it, awaiting the moment when God's faithfulness will be revealed without remainder.

The persistence of suffering, death, and injustice therefore does not negate the messianic claim; it defines its scope. Forgiveness has been offered, yet death remains. The Spirit has been given, yet creation still groans. The kingdom has been announced, yet the nations continue to rage. These tensions are not embarrassments to be explained away. They are the marks of a story that has turned but not concluded.

At this point, the reader stands at the edge of a changed horizon. The questions that governed the earlier chapters — questions of identity, legitimacy, suffering, and covenant — have reached the limits of what the first coming resolves. To press further is not to revisit the same ground, but to look forward. The issue is no longer whether Jesus could be the Messiah, but how the Messiah completes His work.

The prophets had always held this horizon before Israel. Their visions refused to end with restoration alone. They spoke of a day when justice would be established without exception, when death would be undone, when the knowledge of God would fill the earth, when creation itself would be renewed. These promises were not marginal hopes appended to Israel's faith. They were its destination. The Scriptures have never allowed the story to end in compromise.

What emerges, then, is not contradiction but orientation. The Messiah has come, yet the promises have not been exhausted. Recognition has occurred, yet universal acknowledgment has not. Redemption has begun, yet restoration remains incomplete. Scripture itself insists that this tension is purposeful, ordered, and directed toward a final act of God.

The narrative now leans forward. The silhouette that once gathered Israel's hopes has taken form in history, yet the form itself points beyond the present age. The Messiah's work cannot end with forgiveness alone. It must reach resurrection. It cannot stop with reconciliation. It must culminate in renewal. The world that has been claimed must be transformed.

The story therefore stands not at a conclusion, but at a threshold. The promises spoken in Eden, refined through covenant, tested in exile, recognised and resisted in history, now demand their final movement. What lies ahead is not a new hope, but the completion of the old one — the fulfilment toward which Israel's Scriptures have always been leaning.

The Messiah has come.

The kingdom has begun.

The promise remains open.

Part V turns toward that completion.

# V

# THE PROMISE YET TO BE COMPLETED

# 22

# The King Who Will Come Again: The Second Coming and Israel's Hope

Israel's Scriptures speak with a clarity that resists premature closure. From their earliest layers, they insist that history moves toward a decisive divine act that has not yet occurred, an act in which death is overcome, injustice is judged, peace is universal, and God's reign is openly revealed. This horizon is not poetic excess or devotional metaphor. It is the grammar of Israel's hope. The prophets do not merely announce moral improvement or national recovery; they proclaim an end to the present order of corruption itself.

Daniel gives the most explicit articulation of this expectation. He declares that "many of those who sleep in the dust of the earth shall awake, some to everlasting life, and some to shame and everlasting contempt" (Dan 12:2). This is not the restoration of a nation within history, nor the survival of memory through descendants. It is bodily resurrection, the reanimation of those who have entered death, and it is bound to final judgment. Nothing in Israel's historical experience corresponds to this event. Empires rise and fall, exiles end and begin again, but the dead remain in the grave. Daniel's vision therefore presses beyond any completed moment in Israel's past and establishes a future horizon that history itself has not yet crossed.

Isaiah intensifies this horizon. He proclaims a day when the Lord "will swallow up death forever, and the Lord God will wipe away tears from all faces" (Isa 25:8). Death, the ultimate enemy, is not mitigated or spiritualised; it is abolished. Tears are not merely comforted; they are removed. The prophet ties this victory to the public unveiling of God's glory, when "the Lord alone will be exalted" and human pride brought low (Isa 2:11). The vision is universal. Nations stream to Zion, weapons are transformed into instruments of cultivation, and war ceases as a feature of human existence (Isa 2:2–4). No era of Israel's history satisfies these claims. Conflict persists, death reigns, and the knowledge of God does not fill the earth "as the waters cover the sea" (Isa 11:9). The promise remains outstanding.

Ezekiel's visions confirm this incompletion. In the valley of dry bones, he beholds a field of death that no human power can reverse. At the word of the Lord, the bones assemble, are clothed with flesh, and receive breath, standing as a living multitude (Ezek 37:1–10). The prophet interprets the vision as the restoration of Israel, yet the imagery deliberately exceeds metaphor. The act described is creation itself repeated, life summoned from death by divine command. Ezekiel binds this resurrection imagery to a future covenant of peace, the reunification of the tribes, and the everlasting presence of God among His people (Ezek 37:24–28). The scope is total. Israel is restored, creation renewed, and God dwells permanently in their midst. History records no such consummation.

Job's confession, spoken from the depths of suffering, reaches the same horizon. "I know that my Redeemer lives, and at last he will stand upon the earth; and after my skin has been thus destroyed, then in my flesh I shall see God" (Job 19:25–26). This is not abstract hope or moral vindication. Job expects embodied sight of God after death has done its work. His confidence rests on the character of God as Redeemer, not on circumstances that history could supply. The Redeemer's standing "upon the earth" belongs to the same future register as Daniel's awakening of the dead and Isaiah's abolition of death.

These promises converge upon a single conclusion: Israel's Scriptures demand a final act of God that history has not yet delivered. The prophetic vision includes resurrection of the dead, universal peace, final judgment of evil, restored Israel, and the open reign of God. None of these has been realised in their fullness. Partial returns from exile do not end death. Political sovereignty does not heal creation. Moral reform does not abolish injustice. The prophets know the difference between provisional mercy and ultimate restoration, and they speak unambiguously of the latter.

The Day of the Lord functions as the name for this consummation. Joel announces it as "great and terrible," a day when God judges the nations and restores His people (Joel 3:9–17). Zechariah describes a moment when the Lord stands upon the Mount of Olives, when living waters flow from Jerusalem, and when "the Lord will be king over all the earth" (Zech 14:4–9). The nations are judged, Jerusalem is restored, and God's kingship becomes universal. These texts do not describe gradual improvement or symbolic reign. They announce intervention, disruption, and renewal on a scale history has not yet witnessed.

This unresolved horizon is not a defect in Israel's Scriptures; it is their driving force. The prophets are not embarrassed by delay. They write to communities that know exile, oppression, and disappointment. Their hope is sustained precisely because it is anchored beyond immediate fulfilment. The covenant promises are not cancelled by suffering; they are sharpened by it. Israel learns to live oriented toward a future that God alone can bring to pass.

The claim that the Messiah must arrive once and complete all things immediately finds no support here. Israel's own texts resist such compression. They speak of promises that unfold across time, of judgments that precede restoration, of waiting that refines hope rather than negates it. The prophetic imagination assumes that God's faithfulness may involve delay without denial, patience without abandonment. Fulfilment, when it comes, will be unmistakable because it will accomplish what history cannot.

This is the landscape into which any messianic claim must be placed. A Messiah who exhausts Israel's hope within a single historical moment would need to resolve death, judge evil, restore Israel, and renew creation in visible finality. Israel's Scriptures insist on nothing less. Until those realities stand fulfilled, the story remains open, and the horizon of expectation remains future-facing.

This open horizon did not disappear in the centuries leading up to the time of Jesus. On the contrary, it intensified. The literature of the Second Temple period bears consistent witness to a Judaism that understood itself as still waiting for God's decisive act. Far from assuming that messianic hope could be exhausted in a single historical event, Jewish thought during this period is marked by expectation, delay, and anticipation of a future unveiling that would resolve the contradictions of the present age.

The writings collected in *1 Enoch* provide one of the clearest examples. In these texts, a mysterious figure designated as the Son of Man is hidden for a time and later revealed in glory to judge kings and mighty ones, vindicate the righteous, and inaugurate an everlasting kingdom. The timing of this revelation is explicitly future-oriented. The righteous suffer, injustice persists, and the Son of Man does not yet reign openly. Judgment, resurrection, and universal restoration belong to a moment still to come. The structure of expectation is unmistakable: present endurance gives way to future vindication through divine intervention.

A similar pattern appears in *4 Ezra* (also known as *2 Esdras*), written in the aftermath of Jerusalem's destruction. The text grapples with the apparent failure of God's promises and refuses to resolve the tension prematurely. Ezra is told that the age is hastening toward its end, yet the end itself remains delayed for the sake of God's purposes. A messianic figure appears who destroys evil and ushers in judgment, but this occurs only after a period of suffering and waiting. The delay is not interpreted as abandonment but as part of the divine economy. History is incomplete; fulfilment lies ahead.

The *Psalms of Solomon* articulate the same expectation with Davidic focus. They anticipate a future son of David who will purge Jerusalem, judge unrighteous rulers, gather the scattered people, and reign in justice. This king has not yet appeared. The psalms are written in longing, not celebration. The present age is corrupt; the promised reign remains future. The hope is concrete and political in the deepest sense, yet it is explicitly deferred. The messianic task is unfinished because the Messiah has not yet acted in the way Scripture requires.

The Dead Sea Scrolls confirm this posture of expectation. Texts such as 4Q521 describe the signs of the age to come: the blind see, the lame walk, the poor receive good news, and the dead are raised. These are not records of events already accomplished but descriptions of what will accompany God's final intervention. The community at Qumran understands itself as living in the last days, yet still waiting for the decisive act that will transform the world. The gap between promise and fulfilment is assumed, not denied.

Across these diverse texts, a consistent pattern emerges. Second Temple Judaism does not operate with a closed eschatology. The decisive acts of God—resurrection, judgment, restoration, universal peace—belong to the future. The Messiah, however conceived, is expected to participate in this final act. Hope is not resolved; it is sustained. Waiting is not a failure of faith; it is the posture faith demands.

This expectation also clarifies why no single historical moment could plausibly satisfy Israel's messianic criteria. The destruction of the Temple, the persistence of foreign domination, the continuation of death and injustice all testify that the promised restoration has not yet occurred. Jewish writers do not respond by redefining the promises into abstraction. They respond by reaffirming their future fulfilment. The Messiah, when he comes, will complete what history has left unresolved.

The claim that Judaism requires a Messiah who completes all things in one appearance therefore does not arise from Israel's Scriptures or from its lived interpretive tradition. It is a later simplification imposed upon a far more complex and patient hope. The Judaism of the Second Temple period expects stages, delay, and final unveiling. It does not imagine that God's faithfulness must conform to human timetables or immediate expectations.

This context is decisive. Any evaluation of Jesus' messianic claim must take place within a Judaism that already lives between promise and fulfilment. The idea that a messianic mission could unfold across more than one horizon is not foreign to Israel's faith. It is embedded within its most influential texts and sustained by its historical experience. The expectation of a future consummation is not an embarrassment to Jewish hope; it is its defining feature.

Only against this backdrop can the question of Jesus' teaching be addressed. The issue is not whether he failed to complete Israel's hope at once, but whether his own claims align with the future-oriented structure that Israel's Scriptures and interpretive tradition already assume.

The assertion that the Messiah must come once and complete all things immediately collapses when measured against the internal logic of Israel's own history. Scripture itself establishes a recurring pattern in which divine promise precedes fulfilment by long intervals marked by testing, delay, and apparent contradiction. This pattern is not accidental; it is the means by which God forms His people and discloses the depth of His purposes.

The promise to Abraham illustrates this structure at the foundation of Israel's story. God swears to give him land, descendants, and blessing to the nations, yet Abraham dies without possessing the land promised to him, and his descendants enter centuries of slavery before any national fulfilment begins (Gen 12; 15; Exod 1). The promise is not invalidated by delay; it is carried forward across generations. Fulfilment unfolds in stages, each partial, none exhaustive. Scripture does not treat this as failure but as fidelity tested over time.

David's kingship follows the same pattern. He is anointed by Samuel while Saul still reigns, spends years in exile and danger, and only later ascends the throne (1 Sam 16–2 Sam 5). Even then, the covenant sworn to him—that his throne would endure forever—remains visibly unfulfilled within his lifetime and collapses historically with the exile. Yet the prophets do not declare the covenant void. They reaffirm it, projecting its fulfilment into a future horizon beyond the ruins of monarchy (2 Sam 7; Ps 89; Jer 33). The delay sharpens expectation rather than negating it.

The exile itself becomes the paradigmatic example of staged fulfilment.

Israel's sin leads to judgment; the Temple is destroyed; the people are scattered. Restoration follows, but incompletely. A remnant returns, the Temple is rebuilt, yet the glory described by the prophets does not return in fullness (Hag 2; Ezek 43). Foreign domination persists, injustice continues, and death reigns. Israel learns through exile that restoration can be real without being final, genuine without being complete. Scripture offers no expectation that God's promises must resolve themselves in a single act.

This pattern governs prophetic eschatology. Judgment precedes restoration. Suffering precedes glory. Delay refines hope. Isaiah speaks of a Servant who is first rejected and afflicted before being exalted and vindicated (Isa 52–53). Daniel's Son of Man receives dominion only after the beasts have ruled and been judged (Dan 7). Zechariah envisions a shepherd who is struck before the flock is restored and the Lord becomes king over all the earth (Zech 13–14). The structure is consistent: divine purposes unfold through sequence, not simultaneity.

Within this framework, the insistence on a single, instantaneous messianic fulfilment appears not as fidelity to Scripture but as a compression foreign to its witness. Israel's God reveals Himself across time, through covenantal stages, each faithful yet incomplete until the final act. The Messiah, as the agent of God's ultimate purposes, stands within this same economy. Expectation of delay is not a retreat from hope; it is the shape hope takes under covenantal faithfulness.

The rabbinic claim that a true Messiah must resolve all promises at once therefore rests on a selective reading of Scripture. It overlooks the way Israel's story actually unfolds and the manner in which prophecy itself functions. Promises are made, tested, reinterpreted, and ultimately fulfilled in ways that exceed initial expectation. The Scriptures never require fulfilment to be immediate; they require it to be faithful.

This covenantal logic establishes the conditions under which Jesus' own teaching must be evaluated. If Scripture allows for inaugurated fulfilment awaiting consummation, then the presence of unfulfilled promises does not disqualify a messianic claim. The decisive question becomes whether Jesus locates himself truthfully within this structure—whether he claims to bring God's kingdom in a manner consistent with Israel's staged hope, or whether he contradicts it by denying the future horizon altogether.

The answer to that question lies not in later theological construction but in Jesus' own words.

Jesus does not resolve Israel's expectation by collapsing it into the present. He intensifies it by locating Himself at its centre and extending its horizon forward. His teaching consistently affirms that the decisive act of God remains future, even as its inauguration begins in His own ministry. This is not evasive language offered to explain delay; it is the deliberate articulation of a kingdom that has arrived in seed but not yet in harvest.

The title Jesus most frequently uses for Himself, "the Son of Man," draws directly from Daniel's vision of a human figure who comes with the clouds of heaven and receives everlasting dominion from the Ancient of Days (Dan 7:13–14). When questioned by the high priest, Jesus explicitly identifies Himself with this figure, declaring that they will see "the Son of Man seated at the right hand of Power, and coming with the clouds of heaven" (Mark 14:62). The claim is unmistakable. Yet the timing is equally clear. The coming in glory belongs to a future unveiling, not to the present moment of suffering and rejection. Jesus does not claim that Daniel's vision has already been exhausted; He claims that He is the One to whom it refers.

This future orientation governs Jesus' teaching about judgment. He speaks of a day when the Son of Man will come in glory and "all the nations will be gathered before him" (Matt 25:31–32). The language is judicial and universal. Separation, vindication, and condemnation occur at this moment, not gradually across history. The kingdom that grows quietly now will be revealed openly then. Jesus' parables insist on this distinction. Wheat and weeds grow together until the harvest. Nets gather fish indiscriminately until the sorting. Servants labour until the master returns. The pattern is consistent: present activity anticipates future reckoning.

Jesus' teaching on resurrection reinforces this structure. He speaks of "the last day" as the moment when the dead are raised and judgment rendered (John 6:39–40; 11:24). When Martha confesses her belief in resurrection "on the last day," Jesus does not correct her chronology. He affirms it and deepens it by identifying Himself as "the resurrection and the life" (John 11:25). Authority over resurrection belongs to Him, yet the act itself remains future. Later He declares that "the hour is coming when all who are in the tombs will hear his voice and come forth" (John 5:28–29). Resurrection is universal, bodily, and eschatological. It does not occur piecemeal within history.

The kingdom language Jesus employs preserves the same tension. He proclaims that the kingdom of God is at hand, yet He teaches His disciples to pray for its coming. He speaks of a present reign that liberates and heals, and of a future reign that consummates and judges. The present age witnesses signs of God's power; the age to come reveals its fullness. This distinction is not ambiguous in Jesus' teaching. It is essential to it.

What emerges from Jesus' teaching is not a contradiction between presence and expectation, but a deliberate structure. He proclaims the kingdom as already active—breaking into history through His words, works, and person—yet He simultaneously directs attention toward a future unveiling when what is now hidden will be made manifest. The reign of God is announced as present reality and promised consummation. Jesus does not collapse these horizons into one, nor does He allow them to be separated. The kingdom is truly inaugurated, but it is not yet complete. Any account of His messianic mission that ignores either dimension fails to do justice to His own words.

In this way, Jesus situates Himself precisely within Israel's unresolved eschatology. He does not deny the future hope of resurrection, judgment, restoration, and peace. He claims authority over them and places their fulfilment at His return. The Messiah's mission, as Jesus presents it, unfolds across two horizons: inaugurated redemption through His life, death, and resurrection, and final restoration through His coming in glory.

This structure directly addresses the objection that messianic fulfilment must be immediate and exhaustive. Jesus does not retreat from Israel's promises; He reaffirms them. He does not spiritualise them away; He anchors them in His own future action. The delay is not explained as failure but as the outworking of a kingdom that grows before it is revealed.

The question, therefore, is not whether Jesus failed to complete Israel's hope, but whether His claims cohere with the shape that hope already possessed. His teaching answers that question decisively. He claims to be the Messiah precisely because the story is not finished—and because its completion rests in His hands.

The resurrection of the dead stands at the centre of this future horizon and functions as the decisive test of any messianic claim. Israel's Scriptures do not treat resurrection as an optional symbol or peripheral belief. It is the necessary resolution of God's justice. Without it, the righteous suffer in vain, the wicked escape accountability, and the covenant itself collapses into contradiction. A God who binds Himself to His people cannot allow death to remain the final arbiter of history.

Daniel's vision makes this explicit. Resurrection and judgment occur together, binding personal destiny to divine truth (Dan 12:2–3). Isaiah's proclamation that death will be swallowed up forever places resurrection at the heart of Israel's hope for renewal (Isa 25:8). Ezekiel's imagery of bones restored to life unites national restoration with creation reborn by the breath of God (Ezek 37). These texts do not describe inward consolation or symbolic memory. They describe a future act of God that reverses death itself.

Second Temple Judaism recognises this necessity. The martyrs of the Maccabean period confess their hope with striking clarity: "The King of the universe will raise us up to an everlasting renewal of life" (2 Macc 7:9). Their confidence rests not in political success but in bodily restoration. Rabbinic tradition later affirms resurrection as essential to divine justice, precisely because God's covenantal fidelity must extend beyond the grave. Resurrection is not an embarrassment within Judaism; it is its safeguard against despair.

Jesus' own resurrection must be read within this framework. It does not complete Israel's hope; it inaugurates it. Paul describes Christ as the "first fruits" of those who have fallen asleep (1 Cor 15:20), deliberately invoking the logic of promise and fulfilment. The first fruits guarantee the harvest but do not exhaust it. If resurrection is essential to messianic fulfilment—and if resurrection remains future for humanity as a whole—then messianic fulfilment itself cannot be confined to the past.

Paul presses this logic relentlessly. He insists that creation itself awaits liberation, "groaning" until the revealing of the children of God (Rom 8:19–23). Redemption has begun, but it has not reached its terminus. The Spirit is given as a pledge, not as completion. Believers possess resurrection life in promise, not in fullness. This structure mirrors the prophetic vision precisely. What was promised is being realised, but not yet consummated.

The apostolic witness gives this structure conceptual clarity. Paul speaks of salvation as a reality already received and a glory still awaited. Believers are justified, reconciled, and raised with Christ, yet they also "wait eagerly for adoption as sons, the redemption of our bodies" (Rom 8:23). Creation itself has been decisively claimed by Christ's resurrection, yet it remains subject to decay until the final liberation. This tension is not accidental. It reflects a messianic victory that is real but not yet exhaustive—a conquest begun in history and completed at its end. The apostolic proclamation therefore presupposes two moments within the one messianic work: inauguration and consummation.

This future orientation preserves the integrity of Israel's hope rather than dissolving it. A Messiah who abolishes death only for Himself while leaving the world subject to decay would fail Israel's Scriptures. A Messiah who inaugurates resurrection and promises its universal completion preserves them. The resurrection of Jesus therefore functions not as an endpoint but as a sign. It is the proof that death can be defeated and the guarantee that it will be.

The rabbinic objection that messianic fulfilment must be complete at the Messiah's arrival falters here. If resurrection is indispensable to fulfilment, and if resurrection remains future, then fulfilment itself must remain open. Scripture does not allow resurrection to be partial in significance even if it is partial in occurrence. The future resurrection of the dead demands a future act of the Messiah.

This logic carries unavoidable consequences. The Messiah's mission cannot be evaluated solely by what has already occurred. It must be evaluated by whether the trajectory of Israel's hope is preserved and whether the unresolved promises are secured rather than abandoned. Jesus' teaching and resurrection meet this criterion. They insist that the final victory over death lies ahead and that He Himself will bring it to completion.

The Second Coming, then, is not an explanatory device to rescue a failed expectation. It is the only way to remain faithful to the resurrection hope that Israel's Scriptures place at the centre of God's covenantal purpose. Without it, the story fractures. With it, the promise holds.

The messianic hope preserved in Scripture therefore unfolds along two inseparable horizons. In the first, the Messiah enters history to defeat sin, break the power of death, and inaugurate the kingdom of God. In the second, that same Messiah returns to judge evil, raise the dead, restore Israel, and renew creation. These are not two messiahs, nor two unrelated missions, but one coherent vocation revealed in stages. Fulfilment has truly begun, yet fulfilment has not yet reached its fullness. The logic of Scripture itself requires this distinction.

The expectation of a future consummation therefore preserves Israel's hope rather than nullifying it. Far from postponing fulfilment indefinitely, it insists that God's promises retain their full scope. The return of the Messiah does not revise the prophetic vision; it safeguards it from reduction. Without such a horizon, the covenant risks being interpreted as satisfied by partial historical moments that fall short of the promises themselves.

This preservation becomes most evident in the question of Israel's restoration. The prophets consistently speak of a future reunification, purification, and renewal of the people, bound to the definitive reign of God. Ezekiel foresees the gathering of the scattered tribes, the cleansing of their hearts, and the permanent indwelling of God among them (Ezek 36:24–28; 37:24–28). Jeremiah announces a new covenant written on the heart, accompanied by universal knowledge of the Lord and the forgiveness of sin (Jer 31:31–34). These promises are not exhausted by return from exile, nor are they annulled by subsequent suffering. They remain oriented toward a future act in which God's fidelity becomes unmistakable.

Paul addresses this directly in his treatment of Israel's place within God's saving plan. He rejects the notion that Israel's present non-recognition implies rejection, insisting instead that "the gifts and the calling of God are irrevocable" (Rom 11:29). Israel's story, in Paul's account, is not terminated by the coming of the Messiah; it is intensified. A partial hardening serves a larger purpose, allowing mercy to reach the nations while preserving Israel's future turning. The climax of this mystery coincides with the coming of the Deliverer from Zion, who removes ungodliness and fulfils the covenant (Rom 11:25–27). The logic is eschatological, not polemical. Israel's hope is deferred, not denied.

This framework exposes the inadequacy of the claim that Christianity replaces Israel or spiritualises her promises. Replacement would require declaring Israel's future irrelevant. Spiritualisation would require redefining concrete prophetic promises into abstraction. The expectation of the Messiah's return does neither. It affirms that the promises made to Israel retain their literal force precisely because they remain unfulfilled. The future consummation preserves the realism of the prophetic vision.

The same is true of the promise of universal peace. Isaiah's vision of nations beating swords into ploughshares and learning war no more has not been realised in any epoch (Isa 2:4). Human history offers progress, but not the abolition of violence. The prophetic claim remains outstanding. The return of the Messiah provides the only context in which such a promise can be affirmed without denial of reality. Peace is not gradually achieved by human effort alone; it is established by divine kingship.

Zechariah's vision presses this further. He describes a day when the Lord becomes king over all the earth, when living waters flow from Jerusalem, and when the nations come to worship the God of Israel (Zech 14:9, 16). This is not allegory. It is eschatology. The vision presupposes divine intervention that reshapes the world order. Without a future act of God, such language collapses into hyperbole. With it, the promise remains intact.

In this light, the Second Coming functions as a theological necessity rather than a speculative doctrine. It prevents Israel's Scriptures from being hollowed out by partial fulfilment. It maintains the integrity of prophecy by refusing to declare completion where Scripture itself insists on consummation. The Messiah's return is the moment when the promises reach their appointed end.

This necessity also reorients how the present is understood. The interval between inauguration and consummation is not a vacuum but a space of mercy. Judgment is delayed not because God is uncertain, but because His purposes include patience, repentance, and the gathering of the nations. Peter articulates this clearly when he insists that the apparent delay of the Lord's return reflects divine forbearance, not failure (2 Pet 3:8–9). Time itself becomes an expression of covenantal mercy.

This mercy, however, does not undermine certainty. The return of the Messiah remains the fixed horizon of hope. The prophets never imagined a covenant without completion. They spoke to generations that lived and died without seeing the fulfilment, yet they wrote with confidence precisely because God's fidelity does not depend on immediacy. The Messiah's return ensures that the waiting of Israel, the faith of the Church, and the longing of creation converge in a single act of divine faithfulness.

Thus, the Second Coming is not an embarrassment to messianic faith. It is its safeguard. It allows Israel's hope to remain expansive, concrete, and future-oriented. It refuses to close the story before God has finished telling it.

The return of the Messiah therefore brings Israel's story to its proper completion, not by cancelling what has come before, but by revealing its full meaning. The prophets never envisioned an end to history marked by dissolution or escape. They foresaw revelation—God's purposes made visible, His justice made manifest, His covenant fulfilled without remainder. Isaiah announces a day when "the glory of the Lord shall be revealed, and all flesh shall see it together" (Isa 40:5). This is the public unveiling toward which Israel's Scriptures have always pressed.

Jesus adopts this same register. He speaks of a coming that is unmistakable, sudden, and universal, "as lightning flashes from the east and shines as far as the west" (Matt 24:27). The ambiguity of the present age—faith alongside unbelief, righteousness alongside injustice—does not endure indefinitely. The return of the Messiah resolves what history leaves unresolved. Truth is no longer contested; it is revealed. The question of God's kingship is no longer debated; it is displayed.

This unveiling fulfils Israel's deepest covenantal hope: that God will dwell openly with His people. From the tabernacle in the wilderness to the Temple in Jerusalem, Israel lived with the promise of divine presence mediated and partial. Ezekiel's vision of the glory departing and later returning to a restored sanctuary expresses this longing with clarity (Ezek 10; 43:1–7). The return of the Messiah completes this movement. God's presence is no longer veiled or withdrawn. "The dwelling of God is with men" (Rev 21:3). Covenant reaches communion.

This communion does not erase Israel's identity; it vindicates it. The nations are not absorbed into anonymity; they are healed and ordered under God's reign. Zechariah's vision of the Lord as king over all the earth preserves plurality within unity, worship without coercion (Zech 14:9, 16). The return of the Messiah establishes a world reconciled, not flattened—a creation restored, not replaced.

The resurrection of the dead stands as the personal manifestation of this cosmic renewal. Daniel foresaw the righteous shining "like the stars forever and ever" (Dan 12:3). Paul insists that what is sown perishable is raised imperishable, what is sown in weakness is raised in power (1 Cor 15:42–44). Identity is preserved; corruption is removed. The return of the Messiah vindicates the goodness of creation by restoring it rather than discarding it.

Judgment, in this light, is revealed as the final act of mercy. Evil is not explained away; it is overcome. The suffering of the righteous is not justified; it is healed. The delay that once seemed scandalous is unveiled as patience ordered toward salvation. Peter's insistence that the Lord is not slow but merciful finds its fulfilment when mercy and justice meet in the same act (2 Pet 3:9). The return of the Messiah completes what mercy has begun.

For Israel, this moment confirms that hope was not misplaced. The scattering, endurance, and fidelity of the Jewish people are not rendered meaningless by delay. Paul's declaration that "all Israel will be saved" (Rom 11:26) is not a slogan but a confession of trust in God's irrevocable promise. The Messiah's return is the moment when that promise becomes visible, when the covenant spoken to the patriarchs stands fulfilled without dilution.

The Church awaits this same unveiling not as a replacement for Israel, but as a participant in the same covenantal drama. The confession that Jesus is the Messiah does not negate Israel's hope; it intensifies it by insisting that the story remains unfinished until God has completed His work. The return of Christ vindicates both Israel's Scriptures and the Church's faith by showing that neither declared fulfilment prematurely.

The final posture of faith is therefore not calculation but expectation. Jesus does not instruct His disciples to predict the day or hour. He commands vigilance, fidelity, and hope. The Spirit and the Bride together cry, "Come" (Rev 22:17). This cry is not desperation but desire—the longing for the world to be set right, for truth to be unveiled, for God's presence to be unmediated.

Thus the Messiah who came once in humility will come again in glory. The promises made through the prophets are not exhausted; they are secured. Resurrection, judgment, restoration, and peace converge in a single act of divine faithfulness. The Second Coming is not an embarrassment to Israel's hope but its consummation. History moves not toward silence but toward revelation, and the King who once suffered will be recognised by all as Lord.

# 23

# Resurrection and Judgment: The Final Acts of the Messiah

From the earliest prophetic visions, Israel knew that the redemption God promised would not reach its fullness until death itself was undone. The covenant was made with living people in a living land under the blessing of the living God. A salvation that left the grave untouched could never satisfy the hope of Abraham, who believed that God "gives life to the dead" (Rom 4:17). Daniel saw this with astonishing clarity, promising that "many of those who sleep in the dust of the earth shall awake, some to everlasting life, and some to shame and everlasting contempt" (Dan 12:2). The prophet speaks not of disembodied souls but of bodies raised, identities restored, and lives renewed. This moment—when the dead rise and the righteous shine "like the stars forever and ever" (Dan 12:3)—stands at the centre of Israel's eschatological longing.

Isaiah joins his voice to this hope with a vision rich in mercy and triumph. He hears the Lord proclaim, "Your dead shall live; their bodies shall rise. You who dwell in the dust, awake and sing for joy!" (Isa 26:19). And again, he promises that the Lord "will swallow up death forever" and wipe away tears from all faces (Isa 25:8). These are not poetic flourishes but covenantal assurances. The God who created the body will redeem the body. The One who fashioned the world will not abandon it to decay.

Death, the intruder into God's good creation, must be judged and defeated if the promises are to stand.

Ezekiel's vision of dry bones intensifies this hope with dramatic clarity. The Spirit leads the prophet into a valley of scattered skeletons, the remnants of Israel's despair. Yet when the word of the Lord is spoken, bone joins to bone, sinews form, flesh covers the frame, and breath enters once-lifeless bodies. "I will open your graves," the Lord declares, "and raise you from your graves, O my people" (Ezek 37:12). This is more than a metaphor for national restoration. It is a revelation of God's power over death and His intention to reclaim His people in the fullness of their humanity. The resurrection of the dead stands as the ultimate vindication of covenant fidelity.

This hope echoed throughout Second Temple Judaism. In the Psalms of Solomon, the righteous plead for God to raise them and bring justice to those who oppressed them. 4 Ezra envisions the Almighty summoning the dead, judging the wicked, and granting the faithful eternal glory. 1 Enoch speaks of the Son of Man who sits upon a throne of glory, before whom the kings of the earth tremble and the righteous rejoice. Even the Dead Sea Scrolls record the expectation that when God's Messiah comes, "He will heal the wounded, revive the dead, and bring good news to the poor," a remarkable parallel to the signs Jesus Himself offered when identifying His mission (cf. Luke 7:22).

The New Testament does not depart from this Jewish hope; it intensifies and fulfills it. Jesus speaks with divine authority when He declares that "the hour is coming when all who are in the tombs will hear his voice and come forth" (John 5:28–29). The one who forgives sins, heals bodies, and commands creation now claims the power to summon the dead. This is the prerogative of God alone, yet Jesus speaks of it as His own right. His words reveal that resurrection is not merely an event but an encounter—an encounter with Him whose voice called the world into being. The dead rise because the Creator calls them by name.

This authority is revealed most fully in His own resurrection. Paul calls Him "the first fruits of those who have fallen asleep" (1 Cor 15:20). The metaphor is profound: first fruits signify the beginning of a harvest that shares the same nature. The risen body of Jesus is not an anomaly but the pattern. What was sown in dishonour is raised in glory; what was sown in weakness is raised in power. His resurrection is the pledge that the bodies of the faithful will be conformed to His glorious body, as Paul writes: "He will change our lowly body to be like his glorious body" (Phil 3:21). The Messiah does not redeem souls only; He redeems humanity.

The resurrection is inseparable from judgment, for the raising of the dead necessitates the revealing of hearts. Jesus teaches that the resurrection divides not by arbitrary decree but by truth unveiled. Those who have done good rise to life; those who have done evil rise to judgment (John 5:29). He describes the Son of Man arriving in glory, seated on His throne, all nations gathered before Him, and the separation of sheep from goats proceeding as naturally as light from fire (Matt 25:31–46). This judgment is not vengeance; it is the revelation of reality. What is hidden is brought into the open. Evil, long tolerated by the mercy of God, is named and removed so that creation may be restored in peace.

The apostolic witness affirms this with solemn clarity. Paul writes that God "will judge the secrets of men by Christ Jesus" (Rom 2:16). The One who bore human sin on the cross now bears divine authority in judgment. He is entrusted with the final act of the story because He alone has entered every part of it—birth, suffering, death, burial, resurrection, ascension. His judgment is not detached observation but the verdict of the One who knows humanity from within. As Augustine writes, "He shall be the judge, because He was judged" (*City of God*, XX.30). The wounds He carries are the measure of His justice.

The apostles never present judgment as a threat designed to terrify; they present it as the moment when the Messiah completes what He began. Peter speaks of a day when "the heavens will be dissolved" and "righteousness will dwell" in the new creation (2 Pet 3:12–13). The purification of the cosmos and the resurrection of the body are united realities. What God does for the body, He will do for the world; what He does for Christ, He will do for all who belong to Him. The same fire that descended at Sinai, the same fire that appeared at Pentecost, will cleanse creation of every distortion introduced by sin. This is not annihilation but restoration—a renewal that brings forth what the prophets foresaw when they spoke of wolves dwelling with lambs, nations beating swords into plowshares, and the earth being "filled with the knowledge of the glory of the Lord as the waters cover the sea" (Hab 2:14).

Paul's vision in 1 Corinthians 15 brings these threads together with powerful coherence. He insists that "flesh and blood cannot inherit the kingdom of God," which is not a rejection of the body but a rejection of corruptibility. He explains that the mortal must "put on immortality," that what was perishable must be clothed in imperishability (1 Cor 15:53). The language evokes priestly vesting, as though the redeemed body becomes the garment through which humanity enters the sanctuary of God's new world. When this transformation occurs, Paul exults, "Death is swallowed up in victory" (1 Cor 15:54), echoing Isaiah's ancient promise. The Messiah does not merely defeat death for Himself; He destroys it for those united to Him. His triumph becomes theirs.

Judgment flows naturally from this victory, because a world transfigured in righteousness cannot coexist with unreconciled evil. Scripture never portrays judgment as arbitrary punishment. It is the unveiling of truth. Jesus describes it in terms of harvest: wheat separated from chaff, fish sorted after the net is drawn, good fruit distinguished from rotten fruit. These images are not violent; they are diagnostic. They reveal what has grown within the soil of the human heart. When He speaks of the Son of Man sending His angels to "gather out of his kingdom all causes of sin and all law-breakers" (Matt 13:41), the aim is restoration, not destruction. The kingdom cannot be whole until sin is removed from within it.

This is why Jesus is the only one who can judge the world. Judgment requires perfect knowledge of every heart, perfect justice in discerning what each life has become, and perfect mercy in willing the salvation of all. Only the Messiah possesses such knowledge because only He has lived the human condition without sin. Only He has suffered injustice without retaliation. Only He has borne the full weight of human guilt on the cross.

Judgment is entrusted to the crucified one because the crucified one is the measure of love. Gregory the Great writes, "He who came first in mercy shall come again in judgment, so that what He has forgiven in gentleness He may weigh in righteousness" (*Homilies on the Gospels*, II.30). The pierced hands that lifted sinners from shame are the same hands that separate light from darkness at the end.

Resurrection and judgment are therefore not two disconnected events but two movements within a single act of divine restoration. The raising of the dead reveals God's fidelity to His promise; the judgment of the nations reveals God's fidelity to His holiness. The resurrection vindicates the righteous who trusted His word; the judgment puts an end to every form of evil that defaces His creation. In both, the Messiah stands at the centre. He is the one speaking life into the graves of His people; He is the one calling the nations to account; He is the one whose kingdom endures when every earthly throne has fallen.

The imagery used by the New Testament to describe this moment is luminous with authority and tenderness. Christ comes "with a cry of command, with the archangel's call, and with the sound of the trumpet of God" (1 Thess 4:16). He does not whisper to the dead; He summons them. Paul says, "We shall all stand before the judgment seat of God" (Rom 14:10), but then adds, quoting Isaiah, "As I live, says the Lord, every knee shall bow to me, and every tongue shall give praise to God" (Isa 45:23; Rom 14:11). The Lord before whom Israel bowed at Sinai is the Lord before whom humanity bows at the end. Judgment becomes worship because truth becomes unmistakable.

Early Christians welcomed this hope rather than shrinking from it. The *Didache*, one of the earliest Christian writings, ends with a prayer that reflects the Church's eager expectation: "Let grace come, and let this world pass away" (Didache 10). Ignatius of Antioch longed for the day when Christ would be fully revealed, for then, he said, believers would finally be "true disciples." The hope of resurrection made martyrdom intelligible, sanctified suffering with meaning, and filled ordinary lives with quiet courage. They believed the Messiah who rose would raise them; the

Messiah who judged would justify them; the Messiah who reigns would restore all things.

The final judgment is not merely the weighing of individual destinies; it is the moment when God's purposes for Israel and the nations reach their fullest clarity. The prophets envisioned a day when the Lord would gather all peoples, not only to expose the secrets of their hearts but to establish His reign in unmistakable glory. Joel speaks of multitudes in the "valley of decision" where "the Lord roars from Zion" and the heavens and earth tremble (Joel 3:14–16). Zephaniah describes a purifying fire that removes pride and leaves a humble people who "call upon the name of the Lord" with one united voice (Zeph 3:9). Far from the caricature of divine wrath detached from mercy, these visions reveal judgment as the moment when God heals the wound of history by cleansing humanity of the violence, idolatry, and injustice that disfigure creation.

Jesus stands squarely within this prophetic stream, yet He brings an authority no prophet ever claimed. When He speaks of the Son of Man coming in glory, He is not describing another figure. He is describing Himself. "When the Son of Man comes in his glory, and all the angels with him, then he will sit on his glorious throne" (Matt 25:31). No prophet sits upon a throne of judgment; no sage gathers the nations before him. This is divine prerogative, the throne of Yahweh. Yet Jesus speaks of it as naturally as He speaks of the lilies of the field. His authority to judge is not borrowed; it is inherent. It reveals that the Messiah's identity is bound to the identity of Israel's God, who alone judges the earth.

Judgment appears throughout His parables not as a sudden intrusion but as the natural end of a long, patient divine work. A farmer plants seed, allows it to grow, and only at harvest discerns wheat from weeds. A fisherman draws in a net and only afterwards separates what is good from what will not nourish. A king entrusts talents to his servants and later returns to see what fruit their stewardship has borne. Each image conveys that God's justice arrives after a season of mercy, that His patience precedes His verdict, and that His final assessment reveals what human lives have become through freedom. The Messiah who will judge is the

# RESURRECTION AND JUDGMENT: THE FINAL ACTS OF THE MESSIAH

Messiah who first extended every invitation to repentance, healing, and communion.

The apostolic teaching reinforces this unity of justice and mercy. Peter warns that the day of the Lord will come "like a thief," not to promote fear but to awaken vigilance (2 Pet 3:10). The world as presently structured—marred by corruption, driven by rivalries, haunted by death—cannot inherit the kingdom of God. It must be renewed. John's apocalypse gives symbolic expression to this transformation: the old heaven and earth pass away not in annihilation but in transfiguration, making space for the descent of the new Jerusalem, the dwelling place of God with humanity (Rev 21:1–3). Judgment clears the ground for communion. The tears wiped away from every face are the tears that flowed through generations of injustice, oppression, and sorrow; the Judge who wipes them away is the Lamb who bore those wounds.

Paul frames final judgment within the context of resurrection, for the two are inseparable. God "has fixed a day on which he will judge the world in righteousness by a man whom he has appointed," Paul tells the Athenians, and then adds, "of this he has given assurance to all by raising him from the dead" (Acts 17:31). The resurrection is the divine credential of the Judge. The man appointed is the man vindicated. Christ's resurrection is therefore not only the ground of Christian hope but the guarantee that judgment will be administered by the One who conquered death and loves humanity more deeply than humanity loves itself. His rule is not domination but restoration.

The prophets often described the day of the Lord in terms of cosmic upheaval—darkened skies, quaking mountains, collapsing powers. These images speak of the unmaking of all that resists God. Jesus echoes this imagery when He speaks of the sun darkening and the powers of the heavens being shaken (Matt 24:29). Yet in both the prophets and the Gospels, the disruption is not the point; the revelation of God is. The world trembles not because destruction comes but because glory arrives. "Then will appear the sign of the Son of Man," Jesus says, "and they will see the Son of Man coming on the clouds of heaven with power and great glory" (Matt 24:30). The kingdom that began quietly in Galilee, the kingdom that spread through the preaching of fishermen and the breaking of bread, will stand unveiled before every nation.

For those who belong to Christ, this unveiling is not dread but fulfillment. Paul writes that believers "groan inwardly as we wait eagerly for adoption as sons, the redemption of our bodies" (Rom 8:23). Creation itself "waits with eager longing" for this moment (Rom 8:19). The final judgment is therefore the liberation of creation from corruption, the unveiling of the children of God, the harmonisation of heaven and earth. Nothing good is lost; everything true is refined; everything broken is healed. The Messiah stands at the centre of this transformation, not as a distant sovereign but as the firstborn from the dead who leads His people into the life of the new world.

The hope of Israel always moved toward this moment, when God would finally set the world right. The psalmists longed for the day when the Lord would judge with equity, defend the oppressed, and break the power of wickedness. "He will judge the world with righteousness, and the peoples with equity" (Ps 98:9). Far from picturing judgment as arbitrary punishment, the Psalms describe it as the flowering of justice, the healing of a world worn thin by violence. When righteousness reigns, creation rejoices. The rivers clap their hands; the hills sing for joy (Ps 98:8). Judgment is the triumph of the Creator over the forces that oppose His purpose.

This same vision appears in the prophetic books with deeper intensity. Isaiah envisions a branch from the stump of Jesse upon whom the Spirit rests. "With righteousness he shall judge the poor, and decide with equity for the meek of the earth" (Isa 11:4). His rule protects the vulnerable, restrains the violent, and ushers in a peace so profound that predator and prey lie down together. The Messiah judges by seeing reality as God sees it. He discerns the heart, reveals truth, and establishes justice that endures. The earth becomes a place where knowledge of the Lord saturates existence like waters covering the sea (Isa 11:9). Judgment is thus the instrument through which divine peace emerges.

## RESURRECTION AND JUDGMENT: THE FINAL ACTS OF THE MESSIAH

In this context, Jesus' teaching becomes unmistakably messianic. When He says, "The Father judges no one but has given all judgment to the Son" (John 5:22), He is not claiming a delegated role but identifying Himself with the divine prerogative promised in the Scriptures. The Judge of Israel sits on the throne of David; the Messiah of Israel executes the justice of God. Yet Jesus unites these roles with the tenderness of the shepherd who knows His sheep and calls them by name. The Son of Man who comes in glory is the same one who laid down His life for the sheep (John 10:11). Judgment rests in the pierced hands of the crucified Judge.

The early Church clung to this truth with confident hope. In the midst of persecution, believers found strength in the knowledge that Christ's judgment would vindicate their suffering and expose the cruelty of their oppressors. The martyrs of Lyon wrote that Christ "will judge the world in justice and fulfill the promises He made to those who love Him." Their courage flowed from the conviction that no righteous act is forgotten, no faithful endurance wasted. Judgment becomes the moment when the truth of lives long hidden is finally honoured, when the kingdom's values—humility, mercy, love—are revealed as the true currency of eternity.

Paul frames this expectation within the language of divine unveiling. "We must all appear before the judgment seat of Christ," he says, "so that each one may receive what is due for what he has done in the body" (2 Cor 5:10). The word translated "appear" carries the sense of exposure, of being made manifest. The masks that human beings wear—whether of vanity, fear, pride, or shame—fall away before the light of Christ. Judgment reveals who we have become through grace or against it. It is not that Christ delights in exposing sin; rather, He illumines it so that it can no longer wound the world or the soul. The light that reveals also heals.

This unveiling also concerns the nations. Jesus' parable of the sheep and goats shows judgment not merely as personal but as communal. Nations are measured by their response to the hungry, the thirsty, the stranger, the prisoner (Matt 25:31–46). The Messiah judges not only individuals but societies. His kingdom exposes collective sin—oppression, exploitation, indifference—just as it honours collective righteousness—compassion, justice, mercy. The nations stand before Him because the Messiah came for the world, not only for Israel. His rule stretches from Jerusalem to the ends of the earth.

The final judgment also discloses the ultimate fate of evil. Revelation describes the defeat of the powers that enslave humanity—Satan, death, and the forces of rebellion. These scenes are richly symbolic but the truth they communicate is clear: evil has no lasting future. It cannot coexist with a renewed creation. The Messiah's reign requires the removal of all that opposes love. As John writes, death and Hades are thrown into the lake of fire, which is the second death (Rev 20:14). This is not cruelty; it is the final mercy. A world without death is a world without sin; a world without sin is a world fully healed in the presence of God.

The resurrection and judgment also fulfill the deepest longings embedded in Israel's own liturgical and historical memory. Every Passover looked back to deliverance from Egypt yet pointed beyond it, toward a redemption in which slavery itself would be abolished. Every Jubilee proclaimed liberty but anticipated a restoration no earthly cycle could accomplish. Every pilgrimage to Jerusalem rehearsed the hope that God would one day dwell with His people in unbroken communion. The final acts of the Messiah gather all these strands into a single moment of consummation. Death is overthrown, injustice dismantled, and communion restored in its fullness. The kingdom for which Israel prayed in every generation becomes visible.

This final restoration requires the renewal of the human body, for the body is integral to covenant life. The prophets consistently portray salvation in bodily terms—feasting, dwelling, walking in the land, beholding God's glory. Jesus affirms this vision when He promises that the righteous "will shine like the sun in the kingdom of their Father" (Matt 13:43), an image that echoes Daniel's prophecy of the resurrected righteous gleaming like stars. The resurrection is therefore not a concession to ancient imagination but the fulfillment of God's intention for humanity. The body that once bore the marks of suffering becomes the vessel of glory.

The transformation of the body mirrors the transformation of creation. Paul writes that "the creation waits with eager longing for the revealing of the sons of God" (Rom 8:19). Creation is personified as a servant groaning for liberation from the futility imposed by human sin. The resurrection signals that this liberation is near. When the children of God stand in glory, creation itself will be renewed. Isaiah's vision of new heavens and a new earth anticipates this union of cosmic and human restoration. The Messiah does not save souls for escape from the world; He redeems the world so that embodied souls may dwell in it without corruption.

Within this horizon, judgment becomes a moment of incomparable hope. It is the cleansing that precedes the feast, the pruning that allows the vine to bear fruit, the final sorting that makes peace possible. The ancient Church expressed this hope with a paradoxical joy. In the Apostles' Creed, believers professed faith in "the resurrection of the body and the life of the world to come." In the Nicene Creed, they confessed that Christ "will come again in glory to judge the living and the dead," not as a grim inevitability but as a truth that sustains courage and charity. Judgment is the unveiling of Christ's glory, and those united to Him long to see it.

The unity of resurrection and judgment also reveals the coherence of God's covenant. In Genesis, God promises Abraham descendants, land, and blessing. In the prophets, He promises to restore Israel, cleanse sin, and pour out His Spirit. In the Psalms, He promises to judge the world with righteousness. In the New Testament, He fulfills these promises through the Messiah, who rises from the dead, pours out the Spirit, forms a new people, and will return to establish eternal justice. The final acts of the Messiah are therefore the culmination of the covenant story. They do not cancel the promises to Israel; they complete them.

At the heart of this consummation stands Christ Himself. The risen Lord bears the wounds of His passion, not as reminders of suffering but as the seals of victory. When He returns, those wounds will still speak. They will testify to the love that endured rejection, the mercy that overcame sin, the power that raised Him from the grave. The Judge is the Savior; the Savior is the Judge. The one who calls the dead to life is the one who once lay in the tomb. His glory does not erase His humanity; His humanity does not diminish His glory. The world will behold in Him the perfect union of justice and mercy.

And when He calls the dead from their graves and gathers the nations before Him, the story reaches its true end—not in annihilation or despair but in the joy of a redeemed creation. The final judgment is the doorway into the kingdom that has no end, the moment when the Messiah's reign is unveiled in its fullness, and every promise God has ever spoken stands visible in the light of the risen Christ.

The final vision offered by the New Testament reveals a world not abandoned but transfigured, a humanity not erased but fulfilled. John sees a holy city descending from heaven, radiant with the glory of God. "Behold, the dwelling of God is with men," a voice proclaims, "and he will dwell with them, and they shall be his people" (Rev 21:3). This is the goal toward which resurrection and judgment move: not merely the vindication of individuals, nor the punishment of evil, but the restoration of communion. The promise given in Eden—God walking with humanity—is realized beyond all expectation. The curse is lifted; the tears are wiped away; death is no more. The Messiah brings creation to its intended beauty.

The imagery that follows is richly symbolic yet deeply theological. The city needs no temple, for "its temple is the Lord God the Almighty and the Lamb" (Rev 21:22). The worship once localized in Jerusalem now fills creation itself. The Lamb is the lamp of the city, and His light reveals the nations walking in harmony. Kings bring their glory into this new Jerusalem, not as rivals seeking dominance but as stewards who now recognize the true source of authority. This is the fulfillment of the prophetic hope that all nations will stream to Zion, seeking the Lord's instruction and peace.

Ezekiel's vision of a river flowing from the restored temple finds its fulfillment here as water of life flows from the throne of God and of the Lamb (Rev 22:1). Trees bearing twelve kinds of fruit line its banks; their leaves are "for the healing of the nations" (Rev 22:2). The Messiah's mission culminates not only in the healing of individual hearts but in the reconciliation of peoples long set against one another. Judgment clears the ground; resurrection plants the seed; the renewed creation reveals the harvest.

This consummation is not abstract theology; it is the destiny of every person joined to Christ. The righteous who rise in glory behold the face of God and bear His name on their foreheads (Rev 22:4). The intimacy forfeited in the fall is restored. To see God is to live; to live in God is to reign. The servants of the Lamb reign "forever and ever" (Rev 22:5), participating in the kingship of the Messiah who shares His inheritance with His people. The relationship between Creator and creature becomes communion, the fulfillment of grace.

In this final horizon, Israel's hope and the Church's proclamation meet as one. The Messiah who was promised to Abraham, foreshadowed by Moses, anticipated by David, announced by the prophets, rejected by many, and confessed by the nations, completes the story not through force but through the radiance of a love stronger than death. His reign is not another empire among empires; it is the transfiguration of creation. His judgment is not the triumph of power; it is the triumph of holiness. His resurrection is not an isolated miracle; it is the beginning of a new humanity. Every promise God ever whispered to Israel finds its "Yes" in Him (2 Cor 1:20).

The final acts of the Messiah reveal that God's covenant has never wavered, that His mercy has never weakened, and that His fidelity extends beyond death into eternity. The resurrection is the pledge; the judgment is the unveiling; the new creation is the embrace. What began in a garden reaches its fulfillment in a city illuminated by the Lamb, where humanity walks in the light of God and creation itself becomes a temple of unending joy.

# 24

# A New Heaven and a New Earth: Creation Renewed in the Messiah

In the final visions granted to Israel's prophets, creation is never treated as disposable scaffolding or a temporary stage destined to be discarded. From the opening pages of Scripture, the world is declared "very good," and nothing in the long story of covenant ever suggests that God abandoned this judgment. The prophets speak of a future not in which God erases creation but in which He restores it to glory, healing the wounds of sin and drawing the world into the radiance of His presence. When Isaiah announces, "Behold, I create new heavens and a new earth" (Isa 65:17), he is not describing an escape from the world but its transfiguration. The old world that groaned under the burden of violence and idolatry is reborn into harmony and joy. The prophet imagines a creation where sorrow evaporates, where weeping is no longer native to human experience, where life flourishes without threat, and where Jerusalem becomes a place of unbroken delight. The God who once walked with Adam in the garden promises once again to dwell with His people, but now in a renewed creation that can never be undone.

This vision is not an isolated fragment. Isaiah's earlier prophecies paint the same horizon in different colours. He sees a world in which "the wolf shall dwell with the lamb" and "the earth shall be full of the knowledge of the Lord as the waters cover the sea" (Isa 11:6, 9). Peace is not merely the absence of conflict but the reconciliation of nature itself, the healing of relationships among creatures, and the restoration of human vocation as steward and son. In another oracle, the prophet declares that the Lord "will swallow up death forever" and wipe away tears from all faces (Isa 25:8). This promise is breathtaking in scope: death, the universal enemy, is confronted and overcome; grief, the constant companion of human life, is dissolved. Creation is renewed not piecemeal but at its deepest wound.

Even Isaiah's cry that "your dead shall live, their bodies shall rise" (Isa 26:19) belongs to this tapestry. The renewal of creation cannot be separated from the renewal of the body because humanity is the heart of creation's story. The covenant was never with souls alone but with embodied persons called to bear God's image in the world He fashioned. A new heavens and a new earth without resurrected humanity would be a contradiction. Isaiah therefore binds the renewal of creation to the victory over death and the restoration of God's people in glory.

This prophetic hope reshapes how we read the entire biblical narrative. From the beginning, God's purpose was communion: a world filled with His presence, a humanity sharing in His life. The temple in Jerusalem embodied this intention, for it stood as the meeting point of heaven and earth. But even the most glorious sanctuary was only a sign of something greater, a foreshadowing of the moment when God would dwell with His people without veil or boundary. Isaiah's new creation is the flowering of this longing, the day when God's glory covers the earth, when nations come to the light of His presence, and when Jerusalem becomes a joy for all peoples.

The earliest Christians did not read these prophecies as poetic exaggerations. They read them as promises God intended to fulfill through the Messiah. The resurrection of Jesus was the sign that the new creation had already begun. If death had been defeated in Him, then the world's renewal was not a distant fantasy but a living reality breaking into history. When Paul writes that Christ is "the first fruits of those who have fallen asleep" (1 Cor 15:20), he draws upon Israel's agricultural imagery: the first fruits reveal the nature of the harvest to come. The risen body of Jesus, glorified yet still bearing the wounds of love, is the pattern and pledge of the renewed creation God will unveil at the end of the age.

The resurrection of Jesus reveals not merely the destiny of the human body but the destiny of the cosmos itself. When Paul declares that creation "waits with eager longing for the revealing of the sons of God" (Rom 8:19), he is describing a world whose fate is tied to humanity's restoration. The fall did not only distort the human heart; it fractured the harmony of creation. Thorns and thistles, toil and decay, violence and disorder—these are the symptoms of a cosmos groaning under a burden it was never meant to bear. Yet Paul insists that creation's groaning is not the cry of despair but the labour pains of a new birth. The world is waiting, not for destruction, but for transfiguration. It longs for the day when humanity, restored through the Messiah, will once again exercise a royal stewardship that reflects the wisdom and love of God.

The language Paul uses is striking. Creation was "subjected to futility," not willingly but in hope, because the same God who allowed it to share in humanity's fall also willed that it would share in humanity's redemption (Rom 8:20–21). The liberation of creation is inseparable from the liberation of the children of God. When the Messiah redeems humanity, creation itself will be "set free from its bondage to decay" and brought into "the freedom of the glory of the children of God." This is the covenant vision on a cosmic scale: the blessing given to Abraham extends to the nations, and through the nations to creation itself.

The renewal Paul describes is not a metaphor. It is anchored in the reality of the resurrection. Christ's risen body is the first instance of the new creation, the place where immortality has already taken root in the soil of the old world. He is the beginning of what Isaiah foresaw, the dawn of the age in which death is swallowed up and life reigns. The prophets promised a world in which sorrow would cease; the apostles proclaimed the One who had already stepped beyond death and opened the path for the rest of creation to follow. When Paul speaks of the final transformation in which "this mortal body must put on immortality" (1 Cor 15:53), he is describing the same event Isaiah envisioned when he foretold the triumph of life over death. Christ's resurrection is not an isolated miracle but the seed from which the new creation grows.

This connection between Christ's resurrection and the world's renewal shapes the New Testament's vision of the end. Peter speaks of "new heavens and a new earth in which righteousness dwells" (2 Pet 3:13). He does not imagine a world annihilated and replaced, but a world purified and transfigured. The language of fire he uses echoes the prophets: fire that judges, fire that refines, fire that prepares creation for its final destiny. What melts away is corruption, not creation; what perishes is sin, not the world God declared good. The same God who formed the heavens and the earth will unveil them in glory.

In this horizon, the Messiah's reign appears not as a spiritual abstraction but as a renewed reality in which God's presence fills every corner of existence. The prophets always imagined salvation as something embodied: people eating, drinking, celebrating, dwelling in peace, cultivating land that no longer resists them. These images were not childish expectations to be transcended but signposts pointing toward a deeper truth. God intends to restore His creation, not discard it. Human bodies will be raised because they are part of God's enduring purpose; creation will be renewed because it was formed to be God's dwelling place with humanity at its centre.

The vision of a new heaven and a new earth therefore brings the story of Scripture into perfect symmetry. Everything begins with creation; everything ends with creation renewed. The story that opened with a garden closes with a city where the tree of life grows once more. The separation introduced by sin—between God and humanity, humanity and creation, heaven and earth—is healed in the Messiah. His resurrection is the axis upon which the future turns, the moment when the old creation begins to give way to the new.

The apostolic vision of creation renewed reaches its fullest expression in the final pages of Scripture, where John beholds the descent of the holy city, the new Jerusalem. He does not see souls escaping upward into heaven;

he sees heaven coming down to earth. "Then I saw a new heaven and a new earth," he writes, "for the first heaven and the first earth had passed away" (Rev 21:1). The passing here is not annihilation but transformation. The world that groaned in labor is now reborn. What was once scarred by violence, shadowed by death, and divided by sin stands transfigured by the glory of God. This is the moment when the prophetic promise becomes visible: creation renewed, humanity restored, God dwelling in their midst.

John hears a loud voice from the throne proclaim, "Behold, the dwelling of God is with men. He will dwell with them, and they shall be his people" (Rev 21:3). The covenant formula that echoed through the Torah and the prophets—"I will be their God, and they shall be my people"—reaches its final fulfillment. The distance between heaven and earth dissolves. The Creator does not summon His people away from the world; He comes to dwell with them in the world He has renewed. This union is so complete that there is no temple in the city, "for its temple is the Lord God the Almighty and the Lamb" (Rev 21:22). What the temple foreshadowed—God's presence among His people—becomes the very structure of creation itself.

John's description emphasizes not destruction but healing. "He will wipe away every tear from their eyes," he says, "and death shall be no more" (Rev 21:4). Every sorrow that marked human life—betrayal, loss, sickness, violence—finds its end. Death, the last enemy, is not merely defeated; it is expunged from the fabric of creation. The God who first breathed life into Adam breathes eternal life into the renewed world, restoring creation to its intended harmony. This is the world Isaiah anticipated when he spoke of a time when infants would no longer die, when work would bear fruit without frustration, and when God's joy would fill Jerusalem like wine poured into a cup.

The imagery of the new Jerusalem reveals the depth of this transformation. The city shines with the radiance of God's glory, its walls and foundations adorned with precious stones that recall the beauty of Eden. A river of the water of life flows from the throne of God and of the Lamb, echoing both the river in Genesis that nourished the garden and the river in Ezekiel's vision that healed the bitter waters and renewed the land. On either side of the river stands the tree of life, bearing twelve kinds of fruit and yielding its harvest each month. "The leaves of the tree," John says, "were for the healing of the nations" (Rev 22:2). What humanity lost through disobedience—access to the tree of life—is restored through the obedience of the One who died and rose again.

In this renewed creation, the nations walk by the light of the Lamb, and their kings bring their glory into the city. The divisions that fractured humanity are healed; the violence that marked the history of nations is replaced by a common pilgrimage toward the presence of God. The gates of the city never close, for night is no more and nothing unclean can enter. The city embodies the peace promised by Isaiah, the justice longed for by the psalmists, and the joy foreseen by Zechariah when he spoke of a Jerusalem where old men and women sit peacefully in the streets while children play without fear.

This vision is not separate from the Messiah's reign; it is the flowering of it. The Lamb who was slain stands at the centre, His wounds now the fountains of life. The kingship of Christ, revealed in humility at His first coming, is now unveiled in glory. The nations that resisted Him are invited to walk in His light; the creation that groaned under sin is renewed by His grace. Everything is gathered under His lordship, just as Paul declared when he spoke of God's purpose "to unite all things in him, things in heaven and things on earth" (Eph 1:10). The Messiah's reign is the reconciliation and transfiguration of creation.

At the heart of this vision lies a truth that the early Fathers understood with luminous clarity: the renewal of creation is inseparable from the renewal of humanity, and both flow from the incarnation. Irenaeus saw the entire sweep of salvation through this lens. "As the Lord recapitulated in Himself all things," he wrote, "He might have mercy upon all" (*Against Heresies* V.17). For him, the incarnation set in motion the healing not only of human nature but of the cosmos joined to it. Since humanity is the microcosm of creation, the restoration of the human person through Christ brings with it the restoration of the world entrusted to Adam. The second Adam succeeds where the first failed, and creation rejoices in the triumph.

Athanasius also grasped this union of human and cosmic renewal. The Word who became flesh did not merely assume a body for the sake of teaching or example; He united Himself to the fabric of creation so that in rising He might raise all things. In *On the Incarnation*, Athanasius declares that the Word took a body "that He might turn again to in corruption men who had turned back to corruption," a restoration that touches the entire created order because the Word is its source. If creation came into being through Him, then creation will be renewed through Him. The resurrection is not an isolated act but the re-creation of the world from within.

Augustine carries the vision further by contemplating the destiny of the resurrected body. In *City of God* XXII, he describes the resurrected flesh as both fully human and fully transformed, incorruptible yet recognizably continuous with the body that suffered and died. This continuity mirrors the continuity of the new creation with the old. Just as the resurrected body is the same body glorified, so the new creation is this creation transfigured. The world will not be replaced but perfected, freed from decay, harmonized under the rule of Christ, radiant with the glory of God. The final state of creation is not spiritual abstraction but embodied communion.

This patristic vision emerges directly from the resurrection of Christ. When Jesus rose, He did not discard His humanity; He glorified it. He did not abandon the wounds of His passion; He transformed them into signs of victory. His resurrection demonstrates that matter is capable of bearing glory, that the body can become the dwelling place of divine life. The resurrection is therefore the cornerstone of the new creation, for it reveals what God intends not only for humanity but for the cosmos shaped by humanity's vocation. If the head of creation is raised in glory, the body of creation will follow.

In this light, the descent of the new Jerusalem is not a symbol of escape from the world but a symbol of the world's fulfillment. God's intention from the beginning was to dwell with His people in the world He made. The sanctuary of Eden anticipated this presence; the tabernacle and temple made it visible; the incarnation revealed it in flesh; the resurrection inaugurated its final stage; and the new creation will complete it. Humanity restored becomes the living temple of God. The world renewed becomes the holy mountain where all creation worships the Lord. Heaven and earth, once separated by sin, become one.

This union is the ultimate purpose of the Messiah's work. He reconciles heaven and earth in Himself, bridging the chasm introduced by the fall. His kingship gathers the nations; His priesthood cleanses creation; His prophetic word reveals the truth of God's plan. The new creation is therefore not an appendix to the gospel but its climax. It is the world as God intended it: radiant, reconciled, sanctified, overflowing with life. All of Scripture moves toward this moment, when God will be all in all, and creation itself will become the temple of His glory.

The renewed creation restores not only the harmony between humanity and the world but the harmony between heaven and earth. From the beginning, God intended these two dimensions of His creation to be united. Eden was not merely a garden; it was a sanctuary, a place where God walked with humanity in visible intimacy. The separation introduced by sin fractured this communion, driving humanity east of Eden and veiling the divine presence behind curtains of cloud, fire, and stone. Yet even these veils hinted at restoration. Jacob saw a ladder reaching from earth to heaven, angels ascending and descending upon it, a sign that God's presence still reached into the world. Moses climbed Sinai and entered the cloud. The prophets saw visions of the throne room not as distant galaxies but as realities breaking into human history.

In Christ, heaven and earth meet without separation. He is the place where divinity and humanity dwell in perfect unity, the true temple not made with hands. His body becomes the new meeting place of God and man, the fulfillment of every sanctuary that came before. When He ascends, He does not depart from creation but enthrones humanity at the right hand of the Father, beginning the union that the new creation will consummate.

This is why John sees the new Jerusalem descending, not ascending. The movement of salvation is not humanity escaping upward but God coming downward to dwell permanently with His people.

The redeemed humanity becomes the dwelling place of God in a way that surpasses every earlier manifestation. Paul writes that believers are being built into a temple, "a dwelling place of God in the Spirit" (Eph 2:22). This temple is not a symbol but a living reality, for the Spirit given at Pentecost is the same Spirit who hovered over the waters of creation. The renewal of the human heart through grace is the beginning of the renewal of the cosmos. The new creation is already alive within the baptized, awaiting its full revelation when Christ comes again. As Gregory of Nyssa taught, the human person is a microcosm of creation; therefore, when humanity is healed, creation itself is drawn toward healing.

The final union of heaven and earth does not erase their distinction but perfects their communion. Heaven remains the realm of God's unveiled glory; earth remains the realm of embodied life. In the renewed creation, these realms interpenetrate without confusion, as humanity shares in divine life without losing its nature. The incarnation revealed this possibility; the new creation completes it. The Word became flesh so that flesh might dwell in God. The city of God descends so that earth might be lifted into heaven's radiance. The tree of life returns because the exile is over. The Lamb reigns because the victory is complete.

This reconciliation heals every dimension of creation's rupture. Time, once marked by decay, becomes the rhythm of eternal life. Space, once subject to boundaries and conflict, becomes the theatre of divine communion. Relationships fractured by sin—between God and humanity, humanity and creation, and human beings among themselves—are restored in truth and love. Even memory is redeemed, for the wounds of the past are not erased but transfigured, just as Christ's wounds remain visible yet radiant in His resurrected body. Nothing good is lost; everything is gathered and perfected in the Messiah.

The glory of the renewed creation is not static but dynamic participation in God's own life. The nations walk in the light of the Lamb; the kings bring their honour into the city; the servants of God behold His face and reign forever (Rev 22:4–5). Dominion is restored not as domination but as stewardship of love. Humanity, formed in the image of God, finally fulfills its vocation as priest of creation, offering the world back to its Creator in thanksgiving and joy. Creation, healed of corruption, responds with beauty beyond measure. This is the world Israel longed for, the world the apostles proclaimed, the world Christ came to renew.

The renewal of creation is the final disclosure of the Messiah's work, the flowering of promises sown across the whole sweep of Scripture. What began as a covenant with Abraham—blessing for his descendants and for all nations—expands until it embraces the cosmos itself. The land promised to Israel becomes the world promised to the redeemed. "Blessed are the meek," Jesus said, "for they shall inherit the earth" (Matt 5:5). The promise was never that the righteous would float above creation but that they would dwell within it in peace, restored to the vocation first given in Eden. The redeemed earth is the inheritance of the saints, the arena of resurrected life, the place where communion with God becomes the unbroken rhythm of existence.

In this renewed world, the vocation of humanity reaches its perfection. Made in the image of God, humanity was created to reflect His wisdom, exercise His stewardship, and share His communion. Sin fractured this identity, turning dominion into domination, stewardship into exploitation, and communion into alienation. Yet the Messiah restores the image not by erasing human nature but by elevating it into glory. "We shall be like him," John says, "for we shall see him as he is" (1 John 3:2). This likeness is not merely moral but ontological, a participation in the divine life that transforms humanity from within. The resurrected body becomes the vessel of this communion, capable of bearing God's presence without fear, just as Christ's risen body bears the fullness of divine glory.

The world renewed becomes the stage for this communion. The barriers that once separated humanity from God fall away. The curse that shadowed creation is lifted. The Lamb is the lamp of the world, illuminating every corner of existence with truth and love. In this light, human relationships become transparent reflections of divine charity. The nations, once divided by pride and conflict, now walk in unity. Their glory—their culture, wisdom, and contributions—is brought into the new Jerusalem not as competition but as offering. Diversity becomes harmony; difference becomes gift.

This harmony extends to the entire cosmos. The peace Isaiah foresaw—the wolf dwelling with the lamb, the child playing safely by the serpent's den—becomes the lived reality of the world redeemed. Creation no longer resists human stewardship, for humanity no longer abuses creation's trust. The wounds of the land are healed; the violence of nature is pacified; the disharmony of the elements is reconciled. Creation becomes again what God intended: a temple of His glory and a home for His people. As the Psalmist says, "Let the heavens rejoice, let the earth be glad … for he comes to judge the earth. He will judge the world with righteousness and the peoples with truth" (Ps 96:11, 13). Judgment is the doorway to joy because it establishes the righteousness creation has awaited since the fall.

This final state is not monotony but movement, not stasis but participation. The servants of God "reign forever and ever" (Rev 22:5), a reign that reflects Christ's own kingship—not domination but loving governance, not coercion but communion. Reigning with Christ means participating in the divine wisdom that orders creation, the divine love that sustains it, and the divine glory that fills it. Humanity, restored in Christ, becomes what it was always meant to be: the mediator of creation's praise, the bearer of God's presence, the steward of His world.

Here the mission of the Messiah reaches its summit. The One who descended into the womb, the waters, the wilderness, and the grave now reigns over a creation renewed through His obedience. The world He created through His Word becomes the world He restores through His cross. The humanity He assumed becomes the humanity He glorifies. The creation that groaned becomes the creation that sings. And God, who once walked in the garden, now dwells with His people in a city radiant with eternal light.

In the consummation of all things, the Messiah's victory reveals its most expansive horizon—nothing in creation lies outside the reach of His redemptive love. Every fragment of the old world, every story touched by sorrow, every hope deferred by the long ache of history finds its resolution when the One who sits upon the throne declares, "Behold, I make all things new" (Rev 21:5). This is not the announcement of a different world replacing the old but of the old world transfigured, healed, and lifted into a beauty it could never attain on its own. The voice that spoke light into being now speaks renewal over the entirety of creation, and the world responds with the joy for which it was made.

The renewal of creation brings into perfect harmony the divine justice that purifies and the divine mercy that restores. The wounds of history—violence between nations, enmity between peoples, rebellion against God, and the death that reigned over humanity—are judged, healed, and woven into the tapestry of God's glory. Nothing unjust remains, yet nothing good is lost. Human freedom is not erased but fulfilled; the story of every life becomes transparent in the light of the Lamb, where even the scars of suffering shine with redeemed meaning. The Messiah's wounds, radiant in His resurrection, become the pattern by which the wounds of creation are transfigured.

In this new creation, worship and life are no longer distinct realities. The world itself becomes liturgical. Every breath, every movement, every relationship participates in the unending hymn of praise rising from the redeemed cosmos. The nations walk in the Lamb's light; humanity reigns with Him; creation resonates with His glory. The river of life flowing from the throne nourishes existence with divine vitality, while the tree of life—long guarded after Eden—opens its leaves for the healing of the nations. The exile that began in Genesis is finally and irrevocably over. Humanity dwells again with God, not in fragile innocence but in tested and triumphant communion.

The world that emerges in this final vision is the world Israel longed for and the apostles proclaimed: a world without death, without mourning, without corruption, without division. The peace spoken of by the prophets becomes the atmosphere of existence; the joy promised in the psalms becomes the heartbeat of creation; the glory glimpsed in the transfiguration becomes the air humanity breathes. The Lamb and His people share unbroken fellowship. The glory of God illuminates every horizon. The will of God is done on earth as it is in heaven—not as petition but as perpetual reality.

In this consummation, the story of the Messiah finds its completion. He who came to seek the lost brings them home. He who bore sin removes it from creation. He who tasted death abolishes it forever. He who rose in glory shares that glory with the world He fashioned. His kingdom, once hidden like a seed, revealed in weakness, and resisted by many, now fills all things. Heaven and earth, reconciled in Him, sing with one voice the triumph of divine love. And God is all in all.

# 25

# The Question Fulfilment Cannot Avoid

By the close of the messianic promise, the horizon has been fully disclosed. What began as expectation has moved through recognition, rejection, and fulfilment, and has now been carried forward to its final vision. The Messiah returns. The dead are raised. Judgment is rendered. Creation is renewed. The covenant reaches its consummation not in escape from the world, but in its transfiguration. Heaven and earth are joined. God dwells with His people. Nothing remains outside the scope of redemption.

At this point, the story has reached its furthest extent in time. There is nowhere further for history to go.

Yet precisely here, another question presses with quiet force. It does not arise from scepticism or doubt, but from the sheer magnitude of what has been claimed. The Messiah who completes history, who judges the nations, who restores creation, and who fulfils Israel's hope in full cannot be accounted for by function alone. What He does compels inquiry into who He is.

The Scriptures themselves invite this turn. From the beginning, Israel's faith resisted the separation of divine action from divine identity. God alone creates. God alone judges. God alone raises the dead. God alone renews the heavens and the earth. These acts do not belong to intermediaries or delegated agents in the final sense. They belong to the Lord Himself. When the prophets speak of the Day of the Lord, they do not describe an event detached from God's presence. They speak of God coming to His world.

Part V has traced this coming to its end. The Messiah stands not merely as a participant in God's work, but as its centre. The return of the King is not the arrival of a new actor on the stage of history, but the unveiling of the one to whom history has been moving all along. Resurrection and judgment are not assigned tasks within a broader divine economy; they are the decisive acts by which God brings His purposes to completion. The renewal of creation is not an adjustment to the world's structure, but its re-creation from within.

Such claims do not yet answer the question they provoke. They sharpen it.

If the Messiah accomplishes what Scripture attributes to God alone, then messianic fulfilment cannot be understood merely as the resolution of prophecy. It demands a deeper coherence — one that reaches beneath events, beneath timelines, beneath expectation itself. The fulfilment of the promise forces the reader back into the architecture of revelation, to ask how such unity is possible without fracturing the confession that the Lord is one.

Israel's Scriptures have always guarded this confession fiercely. God does not share His glory. He does not relinquish His sovereignty. He does not divide His authority. Yet these same Scriptures repeatedly speak of God acting through figures who bear His presence in ways that exceed ordinary categories. The Word through which creation is spoken. The Wisdom by which God orders the world. The Angel of the Lord who speaks as God and is distinguished from Him. The Glory that fills the Temple yet cannot be contained by it. These realities were not solved within Israel's history. They were lived with, reverenced, and awaited.

The completion of the messianic promise brings these latent tensions to the surface. The Messiah is not merely the endpoint of prophecy; He is the point at which prophecy reveals its depth. The unity of Scripture, traced from promise to fulfilment, now presses toward the unity of the One who stands at its centre. What appeared across centuries as pattern, symbol, and anticipation now demands interpretation at the level of being.

This is not a departure from the story Israel has told. It is its necessary deepening. From the beginning, God's dealings with His people were not merely instructional but revelatory. Covenant was not only law; it was self-disclosure. Worship was not only obedience; it was encounter. Prophecy was not only prediction; it was participation in God's own intention. As the story reaches its fulfilment, revelation does not retreat. It intensifies.

The Messiah who brings history to its end cannot be understood apart from the God who authored history from its beginning. Fulfilment, therefore, does not close the question of identity; it opens it. The coherence of Scripture now demands coherence at its centre. The promise has been kept. The question is how.

At this threshold, typology ceases to be merely illustrative and becomes architectural. The figures, patterns, and symbols that once pointed forward now reveal the shape of divine intention itself. Adam and the new humanity, the flood and new creation, Abraham and universal blessing, Moses and definitive mediation, David and eternal kingship, the Temple and divine indwelling — these were never isolated correspondences. They were the grammar by which God taught Israel how to recognise His presence when it came in fullness.

The fulfilment of the promise therefore compels a return to Scripture, not to re-read predictions, but to discern design. The unity of God's action across time reveals a unity of authorship. History does not converge upon the Messiah by coincidence. It is drawn toward Him. Prophecy is not alignment after the fact; it is intention unfolding.

This realisation also clarifies the relationship between Israel and the Church. If Christ completes rather than replaces Israel's story, then continuity is not an afterthought but the very logic of fulfilment. The Messiah does not interrupt Israel's vocation; He embodies it. The Law is not discarded; it is fulfilled. The covenant is not annulled; it is brought to its intended form. The Church does not stand beside Israel as an alternative people; it stands within Israel's story as its redeemed extension.

At this point, fulfilled prophecy reveals its deepest function. It does not merely demonstrate that God keeps His word. It discloses who God is. The same God who promised, acted. The same God who spoke, came. The same God who shaped history now stands at its centre.

The story has moved from expectation to completion. The horizon of time has been traversed. What remains is not another chapter in history, but a question about the heart of reality itself. The Messiah who judges, raises, renews, and reigns must be more than a servant within creation. He must belong to the mystery of the Creator.

Part VI turns to this question — not as a speculative detour, but as the unavoidable consequence of fulfilment. If the promise has been completed, then the Messiah must be understood not only as the one who comes from God, but as the one in whom God comes.

The story now moves inward, from what God has done to who God has revealed Himself to be.

# VI

# THE MESSIAH WHO IS GOD

# 26

# The Architecture of Prophecy: Typology and Divine Design

From its opening pages, Scripture resists being read as a loose anthology of religious reflections. It presents itself instead as a continuous history shaped by promise, judgment, renewal, and expectation. The story moves with direction. Events echo earlier events; figures emerge who resemble those who came before them; institutions appear, fail, and are promised renewal. This internal coherence is not accidental. It is already signalled in the earliest chapters of Genesis, where the fall of humanity is answered not with abandonment but with a word of promise spoken into history itself: "I will put enmity between you and the woman, and between your seed and her seed; he shall bruise your head, and you shall bruise his heel" (Gen 3:15). The narrative does not close this wound; it carries it forward.

Adam stands at the head of this story not merely as the first man, but as a representative figure whose disobedience shapes the destiny of those who come after him. Paul later reads Adam precisely this way, writing that "sin came into the world through one man and death through sin" (Rom 5:12), and then daring to speak of Christ as "the last Adam" (1 Cor 15:45). Such language does not emerge from speculative theology; it arises from the recognition that the pattern of humanity's fall and restoration is already inscribed in the structure of the story. Adam is not merely an individual; he is a type, a beginning whose meaning is clarified only at the end.

This pattern deepens with Noah. Once again the world descends into corruption, and once again judgment and mercy are intertwined. The flood destroys, yet it also saves. A single righteous man passes through the waters into a renewed creation. Peter later reflects on this event and insists that it was never merely about ancient catastrophe: "God's patience waited in the days of Noah… in which a few, that is, eight persons, were saved through water" (1 Pet 3:20). The language of salvation through judgment recurs, not as repetition, but as design. History is being shaped to teach humanity how God redeems.

The figure of Abraham advances the pattern further. The promise narrows. No longer is the hope cast broadly over humanity in general; it is now lodged within a family. Abraham is summoned by a word, sustained by a promise, and tested by command. The near-sacrifice of Isaac exposes the logic of this design with particular force. God binds Himself to His promise through the demand for the son, only to provide a substitute at the last moment. "God will provide for himself the lamb for a burnt offering" (Gen 22:8). The story does not resolve the tension it creates. It leaves behind a question suspended in the narrative itself: where, and when, will God finally provide what He has promised?

Moses intensifies the architectural coherence of Scripture. He is deliverer, lawgiver, mediator, and intercessor. Through him, Israel passes from slavery into covenant, from chaos into ordered life under God's word. Yet Moses himself anticipates another. "The Lord your God will raise up for you a prophet like me from among you; him you shall heed" (Deut 18:15). The promise is not metaphorical. It is programmatic. Israel's future hope will be shaped by the memory of exodus, the authority of Torah, and the expectation that God will act again with comparable power.

David introduces kingship into this design. With him, covenant and throne are bound together. God promises not merely a dynasty, but an enduring kingdom: "Your house and your kingdom shall be made sure for ever before me; your throne shall be established for ever" (2 Sam 7:16).

The language strains against historical reality almost immediately. David's successors fail; the kingdom fractures; exile follows. Psalm 89 voices the crisis without restraint: "Lord, where is thy steadfast love of old, which by thy faithfulness thou didst swear to David?" (Ps 89:49). The promise remains, but its fulfilment is deferred. Kingship itself becomes a sign pointing beyond itself.

The Temple and its sacrificial system function in the same way. The tabernacle is constructed "according to the pattern" shown on the mountain (Exod 25:40), suggesting that Israel's worship mirrors a deeper reality. The Day of Atonement enacts reconciliation annually, yet its repetition exposes its own incompleteness. "In sacrifices and offerings thou hast not delighted... burnt offering and sin offering thou hast not required" (Ps 40:6). Scripture itself insists that these rites gesture toward something more final, more complete.

The prophets do not abandon this architectural logic; they intensify it. Jonah's descent into the depths and return to life becomes a living parable of judgment and mercy. Isaiah speaks of a servant who embodies Israel's calling yet fulfils it through suffering. Daniel envisions a human figure who receives dominion from God Himself. None of these strands resolves independently. They accumulate. They converge.

The New Testament does not impose this coherence retrospectively. It recognises it. Jesus Himself insists that Moses, the Prophets, and the Psalms speak with a single voice. "Beginning with Moses and all the prophets, he interpreted to them in all the scriptures the things concerning himself" (Luke 24:27). Paul reads Israel's wilderness history as "written for our instruction" (1 Cor 10:11), while the author of Hebrews declares that earthly worship consists of "a copy and shadow of the heavenly sanctuary" (Heb 8:5). Such claims presuppose a guiding intelligence behind history itself.

The Fathers of the Church did not invent this vision. They received it. Irenaeus spoke of Christ as the one who "recapitulated in Himself the long history of mankind" (*Against Heresies* III.18.1), while Justin argued that the Law and the prophets were given as preparation, not replacement

(*Dialogue with Trypho*). Augustine would later summarise the logic with stark simplicity: the New Testament is hidden in the Old, and the Old is revealed in the New (*City of God* XVI).

Typology, then, is not literary cleverness or theological artifice. It is the recognition that Scripture unfolds according to design. History is shaped to teach, to prepare, and to converge. Such coherence demands more than human explanation. It presses the reader toward a conclusion not yet fully stated, but increasingly unavoidable: the one who fulfils these patterns does not merely stand at the end of the story. He stands at its source.

As the biblical narrative advances, typology ceases to be merely suggestive and becomes unmistakably structural. The figures of Israel's past do not fade as the story moves forward; they reappear in heightened form, carrying with them unresolved tensions that press toward fulfilment. Moses dies outside the land he delivered his people to. David's throne collapses under the weight of his descendants' failures. The Temple, built as the dwelling place of God, is destroyed—rebuilt—and destroyed again. Scripture does not tidy these loose ends. It preserves them. The unresolved nature of Israel's history is itself part of the design.

This becomes especially clear in the logic of covenant. Each covenant deepens what came before while exposing its limits. The covenant with Noah preserves creation but does not heal the human heart. The covenant with Abraham promises blessing but awaits realisation. Sinai reveals God's will but cannot guarantee obedience. The Davidic covenant establishes kingship but cannot secure fidelity. Jeremiah names the problem without ambiguity: "The days are surely coming, says the Lord, when I will make a new covenant... not like the covenant which I made with their fathers" (Jer 31:31–32). The structure of covenantal history itself demands completion beyond repetition.

The Temple intensifies this demand. Exodus insists that the tabernacle is constructed according to a heavenly pattern, not human preference: "See that you make them after the pattern for them, which is being shown you on the mountain" (Exod 25:40). The language is architectural, not symbolic. Worship on earth is shaped to correspond to a prior reality. When Solomon dedicates the Temple, he already acknowledges its insufficiency: "Will God indeed dwell on the earth? Behold, heaven and the highest heaven cannot contain thee; how much less this house which I have built!" (1 Kgs 8:27). The Temple exists as a sign pointing beyond itself.

Second Temple Judaism did not miss this tension. The Dead Sea Scrolls testify to an expectation that transcended literal restoration. In 4QFlorilegium, the promise of 2 Samuel 7 is read eschatologically, not as exhausted by Solomon. The text speaks of a future figure through whom God would establish His dwelling definitively. Even more striking, 11QMelchizedek interprets Levitical and jubilee imagery as referring to a heavenly deliverer who proclaims liberty and effects atonement. These texts do not anticipate Christianity, but they do reveal a pattern-conscious reading of Scripture in which history is guided toward an ultimate act of divine intervention.

The New Testament writers speak from within this same consciousness. Hebrews insists that the cultic life of Israel is provisional by design: "They serve a copy and shadow of the heavenly sanctuary" (Heb 8:5). The author goes further, claiming that the law possesses "only a shadow of the good things to come instead of the true form of these realities" (Heb 10:1). This is not a rejection of Israel's worship but an interpretation of its purpose. Shadow implies intention. Copy presupposes an original. The argument rests on the conviction that God has authored history toward a specific end.

Paul's Adam–Christ parallel makes the same claim in anthropological terms. Adam is not simply a historical ancestor; he is "a type of the one who was to come" (Rom 5:14). Humanity's beginning is shaped in light of its consummation. What is fractured in the first man is healed in the second. Paul's logic does not treat this as an exegetical curiosity but as the foundation of salvation itself: "For as by one man's disobedience many were made sinners, so by one man's obedience many will be made righteous" (Rom 5:19). History, here, is not cyclical or random. It moves from pattern to fulfilment.

Jesus' own use of typology confirms that this is not a later theological overlay. When He identifies Jonah as a sign—"as Jonah was three days and three nights in the belly of the whale, so will the Son of man be three days and three nights in the heart of the earth" (Matt 12:40)—He is not offering a clever analogy. He is claiming that Israel's Scriptures have been shaped to prefigure His mission. The past was written with the future in view.

The early Church recognised the implications immediately. Justin Martyr argued that the events of Israel's history were "types" given by God to prepare for Christ, not riddles invented after the fact (*Dialogue with Trypho* 40). Irenaeus pressed the point further, insisting that the same God who formed Adam, called Abraham, and spoke through the prophets also acted decisively in Christ, "summing up all things in Himself" (*Against Heresies* III.16.6). For Irenaeus, recapitulation was not metaphor but metaphysics: history is gathered into Christ because Christ is its source.

What emerges from this convergence is not merely a method of reading Scripture, but a claim about reality itself. Typology assumes that time is not autonomous, that events are not self-contained, and that meaning is not imposed from without. History bears coherence because it is authored. Scripture converges because it is guided. Fulfilment surpasses the type because the type was never the goal.

By the time this architectural vision comes fully into view, the question is no longer whether Christ fulfils prophecy in isolated ways. The question becomes whether any merely human figure could stand at the centre of such design. The patterns do not point toward a clever interpreter of Scripture or a charismatic reformer. They point toward one in whom creation, covenant, worship, and humanity itself find their unity. The logic of typology presses beyond function toward identity, beyond fulfilment toward origin.

The convergence of these patterns raises a question that cannot be evaded without distorting the text itself. If Scripture unfolds through recurring figures, institutions, and events that anticipate a final fulfilment, then prophecy cannot be reduced to foresight alone. It must be understood as the shaping of history by intention. The biblical narrative does not merely predict; it prepares. Its coherence rests not in human memory, but in divine authorship.

This becomes especially evident when typology moves beyond persons to encompass sacred space. The Temple is not simply the location of Israel's worship; it is the spatial expression of God's desire to dwell with humanity. Exodus presents the tabernacle as a microcosm of creation, ordered from outer court to inner sanctuary, mirroring the movement from chaos to communion. When Solomon consecrates the Temple, he recognises the paradox at its heart: "Heaven and the highest heaven cannot contain thee" (1 Kgs 8:27). The Temple both affirms God's nearness and confesses its own insufficiency. It is a dwelling that gestures beyond itself.

The sacrificial system functions in precisely the same way. Leviticus orders Israel's life around offerings that cleanse, reconcile, and restore. Yet Scripture refuses to allow sacrifice to become an end in itself. The Psalms protest against ritual severed from obedience: "For thou hast no delight in sacrifice; were I to give a burnt offering, thou wouldst not be pleased" (Ps 51:16). Isaiah speaks even more sharply, condemning worship that masks injustice (Isa 1:11–17). These texts do not abolish sacrifice; they expose its provisional role. Atonement is enacted repeatedly because it is incomplete. The very rhythm of repetition prophesies a final act that will not need renewal.

Hebrews draws this logic to its unavoidable conclusion. The author insists that the law contains "a shadow of the good things to come instead of the true form of these realities" (Heb 10:1). The language is exact. Shadow presupposes substance. Pattern implies fulfilment. The priest who enters the sanctuary annually does so "with blood not his own" (Heb 9:25), a detail that reveals the inadequacy of the system while preserving its purpose. Worship, like kingship and covenant, is shaped toward completion.

Second Temple texts confirm that this sense of anticipation was not a Christian invention. The community at Qumran read Israel's Scriptures with a keen awareness of unfinished business. In 11QMelchizedek, jubilee imagery from Leviticus is interpreted as the work of a heavenly agent who brings definitive release and atonement. The text speaks of Melchizedek as one who proclaims liberty and judges wickedness, a figure operating at the intersection of divine authority and historical fulfilment. This is not naïve literalism. It is architectural expectation. The patterns of Torah are understood to require eschatological completion.

What matters here is not whether these groups anticipated Jesus of Nazareth, but that they recognised the nature of prophecy itself. History, for them, was moving toward a climax beyond ordinary repetition. The biblical story was understood as directed, purposeful, and incomplete. Christianity emerges from this same interpretive world, not as its negation but as its radical claim of fulfilment.

The New Testament's use of typology is therefore neither arbitrary nor opportunistic. When Paul declares that "all these things happened to them as a warning, but they were written down for our instruction" (1 Cor 10:11), he presupposes that Israel's history possesses a didactic shape. Events are not merely remembered; they are inscribed with meaning for later generations. Time itself becomes a medium of revelation.

The Fathers grasped the implications with clarity. Irenaeus insisted that the unity of Scripture depends upon the unity of its Author. "There is one and the same God who spoke through the prophets and who was revealed in Christ" (*Against Heresies* IV.9.1). For him, typology was not a technique but a confession. To recognise Christ in the patterns of Scripture was to confess that God governs history toward a single end. Augustine would later echo this conviction, arguing that history possesses intelligibility only because it unfolds under divine providence (*City of God* XI).

At this point, the architecture of prophecy stands fully exposed. The convergence of Adam and Christ, exodus and redemption, Temple and presence, sacrifice and atonement, is too integrated to be explained by retrospective ingenuity. The patterns precede their fulfilment. They persist across centuries. They survive the collapse of institutions and the failure of leaders. They endure because they are not grounded in human planning.

The logic presses the reader toward a conclusion that is not yet named but increasingly unavoidable. If history itself has been shaped to converge upon a single figure, then that figure cannot be understood merely as a participant within the story. He stands as its interpretive key. Typology does not simply point forward; it reveals backward intention. The fulfilment does not merely complete the pattern; it discloses the mind that formed it.

By this stage the reader has been carried to the edge of a claim that Scripture itself is preparing, even if it has not yet been spoken aloud. The question is no longer whether typology exists, nor whether the patterns are real. The question is whether the convergence of these patterns can be accounted for without reference to divine agency acting *within* history rather than merely upon it. The architecture of prophecy does not resemble a roadmap marked with isolated destinations; it resembles a structure in which every beam, arch, and foundation stone bears weight only in relation to the whole.

This becomes unmistakable when one attends carefully to the way Scripture speaks about time itself. The biblical authors do not treat history as a neutral container in which religious events occasionally occur. Time is shaped, directed, and interpreted as the arena of God's action. Isaiah hears the Lord declare, "I am God, and there is none like me, declaring the end from the beginning and from ancient times things not yet done" (Isa 46:9–10). The force of the claim lies not merely in foreknowledge, but in authorship. God does not simply foresee what will happen; He brings His purposes to completion through the unfolding of events.

This understanding of divine action governs the New Testament's insistence that Scripture speaks with a single voice. When Jesus confronts His opponents, He does not accuse them of ignorance of individual texts, but of failing to perceive their direction. "You search the Scriptures, because you think that in them you have eternal life; and it is they that bear witness to me" (John 5:39). The problem is not lack of information, but resistance to recognition. The Scriptures testify, but their testimony requires interpretation in light of God's decisive act.

Paul's letters make this point with particular sharpness. Writing to the Corinthians, he insists that the events of Israel's wilderness journey were not only historical realities but pedagogical acts: "These things happened to them as types" (1 Cor 10:11). The Greek term *typoi* carries the sense of imprint or pattern. Israel's history bears the mark of intention. It is shaped so as to instruct those who come later, not because later readers are clever, but because God has fashioned the story with future fulfilment in view.

The Epistle to the Hebrews presses this logic further by grounding typology in ontology rather than analogy. Earthly realities are "copies" (*hypodeigmata*) of heavenly ones (Heb 9:23). The sanctuary is not merely symbolic; it is derivative. The priesthood is not merely instructive; it is provisional. Such language presupposes a hierarchy of reality in which the visible participates in the invisible. History, in this account, is not self-contained. It is porous, open to a deeper order that governs it from within.

The patristic tradition recognises the implications without hesitation. Origen argues that Scripture possesses a unified *logos* precisely because it proceeds from the one Logos of God (*On First Principles* IV). The coherence of the text reflects the coherence of the divine mind. Augustine, reflecting on the long arc of history, insists that God's providence orders events so that meaning emerges not immediately, but through patient unfolding. What appears fragmented in the moment reveals its unity only when viewed from the end (*City of God* XI).

Jean Daniélou would later describe this logic as divine pedagogy: God educates humanity through history itself, shaping events so that understanding grows through encounter and fulfilment rather than abstraction. The point is not ingenuity, but intention. Typology functions because God is faithful to His own design.

At this point, the claim implicit in Scripture can no longer be deferred. If history bears coherence, if prophecy operates through pattern rather than prediction alone, if fulfilment surpasses every type while remaining faithful to it, then the figure in whom all these lines converge cannot be explained merely as an inspired reader of Scripture or a gifted religious leader. The architecture points beyond function to identity. The fulfilment

## THE ARCHITECTURE OF PROPHECY: TYPOLOGY AND DIVINE DESIGN

reveals not only what was promised, but who has been acting all along.

The argument has not yet named this identity explicitly. That restraint is deliberate. Scripture itself often leads the reader to recognition before articulation. What can be said, without anticipation, is this: the one who fulfils the architecture of prophecy stands in relation to Israel's history not as its final chapter alone, but as its organising principle. Typology does not simply culminate in Him; it discloses Him as the centre from which the story has always been told.

What remains, before this architecture gives way to explicit confession, is to recognise the restraint built into Scripture's own pedagogy. The biblical text does not rush its reader toward metaphysical conclusions. It forms perception before it demands assent. Pattern precedes proclamation. Fulfilment clarifies what promise alone could not. This is why typology functions as a mode of revelation rather than a technique of argument. It trains the reader to see history itself as meaningful, directed, and internally coherent.

This restraint is evident even in the way Scripture speaks about God's dwelling with humanity. From Eden onward, divine presence is mediated, approached through veils, guarded spaces, and appointed times. The garden becomes tabernacle; the tabernacle becomes Temple; the Temple becomes memory and hope. Each stage intensifies the desire for communion while preserving distance. God draws near, yet remains elusive. Exodus insists that no one may see God and live (Exod 33:20), even as it promises that God will dwell among His people. The tension is not resolved by explanation, but by movement. History advances toward a form of presence that will not negate transcendence while finally overcoming separation.

The prophets give voice to this longing without dissolving its mystery. Ezekiel envisions a restored Temple filled with glory, yet its measurements exceed any historical structure (Ezek 40–48). Zechariah speaks of a king who is humble and victorious, pierced and vindicated (Zech 9; 12). Isaiah dares to proclaim that God Himself will come to save His people (Isa 35:4), even as he speaks of a servant who suffers and is rejected. The prophetic imagination stretches language to its limits, not because it is confused, but because the reality it anticipates exceeds prior categories.

The New Testament writers inherit this tension rather than resolving it prematurely. John begins his Gospel not with argument but with declaration: "The Word became flesh and dwelt among us" (John 1:14). The verb deliberately echoes tabernacle imagery. God's dwelling has entered history in a form both familiar and unprecedented. Yet John does not immediately unpack the metaphysical implications. He narrates encounters, signs, misunderstandings, and recognition. The reader is invited to see before being told what seeing means.

Paul adopts the same method. When he speaks of Christ as the "image of the invisible God" (Col 1:15), he does so within a hymn that gathers creation, redemption, and reconciliation into a single vision. Christ is not introduced as a solution to a puzzle, but as the one in whom "all things hold together" (Col 1:17). The architecture of prophecy gives way to an architecture of being. The coherence of history reveals the coherence of reality itself.

The Fathers follow this pattern with remarkable fidelity. Irenaeus insists that God prepared humanity gradually, accustoming it to receive Him through stages of revelation. Christ appears not as a disruption, but as the moment when humanity becomes capable of what was always intended (*Against Heresies* IV.38). Augustine, reflecting on the long delay of fulfilment, argues that God educates desire through waiting, so that fulfilment may be received as gift rather than seized as possession (*Confessions* I).

At the threshold of explicit Christology, then, the reader stands equipped but not coerced. The architecture of prophecy has done its work. It has shown that Scripture is not a patchwork, that history is not inert, and that fulfilment is not accidental. It has revealed a pattern of divine action that cannot be reduced to foresight or coincidence. What remains is to name the implication that Scripture itself has been preparing: if the story converges upon one figure with such totality, then that figure cannot be understood merely as the recipient of prophecy. He must be understood as the one through whom prophecy was given, history was shaped, and meaning itself was disclosed.

The movement from architecture to confession is now inevitable. The question that follows is no longer whether prophecy has been fulfilled, but what such fulfilment reveals about the identity of the fulfiller. That question belongs to what comes next.

The architecture of prophecy has now carried the reader to the point where recognition becomes unavoidable. Scripture has trained the eye through repetition, escalation, and convergence. Figures have risen and fallen, institutions have been established and judged, covenants have been given and strained to their limits. None of these realities collapses into irrelevance; each remains indispensable, precisely because none is sufficient on its own. The coherence of the story lies not in any single element, but in the way all of them lean forward together.

This forward pressure reveals something decisive about the nature of revelation itself. Biblical prophecy does not function as a catalogue of future facts awaiting verification. It operates as divine self-disclosure through time. God reveals who He is by what He does, and what He does is shaped so that its meaning unfolds gradually. The delay between promise and fulfilment is not a problem to be solved; it is the means by which understanding is formed. History becomes intelligible only when its end is disclosed, and its end reveals that its beginning was already ordered toward that disclosure.

This is why the unity of Scripture cannot be explained by shared religious sensibility alone. The biblical authors span centuries, cultures, empires, and crises. They write under radically different circumstances, yet the same structures persist. Covenant, sacrifice, kingship, exile, return, judgment, mercy—these themes recur with increasing density. They do not cancel one another out; they accumulate. The effect is cumulative pressure toward a fulfilment that is at once faithful to all that preceded it and greater than any prior expression.

The recognition of this pressure is already present within Scripture itself. The Psalms wrestle openly with delayed fulfilment, refusing to abandon either promise or reality. "How long, O Lord?" becomes a refrain not of despair, but of fidelity. The prophets intensify this tension, speaking of future glory while standing amid ruin. Their hope is not abstract optimism; it is grounded in the conviction that God's word cannot fail, even when history appears to contradict it. This conviction presupposes that God is not merely reacting to events, but directing them toward an end known to Him.

The New Testament writers inherit this conviction fully formed. They do not present Jesus as a fortunate alignment of prophecy, but as the moment when Scripture's internal logic is disclosed. The risen Christ does not offer His disciples new texts; He reopens the old ones. "Then he opened their minds to understand the Scriptures" (Luke 24:45). Understanding comes not from additional data, but from the revelation of meaning. The Scriptures were already complete; what was lacking was sight.

This sight transforms how the past is read. Adam is no longer merely the first sinner; he is the head of a humanity awaiting restoration. Moses is no longer only a lawgiver; he is the mediator whose work anticipates a deeper deliverance. David is no longer simply a king; he is the bearer of a promise that outlives his throne. The Temple is no longer only a building; it is the sign of God's intention to dwell with His people in a manner yet unrealised. None of these readings negates the historical reality. Each reveals its depth.

The Church Fathers articulate this recognition with clarity precisely because they stand close to the apostolic witness. Irenaeus insists that God educates humanity through history so that it may learn to receive Him without fear. The long preparation is not evidence of divine hesitation, but of divine wisdom. Augustine deepens this insight by insisting that time itself is a creature, ordered by God for the sake of revelation. History unfolds not randomly, but according to providence that accommodates human limitation while remaining faithful to divine purpose.

At this point, the reader has been shown enough to understand the shape of the claim without yet hearing it named. The architecture of prophecy does not terminate in a mere solution to textual puzzles. It reveals a reality in which history, Scripture, and meaning converge upon a single centre. The convergence is too comprehensive to be explained by human agency alone. It implies intention at the level of authorship, not merely foresight.

The fulfilment toward which Scripture moves is therefore not simply the arrival of a figure within history, but the disclosure of the one who has been acting through history all along. The patterns do not merely anticipate Him; they originate from Him. The story does not merely end with Him; it is held together by Him. To acknowledge this is not yet to articulate doctrine, but it is to stand at the threshold of confession.

The architecture has done its work. It has trained the reader to recognise coherence where fragmentation once seemed inevitable, intention where chance once appeared sufficient, and design where accident once seemed plausible. What remains is the step Scripture itself now demands: to ask what kind of Messiah could stand at the centre of such a story, and what that centrality reveals about His identity. The answer, once spoken, will not arrive as an intrusion. It will arrive as the only conclusion the story itself permits.

The history preserved in Scripture moves toward fulfilment without collapsing into repetition. Each covenant establishes something real, yet leaves something unfinished. Each institution mediates God's presence, yet confesses its own insufficiency. Kings rule and fall. Prophets speak and suffer. Sacrifice reconciles and yet must be offered again. These realities do not negate one another; they accumulate. The weight of the story increases precisely because nothing resolves it from within. The persistence of promise in the face of failure reveals not error, but intention.

This intention becomes visible in the way Scripture speaks of God's nearness. From Eden onward, divine presence is given under conditions— walked with, heard, approached, guarded. The garden becomes sanctuary; sanctuary becomes tabernacle; tabernacle becomes Temple. Each stage intensifies intimacy while preserving distance. God dwells with His people, yet remains uncontained. Even at the height of Israel's cultic life, the tension remains unresolved. "Behold, heaven and the highest heaven cannot contain thee" (1 Kgs 8:27). Presence is real, yet incomplete.

Communion is promised, yet deferred.

The prophetic writings deepen this tension rather than resolving it. Ezekiel's vision of a restored Temple exceeds historical realisation. Isaiah dares to proclaim that God Himself will come to save, even as he speaks of a servant who is despised and rejected. Zechariah speaks of a king who is both humble and victorious, pierced and vindicated. These visions are not contradictions; they are expansions. Language is stretched because the reality toward which it points surpasses existing forms.

The New Testament bears witness to the same logic. Israel's history is treated not as a closed past, but as a pattern whose meaning becomes visible only in fulfilment. Adam is read as the head of a humanity awaiting restoration. Moses is understood as mediator of a covenant that anticipates a deeper deliverance. David's throne is recognised as the bearer of a promise that outlives political sovereignty. The Temple is interpreted as a sign of God's intention to dwell with humanity in a manner not yet realised. None of these readings abolishes the historical reality. Each discloses its depth.

The coherence of this disclosure cannot be explained by foresight alone. Prediction accounts for isolated correspondences; it cannot account for structural convergence across centuries, genres, and institutions. What emerges instead is a vision of history shaped by purpose. Events are not merely foreseen; they are formed. Meaning is not imposed retrospectively; it is woven into time itself. The patterns persist because they are grounded in a will that precedes them.

This coherence reveals something decisive about fulfilment. Fulfilment does not merely complete what was lacking; it reveals what was always intended. The type is not rendered obsolete by fulfilment; it is illuminated. The promise is not negated by realisation; it is shown to have been truthful beyond what could previously be grasped. History's unity emerges only when its centre is disclosed.

When the lines of covenant, kingship, sacrifice, and presence are traced together, they converge upon a single reality that holds them in unity without dissolving their distinctiveness. The fulfilment toward which

Scripture moves is not external to the story it completes. It stands within it as its organising principle. The coherence of prophecy reveals not merely that God keeps His word, but that the one in whom prophecy converges belongs on the side of authorship rather than reception.

At this point the structure of Scripture has said as much as it can without explicit declaration. The patterns have spoken. The unity has been displayed. The question that remains is not whether prophecy has been fulfilled, but what such fulfilment reveals about the identity of the one in whom the entire design comes to rest.

# 27

# Fulfilment, Not Replacement: Christ and the Story of Israel

Jesus' claim that He came not to abolish the Law and the Prophets but to fulfil them stands as one of the most densely charged statements in the Gospels. "Do not think that I have come to abolish the law or the prophets; I have come not to abolish them but to fulfil them" (Matt 5:17). The verb He chooses, *plērōsai*, does not suggest negation or replacement, but completion—bringing something to its intended fullness. The claim presupposes continuity. One does not fulfil what one discards. From the outset, Jesus situates His mission within Israel's story, not over against it.

This insistence on fulfilment governs the way Jesus inhabits Israel's Scriptures. When He enters the synagogue at Nazareth and reads Isaiah's proclamation of good news to the poor and liberty to the captives, He closes the scroll and declares, "Today this scripture has been fulfilled in your hearing" (Luke 4:21). The force of the statement lies not merely in timing, but in identity. The prophecy is not exhausted by proclamation; it is realised in the one who speaks it. Fulfilment here is personal before it is doctrinal. Scripture reaches its goal not in an event alone, but in a life that embodies its meaning.

The Gospels repeatedly present Jesus as reliving Israel's history in concentrated form. Matthew's citation of Hosea—"Out of Egypt I called my son" (Hos 11:1; Matt 2:15)—is not an arbitrary proof-text. Hosea's original reference is corporate, describing Israel's exodus. Matthew's application assumes that Jesus stands as Israel-in-person, the faithful Son who re-enacts the nation's journey. This pattern continues in the wilderness temptations, where Jesus responds to Satan exclusively with words drawn from Deuteronomy (Matt 4:1–11). Where Israel faltered in the wilderness, the Son remains obedient. The Law is not set aside; it is lived.

The Sermon on the Mount intensifies this logic. Jesus does not repeal Torah; He internalises it. "You have heard that it was said... but I say to you" (Matt 5:21–48) does not pit Jesus against Moses, but reveals the depth toward which the Law was always oriented. Commandment is drawn inward to intention, obedience to desire. The Law's true aim—formation of the heart—is disclosed rather than abandoned. This movement corresponds precisely to the prophetic promise of covenant renewal. Jeremiah announces a covenant not written on stone but on the heart: "I will put my law within them, and I will write it upon their hearts" (Jer 31:33). The new covenant does not erase Torah; it completes its purpose.

The Transfiguration gathers this continuity into a single moment. Moses and Elijah—representing Law and Prophets—appear in glory and speak with Jesus "of his exodus, which he was to accomplish at Jerusalem" (Luke 9:31). The language is deliberate. Jesus' passion is interpreted not as rupture, but as fulfilment of Israel's foundational act of redemption. Exodus, covenant, and suffering converge. The voice from the cloud does not dismiss the past; it identifies the Son as the one to whom it points: "This is my Son, my Chosen; listen to him" (Luke 9:35).

Paul articulates the same logic through covenantal progression. The promise given to Abraham precedes the Law and cannot be nullified by it. "The law, which came four hundred and thirty years afterward, does not annul a covenant previously ratified by God" (Gal 3:17). For Paul, Christ does not interrupt the Abrahamic promise; He brings it to fruition. The inheritance promised to Abraham's seed finds its concrete realisation "in Christ" (Gal 3:16). Fulfilment here is organic. What was pledged in promise is realised in person.

Romans 9–11 presses this continuity further by addressing Israel's ongoing place in salvation history. Paul refuses to frame the Gospel as displacement. Israel's privileges remain real: "to them belong the adoption, the glory, the covenants, the giving of the law, the worship, and the promises" (Rom 9:4). Even Israel's unbelief does not cancel God's fidelity. "The gifts and the call of God are irrevocable" (Rom 11:29). The olive tree remains one. Gentiles are grafted in; they do not replace the root (Rom 11:17–24). The Church exists within Israel's covenantal story as its expansion, not its negation.

The Fourth Gospel articulates this fulfilment with striking theological density. "The Word became flesh and dwelt among us" (John 1:14). The verb translated "dwelt" (*eskēnōsen*) evokes the tabernacle. The divine presence once mediated through tent and Temple is now embodied. John immediately places Moses and Torah within this movement: "The law was given through Moses; grace and truth came through Jesus Christ" (John 1:17). The contrast is not between falsehood and truth, but between gift and completion. What was given through Moses reaches its fullness in the Word made flesh.

The early Fathers recognised this continuity as essential to the faith. Irenaeus insists that Christ "did not reject the ancient covenant, but fulfilled it, and by fulfilling it extended it to all" (*Against Heresies* IV.9.1). Justin Martyr argues that the Law was preparatory, given to form a people capable of recognising its fulfilment, not to be discarded as error (*Dialogue with Trypho* 11). Augustine would later summarise the relationship with characteristic clarity: the Old Testament is revealed in the New, and the New is hidden in the Old (*City of God* XVI).

Fulfilment, then, names neither rupture nor replacement. It names completion from within. Christ stands not as a foreign solution imposed upon Israel's Scriptures, but as the one in whom their deepest intention becomes visible. The Law reaches its goal in obedience perfected, covenant in communion restored, and promise in presence realised. What Israel awaited is not abandoned. It is accomplished.

The claim that Christ fulfils Israel from within gains further clarity when the covenants themselves are traced as a single, organic movement rather than as discrete legal arrangements. Scripture presents covenant not as a sequence of discarded contracts, but as a deepening relationship between God and His people. Each covenant preserves what came before while pressing toward a fuller expression of communion. Creation establishes humanity as God's image-bearing partner. Abraham is chosen so that blessing might extend to the nations. Sinai orders Israel's life around God's holiness. Davidic kingship unites covenant and rule. None of these stages is negated by what follows. Each remains intelligible only because it is taken up into a greater whole.

Jeremiah's promise of a new covenant must be read within this logic. "Not like the covenant which I made with their fathers... but this is the covenant which I will make... I will put my law within them, and I will write it upon their hearts" (Jer 31:32–33). The contrast is not between law and lawlessness, but between external inscription and interior transformation. The Torah remains God's gift; what changes is the mode of its reception. Ezekiel speaks in the same register when he announces that God will remove the heart of stone and give a heart of flesh, placing His Spirit within His people so that they may walk in His statutes (Ezek 36:26–27). Covenant renewal intensifies obedience by healing the human subject who receives it.

Jesus' ministry unfolds precisely along this line. He gathers disciples not to form a rival community to Israel, but to constitute a renewed Israel centred upon Himself. The selection of twelve is neither symbolic flourish nor administrative convenience. It signals restoration. The twelve tribes are gathered again, not through territorial reconstitution, but through communion with the one who embodies Israel's vocation. When Jesus speaks of sitting on twelve thrones judging the tribes of Israel (Matt 19:28), He does not dissolve Israel's identity; He reconfigures it around fidelity to Himself.

The Gospel narratives confirm this repeatedly. Jesus forgives sins apart from Temple sacrifice, yet He does not despise the Temple; He identifies Himself as its fulfilment. He announces the coming destruction of the sanctuary not as a rejection of Israel's worship, but as judgment for infidelity and as the prelude to a new mode of divine presence. "Destroy this temple, and in three days I will raise it up" (John 2:19). John immediately clarifies that He was speaking of the temple of His body (John 2:21). Sacred space is not abolished; it is transposed. Presence is no longer localised in stone, but embodied in a person.

The apostolic witness preserves this continuity with care. The council of Jerusalem in Acts 15 does not abandon Torah as irrelevant. It discerns how Gentiles may be incorporated into Israel's covenantal life without bearing the full yoke of the Mosaic law. James appeals to the prophets, citing Amos' vision of the restored tent of David so that "the rest of men may seek the Lord" (Acts 15:16–17). Gentile inclusion is not innovation; it is fulfilment of Israel's mission. The covenant expands without dissolving its roots.

Paul's olive tree metaphor remains decisive. Israel is not uprooted. Gentiles are grafted in "contrary to nature" (Rom 11:24). The image presupposes continuity of life flowing from the same root. Warning accompanies privilege. Those who stand by faith are cautioned against arrogance, for they share in what they did not originate. Israel's stumbling is neither final nor total. "As regards election they are beloved for the sake of their forefathers" (Rom 11:28). Fulfilment does not cancel election; it intensifies responsibility.

Patristic theology recognises this pattern as intrinsic to revelation. Irenaeus insists that God "recapitulated" humanity in Christ, gathering Israel's history into a single obedient life (*Against Heresies* III.18.1). The covenants are not stages of abandonment, but stages of maturation. Augustine speaks of salvation history as a divine pedagogy, in which God educates desire through time so that fulfilment may be received as gift rather than seized as possession (*Against Faustus* XII). Fulfilment, in this vision, preserves the past by bringing it to its intended end.

Christ's relationship to Israel, then, cannot be described adequately in terms of succession or substitution. He does not take Israel's place; He takes Israel's calling upon Himself. What Israel was chosen to be—a light to the nations, a priestly people, a bearer of God's presence—He lives in perfect obedience. In Him, covenant becomes communion, law becomes life, and promise becomes presence. The story Israel began is not concluded by being set aside. It is concluded by being fulfilled.

The claim that Christ fulfils Israel by embodying its vocation reaches its deepest expression in the way Scripture speaks of Torah itself. The Law is never presented merely as regulation; it is revelation. Through it, Israel learns who God is and what covenant fidelity requires. "The law of the Lord is perfect, reviving the soul" (Ps 19:7). To be faithful to Torah is to live in alignment with God's will. Any fulfilment worthy of the name must therefore preserve Torah's revelatory function even as it discloses its ultimate aim.

Jesus' teaching consistently operates within this framework. When questioned about the greatest commandment, He does not innovate; He gathers Torah's heart into unity. "You shall love the Lord your God with all your heart… and your neighbour as yourself" (Deut 6:5; Lev 19:18; Matt 22:37–40). On these commandments, He insists, "depend all the law and the prophets" (Matt 22:40). The Law is neither relativised nor bypassed. It is unveiled in its inner coherence. Love is not offered as an alternative to obedience, but as its true form.

John's Gospel articulates this unveiling with striking precision. "The Word became flesh and dwelt among us" (John 1:14). The language deliberately evokes the tabernacle, the place where Torah and presence once met. John immediately situates Moses within this movement: "The law was given through Moses; grace and truth came through Jesus Christ" (John 1:17). The contrast is not between falsehood and truth, but between anticipation and fulfilment. Grace and truth do not negate the Law; they disclose what the Law was ordered toward. The Word who speaks the command now lives it.

Paul's letters press the same insight through a different register. He insists that the righteous requirement of the law is fulfilled not by external conformity but by life in the Spirit: "The law of the Spirit of life in Christ Jesus has set me free from the law of sin and death" (Rom 8:2). What the Law could command but not effect—obedience from the heart—God accomplishes by transforming the human subject. Fulfilment here is not legal substitution, but ontological healing. The Law's intention is realised because the human person is renewed.

The Epistle to the Hebrews situates this fulfilment within covenantal logic. Quoting Jeremiah's promise of a new covenant, the author insists that what is new does not arise from divine regret, but from maturation. "In speaking of a new covenant, he treats the first as obsolete" (Heb 8:13). Obsolescence here is not error, but completion. What was provisional yields to what is definitive. The sacrificial system gives way to a single offering because its purpose has been achieved. "By a single offering he has perfected for all time those who are sanctified" (Heb 10:14). The Law's pedagogy reaches its end in perfected communion.

Second Temple Judaism itself anticipated this kind of covenantal deepening. The Community Rule from Qumran speaks of a renewed covenant in which obedience flows from purification of the heart rather than mere conformity to command. The expectation was not abandonment of Torah, but its interiorisation. Restoration meant more than return from exile; it meant transformation of the people who would keep the covenant. This expectation forms the background against which Jesus' teaching is heard and contested.

The patristic witness recognises the stakes clearly. Irenaeus insists that Christ fulfils the Law precisely because He embodies obedience without fracture. "What we had lost in Adam... this we recover in Christ Jesus" (*Against Heresies* III.23.1). The Law is not bypassed; it is honoured by being fulfilled in flesh. Origen, reflecting on the unity of Scripture, argues that the spiritual sense of the Law does not negate its historical reality, but reveals its depth (*On First Principles* IV). The Law's true meaning emerges only when it is lived perfectly.

Augustine articulates the same logic with characteristic economy. The Law, he writes, was given so that grace might be sought; grace was given so that the Law might be fulfilled (*On the Spirit and the Letter* 19). Fulfilment here is not the erasure of command, but the gift of capacity. Obedience becomes possible because love has been poured into the heart (Rom 5:5). What was once external instruction becomes interior life.

Christ's fulfilment of Torah thus reveals continuity at its deepest level. Command becomes communion. Instruction becomes incarnation. Promise becomes presence. The Law is not set aside; it is brought to life. In the obedience of the Son, Israel's vocation reaches its goal, and the covenant's intention is disclosed in full.

The continuity between Israel and the Church becomes most visible when the question of belonging is addressed without abstraction. Scripture refuses to speak of God's people in terms of replacement or displacement. It speaks instead of inheritance, grafting, and enlargement. Paul's olive tree image in Romans is not illustrative rhetoric; it is theological precision. Israel remains the cultivated tree. The patriarchal promises remain the root. Gentiles, Paul insists, do not constitute a new planting. They are grafted in "contrary to nature" (Rom 11:24), sharing in nourishment they did not generate. The warning is as strong as the promise: "Do not boast over the branches" (Rom 11:18). Fulfilment does not permit triumphalism; it demands humility.

Paul's argument depends on a prior conviction: God's covenantal fidelity does not fail. "Has God rejected his people? By no means!" (Rom 11:1). Israel's stumbling, however grave, does not annul election. The language Paul uses is unambiguous: "the gifts and the call of God are irrevocable" (Rom 11:29). Fulfilment, therefore, cannot be construed as divine reversal. It is not the abandonment of Israel for another people, but the unfolding of God's mercy in a way that remains faithful to what He first promised. Even judgment serves restoration. Even exclusion remains ordered toward inclusion.

This conviction governs the Church's self-understanding in the New Testament. The Church is not portrayed as a parallel entity with a separate origin story. It is presented as the extension of Israel's calling into the nations. Peter addresses Gentile believers using titles drawn directly from

Exodus: "a chosen race, a royal priesthood, a holy nation" (1 Pet 2:9; cf. Exod 19:6). These titles are not transferred as spoils; they are shared as vocation. What Israel was called to be, the Church is called to live in Christ, not apart from Him.

The Book of Acts reinforces this continuity at every turn. The apostolic mission begins in Jerusalem, moves through Judea and Samaria, and only then reaches the Gentile world (Acts 1:8). This movement is not strategic; it is theological. Salvation flows outward from Israel's centre. Even the controversy surrounding Gentile inclusion does not result in Torah being dismissed as error. At the Jerusalem council, James interprets the Gentile mission through the prophets: "After this I will return, and I will rebuild the dwelling of David" (Acts 15:16, citing Amos 9). The inclusion of the nations is read not as innovation, but as fulfilment of Israel's restoration.

This pattern confirms that Christ's fulfilment of Israel does not exhaust Israel's significance. It intensifies it. Israel's story does not end with Christ; it is reoriented around Him. The Church does not stand over Israel as judge; it stands within Israel's promises as beneficiary. Augustine captures this posture when he insists that the Church reads Israel's Scriptures not as a conquered past, but as her own inheritance (*City of God* XVII). The Old Testament remains indispensable because it is the story Christ fulfils.

Second Temple literature reinforces this covenantal logic. Texts such as 4 Ezra and 2 Baruch wrestle with the apparent delay of fulfilment after the destruction of the Temple. Their anguish arises precisely because covenant is presumed to be enduring. God's fidelity is not questioned because covenant exists; it is questioned because covenant has not yet reached its promised resolution. Expectation of restoration presupposes continuity. Fulfilment remains future, but covenant remains intact.

The Fathers read these developments not as theological improvisation, but as divine consistency. Irenaeus insists that God educates humanity gradually, shaping capacity for communion through time. "It was necessary that man should first be made, and having been made, should receive growth, and having received growth, should be strengthened" (*Against Heresies* IV.38.3). Fulfilment, in this vision, is maturation, not replacement.

God does not change His purpose; He brings it to completion.

Christ, then, stands at the centre of Israel's story as its living convergence point. He gathers covenant, law, worship, and promise into Himself without dissolving their meaning. In Him, Israel's election is neither negated nor postponed. It is fulfilled in a way that preserves God's faithfulness and expands His mercy. The Church lives from this fulfilment only insofar as it remains grafted into Israel's root, nourished by promises it did not originate, and sustained by a covenant that reaches its completion not by being set aside, but by being brought to life.

What finally emerges from this convergence is a definition of fulfilment that resists reduction to chronology or proof. Fulfilment is not simply that events predicted in Israel's Scriptures occurred in Jesus' life, though they did. It is that the entire meaning of Israel's covenantal existence finds coherence in Him. Promise, law, worship, suffering, hope, and vocation are gathered without loss into a single, living centre. Scripture's unity is no longer merely conceptual; it becomes personal.

This is why the New Testament consistently speaks of Christ not only as the fulfiller of Scripture, but as its interpretive key. On the road to Emmaus, the risen Jesus does not introduce new revelation. He "interpreted to them in all the scriptures the things concerning himself" (Luke 24:27). The text does not say that He replaced Moses and the prophets, but that He unveiled their inner logic. Their meaning had always been ordered toward Him. Recognition, not revision, is what transforms confusion into understanding. Hearts burn not because the past is discarded, but because it is finally intelligible.

This recognition also explains why the earliest Christian proclamation was inseparable from Israel's Scriptures. Apostolic preaching does not appeal to novelty. It appeals to fulfilment. Peter's Pentecost sermon moves effortlessly between Joel, the Psalms, and Davidic promise because he assumes a single narrative arc (Acts 2). Paul reasons from the Scriptures in synagogues precisely because he believes Christ completes what those Scriptures announce (Acts 17:2–3). The Gospel advances not by severing continuity, but by revealing it.

The theological weight of this fulfilment presses beyond historical correspondence. If Christ fulfils Israel's law by embodying obedience, Israel's worship by becoming the living Temple, Israel's kingship by reigning through self-giving love, and Israel's vocation by drawing the nations into covenant, then fulfilment cannot be explained merely by role or function. The coherence is too total. What converges in Him is not one thread of Israel's hope, but all of them at once. Such convergence demands a deeper explanation.

The Scriptures themselves gesture toward this depth without naming it prematurely. The Word through whom Torah was given now dwells among His people (John 1:14). The divine glory once filling the Temple now rests upon a human life (John 1:14; Exod 40:34). The covenant mediated through prophets and priests is now mediated through a person who speaks and acts with divine authority. Fulfilment begins to look less like succession and more like presence.

The Fathers did not hesitate to follow this logic to its conclusion. Irenaeus insists that the same Word who spoke through the prophets has now appeared visibly, not as a break in God's self-disclosure, but as its culmination. Augustine argues that Christ is the one in whom Scripture's dispersed meanings are unified, not by force, but by truth. Fulfilment reveals authorship. The unity of the story reflects the unity of the speaker.

At this point, the reader stands at a threshold. Israel's story has not been replaced. It has been completed in a way that preserves its integrity while revealing its deepest meaning. Covenant continuity has not flattened difference; it has disclosed purpose. What remains is to speak explicitly what has thus far been implied: that the fulfilment of Israel's Scriptures in Christ discloses not only the faithfulness of God, but the identity of the one who fulfils them. The Messiah who completes Israel's story does not merely belong to it. He stands as its source and its goal.

The architecture is now visible. The question that remains is unavoidable. If prophecy, covenant, and history converge so completely in Christ, then fulfilment itself becomes revelation. The story Israel tells about God has reached its centre. What follows must address what this centre reveals about the Messiah Himself.

Fulfilment, then, is not an abstract principle layered onto Israel's Scriptures after the fact. It is the form those Scriptures were always taking as they unfolded through history. The coherence now visible does not arise from selective reading or retrospective harmonisation. It arises from the conviction, shared by prophets, apostles, and the Church's earliest theologians, that God has spoken with a single voice across time. The unity of the story reflects the unity of its Author.

This is why Christian faith has never understood itself as a departure from Israel's God, but as allegiance to Him revealed at last without veil. The God who called Abraham, who spoke at Sinai, who dwelt in the Temple, and who sustained Israel through exile is the same God encountered in Christ. The continuity is not merely conceptual. It is covenantal, historical, and personal. What was once known through promise is now known through presence.

Yet this presence does not exhaust Israel's mystery. Paul's language resists closure. Israel remains beloved "for the sake of their forefathers" (Rom 11:28). The covenantal story remains open, not because it is unresolved, but because God's mercy exceeds human timetables. Fulfilment has occurred, yet its effects unfold through history. The Messiah has come, yet the fullness of His reign continues to be received. Continuity and expectation remain intertwined.

This tension preserves humility. The Church does not possess fulfilment as an achievement. She receives it as gift. She lives from promises she did not initiate and Scriptures she did not author. Her confidence rests not in superiority of insight, but in fidelity to what has been revealed. To sever herself from Israel would be to sever herself from the very story that gives her identity. To honour Israel's Scriptures is not an act of nostalgia; it is an act of faithfulness to Christ.

The chapter thus closes where it must: not with finality, but with recognition. Israel's story has not been replaced. It has been completed in a way that preserves its integrity while unveiling its deepest meaning. Covenant has not been annulled; it has been fulfilled. Law has not been discarded; it has been embodied. Promise has not failed; it has taken flesh.

What now stands before the reader is not a theory of fulfilment, but a person in whom fulfilment lives. The question that follows is no longer whether prophecy coheres, but what that coherence reveals about the one in whom it converges. If Israel's Scriptures reach their fullness in Christ, then the nature of that fulfilment must disclose something decisive about who the Messiah truly is. The story now presses beyond fulfilment toward identity.

# 28

# Why Prophecy Matters: Faith, Evangelisation, and Discipleship

Fulfilled prophecy confronts the human person first with the character of God, not with an abstract proof. In Scripture, prophecy is never presented as speculative foresight or religious poetry. It is covenantal speech, bound to God's own faithfulness. Moses instructs Israel that the truth of a prophet is measured not by eloquence or intensity, but by fulfilment: "When a prophet speaks in the name of the Lord, if the word does not come to pass or come true, that is a word which the Lord has not spoken" (Deut 18:22). God binds His name to His word. What He promises, He is obligated—by His own fidelity—to accomplish.

The Psalms repeatedly return to this theme, not as theory but as worship. "The Lord is faithful in all his words, and gracious in all his deeds" (Ps 145:13). Faithfulness here is not one attribute among others; it is the ground of trust. Israel worships the God who *keeps His word*. The history of promise and fulfilment is therefore not ancillary to faith; it is its foundation. Abraham believes not because he can see the outcome, but because he trusts the promiser. "He believed the Lord; and he reckoned it to him as righteousness" (Gen 15:6). Fulfilled prophecy vindicates that trust across time. It reveals that faith was never misplaced.

The Letter to the Hebrews draws this logic to its sharpest point. God, it insists, does not merely promise; He swears. "When God made a promise to Abraham, since he had no one greater by whom to swear, he swore by himself" (Heb 6:13). The oath is not for God's sake but for ours. "So that through two unchangeable things, in which it is impossible that God should prove false, we who have fled for refuge might have strong encouragement to seize the hope set before us" (Heb 6:18). Fulfilled prophecy matters because it discloses a God who cannot lie. Faith rests not on probability, but on demonstrated fidelity.

The New Testament presents the fulfilment of prophecy precisely as the decisive manifestation of this divine character. When the risen Christ encounters the disciples on the road to Emmaus, He does not begin with exhortation or command. He begins with Scripture. "Beginning with Moses and all the prophets, he interpreted to them in all the scriptures the things concerning himself" (Luke 24:27). The text does not say that Jesus replaced Moses and the prophets, but that He unveiled their inner coherence. Fulfilment is not imposed upon the text; it is disclosed from within it. Recognition precedes response. Only after Scripture is opened do hearts begin to burn (Luke 24:32).

This pattern governs apostolic proclamation from the beginning. Peter's sermon at Pentecost is structured entirely around fulfilled prophecy. Joel's promise of the Spirit poured out on all flesh is declared realised: "This is what was spoken by the prophet Joel" (Acts 2:16). David's psalms concerning the Holy One who would not see corruption are read in light of the resurrection: "This Jesus God raised up, and of that we all are witnesses" (Acts 2:32). The conclusion follows with inevitability rather than coercion: "Let all the house of Israel therefore know assuredly that God has made him both Lord and Christ" (Acts 2:36). Fulfilment demands recognition because it reveals that God has acted in continuity with His word.

Paul preaches in the same register. In Pisidian Antioch he traces Israel's history deliberately, not as background but as promise unfolding toward Christ. "What God promised to the fathers, this he has fulfilled to us their children by raising Jesus" (Acts 13:32–33). The language is juridical.

Promise has been honoured. God has acted consistently with His covenant. Faith, in this context, is not blind assent but acknowledgment of fulfilled truth. It is recognition that God has done what He said He would do.

Scripture therefore treats fulfilled prophecy not as neutral information but as revelation that claims the conscience. Jesus Himself makes this explicit. In the parable of the rich man and Lazarus, the sufficiency of revelation is not in question: "They have Moses and the prophets; let them hear them" (Luke 16:29). The problem is not lack of evidence, but refusal to listen. Fulfilment removes ambiguity. To encounter it and remain unmoved is not caution; it is resistance. "If I had not come and spoken to them, they would not have sin; but now they have no excuse for their sin" (John 15:22).

The Epistle to the Hebrews intensifies this moral dimension. "In many and various ways God spoke of old to our fathers by the prophets; but in these last days he has spoken to us by a Son" (Heb 1:1–2). The contrast is not between false and true speech, but between partial and definitive address. God's speech has reached its fullness. The response it requires is therefore decisive. "How shall we escape if we neglect such a great salvation?" (Heb 2:3). Fulfilled prophecy does not merely inform; it summons.

The Fathers grasped this with clarity. Augustine insists that fulfilled prophecy leaves no room for neutrality. "He who foretold these things has done them; he who has done them calls us to believe" (*Sermon* 131). Faith, for Augustine, is not assent to probability but obedience to truth revealed. John Chrysostom speaks in the same register when he warns that knowledge of Scripture without submission becomes indictment. The prophets, he insists, were sent not merely to inform, but "that men might change their lives" (*Homilies on Matthew*). Revelation either heals or hardens, depending on response.

Origen presses the point even further. Scripture, he argues, is not merely read; it addresses. The same word that enlightens can judge if resisted. Fulfilled prophecy therefore stands as mercy and judgment at once (*Homilies on Jeremiah*). It reveals a God who has kept His word and a humanity summoned to answer. To recognise fulfilment is already to stand under obligation.

Prophecy matters, then, because it reveals a God whose promises are trustworthy and whose speech is binding. Faith is not the creation of meaning but submission to meaning disclosed. The Gospel does not ask whether fulfilment is persuasive. It asks whether it is true—and whether the one who sees it will receive it as such.

Fulfilled prophecy sharpens not only faith but responsibility. Scripture never permits revelation to remain a neutral possession. Once God has spoken and acted, the hearer stands accountable to what has been disclosed. Jesus articulates this with disarming clarity when He rebukes the cities that witnessed His mighty works yet refused repentance: "Woe to you, Chorazin! Woe to you, Bethsaida! For if the mighty works done in you had been done in Tyre and Sidon, they would have repented long ago" (Matt 11:21). The judgment is not based on ignorance, but on proximity to fulfilled signs. The nearer one stands to revelation, the heavier the moral weight of refusal.

This logic appears again in Jesus' lament over Jerusalem. "Would that even today you knew the things that make for peace! But now they are hid from your eyes" (Luke 19:42). The tragedy is not that peace was unavailable, but that it was unrecognised. Fulfilment has occurred, yet blindness persists. Revelation intensifies rather than alleviates the stakes of decision. "This is the judgment," John records, "that the light has come into the world, and men loved darkness rather than light" (John 3:19). Fulfilled prophecy unmasks preference. It reveals not only what one knows, but what one loves.

The apostolic witness treats this dynamic with unflinching seriousness. Peter's Pentecost sermon concludes not with an invitation to admire coherence, but with a summons to conversion: "Repent, and be baptized every one of you in the name of Jesus Christ for the forgiveness of your sins" (Acts 2:38). Fulfilment presses toward repentance because it confronts the hearer with truth that cannot be indefinitely deferred. Paul echoes this urgency when he warns that God "commands all men everywhere to repent, because he has fixed a day on which he will judge the world in righteousness" (Acts 17:30–31). The ground of the command is not fear, but fulfilment: God has given assurance "by raising him from the dead."

Romans frames this accountability within the obedience of faith. Paul insists that the Gospel creates responsibility precisely because it has been announced in continuity with Israel's Scriptures. "They have not all heeded the gospel; for Isaiah says, 'Lord, who has believed our report?'" (Rom 10:16; Isa 53:1). The report has been given. Hearing has occurred. Faith or refusal now becomes the decisive act. Revelation is not information awaiting analysis; it is address demanding response.

The Epistle of James distils this truth into a stark admonition: "Be doers of the word, and not hearers only, deceiving yourselves" (Jas 1:22). Self-deception becomes possible precisely where revelation is treated as inert knowledge. Fulfilled prophecy renders such deception untenable. Once God's promises have been shown trustworthy in history, to hear without obedience is to resist truth knowingly.

The Fathers recognised this moral dimension as intrinsic to prophecy itself. John Chrysostom warns that Scripture read without submission becomes judgment rather than gift. Knowledge, he insists, increases condemnation if it does not lead to repentance (*Homilies on Matthew*). Augustine speaks even more sharply: unbelief in the face of fulfilled prophecy is not mere error but culpable blindness of the will (*Tractates on John*). To refuse what God has made plain is to prefer darkness to light.

This is why fulfilled prophecy abolishes neutrality. One cannot indefinitely suspend judgment once God has acted. The convergence of Scripture in Christ does not merely persuade; it exposes. It reveals a God who has kept His word and a humanity called to answer. Faith becomes obedience, and refusal becomes judgment. Revelation fulfilled presses beyond recognition toward decision, beyond understanding toward conversion.

Fulfilled prophecy also creates an imperative that cannot remain private. The apostolic Church never understood fulfilment as an inward certainty reserved for personal consolation. It understood it as a truth that demanded public witness. The resurrection of Jesus, proclaimed as the fulfilment of Scripture, is never treated as esoteric knowledge. It is announced openly, often at great cost. "We cannot but speak of what we have seen and heard" (Acts 4:20). Fulfilment imposes obligation. Silence becomes a form of denial.

This pattern is evident throughout the Acts of the Apostles. Evangelisation consistently unfolds as exposition of Scripture culminating in fulfilment. Stephen's address before the Sanhedrin is not a philosophical defence but a retelling of Israel's history ordered toward Christ (Acts 7). Paul's preaching in the synagogues is described with precision: he "argued with them from the scriptures, explaining and proving that it was necessary for the Christ to suffer and to rise from the dead" (Acts 17:2–3). The verbs are significant. Paul does not invent a message; he demonstrates necessity. Fulfilment is shown to arise from the inner logic of Israel's Scriptures themselves.

The apostolic insistence on fulfilment also guards evangelisation from manipulation. Because the Gospel rests on what God has already done, proclamation is not coercive. Peter exhorts believers to be prepared to give an account of their hope, yet insists that it be offered "with gentleness and reverence" (1 Pet 3:15). Fulfilment frees the Church from anxiety about reception. Truth does not require force. It requires witness. God's fidelity does not depend on human acceptance.

Paul articulates this restraint most clearly in Romans. The same apostle who proclaims fulfilment with confidence also confesses profound anguish over those who do not yet recognise it. "I have great sorrow and unceasing anguish in my heart" for his own people (Rom 9:2). Evangelisation rooted in fulfilled prophecy does not despise resistance; it bears witness while remaining patient. Paul's hope rests not in rhetorical success but in God's mercy. "God has consigned all men to disobedience, that he may have mercy upon all" (Rom 11:32). Fulfilment initiates mission, but it does not terminate God's patience.

This patience does not weaken proclamation. It purifies it. The apostolic Church preaches precisely because history has meaning. Prophecy fulfilled assures believers that time is not random and that witness is not futile. "Knowing the fear of the Lord, we persuade others" (2 Cor 5:11). The persuasion is moral and existential, not manipulative. It flows from conviction that God has acted definitively in Christ and that this action concerns every human life.

The Fathers consistently frame evangelisation as participation in God's own fidelity rather than as triumph over opponents. John Chrysostom insists that preaching is effective only insofar as it bears witness to what God has already shown to be true through fulfilled prophecy (*Homilies on Acts*). Augustine likewise describes proclamation as obedience to a trust received. Those who preach Christ do so not as innovators but as stewards of a mystery already revealed (*On Christian Doctrine*). Evangelisation is therefore an act of humility before it is an act of courage.

Fulfilled prophecy thus grounds mission in truth rather than technique. The Church is liberated from the need to manufacture relevance or novelty. What she proclaims is not a new idea but a fulfilled promise. She speaks because God has spoken and acted. Witness becomes obedience rather than self-assertion. Prophecy matters because fulfilment, once seen, cannot be kept silent.

Fulfilled prophecy also reshapes the interior form of Christian life. It determines not only what the believer confesses, but how the believer endures. Scripture never presents fulfilment as the elimination of struggle. Instead, it insists that fulfilment renders struggle intelligible. The risen Christ Himself interprets His suffering in precisely these terms: "Was it not necessary that the Christ should suffer these things and enter into his glory?" (Luke 24:26). Necessity here is not fate, but divine coherence. Suffering is not evidence against fulfilment; it is the path through which fulfilment is disclosed.

The apostolic Church internalises this logic immediately. Paul and Barnabas strengthen the churches not by promising escape from hardship, but by naming its place within God's design: "Through many tribulations we must enter the kingdom of God" (Acts 14:22). Fulfilled prophecy does not anesthetise discipleship; it fortifies it. Because God has already acted decisively in history, present affliction is no longer meaningless delay. It becomes participation in a story whose end is assured.

The Letter to the Hebrews situates perseverance explicitly within the memory of fulfilled promise. The catalogue of witnesses in Hebrews 11 is not a celebration of success, but of fidelity under incompletion. "All these died in faith, not having received what was promised, but having seen it and greeted it from afar" (Heb 11:13). Their endurance is grounded not in possession, but in recognition. Fulfilment is trusted before it is seen. The author then turns to the Church and draws the conclusion with urgency: "Let us run with perseverance the race that is set before us, looking to Jesus" (Heb 12:1–2). Christ, as the fulfiller of prophecy, becomes the anchor of endurance.

Peter frames prophecy itself as a resource for perseverance amid darkness. He reminds the Church that apostolic proclamation is not myth, but grounded in historical encounter, and then adds: "You will do well to pay attention to this as to a lamp shining in a dark place, until the day dawns and the morning star rises in your hearts" (2 Pet 1:19). Fulfilled prophecy does not remove darkness at once. It provides light sufficient to walk faithfully within it. Hope is sustained not by constant clarity, but by trustworthy illumination.

The early martyrs understood this instinctively. Ignatius of Antioch, on his way to execution, speaks not of despair but of completion. His confidence rests not in personal courage, but in the certainty that Christ has already fulfilled God's promises through suffering. Polycarp, facing death, gives thanks that he has been counted worthy to share "in the cup of Christ." Their witness is unintelligible apart from fulfilled prophecy. They endure because history has meaning and because God has already shown Himself faithful.

Augustine reflects on this dynamic with characteristic depth. He describes the Church as living between memory and hope—remembering what God has done and awaiting what God will yet reveal. Fulfilment, for Augustine, guarantees hope without exhausting it. "We walk by faith, not by sight," precisely because God has already proven Himself trustworthy

(*City of God* XIX). The believer perseveres not by denial of suffering, but by confidence that suffering does not have the final word.

This perseverance shapes Christian hope without illusion. The New Testament refuses to collapse fulfilment into closure. Christ has come; His reign has begun; yet the world remains marked by contradiction. This tension is not failure; it is vocation. Fulfilled prophecy teaches the Church how to inhabit time faithfully—neither despairing at delay nor presuming completion. Faith learns patience because God has already kept His word once and therefore can be trusted again.

In this way, prophecy matters not only for belief and proclamation, but for endurance. It trains the soul to trust history itself. Because God has fulfilled His promises in Christ, the believer can remain faithful amid suffering, confident that present trials stand within a story already proven true.

Fulfilled prophecy also governs how the Church understands her posture toward Israel and the world. Revelation does not grant mastery over history; it confers responsibility within it. Nowhere is this clearer than in Paul's sustained meditation on Israel in Romans 9–11. After affirming that the promises, covenants, worship, and law belong to Israel (Rom 9:4), Paul refuses any conclusion that would imply divine abandonment. He asks the question directly and answers it without qualification: "Has God rejected his people? By no means!" (Rom 11:1). Fulfilment does not cancel election. It discloses its depth.

Paul's argument proceeds with deliberate restraint. Israel's stumbling, he insists, is neither total nor final. "A hardening has come upon part of Israel, until the full number of the Gentiles come in" (Rom 11:25). The language is provisional. History remains open. Fulfilment has occurred, yet its effects unfold through time according to God's wisdom rather than human urgency. The Church is warned against triumphalism precisely because she lives by grace. "Do not boast over the branches," Paul cautions; "remember it is not you that support the root, but the root that supports you" (Rom 11:18). Fulfilled prophecy grounds humility rather than superiority.

This humility does not weaken witness. It purifies it. Paul's confidence rests not in human persuasion but in God's fidelity. "The gifts and the call of God are irrevocable" (Rom 11:29). Because God does not revoke His promises, hope remains legitimate even when recognition is delayed. The Church's task is therefore not to coerce assent but to bear patient witness to fulfilment already accomplished. Fulfilled prophecy authorises proclamation without authorising domination.

The prophets themselves anticipated this posture. Zechariah envisions a future turning marked not by force but by recognition: "They shall look on him whom they have pierced, and mourn for him" (Zech 12:10). The movement is interior before it is public. Recognition precedes reconciliation. The text does not depict triumph, but repentance. Fulfilment awakens sight rather than imposing victory.

The Fathers preserve this balance with care. Augustine speaks of Israel as a living witness to Scripture's truth, preserved within history not as an enemy of the Church but as a sign of God's fidelity (*City of God* XVIII). Israel's continued existence testifies that God does not abandon His promises even when they are misunderstood or resisted. Origen, reflecting on divine pedagogy, insists that God educates humanity through time, allowing resistance to serve a purpose within mercy (*Homilies on Jeremiah*). Fulfilment does not collapse patience; it intensifies hope.

This patient witness shapes how the Church engages the world at large. Evangelisation rooted in fulfilled prophecy remains confident without becoming aggressive. The Church testifies because God has acted, not because she controls outcomes. Paul captures this paradox when he writes, "We are ambassadors for Christ, God making his appeal through us" (2 Cor 5:20). The ambassador speaks with authority, yet does not compel. Fulfilled prophecy authorises speech while entrusting conversion to God.

The same restraint governs Christian hope amid delay. Paul's confidence that "all Israel will be saved" (Rom 11:26) is not a timetable but a confession of trust. God's mercy exceeds human calculation. Fulfilment has occurred decisively in Christ; consummation remains awaited. The Church lives between these poles not in anxiety, but in expectation. Faith learns patience because God has already shown Himself faithful.

This posture guards the Church from despair on one side and presumption on the other. Fulfilled prophecy assures believers that history has meaning, yet it forbids them from seizing control of its outcomes. The Church waits and witnesses, confident that the God who has fulfilled His word once will complete His work in His time. Hope remains disciplined by memory. Witness remains tempered by humility.

In this way, prophecy matters for the Church's posture as much as for her message. It teaches her how to speak without coercion, how to hope without impatience, and how to remain faithful without fear. Fulfilment does not close history; it opens it toward mercy.

Fulfilled prophecy also reorients the believer toward judgment and consummation. Scripture never treats fulfilment as the abolition of accountability. Instead, it intensifies it. The same God who proves faithful to His promises proves faithful to His warnings. Jesus makes this explicit when He links recognition of fulfilment to final reckoning: "Every one to whom much is given, of him will much be required" (Luke 12:48). Revelation increases responsibility. To see prophecy fulfilled is to stand closer to the truth by which all things are measured.

The New Testament repeatedly frames judgment as disclosure rather than surprise. Paul tells the Athenians that God "has fixed a day on which he will judge the world in righteousness by a man whom he has appointed," and then adds that God has given assurance of this "by raising him from the dead" (Acts 17:31). Resurrection is not merely consolation; it is credential. Fulfilment establishes the criterion of judgment. The risen Christ becomes the measure of history because He is the one in whom God's promises have been confirmed.

Hebrews presses this point with sobering clarity. The author reminds the Church that the God who once spoke through angels and prophets now speaks through the Son, and draws the unavoidable conclusion: "See that you do not refuse him who is speaking" (Heb 12:25). Refusal here is not ignorance but rejection of fulfilled truth. The warning is grounded not in threat but in revelation. God has acted decisively; therefore response is decisive.

This eschatological seriousness does not collapse into fear. It deepens hope. Paul insists that the same Christ who judges is the one who intercedes. "Who is to condemn? Is it Christ Jesus, who died, yes, who was raised, who is at the right hand of God, who indeed intercedes for us?" (Rom 8:34). Judgment and mercy meet in the same person. Fulfilled prophecy assures believers that the judge is the fulfiller—the one who has already borne sin and conquered death.

The Fathers consistently interpret judgment through this Christological lens. Augustine rejects the notion of arbitrary divine reckoning, insisting that judgment is the revelation of truth already present. "God will judge not by new laws, but by the law of truth already revealed" (*City of God* XX). Fulfilment renders judgment intelligible. Humanity is not judged by an unknown standard, but by the Word made flesh who has already shown what obedience looks like.

The Book of Revelation gathers these strands into a final vision. History does not drift toward annihilation but toward disclosure. The Lamb who was slain stands at the centre of the throne (Rev 5:6). Authority belongs not to violence but to self-giving love. Fulfilment reaches its climax not in domination but in unveiling. "Behold, I am coming soon, bringing my recompense, to repay every one for what he has done" (Rev 22:12). The one who speaks is the same who declares, "I am the Alpha and the Omega" (Rev 22:13). Promise and fulfilment, beginning and end, converge in the person of Christ.

This convergence restores moral seriousness without despair. Revelation does not ask whether prophecy has been fulfilled; it proclaims that it has—and that history therefore has direction. Time moves toward encounter. The Church waits not in uncertainty, but in vigilance. Fulfilled prophecy becomes the grammar of hope. It teaches believers how to live between what has been accomplished and what will be revealed.

In this final orientation, prophecy matters because it prevents faith from dissolving into sentiment. It anchors discipleship in truth, perseverance in memory, mission in obedience, and hope in promise already kept.

Fulfilment does not remove the future; it guarantees it. The God who has acted will act again. History, having been spoken into coherence, will be gathered into glory.

Fulfilled prophecy therefore gathers the entire Christian life into a single posture of watchful obedience. Faith is no longer speculative belief, mission no longer anxious persuasion, perseverance no longer stoic endurance. All are ordered toward encounter. Scripture closes not with an explanation but with an address. The risen Christ speaks as the fulfiller of all that has been promised: "Surely I am coming soon" (Rev 22:20). The response placed on the lips of the Church is not argument but assent: "Amen. Come, Lord Jesus."

This final word does not negate history; it transfigures it. The New Testament consistently frames Christian existence as living between fulfilment and consummation. "Our citizenship is in heaven," Paul writes, "and from it we await a Savior, the Lord Jesus Christ" (Phil 3:20). Awaiting does not imply passivity. It names a form of life shaped by what has already occurred. Because prophecy has been fulfilled in Christ, the future is not open-ended. It is oriented. Waiting becomes vigilance rather than uncertainty.

Jesus Himself binds fulfilment to readiness. In the parables of watchfulness, the decisive issue is not ignorance of the master's return, but negligence in light of what is known. "Blessed are those servants whom the master finds awake when he comes" (Luke 12:37). The servant's vigilance is grounded in trust that the promise will indeed be kept. Fulfilled prophecy trains the soul to live as though God means what He says—because He has already shown that He does.

The apostolic exhortations consistently return to this eschatological sobriety. Peter urges believers to live in holiness precisely because the prophetic word has proven reliable. "The end of all things is at hand; therefore keep sane and sober for your prayers" (1 Pet 4:7). Sobriety here is not fear, but clarity. Fulfilment strips illusion away. It exposes what endures and what passes. The believer learns to order life according to what will last.

Paul presses the same logic in a different register. "Knowing the time, that the hour has come for you to wake from sleep" (Rom 13:11). The awakening is not toward novelty but toward recognition. The Messiah has come. The decisive act of God has occurred. Life must now conform to reality. Fulfilled prophecy therefore becomes ethical in the deepest sense. It calls the believer to live truthfully within a world already redeemed in principle, though not yet fully unveiled.

The Fathers grasped this eschatological tension with remarkable precision. Augustine insists that the Church lives in the *saeculum*, the in-between time, where fulfilment is real yet contested. Hope, he writes, is anchored not in what is visible, but in what has already been promised and accomplished in Christ (*Enchiridion*). The certainty of fulfilment makes patience possible. Gregory the Great similarly describes Christian vigilance as memory turned toward the future. The soul watches because it remembers what God has already done.

This final summons also restores gravity to discipleship. Fulfilled prophecy eliminates the illusion that faith is a matter of taste or temperament. To know that God has kept His word is to know that life has direction. "The night is far gone, the day is at hand" (Rom 13:12). The Church does not drift toward the future; she walks toward it with lamps lit, nourished by the memory of fulfilment and the promise of glory.

Revelation gathers this posture into a final vision. The Spirit and the Bride speak together, not with analysis but invitation: "Come" (Rev 22:17). The call is universal and unforced. Truth stands open. Fulfilment has been declared. Response remains free, yet urgent. The water of life is offered without price, but it must be received. History closes not with coercion, but with appeal.

Prophecy matters, then, because it reveals the God who acts, the Christ who fulfils, and the future toward which all things move. It grounds faith in fidelity, mission in obedience, perseverance in hope, and judgment in truth. It leaves no room for indifference, yet no room for despair. The God who spoke has acted. The Messiah has come. The King will come again.

Between promise kept and promise consummated, the Church learns to pray with clarity and courage:

"Come, Lord Jesus."

# 29

# Conclusion

The Scriptures do not end by leaving the reader with a solved puzzle. They end by leaving the reader before a Person. Every promise, every pattern, every act of divine speech traced across these pages has been moving toward recognition rather than resolution. The danger at the end of a long argument about prophecy is not disbelief but distance—the temptation to remain with texts and patterns while avoiding the One to whom they testify. Jesus Himself warned against this posture with unsettling clarity: "You search the scriptures, because you think that in them you have eternal life; and it is they that bear witness to me; yet you refuse to come to me that you may have life" (John 5:39–40). The tragedy He names is not ignorance of Scripture but resistance to encounter.

From the beginning, Israel's Scriptures were shaped not to terminate in ideas but to lead toward presence. When the risen Christ walks with the disciples on the road to Emmaus, He does not offer them a new method or a novel synthesis. He opens what was already there. "Beginning with Moses and all the prophets, he interpreted to them in all the scriptures the things concerning himself" (Luke 24:27). The text is striking not only for what Jesus explains, but for what happens afterward. The turning point is not comprehension but recognition. "Their eyes were opened and they recognized him" (Luke 24:31). Fulfilment completes its work only when the heart moves from understanding to sight.

## CONCLUSION

This movement—from text to person—reveals the deepest meaning of prophecy itself. Prophecy is not primarily about foretelling events, but about forming expectation. It trains the people of God to wait, to watch, to desire rightly. When fulfilment comes, it does not abolish waiting; it transfigures it. The one awaited now stands present. The promises are no longer only words spoken long ago; they have taken flesh. "The Word became flesh and dwelt among us, full of grace and truth" (John 1:14). Fulfilment is not merely confirmation that God was correct. It is the unveiling of who God is.

The unity of history becomes visible only at this point. From Adam to Abraham, from Moses to David, from prophet to priest, the figures and institutions of Israel do not dissolve into Christ; they are gathered into Him. Paul expresses this with serene confidence when he writes that God's purpose was "to unite all things in him, things in heaven and things on earth" (Eph 1:10). Christ does not stand at the end of the story as a solution imposed from outside. He stands at its centre as the one in whom its scattered threads finally cohere. History, which appeared fragmented when read from within time, reveals its shape when read from Him outward.

The Fathers saw this with remarkable clarity. Irenaeus spoke of Christ as the one who "recapitulates" all things, gathering the entire human story into Himself so that nothing is lost, nothing discarded, nothing wasted (*Against Heresies* III.18). Athanasius went further, insisting that the Incarnation is not an afterthought but the key to creation itself. Humanity was made with Christ in view, and history only becomes intelligible when read through Him (*On the Incarnation*). Fulfilment, in this sense, is not simply the completion of prophecy; it is the revelation of the logic that was always there.

This recognition reshapes how one reads Israel's story. The Law, the covenants, the sacrifices, the kingship, the exile—all of it presses forward toward communion. The temple was never meant to contain God, but to signal God's desire to dwell with His people. The sacrifices were never meant to satisfy divine need, but to teach humanity the cost of reconciliation. The kingship was never meant to glorify human power, but to image divine justice. In Christ, these meanings are not cancelled but fulfilled. He is the true temple (John 2:21), the true sacrifice (Heb 9:26), the true king whose throne is established not by domination but by self-giving love (Phil 2:8–11).

Yet this gathering into Christ does not flatten history into nostalgia. Fulfilment does not close the future; it opens it. The same Jesus who fulfils the promises of Israel stands also as the one who will bring them to consummation. The angelic words spoken at the Ascension preserve this tension with deliberate simplicity: "This Jesus, who was taken up from you into heaven, will come in the same way as you saw him go into heaven" (Acts 1:11). The Messiah who came in humility will return in glory. History moves not toward repetition but toward revelation.

The New Testament holds these two moments together without confusion. Paul's great Christological hymn in Philippians refuses to separate humiliation from exaltation. The one who "emptied himself, taking the form of a servant" is the same one before whom "every knee should bow" (Phil 2:7, 10). Fulfilment, therefore, is not exhausted by the past. It establishes the pattern by which the future will unfold. The Lamb who was slain stands at the centre of the throne (Rev 5:6). Glory bears the marks of sacrifice. The face revealed at the end of history is the same face revealed on the cross.

This reality gives prophecy its final gravity. Recognition is never neutral. To see the coherence of Scripture in Christ is to be placed before a choice. Jesus Himself names this moment of division: "For judgment I came into this world, that those who do not see may see, and that those who see may become blind" (John 9:39). Judgment here is not primarily condemnation but disclosure. The light reveals what was already present. Fulfilment uncovers the posture of the heart.

The Letter to the Hebrews presses this point with quiet urgency. After rehearsing the long history of God's patient speech, it asks a question that admits no evasion: "How shall we escape if we neglect such a great salvation?" (Heb 2:3). The danger is not hostility but neglect. To encounter fulfilled prophecy and remain unmoved is to stand before truth and turn away. Augustine understood this deeply. He warned that Scripture, when read without humility, becomes not illumination but accusation (*Tractates on John*). The same word that heals can judge if resisted.

Yet the final word of fulfilment is not threat but invitation. Scripture closes not with an argument but with a call. "The Spirit and the Bride say, 'Come'" (Rev 22:17). The God who keeps His promises does not force recognition. He invites it. The Messiah stands at the centre of history and at the threshold of the human heart. The face behind the promises does not compel; He waits.

This is where prophecy ultimately leads. Not to mastery of texts, not to intellectual closure, but to encounter. The reader who has followed the promises from Genesis to Christ now stands where Israel once stood, where the disciples once stood, where the Church always stands—before the fulfilled word, asked not merely to understand, but to remain.

The invitation that closes Scripture does not suspend thought; it gathers it. Fulfilment, rightly understood, does not ask the reader to abandon reason but to let reason arrive where it was always meant to arrive: before a living centre. The promises of Israel were never an end in themselves. They were signs, pathways, preparations. When they converge in Christ, they do not dissolve into abstraction; they reveal a face. Paul names this convergence with sober precision when he writes that "all the promises of God find their Yes in him" (2 Cor 1:20). The word *Yes* is not a concept. It is consent, presence, commitment. God's fidelity has taken personal form.

This personal centre reshapes how time itself is understood. Before fulfilment, Israel lived by expectation; after fulfilment, the Church lives by remembrance and hope held together. Memory becomes sacramental. The past is no longer merely past; it is the place where God has shown His hand. Hope becomes disciplined. The future is no longer an open question; it is oriented toward a promised return. Christian time is therefore neither cyclical nor linear in the modern sense. It is christological. History turns around a person who has entered it and will gather it to completion.

The Gospels quietly insist on this temporal transformation. When Jesus announces the kingdom, He does not speak of it as a distant ideal but as a present reality: "The time is fulfilled, and the kingdom of God is at hand" (Mark 1:15). Fulfilment compresses time. What was long awaited now stands near. Yet the same Jesus teaches His disciples to pray, "Thy kingdom come" (Matt 6:10). Presence and expectation are held together without contradiction. The kingdom has arrived, yet it is still arriving. Fulfilment inaugurates a way of living that neither clings to the past nor escapes into the future.

This tension guards against two opposite errors. On one side lies triumphalism—the belief that fulfilment exhausts the mystery and places history under human control. On the other lies scepticism—the belief that fulfilment is merely symbolic and therefore inconsequential. Scripture resists both. The resurrection of Jesus is neither metaphor nor final closure. It is the beginning of a new creation whose fullness remains awaited. Paul expresses this with measured confidence: "If anyone is in Christ, he is a new creation; the old has passed away, behold, the new has come" (2 Cor 5:17). Something decisive has occurred. Yet the same apostle confesses that creation still "groans" as it waits for redemption (Rom 8:22–23). Fulfilment is real, but not yet complete.

The Church lives precisely within this interval. She remembers what God has done and waits for what God will yet reveal. This posture shapes her identity more deeply than any institutional structure or cultural expression. Peter describes believers as those "who through him are believers in God, who raised him from the dead and gave him glory, so that your faith and hope are in God" (1 Pet 1:21). Faith looks backward to resurrection; hope looks forward to glory. Both are anchored in the same divine act. Prophecy fulfilled trains the Church to inhabit this tension faithfully.

The Fathers return to this point repeatedly. Augustine insists that Christian hope is neither impatience nor resignation, but steadfast expectation grounded in memory (*Enchiridion*). The Church waits because she remembers. Gregory of Nyssa speaks of the soul's continual stretching toward God, a movement made possible because God has already drawn near in Christ. Fulfilment does not end desire; it purifies it. The believer learns to long rightly, not for escape from history, but for its transfiguration.

This transfiguration is not abstract. It bears concrete moral weight. To recognise fulfilment is to accept that life has direction and meaning. Jesus' parables of readiness press this truth with simplicity. The wise servant is not the one who predicts the master's return, but the one who lives faithfully in light of it (Luke 12:42–44). Fulfilment reorders daily life. It renders obedience intelligible and vigilance necessary. Faith becomes not a moment of insight but a sustained way of living under truth.

Paul frames this ethical seriousness in eschatological terms. "The night is far gone; the day is at hand" (Rom 13:12). The imagery is not dramatic flourish. It is moral orientation. Because the decisive act of God has occurred, believers are called to live as children of the day even while night lingers. Fulfilled prophecy thus becomes the grammar of holiness. It teaches the believer how to live between what has been revealed and what will be unveiled.

Yet the face behind the promises remains gentle. The same Christ who warns of judgment invites rest. "Come to me, all who labor and are heavy laden, and I will give you rest" (Matt 11:28). The authority that fulfils prophecy is the authority that bears burdens. The one who will return in glory is the one who washed the feet of His disciples. Fulfilment, therefore, does not produce fear in those who recognise it rightly. It produces trust.

This trust is the final fruit of prophecy. The God who has kept His word once can be trusted again. The Messiah who has come will come again. Between these two certainties, the believer learns to live without illusion and without despair. The Scriptures, having led the reader to this point, grow quiet. They have done what they were meant to do. They have brought the reader face to face with the One behind every promise.

The Scriptures do not hurry the reader away from this recognition. They linger, not to multiply explanations, but to allow the weight of fulfilment to settle. The face behind the promises is not revealed as an abstraction but as a presence that calls for response. This is why the New Testament so often frames belief not as intellectual assent but as coming, remaining, abiding. Jesus does not say, "Understand me," but "Follow me" (Matt 4:19). Fulfilment draws the reader out of spectatorship and into relation.

The Gospel of John articulates this movement with particular intensity. After narrating signs that echo Israel's hopes—bread in the wilderness, light in darkness, life from death—John pauses to name their purpose: "These are written that you may believe that Jesus is the Christ, the Son of God, and that believing you may have life in his name" (John 20:31). Belief here is not mere recognition of identity. It is participation in life. Prophecy fulfilled is meant to generate communion, not conclusion.

This communion reshapes how one understands both God and humanity. In Christ, God's faithfulness is no longer inferred; it is encountered. "He who has seen me has seen the Father" (John 14:9). The promises made across centuries converge in a single human face, revealing not only divine power but divine character. The God of Israel proves Himself not distant or arbitrary, but patient, self-giving, and faithful unto death. Fulfilment, therefore, is not simply confirmation that God acts; it is revelation of how God loves.

At the same time, humanity's vocation comes into focus. To recognise the Messiah is to recognise what humanity was made for. Paul expresses this with audacious clarity when he writes that believers are being "conformed to the image of his Son" (Rom 8:29). Fulfilled prophecy does not merely tell us who Christ is; it discloses who we are called to become. The image of God, obscured by sin and exile, is restored not by law or effort but by communion with the One who fulfils the law and embodies obedience.

The Fathers understood this transformative dimension instinctively. Athanasius famously declared that the Son of God became man so that man might become god—not by nature, but by participation (*On the Incarnation*). This was not speculative mysticism but the logical consequence of fulfilment. If the promises of God culminate in the Incarnation, then their purpose is not only to reveal truth but to communicate life. Fulfilment aims at transfiguration.

This transfiguration unfolds within history, not apart from it. The

Church does not retreat from the world in order to safeguard fulfilment; she bears fulfilment into the world as witness. The Acts of the Apostles portrays this movement vividly. The disciples do not remain on the mountain after the Ascension, gazing upward. They return to Jerusalem to wait, pray, and then speak (Acts 1:11–14). Fulfilment sends them back into history, not away from it. Recognition becomes mission.

Yet mission, as Scripture presents it, is never anxious. The Church does not carry the burden of proving fulfilment by force. She bears witness to what God has already done. Paul captures this posture when he writes, "We have this treasure in earthen vessels, to show that the transcendent power belongs to God and not to us" (2 Cor 4:7). Fulfilment rests on divine action; human witness remains fragile, provisional, and humble.

This humility safeguards hope. Because fulfilment belongs to God, its completion does not depend on human success. The Church can therefore endure apparent failure without despair. The parables of growth that Jesus tells—the seed that grows unseen, the leaven hidden in dough—assume a history whose meaning is not immediately visible (Mark 4:26–29; Matt 13:33). Fulfilled prophecy teaches patience. What has begun in Christ will reach completion in God's time.

The New Testament returns repeatedly to this assurance. "He who began a good work in you will bring it to completion at the day of Jesus Christ" (Phil 1:6). The promise applies not only to individual believers but to creation itself. Paul dares to speak of the entire cosmos waiting for revelation, "groaning in travail" as it longs for redemption (Rom 8:19–22). Fulfilment has cosmic scope. The Messiah does not redeem souls alone; He restores creation.

This breadth restores confidence without presumption. The Church does not need to manufacture meaning or accelerate outcomes. She lives by trust. The God who has shown His faithfulness in Christ will not abandon His work. Augustine returns to this point often, reminding believers that hope is sustained not by visible success but by trust in God's promises already kept (*City of God* XXII). Fulfilment in the past becomes the ground of hope for the future.

As the conclusion draws nearer to silence, the tone of Scripture itself becomes prayer. The final chapter of Revelation does not rehearse arguments or restate doctrines. It speaks directly, personally, urgently. "Behold, I am coming soon" (Rev 22:12). The voice is the same that spoke in creation, in covenant, in incarnation. The response it seeks is not analysis but readiness. The Church answers not with explanation but with desire.

The face behind the promises stands revealed. History has been given meaning. The promises have been kept. What remains is not proof but response—whether the reader will turn away, or remain, and learn to live in the light of fulfilment.

The final word Scripture gives is neither explanation nor closure. It is invitation. After all visions have been shown, after judgment and mercy have been named, after history has been gathered into coherence, the Bible ends not with an answer but with a voice. "Surely I am coming soon" (Rev 22:20). The promise is not new. It is the same promise that has echoed from the beginning, now spoken with unveiled clarity. The response placed upon the lips of the Church is spare and sufficient: "Amen. Come, Lord Jesus."

This exchange reveals what prophecy has always been for. It has not been given merely to inform the intellect or to settle disputes, but to teach the human heart how to wait. Waiting, in the biblical sense, is not passivity. It is fidelity shaped by memory. Israel waited because God had acted before. The Church waits because God has acted decisively in Christ. Fulfilment has already entered history, and because of that, hope is no longer wishful thinking but trust grounded in experience.

The New Testament repeatedly frames Christian existence in these terms. "For here we have no lasting city, but we seek the city which is to come" (Heb 13:14). The believer does not flee history, but does not absolutise it either. Fulfilment relativises every earthly power and ambition. Kingship has been revealed in humility, victory in sacrifice, glory in love. The face behind the promises has shown what endures. Everything else passes.

This recognition restores sobriety without despair. Jesus' warnings

## CONCLUSION

about readiness are not threats designed to paralyse, but truths meant to awaken. "Watch therefore, for you know neither the day nor the hour" (Matt 25:13). Watchfulness is possible only because the promise is trustworthy. One waits because one expects. Fulfilled prophecy makes vigilance rational. It teaches the believer to live as though God means what He says—because He has already shown that He does.

Paul brings this posture into daily life with quiet authority. "Set your minds on things that are above, not on things that are on earth" (Col 3:2). This is not withdrawal from responsibility but alignment with reality. Because Christ has been raised and enthroned, because the promises have been kept, life can be ordered according to what is true rather than what is urgent. Fulfilment frees the believer from the tyranny of the moment.

The Fathers speak of this freedom with tenderness. Augustine describes the Christian life as a pilgrimage sustained by love—love made possible because God has already drawn near (*Enchiridion*). Gregory the Great speaks of hope stretching the soul toward God, not in restlessness but in confidence. Fulfilment does not exhaust desire; it purifies it. The believer learns to desire what will last.

This desire is finally directed not toward an outcome but toward a person. The Scriptures have led the reader, patiently and persistently, to Christ Himself. Not Christ as an idea, not Christ as a symbol, but Christ as the living fulfilment of God's promises. The Messiah who came in humility, who suffered, who rose, who reigns, now stands at the end of history as its meaning. He does not erase Israel's hope; He embodies it. He does not abolish the promises; He reveals the one who was speaking all along.

What remains, then, is not argument but encounter. The Bible closes as it began—with God addressing humanity. "Let him who is thirsty come, let him who desires take the water of life without price" (Rev 22:17). Fulfilment does not coerce. It offers. The face behind the promises waits, not because He is absent, but because love does not force recognition.

The reader stands where generations have stood before. The promises have been traced. The fulfilment has been shown. The Messiah has been revealed. The question that remains is not whether God has kept His word, but whether the heart will receive what has been given. Scripture leaves that question open—not unresolved, but alive.

And so the book ends where Scripture ends: not with possession, but with hope; not with certainty without cost, but with trust grounded in fidelity. History moves toward the One who has already entered it. The Messiah has come. The Messiah will come again. Between these two certainties, the Church learns to live, to wait, and to pray with quiet confidence:

Amen.

Come, Lord Jesus.

# About the Author

www.ingramcontent.com/pod-product-compliance
Lightning Source LLC
Chambersburg PA
CBHW060107230426
43661CB00033B/1421/J